Hybrid Factory

HYBRID FACTORY
The Japanese Production System in the United States

Edited by

Tetsuo Abo

New York Oxford
OXFORD UNIVERSITY PRESS
1994

Oxford University Press

Oxford   New York   Toronto
Delhi   Bombay   Calcutta   Madras   Karachi
Kuala Lumpur   Singapore   Hong Kong   Tokyo
Nairobi   Dar es Salaam   Cape Town
Melbourne   Auckland   Madrid

and associated companies in
Berlin   Ibadan

Library of Congress Cataloging-in-Publication Data
Amerika ni ikiru Nihon-teki seisan shisutemu.
English.   Hybrid factory :
the Japanese production system in
the United States / edited by Tetsuo Abo.
p. cm.   Includes bibliographical references and index.
ISBN 0-19-507974-4
1. Industrial management—Japan.
2. Corporations, Japanese-United States—Management.
I. Abo, Tetsuo, 1937–   . II. Title.
HD70.J3A45713   1994   338.8′8952073—dc20   93-19546

9 8 7 6 5 4 3 2 1

Printed in the United States of America
on acid-free paper

Preface

This book describes the results of a study of Japanese automotive and electronics firms with manufacturing operations in the United States. It explores the potential for the effective transfer of Japanese management and production systems, credited with providing Japanese manufacturing firms much of their competitive superiority, to a much different national culture. It seeks an answer to the question of what specific elements of production systems employed in Japan can be successfully transferred to factories operating in the United States.

The study on which the book is based was conducted jointly by Japanese and American scholars and lasted nearly 10 years. The project focused on Japanese manufacturing firms that, beginning in the 1970s, and increasingly in the 1980s, vigorously embarked on overseas production in the United States. Of special importance was testing whether the human factors that are assumed to underlie and provide strength to Japanese production systems can survive the transfer to a foreign environment. Or, whether the radically different social and cultural environment in the United States will make such transfer very difficult.

With support from the Toyota Foundation—given at two times during the study—a 1-year preliminary study was carried out in 1986. This was followed by a more comprehensive research study conducted over a 2-year period beginning in 1988.

THE RESEARCH STUDY

The research methodology involved the comparative study of parent companies of manufacturing firms located in Japan and their United States subsidiaries. The objective was to reveal the precise extent to which each constituent element of the production system observed at the parent companies in Japan was implemented in the subsidiaries located in the United States. The basis of comparison was a model that we constructed called the Application-Adaptation Hybrid Model.

We constructed separate models for Japanese and American plant production systems and then compared where the U.S subsidiaries could be positioned relative to their Japanese parents, or between the above two models, on a five-point scale. A preliminary field study was published in English in report form in 1990 under the title *The Local Production of Japanese Auto and Electronics Firms in the United*

States: The Application and Adaptation of Japanese-style Management, Institute of Social Science, Univ. of Tokyo (edited by Tetsuo Abo). The report applied the model to the data that we had collected through 1986. However, we do not take it for granted in the present book that readers will be familiar with this early report. Therefore, though we refer to the report at several points in this book, especially in Chapter 1, we have tried to provide enough background to make the discussion clear to anyone who has not read it.

We were encouraged by the generally favorable response to the earlier report to proceed with the more ambitious and comprehensive phase of the study on which this book is based. As we will describe in this book, we have progressed beyond the original model in a number of ways, including content, evaluation standards, treatment, and analytical methods—though the basic model has remained fundamentally the same.

RESEARCH TEAM

The research team, the Japanese Multinational Enterprise Study Group (JMNESG headed by Tetsuo Abo), consisted of nine Japanese and four Americans. It became apparent to the team that the amount of data collected and organized since 1987, including the results of its analysis, was far too large to publish as a single volume. The team therefore decided to divide the work into two parts in the Japanese edition. Part I, titled in the Japanese edition, *America ni Ikiru Nihon-teki Seisan System,* T. Abo, H. Itagaki, K. Kamiyama, T. Kawamura, and H. Kumon, Toyo Keizai Inc., 1991, was a collaboration among the five Japanese members who constituted the "small group." These five members made this project virtually their chief undertaking from the time that the preliminary studies were first carried out. They participated in the construction of the "application-adaptation model," as well as the plant visits, and the data collection, analysis, and evaluation. It would have been extremely difficult to complete such a long-term, tightly scheduled project with a larger team. The enormous demands on time and energy required tightly knit teamwork that could efficiently share the many burdens that this work entailed. Members of the team visited each of the different plants and head offices, as well as union offices, and government agencies located in places as far afield as Aizu and Kumamoto in Japan, and on both coasts, in the southern interior, and in the Great Lakes regions of the United States, not to mention Mexico and Canada. Driving distances covered in North America alone amounted to roughly 19,000 miles. Collating and analyzing all of the data gathered from each of these plants, performing comprehensive evaluations, and repeating the process as additional data were introduced involved considerable time and effort. Most of this work took place at the Institute of Social Science, University of Tokyo, but on occasion the locale changed to the Hosei University Tama campus, Teikyo University, or the homes of the various team members.

Other coresearchers not in the "small group," including the four Americans, participated in this project concurrently with their other research obligations. Consequently, their involvement in the project was of a more limited nature. In principle, the Japanese coresearchers attended all of the regular meetings in Japan, and in the summer of 1988, Duane Kujawa, Professor, Univ. of Miami, and Mamoru Yoshida, Assistant Professor, Florida Atlantic Univ., came to Japan in order to take part in plant visits and participate in discussions. Kujawa and Mira Wilkins, Professor, Florida International Univ., from the United States and Michio Nitta, Associate Professor, Univ. of Tokyo, and Koichi Shimokawa, Professor, Hosei Univ., from Japan conducted the field studies at U.S. plants in 1989. Kujawa, as the American-side representative of our group, carried out the questionnaire survey jointly with Kumon, as well as other important roles such as the arrangements of the visits to the plants of the U.S. firms. The members of this "large group" (including the "small group") thus contributed data, materials, and suggestions that were connected with each of their individual areas of specialty.

To report this wealth of data, it was decided to publish a second volume, Part II, in Japanese consisting of a collection of interrelated papers written by the coresearchers involved in this project, tentatively titled in Japanese, *Seisan Sisutemu no Nichi-bei Hikaku (Comparative Studies of Japanese and U.S. Production Systems)*, T. Abo, ed., Minerva-Shobo, to be published in 1994.

THE PRESENT BOOK

This book is a translation of Part I of the Japanese edition. However, two chapters were added from Part II, those by the American members, Kujawa and Wilkins. Members not directly involved in the present book and not mentioned above were Etsuo Abe, Professor, Meiji Univ., Jeffrey S. Arpan, Professor, Univ. of South Carolina, Fumie Kumagai, Professor, Kyorin Univ. (an author of Part II), Haruo Horaguchi, Lecturer, Hosei Univ., Masaki Takenouchi, Associate Professor, Univ. of Tokyo, and Hiroaki Yamazaki, Professor, Univ. of Tokyo. These Japanese members attended regular meetings of the research group and took an active part in many of the discussions and in some plant visits in Japan and the United States. They thus made an important contribution to this book. We would like to express our sincere gratitude to these members.

Tokyo   T. A.
May 1993

Acknowledgments

There are a great many persons and organizations to whom we owe a large debt of gratitude for assistance and support in bringing this project and the publication of its results to fruition.

For research funding, we would like to express our appreciation to the Toyota Foundation, from which we received awards in 1985 and 1987–88, and in particular to their program officer, Yoshinon Yamaoka. Their strict request for reports on our research results and their forbearance in regard to our business procedures were both appreciated.

For the English publication, our greatest debt is to Professor John Zysman of the University of California, who strongly recommended our research for publication by Oxford University Press and who kindly took the time to write an excellent foreword to this book. The Japan Foundation generously provided financial support both for translation and production (1991–92), as did the Japan Ministry of Education for translation (1992). When we applied to the Japan Foundation for translation assistance, Professor Kazuo Noda, president of the Tama Institute of Management & Information Sciences, and Professor Haruo Shimada of Keio University were particularly helpful in writing impressive letters of recommendation on our behalf.

We are also very grateful to Akihiko Watanebe, editor of the Toyo Keizal, Inc., for help with the Japanese edition.

As translators of the primary manuscript, Herbert E. Brauer and Jon Babcock did a very skillful job in smoothly translating the language as well as technical terms, including plant-level terminology. Their competent translation gave the Japanese authors much confidence in the quality of the final English manuscript.

We were very impressed with the coordination of the large editorial staff at Oxford University Press in systematically progressing from the initial overall editing, design, copy-editing, and production of the manuscript, to the promotion and marketing of our new book. At Oxford, we wish to express particular thanks to Herbert J. Addison, vice-president and executive editor, Mary L. Sutherland, assistant editor, Ellen B. Fuchs, managing editor, Caroline Tzelios, copywriter, Peter A. Knapp, marketing manager, and associate editors, Ruth Sandweiss and Dolores Oetting.

The Institute of Social Science at the University of Tokyo, where we established our research headquarters, was very generous in putting personnel and various facilities including office equipment at our disposal. We also received a number of helpful suggestions from related research which was in progress at the Institute at that time.

Finally, we would like to express our great appreciation to the Japanese, American, and Korean companies, which were a part of this study. It goes without saying that none of this would have been possible without the cooperation of the following:

AUTOMOBILE INDUSTRIES (ASSEMBLY AND PARTS)

Japanese Companies

Akebono Brake Industry Co., Ltd. (1), Calsonic Corporation (1), Delta Kogyo Co., Ltd. (1), Fuji Heavy Industries, Ltd. (1), Honda Motor Co., Ltd. (1), Isuzu Motors, Ltd. (1), Jidosha Denki Kogyo Co., Ltd. (1), Kansei Corporation (1), Mazda Motor Corporation (1), Mitsubishi Motors Corporation (1), NHK Spring Co., Ltd. (1), Nippondenso Co., Ltd. (1), Nippon Eagle Wings Industries, Ltd. (1), Nissan Motor Co., Ltd. (1), Ogihara Iron Works Co., Ltd. (1), Suzuki Motor Co., Ltd. (1), Toyota Motor Corporation (3), Yazaki Corporation (1).

American Companies

Chrysler Corporation (1), Ford Motor Company (2), General Motors Corporation (1).

Korean Company

Hyundai Motor Company (1).

ELECTRIC AND ELECTRONICS INDUSTRIES (ASSEMBLY AND PARTS)

Japanese Companies

Fujitsu, Ltd. (2), Hitachi, Ltd. (2), Matsushita Electric Industrial Co., Ltd. (2), Mitsubishi Electric Corporation (2), NEC Corporation (1), Sanyo Electric Co., Ltd. (2), Sharp Corporation (1), Sony Corporation (1), Tabuchi Electric Co., Ltd. (1), Toshiba Corporation (4), Rohm Co., Ltd. (1), Victor Company of Japan, Ltd. (1).

American Companies

Motorola, Inc. (1), National Semiconductor Corporation (1), Texas Instruments, Inc. (1).

Contents

Foreword
Globalization and Production

As Japanese companies open production facilities in Europe and the United States, what elements of the Japanese production system are actually being transplanted? *Hybrid Factory: The Japanese Production System in the United States* provides a remarkably valuable, well researched, and detailed response. The book also forces us to consider a broad and significant question. The Japanese transplants are a symbol both of Japanese competitive surge in consumer durable sectors over the past fifteen years and of the radical restructuring of production processes going on in all advanced countries.

Large manufacturers are reorganizing their entire operations, from design through assembly and distribution. The slogans of this shift are familiar ones—flexibility, total quality control, just in time, continuous improvement, to name a few. These emblems, popularly associated with Japanese "lean production" innovations, make it tempting to conclude that traditional mass production is being superseded by a single, new model of organizing production invented in Japan and now diffusing to the United States and Europe.

While traditional mass production as the ascendent and dominant mode of production organization may well have reached its limits, however, lean is not the last word in innovation. In fact, research at the Berkeley Roundtable on the International Economy (BRIE) indicates that multiple innovative methods are originating in a variety of places. That is, rather than the emergence of a single, dominant mode of innovation, the current period of globalization is characterized by multiple geographic sources of diverse innovations that are combined into several quite different approaches to production. For instance, production within industrial districts in Italy and Germany has been characterized by a model of "flexible specialization," in many ways distinct from the Japanese "lean" model. The technologies to implement these models emerge, likewise, from different places. Robotics innovations, along somewhat different lines, are developing in Japan and Europe, while corporate telecommunications networking strategies come out of the United States. Jap-

This foreword draws on work by Francois Bar, Judith Biewener, Michael Borrus, Stephen Cohen, Jay Stowsky, Tim Sturgeon, Jay Tate, Laura Tyson, and John Zysman, all members of BRIE. BRIE, the Berkeley Roundtable on the International Economy, is an interdisciplinary research project at the University of California at Berkeley that focuses on international economic competition and the development and application of advanced technologies.

anese "lean production," then, is just one of several competing approaches emerging in response to the new global competition.

The distinctive character of these innovative approaches reveals that differences in place shape the capacity for and the character of production innovation as a response to global market opportunities. While many argue that increasing globalization points to the erosion of differences in national production systems, the particulars of place continue to play an essential role in shaping corporate and government strategies. The market for the diffusion of technology—the "exploitation" of technology—may becoming increasingly global, but the sources of technology remain distinctly national. Thus as each place builds its response to the changing competitive environment, the variety, multiplicity, and importance of place is reinforced by globalization itself.

WHAT'S JAPANESE IN "LEAN"

Production innovation must be understood in terms of national political economies and the markets they generate. The very origins of "lean" in Japan reflect this. The lean production model, now taken as the major paradigm in international competitiveness debates, emerged in a very particular Japanese context. When Japanese firms found themselves inventing lean production they were trying to imitate such mass producers as Ford Motor Company and the Aluminum Company of America (Alcoa)—but in a situation characterized by weak suppliers using backward technologies. In other words, lean started out as "fragile" production, limited in scale and resources and, therefore, competitively vulnerable. This system evolved into "lean" as a result of specific national institutions and policies, particularly trade and technology development policies that helped strengthen the weaker elements within the Japanese system.

The Japanese government's trade protection and export orientation, for instance, created a steady and stable increase of demand, at home and from abroad, that could sustain and eventually strengthen the fragile system. Beyond protective trade policy, the government made efforts to rationalize industry structure, offer discounted financing, and provide administrative guidance through a variety of government-sponsored trade associations. In particular, the government played an important role in nourishing an increasingly talented pyramid of suppliers to final assemblers. This led to the development of an industrial structure in which suppliers could be expected to upgrade production capabilities regularly and provide increasingly complex and completed sub-units to final assemblers.

Just as context shaped the lean production model, so will the particular circumstances of other places shape responses to the global market, unveiling distinctive approaches and innovations. Even the lean model must change in response to new circumstances. Structural shifts in Japanese financial and asset markets have forced Japanese producers to confront capital costs and return-on-investment requirements that resemble those of their European and American competitors. Increased protection of markets abroad and escalating costs at home have simultaneously obliged them to locate production outside of Japan—and not just assembly. Thus economic downsizing in Japan may well strain the lean system, leaving Japanese firms vulnerable to production innovations abroad.

NATIONAL ROOTS OF TECHNOLOGICAL DEVELOPMENT

Firm strategies and tactics for production innovation are formed within particular institutional arrangements that at once constrain and direct firm choices. Nations follow different paths of development that rest on differences in industrial structure, social organization, and the role of government in the economy. Different trajectories imply not only that some countries will have faster growth because of higher savings rates, for instance, but that industries in one nation may make innovations or begin lines of development that are not readily transferable to others.

The emergence of distinct national trajectories derives from the nature of technological development itself. Technological knowledge tends to develop through a step-by-step process, an iterative interaction between opportunities and knowledge in specific settings. Technological innovations are not a set of blueprints produced by scientific advances that occur independently of the production process, but often are a joint output of the production process itself—a result of learning-by-doing. Such knowledge cannot be simply bought or sold; rather it is constituted through a subtle set of insights that develop only in conjunction with both design and production.

Thus technological knowledge is often local in nature and advances incrementally. As a consequence, much of the know-how that is necessary—to use a new product or piece of production equipment, for example—remains lodged in the people and organization that created it. Such knowledge does not necessarily move between regions within countries, let alone between nations. It accumulates in the firm in the particular know-how of workers. It accumulates in communities in the experience of suppliers and repair services. It accumulates in nations in the skills and experiences of the workforce in general and in the institutions that train workers and diffuse technology. Hence, technology's evolution follows trajectories that reflect the community and market context in which it develops.

This kind of local or non-traded knowledge is crucial during the initial development phase of new products and processes. Technology is malleable—its particular form is set by social molds in which it emerges—but broad market acceptance of a new technology excludes new possibilities. After positions freeze, a radically new technology will not be developed unless it is so attractive that producers and users are willing to walk away from their investments in earlier technologies; sunken investment becomes so great that the alternatives are too pricy. Hence, while technology does not begin as a binding parameter, over time it becomes one. The distribution of technological "bets" is set by the nature of the community. Over time the bets accumulate, making it less likely that alternate possibilities will be adopted. Firms forego abstractly attractive possibilities because they push the frontier of more limited and mature approaches.

National industrial trajectories are channeled and reinforced by technological and market linkages among firms and industries. These linkages between activities in an economy are not fully described by a simple model of market exchange, an assessment of who buys what from whom. Activities are linked together in different ways; some are more tightly bound than others. For instance, technological knowledge in one sector or activity can provide the basis for innovation in another—knowledge "spills" from its point of origin. The tighter the linkages, the greater the spillovers and the more the course of a few industries and technologies can shape an entire economy.

The way technological learning and knowledge accumulates in a particular industry within a national community will turn on the character of these organizational market linkages. In this sense, the growth and technological development of a nation is molded by the current composition of its industries and activities. In other words, what a country makes matters: it affects the areas in which technical skills are accumulated, innovation undertaken, and economies of scale reaped. Industrial composition and industrial structure set the environment for the learning. When the spillover from a sector is great and the knowledge is tacit—passing through community institutions and not markets—that sector can become a piece of infrastructure to the whole economy.

Hence, corporate capacities are rooted in national and regional expertise and advantage. Because technological development reflects, at least in part, the historical roots and national needs of a specific community, it gives at least an initial advantage to the innovating country. The technology emerges from, and plays to, the national strength of that country. "Winning" technology always imposes its own constraints and, once set, it can shape the patterns of trade. Technological externalities will vary with industry and national organization; the issue is as much one of political and social organization as one of economic logic. If an industry is structured within a country so that technological knowledge remains captive and is not available readily on the market, then other countries that would benefit from the technological spillovers from that industry must develop their own domestic producers.

Together the composition of a country's production activities and how those activities are linked constitute a distinct production architecture, a particular supply base that shapes the possibilities confronting users by enabling or deterring access to appropriate technologies in a timely fashion and at a reasonable price. Supply bases act as a structural constraint on individual company choices since, as firms innovate, they must draw on the skills of others through supplier networks. Close interactions between firm and supplier permit more mutual learning to take place between parties. Whereas more distant interactions may impede the resident capability to supply the component, machinery, materials, and control technologies—and their associated know-how—that producers use to develop and manufacture products. The national dynamics of innovation are thus likely to shape the industrial trajectory of each country as well as the terms and character of international competition.

REGIONAL SUPPLY BASES IN A GLOBAL ECONOMY

BRIE's ongoing research suggests the emergence of three distinct, though interconnected, regional supply bases in the industrialized world: a North American region comprising the United States and Canada, a Western European region, and a Japanese-led region including the four NICs. Each of these regions is distinguished by a distinct architecture of skills, component producers, subsystems capacities, and final assemblers—different "know-how" sets. For instance, many of the relevant hardware technologies, their associated know-how and manufacturing skills now reside in Asia, while control technologies—novel architectures, design, software, systems integration—reside in the United States.

Despite enormous discussion of the expansion of global trade, each of these regions is heavily focused inward. Foreign trade is, in fact, quite a limited part of the GDP of each region, while trade within the regions is growing far more rapidly than inter-regional trade. Consider Europe which, as a relatively self-contained unit, already exists. Trade within the European Economic Community has grown faster than the trade between the Community and the rest of the world since the establishment of the EEC in 1958. That trend is likely to continue with the creation of the Single Market and the adherence of the EFTA countries to it, whether they formally join or not. As in Asia, financial ties now reinforce regional trade ties. The European currencies are increasingly bound to each other and progress is being made toward formal coordination of fiscal and monetary policy, which could eventually culminate in a European Central Bank.

Evidence for the emergence of distinct regional know-how sets is most striking in the case of Japan and Asia where a regional supply base has emerged with a broad range of sub-system, component, machinery, and materials technologies. The concentration of new consumer durable manufacturing know-how in Japan and the rest of the Asian region represents a distinct technology trajectory, what we call "high-volume flexible production." It is an example of flexible automation, lean manufacturing, in which scale continues to matter enormously, creating product differentiation and speed to market.

The case is clearest in electronics. Its distinguishing characteristic is the manufacturing of products containing sophisticated, industrially significant technologies, in volumes and at cost traditionally associated with consumer demand. Such products include the latest consumer items like camcorders, electronic still cameras, compact disc players, hand-held televisions, and new micro-systems like portable faxes, copiers and printers, electronic datebooks, lap-top computers, optical disk mass-storage systems, smartcards, and portable telephones. This "high-volume" electronics industry is beginning to drive the development, costs, quality, and manufacture of technological inputs critical to computing, communications, military, and industrial electronics.

This trajectory signifies a new production architecture for Japan in the Asian region. Japanese technology lies at the heart of an increasingly complementary relationship between Japan and its major Asian trading partners. Japanese companies supply technology-intensive components, subsystems, parts, materials, and capital equipment to their affiliates, sub-contractors, and independent producers in other Asian countries for assembly into products. These final products are sold via export in third country markets (primarily in the United States and other Asian countries). Conversely, non-affiliated, labor-intensive manufactures flow back into Japan from other Asian producers.

In electronics there seem to be two key elements to the regional strategy. Japanese companies are spreading subsystems assembly and low value-added systems production throughout Asia, while persuading local governments to treat subsystems originating in other Asian countries as being of 'domestic origin.' Meanwhile, Japanese companies are keeping tight control over the underlying component, machinery, and materials technologies by regulating their availability to independent Asian producers and keeping advanced production at home.

By the end of 1990, Japanese producers had moved most of their low-end consumer electronics production off-shore into the NICs and Southeast Asia—including most audio systems (cassette recorders, headphones, low-end tuners, etc.), under-20-inch televisions, calculators, and low-end appliances like microwave ovens. Different Asian producers were concentrating on production of different systems and subsystems. Local Asian content had risen to over 60%, but key technological inputs—e.g., magnetrons in microwave ovens, advanced semiconductor logic chips, precision mechanical components—were exclusively sourced from Japan. Overall, the regional architecture appears to ensure that leading-edge production know-how remains localized in Japan, while selected production know-how diffuses asymmetrically throughout the rest of Asia.

Production innovations within the U.S.-led and European regions will accommodate the imperatives, constraints, and paths perceived as open in those market and institutional environments. Such innovations will develop differently than in the Asian region due to different regional supply bases and know-how upon which firms are reorganizing.

For the last two generations, Europe's economic position has rested on a set of implicit bargains with the United States. Europe had access to American technology. In trade, the American market was relatively open and the United States accepted and encouraged the creation of the Community. Suddenly, crucial technologies often appear to be only available from Japan. Relative dependence on Japan in finance and technology with asymmetrical market access in trade makes it unattractive to exchange America for Japan as a source of technology and production know-how. While it is weak in electronics, Europe's regional trajectory will likely be based on its strength in a range of sectors including aircraft, specialty chemicals, and production equipment. Moreover, the integration of southern Europe, with lower-wage and lower-skilled labor, and Central Europe, with its relatively high-skilled and potentially middle-waged labor force, creates the possibility of a much more differentiated supply base than that of the Japanese-led region.

In the case of the North American region, production innovations reflect the fact that the United States has ceded many critical areas of its supply base by losing its position in traditional traded industries (autos, consumer electronics, apparel, steel). At the same time, control technologies—novel architectures, design, software, systems integration—generally reside in the United States. As a result, it is likely that U.S. firms will rely far more heavily than have the Japanese on technology in responding to global competition, particularly information technology. In addressing changes in their competitive environment, Japanese firms predominantly innovated around blue-collar work organization. The resulting form of production organization strongly reflected the specifics of the Japanese environment. U.S. companies have had different opportunities to innovate—in design, engineering, and manufacturing processes—around white-collar organization.

The most enduring competitive benefits for the United States are likely to arise from the ability of firms to reorganize their business activities around the possibilities advanced information networks create, to experiment with alternative ways of organizing those activities, and to learn cumulatively by doing so. Companies are using network technologies not simply to improve existing processes, but more fundamentally as a way to recast the organization. Network facilitated transactions are helping reorganize sequential design processes into concurrent engineering, to draw suppliers into real-time product development, to tap and integrate know-how in remote locations (both inside and outside the firm), and to reconstruct logistics throughout the entire industrial sector.

Telecommunications networks have enormous implications for manufacturing. Firms face drastically shorter product cycles, which force them to rethink both their production and commercial organizations. Competitiveness increasingly rests on a firm's ability to use telecommunications networks to differentiate and adapt its products, to do so rapidly in response to changes in demand or to anticipate such changes. Firms must introduce enough organizational or technological flexibility within their mass production operations to differentiate products during production, to move from large volumes of standardized products to differentiated batches, without losing the benefits of traditional mass production. Telecommunications networks often constitute the very backbone around which firms reorganize production processes.

Our hypothesis, then, is that American firms are not reorganizing themselves by copying or adopting the specific linkage structures that defined lean production in the Japanese environment, even though their efforts are often promoted and conceived that way. Rather, U.S. firms are attempting to develop new linkages that define alternative production organizations. Information technology will serve to rearrange linkages between design, engineering, manufacturing, assembly, distribution, and service operations within the firm and among firms, their suppliers, partners, and customers.

TRANSPLANTING LEAN

The enduring importance of place in shaping the character of production innovation suggests that models of innovations are not readily transferable from one country to the next. In the United States, Japanese "lean" production is often portrayed as the winning ticket to gaining the competitive edge U.S. industries have lost in the global economy. Such views make it seem as though it is not only possible to imitate the Japanese experience in the U.S. context, but the very "superiority" of lean will lead to its inevitable diffusion in the United States and elsewhere.

We have argued that technological development and production innovation emerge out of distinct institutional and industrial contexts—through trade and technological development policies, the networks of relationships between producers and suppliers, and the experience and skills of workers and organizations. The importance of national systems is borne out in the following investigation of Japanese manufacturing companies operating in the United States. The authors of this book highlight the importance of national context in the development of production innovation by looking at attempts to "apply" the Japanese system in a range of industries and companies in the United States. The results of their study lead them to challenge the notion that such a system can be transferred to other national contexts without being significantly shaped by the conditions existing in each country.

The research of Abo and colleagues suggests that the core elements of the Japanese production model developed within the context of a specific national system. In attempting to introduce this model into the U.S. context, a tension arises between application and the parameters set by national-specific conditions, resulting in a model that differs significantly from the original. In key areas of the production system—work organization, production control, supplier networks, and procurement—this book examines the core elements of the Japanese system and finds that the tradeoffs between application and adaptation result in a revised, or hybrid, Japanese system or even, in some case, the adoption of American-style practices.

Hence, U.S. firms can adopt "lean" practices. Japanese companies can even introduce "lean" innovations into their production operations in the United States. But, as the authors of this book argue, the outcome of these practices will unlikely resemble "lean production" in Japan. Rather, those practices are likely to take on a particular character, to be transformed by the industrial architecture of the United States. The United States' real hope, then, lies in generating its own distinctive, innovative responses to the new global competition.

BRIE

Contributors

TETSUO ABO
University of Tokyo

HIROSHI ITAGAKI
Saitama University

KUNIO KAMIYAMA
Josai University

TETSUJI KAWAMURA
Teikyo University

DUANE KUJAWA
University of Miami

HIROSHI KUMON
Hosei University

MIRA WILKINS
Florida International University

Hybrid Factory

1

The Analysis of Japanese Factories Located Overseas

TETSUO ABO

ANALYTICAL PERSPECTIVES ON JAPANESE OVERSEAS PLANTS

To understand how Japanese firms have transferred their management and production systems to subsidiaries operating in the United States, it is important first to understand the context in which it has occurred. This chapter will begin by discussing the general phenomenon of foreign direct investment (FDI) as practiced in Japan since the early 1970s. It then describes two theories of multinational enterprises and contrasts them with the emerging model of the Japanese multinational enterprise. It concludes with an explanation of the theoretical framework and methodology of the research on which this book is based.

FOREIGN DIRECT INVESTMENT BY JAPANESE MANUFACTURING COMPANIES IN THE UNITED STATES

The aggregate macroeconomic value of overseas business activity is usually described in terms of FDI. Accordingly, Figure 1–1 shows that the flow of FDI from Japan, on a reported basis, began to surge after the 1970s. (Regarding the historical development of Japanese FDI, see the Epilogue.) Japan's performance in this area soon ranked among that of the other industrially advanced countries. Growth in Japan's FDI was particularly pronounced in the 1980s. A sharp and persistent increase in the current account surplus gave rise to fundamental changes in the economic structure of Japan and her trading partners, and although it does not compare with the dramatic growth in foreign securities investment stimulated by the money-boom, Japanese FDI did increase in two very conspicuous stages. In 1986, FDI had doubled from the previous year to the U.S.$20 billion level in spite of economic pressure in the form of trade friction and the sharply appreciated yen; by 1989 it had more than tripled over the previous 3 years to reach US$67 billion while domestically, the "bubble" economy triggered a boom in stock and foreign real-estate investment. It is of course necessary to discount this increase in FDI somewhat in order to account for the steep yen appreciation, which reached 70 percent

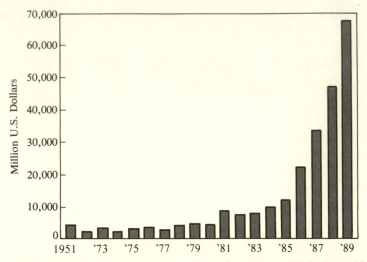

Figure 1–1 Foreign Direct Investment Flows from Japan, JFY* 1951–1989
*Japanese Fiscal Year: April of current year to end of March of subsequent year
Source: Japanese Ministry of Finance statistics

at its peak in 1988. However, the trend remained unchanged even in 1989, when the value of the yen began to moderate.

On a reported basis, the figure for the flow of FDI in 1989 decreases to US$44 billion, but the trend remains virtually unchanged. In 1990, a combination of factors, such as the U.S. recession, the completion of major plant construction projects by Japanese firms in the United States, and the bursting of Japan's "bubble" economy, resulted in an extremely sluggish growth of FDI, with the value reaching only about US$48 billion. It is notable, however, that such macroeconomic factors had a far more severe impact upon investment in foreign securities, where the value plummeted to one-third that of the previous year, and at US$39.7 billion (as reported by the Bank of Japan), fell below that of FDI. Nevertheless, by the end of 1988, the cumulative total of FDI registered US$110.8 billion, which was the third highest in the world (Table 1–2). When other forms of capital investment such as securities are added to this figure, the grand total for external assets swells to US$1.469 trillion; Japan had become the world's largest exporter of capital. Although Japan's FDI is not likely to increase by large amounts in the future, it is expected to maintain a relatively steady increasing trend, and become the core of Japan's foreign investment.

Table 1–1 shows the composition and amount of Japanese FDI in North America relative to that in other regions. These figures represent cumulative totals on a reported basis, not total values in real terms, and are suitable for examining the relative amounts and compositions by industry and region. The table shows that in 1989, North America received 42.9% of the total investment of US$254 billion (Canada 1.8%), followed far behind by Europe with less than 17.7%. In 1971, North America accounted for 25.1% of the total investment, just barely more than the

22.6% invested in Asia. Concerning investment in the manufacturing sector, in 1989 North America was far ahead with 50.7%, compared with Asia at 23.6%. In 1971, North America's share of total investment in the manufacturing sector was only 21.5%, lagging behind Asia, which received 36.8%. Most notable is North America's substantial lead in investment in areas such as real estate, commerce, and services. Of these, the rapid increase in real estate investment is particularly conspicuous.

Turning to the composition of Japanese FDI in North America, it is apparent that the manufacturing sector accounted for 30.8% of this investment. This was second highest after Asia, where 38.5% of FDI was directed to manufacturing, and very high relatively to the 26.6% total share that the manufacturing sector received from overall Japanese FDI in every region. Incidentally, Japan's proportion of manufacturing sector investment to total FDI is low in comparison with 40.9% for the United States, and 60.4% for former West Germany (JETRO, 1987). Also, it is clear that the proportion of investment in the U.S. manufacturing sector rose substantially from the 23.9 percent recorded in 1971. Of course a salient characteristic of Japanese FDI in the United States in recent years is the rapid increase in the proportion directed towards the nonmanufacturing sector such as real estate, finance, and services. However, when prospects for future investment are taken into account, there is no question that the steadiest increase will be seen in the manufacturing sector.

As these figures readily demonstrate, the past 15 years or so have witnessed a tremendous growth in FDI by Japanese corporations, as well as a rapid increase in its global rank. There has also been a markedly different pattern in the growth of Japanese FDI compared with that of the other industrially advanced countries that carry out this type of investment. This point is related to our research objectives and theoretical framework and therefore merits particular attention. First, Table 1–2 shows that by the end of 1988, Japanese FDI had surpassed that of former West Germany to become the third largest in the world. At the same time, the proportion of FDI to GNP in the case of Japan was still very low compared to that of the other major investing countries. Japan's FDI, which figures only 3.9% of GNP, is far lower than the 20 to 30% of GNP in the case of Great Britain or the Netherlands. It is also low in comparison with the 6.7% for the United States, and 8.1% for former West Germany. Moreover, as is clear from the above discussion of structural composition of FDI, an international comparison of Japan's direct investment in the manufacturing sector as a proportion of GNP would produce an even smaller figure. This is well illustrated by the "overseas production ratio" (sales by overseas subsidiaries/domestic sales) for the Japanese manufacturing industry. In the mid-1980s, the ratio for Japan was a mere 3 to 4 percent, while that for the United States or former West Germany hovered in the range of 16 to 19 percent. (MITI, 1988).

This large discrepancy between Japan and Western countries cannot be explained in terms of an inevitable "catching up" that Japanese capitalism will experience. In the first place, as the 1989 export-to-GNP ratios for Japan (9.6%), the United States (7.5%), and West Germany (28.3%) reveal, this gap does not reflect a low degree of Japanese dependence upon exports. Second, the share of 1988 world exports for Japan (10.2%), the United States (12.4%), and West Ger-

Table 1-1. Cumulative Japanese Foreign Direct Investment by Industry and Area as of the End of JFY 1971, and JFY 1989* (Million U.S. dollars, %)

Areas Industries	North America 1971	North America 1989	Asia 1971	Asia 1989	Europe 1971	Europe 1989	Others 1971	Others 1989	Total 1971	Total 1989
Mfg Industries										
Foods	9	1,485	36	1,049	6	311	30	419	80	3,265
Textiles	7	651	161	1,569	1	489	85	494	254	3,203
Wood & pulp	208	1,847	17	450		17	37	340	262	2,654
Chemicals	11	3,581	36	2,077	18	1,110	10	1,882	76	8,649
Metals	1	3,656	40	2,578	9	395	138	2,631	188	9,261
Machinery	10	3,277	20	1,387	14	1,339	46	475	91	6,479
Electrical	3	8,686	65	3,348	1	2,016	30	625	98	14,676
Transportation equipment	15	4,453	14	1,326	4	1,352	83	1,877	116	9,009
Others	4	5,894	72	1,807	3	917	10	314	88	8,932
Subtotal %→	(21.5)	(50.7)	(36.8)	(23.6)	(4.6)	(12.8)	(37.2)	(13.7)	(100.0)	(100.0)
	269	33,529	461	15,591	58	7,949	465	9,058	1,253	66,127
%↓	[23.9]	[30.8]	[45.5]	[38.5]	[8.1]	[17.7]	[29.5]	[15.2]	[28.0]	[26.0]

Non-mfg Industries

Agriculture & forestry	5	430	50	297	—	8	14	570	68	1,205
Fisheries	3	158	15	177	6	18	21	326	39	678
Mining	191	1,889	320	7,124	1	1,416	837	4,782	1,355	15,211
Construction	7	1,015	6	643		84	27	346	41	2,089
Commerce	413	14,146	29	2,575	44	5,404	60	3,035	546	25,159
Finance	142	16,996	72	3,588	68	21,258	111	15,429	393	57,271
Services		12,038		4,815		2,487		4,036		23,375
Transportation		411		982		157		13,719		15,269
Real estate	96	24,637	60	2,351	539	3,669	89	4,085	784	34,742
Others		2,215		1,632		1,056		2,341		7,515
Subtotal %→	(26.6)	(40.5)	(17.1)	(13.2)	(20.4)	(19.5)	(36.0)	(26.8)	(100.0)	(100.0)
Subtotal	856	73,935	552	24,183	658	35,556	1,160	48,842	3,226	182,516
%↓	[76.1]	[60.8]	[54.5]	[59.8]	[91.9]	[79.9]	[71.4]	[82.1]	[72.0]	[71.9]
Branch expansion		1,044		654		1,430		1,531		4,659
Acquisition of real estate		485		37		38		35		595
Total %→	(25.1)	(42.9)	(22.6)	(15.9)	(16.0)	(17.7)	(36.3)	(23.4)	(100.0)	(100.0)
Total	1,125	108,993	1,013	40,465	717	44,972	1,625	59,466	4,481	253,896
%↓	[100.0]	[100.0]	[100.0]	[100.0]	[100.0]	[100.0]	[100.0]	[100.0]	[100.0]	[100.0]

*JFY-Japanese Fiscal Year (April of current year to end of March of subsequent year)

Source: Japanese Ministry of Finance

Table 1-2. Outstandings of Foreign Direct Investment by Major Countries

(Billion U.S. dollars)

Country	1987 Year-end	1988 Year-end	Rate of Increase (%)	Relative to GNP (%, end of 1988)
United States	308.0	326.9	6.1	6.7
United Kingdom	169.2	183.7	8.6	22.1
Japan	77.0	110.8	43.9	3.9
Germany (West)	99.8	97.3	−2.5	8.1
Netherlands	74.8	70.2	−6.1	30.9
France	51.7	58.1	12.4	6.1
Canada	43.8	50.7	15.8	10.8
Total (7 countries)	824.3	897.7	8.9	
World Total*	947.5	1031.8	8.9	

*Estimates

Notes:
1. Domestic currency balances have been converted to U.S. dollars at the exchange rate in effect at the end of the year.
2. World estimates have been calculated on the flow basis of data for 1970 to 1987 (IMF International Balance of Payments Yearbook basis), which indicates that FDI from the seven listed countries represented 87 percent of the world balance.
3. Japanese FDI balance has been calculated on the basis of international balance of payment data and varies somewhat from figures reported from the Japanese Ministry of Finance (in Table 1–1).

Sources: JETRO, JETRO White Paper: Foreign Investment,1990, and so on.

many (12.4%) proves that it does not reflect a lack of international competitiveness on the part of Japanese industry (Bank of Japan, 1990). When examining this export-share data, it is necessary to note that voluntary export restraints that affect virtually all of Japan's major export commodities, and the fact that 54.8 percent of West Germany's exports were confined to the EC (the U.S., which is Japan's largest foreign market, only absorbs 36.5 percent of Japanese exports) disguise Japan's true export potential.

The type of data described above illustrates two important characteristics of Japanese industry, namely the export-led growth of the Japanese manufacturing industry, and the "reluctance" with which Japanese industry finally yielded to pressure to expand into overseas production. Examining these characteristics of Japanese MNEs is the starting point of this joint research project.

THEORETICAL IMPLICATIONS OF THE EMERGENCE OF JAPANESE MULTINATIONAL ENTERPRISES (MNEs)

This study relies largely upon MNE theory in attempting to identify the practical results of the international transfer of the Japanese management and production system in the auto and electronics industries. A sound theoretical framework for this research therefore required a solid grasp of the important points of MNE theory.

MNE Theory and the Japanese Multinationals

As we emphasized in the previous publication, however, existing MNE theory, which is based upon a Western model, was inadequate for describing the important characteristics of Japanese multinationals and that it was therefore necessary to develop a new analytical perspective that would more completely incorporate the Japanese model. As mentioned above, Japanese manufacturing companies only began to expand into overseas production in the second half of the 1960s, and did not aggressively pursue this type of activity until the 1980s. Consequently, early research into the behavior of Japanese multinationals was essentially an application of the American MNE model. As this research gradually began to include elements of the theory of Japanese-style management,[1] it began to direct its attention towards those characteristics of the Japanese system that differed from the American model. Nevertheless, such research has yet to produce any meaningful results.

A simple but powerful hypothesis underlying the American MNE model is also the starting point for the analysis of Japanese multinationals. This hypothesis states that when an enterprise attempts to multinationalize by engaging in direct foreign investment, it must have some advantage relative to its local competitors (Heimer, 1960). The problem lies in identifying that advantage, or competitive superiority. According to conventional wisdom, on a macroeconomic level, the factors accounting for this superiority are typically production factors such as capital and labor. On a microeconomic level they are represented by ownership-specific managerial resources such as "hard" and "soft" technology, specialized knowledge, and experience or know-how. A major premise of this hypothesis was that, qualitatively, such superiority-determining factors existed to an equal extent in any country or region, and that the only important differences were quantitative. Of course, technical difficulties accompanied the transfer of some of these managerial (micro) resources. Especially where it concerned industrial secrets or other sensitive "soft" technology, measures were sometimes adopted to prevent the uncontrolled dissemination of such information. This behavior will be examined below as one of the explanations for the theory of internalization. However, it was assumed that such conditions existed equally in every country and that the only differences were those existing among enterprises.

In fact, even the most fundamental factors of production, such as capital and labor, differ considerably in terms of how they react to identical economic stimuli depending upon the different countries, regions, and cultures of which they are a part. This becomes even more pronounced at the corporate level where business practices, methods of administration, and types of organization more directly reflect the history, society, and culture from which they originate. The social sciences have tended to construct models and theories based on rational economic and social mechanisms perceived as universal and therefore culturally neutral. Those elements mentioned above, which were considered characteristic of and peculiar to specific regions or societies, were excluded from such general laws of social science. They were considered aberrations that were of no particular significance for understanding the dynamics behind the development of international economies. In those cases where studies analyzing individual countries did actively address these special characteristics, they were generally perceived as reflecting historical backwardness. In fact, a number of "late development hypotheses" comprising part of an "historical development stage theory" merely asserted that backwardness could even sometimes constitute superiority.

The history of capitalism shows that unique societal factors have always played important roles in the development of countries such as England, Germany, and the United States, to positions of economic world leadership. The transfer of technology developed by the advanced countries may be a necessary precondition for late developing countries to catch up, but by itself it is insufficient to explain their ability to jump into the lead. For example, between the middle of the nineteenth century and the end of World War I, American industry dominated the world market with technology that consumed massive quantities of natural resources and made economical use of labor. In addition to special geographical and historical conditions, America's unique sociocultural background, namely a society made up almost entirely of immigrants, resulted in an extremely diverse labor force that was therefore very difficult to integrate into a single, cohesive element. These factors played a vital role in the formation of the management and production system that sustained the fundamental productivity that characterized Pax Americana and that was represented by Taylorism or the Ford system. Although many researchers have attempted to show that parts of this established system and method can be theoretically separated from their place of origin and abstracted as a set of general "principles," there is no other country to which the American system has been successfully transferred in its original state. In Japan, many years of attempting to imitate U.S. industry have produced a system to which a number of elements that differ considerably from the U.S. model have been added. The competitive strength of Japanese industry that results from these characteristic Japanese management methods, has now forced a closer reexamination of the issue concerning special characteristics.

"Technology" and "technical skills" consist of a number of aspects and a variety of different elements. Depending upon the country, region, or period of history in which a given technology has developed, different combinations of these aspects and elements result in different types or patterns of technology. This is an important point to remember when considering the international transfer of technology and its related systems. Researchers in this field have proposed a number of dichotomies for describing the types or patterns of technology that they encounter: Abernathy described "product technology" and "process technology"; Vernon distinguishes between "labor-saving innovation" and "material-saving" innovation. The present research identifies a number of related technology-types, including "system-oriented technology" and "accumulation-oriented technology," or the mechanics- and electronics-oriented technology (combined in Japanese as "mechatronics" or ME (micro- electronics technology). Although a detailed explanation is not possible here, Japanese society or corporate organization generally corresponds to the latter part of these dichotomies. In America (and most of Europe) society and corporate organization seem to follow the former.[2] Of course it is also possible for a system to occupy an intermediate position or to represent a combination of the opposing paradigms, but the tendency is to favor one or the other.

As each country's characteristic social and cultural factors are interrelated with the factors that determine relative manufacturing superiority, it is clearly insufficient for MNE theory, in its attempts to account for the international transfer of management systems, to focus solely upon those aspects of the systems that all countries have in common. Approaches such as the theory of Japanese management address this problem directly. Before taking a closer look at that theory, we shall briefly examine two other MNE theories that hold particular significance for this type of approach.

The first of these is Dunning's "eclectic theory." According to this theory, the factors that govern international production through FDI are not only ownership or firm-specific factors but also location-specific factors. This has proved very useful for practical research and analysis. Particularly noteworthy is the point that the factors of a superior production system that are first recognized in a foreign environment are not owner- or company-specific, but rather country-specific. In other words, they are primarily a product of their national economies. This leads to the conclusion that superior technology or management systems are created within the context of a specific social system.[3] In regard to location-specific superiority, this theory emphasizes the importance of management elements that already exist in the local environment, such as characteristics of the labor force, or differences in pricing systems or adaptation by the MNE towards local government policies (localization policy). In highlighting qualitative differences between the managerial environment in the investing and investment-receiving countries, this theory provides an important perspective for the debate on international transfer.

This theory's shortcoming lies precisely in the fact that it is so eclectic and merely presents two views without offering any insight as to their interrelationship. In a similar argument, Abo proposed that the essential characteristic of MNEs lies in the dynamism that springs from the strained relationship between "integration logic" of parent companies and "localization logic" of subsidiaries.[4] If the eclectic theory included this perspective, it would show that subsidiaries cannot simply apply original overseas business strategies developed by their parent companies, but must modify the system in order to adapt. This is part of a fundamental awareness behind the theoretical framework employed in the present research.

Another interesting, and currently popular approach has been the promotion of R. H. Coase's internalization theory as a general MNE theory by people such as Buckley and Casson.[5] This attempts to offer a general explanation for the development of enterprises through the application of internalization to MNE theory. It attempts to offer a comprehensive and consistent explanation for the systematic (export ≫ licensing ≫ local production) developmental sequence of overseas business activities motivated by reduced transaction costs. The theory contains some questionable points, such as the idea that companies can only be explained through the assumption of an imperfect market. However, if this is interpreted in the opposite sense, as a theory about the relationship between the market and enterprise organization, then it has some interesting implications for the transfer between enterprises, and in particular the international transfer, of managerial resources that are difficult to trade in the market. This is because the international transfer of special knowledge, "soft" technology, or know-how possessed by an enterprise, especially the managerial methods or shop-floor human organization systems characteristic of Japanese-style management, is greatly facilitated by internalized parent-subsidiary transactions. In other words, external contracts or arms-length transactions pose a major obstacle to this type of international transfer.

This was a brief review of two major MNE theories, and a look at the elements and approaches that might prove helpful in carrying out an analysis of the Japanese MNE pattern. However, there are limitations to applying existing theories in this manner. This is because the managerial environment that surrounds investing and investment-receiving countries is not clearly and systematically explored. There is no framework and no provisions to account for or to examine qualitative differences in technology or special problems with the international transfer of management organizations and methods related to such qualitative differences. With this in mind, we now turn to a consideration of the major elements of the theory of Japanese-style management and how they have contributed to MNE theory.

Impact of Japanese Style Management

The fundamentals of conventional Japanese MNE theory were first established by Yoshino.[6] He argued that the strengths of Japanese management derive from factors related to special characteristics of Japanese society such as group orientation or the ethnic homogeneity of the work force. He stressed that problems and difficulties experienced by Japanese multinationals were the result of attempting to transfer this management system across national boundaries and into an entirely different cultural and social environment. By examining the international adaptability of the Japanese management system in light of the cultural characteristics of Japanese society, Yoshino's research can be considered an important milestone in this field. However, the important issue of whether to consider Japanese management as an exception and therefore to regard the treatment of special characteristics as relevant only to Japanese MNE theory, or whether to reconstruct general MNE theory so that it accounts for qualitatively different management methods and economic systems, has been left unexplored.

On the one hand, Yoshino's theory is a standard interpretation of the three "sacred treasures" of Japanese management, and it focuses upon characteristics of the system at the white collar level. Management methods concerning fundamental elements at the shop-floor level, such as worker organization, job assignment, production control, or procurement method, are not taken up.

On the other hand, the multinationals that were the subject of Yoshino's theory were mainly those Japanese enterprises that established plants in Southeast Asia before and during the early 1970s. That theory is not well-suited to the new type of Japanese MNE that began to appear after the early 1970s as Japanese firms expanded their presence to industrially advanced countries such as the United States. In other words, Yoshino emphasized the difficulties of transferring Japanese-style management to a foreign environment, even though in comparison to the West, Southeast Asia is culturally and socially relatively similar to Japan. Although it is not possible to arrive at a firm conclusion without detailed, plant-level analysis, the implication is that the transfer of Japanese-style management to countries such as the United States would be even more difficult.

In contrast, research conducted by Trevor sheds light upon the characteristics of Japanese multinationals operating in industrially advanced countries.[7] Trevor focuses upon Japanese MNEs located in Britain. Based upon a systemic study of the historical and cultural background of Japanese management, as well as the actual conditions existing among these enterprises, Trevor concludes that the Japanese MNEs are "reluctant multinationals". His important observations are that Japanese-style management methods cause much stress at the manager level, where orientation is towards the principle of skill development, but that the blue collar workers welcome the equality that these methods bestow upon their ranks. Similar observations regarding the latter point have been made in Japan, but Trevor's study is exemplary because of its timing and excellent documentation.

In spite of some limiting conditions, this is an extremely noteworthy attempt at showing the universality with which Japanese management is applied in industrially advanced countries. However, it is important to remember that this study does not extend to actual observations of shop-floor operations but relies primarily upon questionnaires for data collection. For example, it is an oversimplification to say that regular shop-floor workers at Japanese plants are all treated equally. In fact, these workers are individually assessed and treated (promoted, paid) accordingly. One wonders how this practice would be received in Britain.[8] Consequently, our research requires a survey method that examines, within the overall MNE plant system, precisely how and to what extent the implications of Trevor's findings are valid, as well as whether these findings extend to countries other than Britain.

It is interesting that the characteristics of Japanese MNEs, as well as those of Japanese-style management, attracted the attention of researchers outside of Japan so quickly.[9] These studies stimulated Japanese scholars, particularly in recent years, to undertake their own studies of Japanese MNEs or of the international transfer of the Japanese system through the analysis of Japanese labor relations or Japanese management theories. Before we begin to describe the research that is the subject of the present book, we shall briefly review some of the work in this area that has been done in Japan.

Potential for the International Transfer of the Japanese System

The theories of the international transfer of Japanese management described above include several that were reviewed in our previously published study. Below, we shall consider these theories in terms of the international transferability of the Japanese production system, as well as the theoretical significance of the Japanese multinational enterprise.

The potential for the international transfer of the Japanese management and production system has recently become the subject of great debate. Of course the transfer of the American model, which developed around the time of the World War I and was exemplified by the Ford system, Taylorism, or Sloan's principles (decentralization and coordination adopted by General Motors), to countries such as Germany and Japan was also an important development. These countries were eager to catch up to the United States and in their attempt they underwent a large-scale industrial rationalization movement during the inter-war period. In that case the issue was not the universality or general applicability of the American system so much as the essentially quantitative issues of bridging the gap between the general level of technology or between market scale or capital concentration which existed in the United States and or in the other industrialized countries. There is no question that certain theories we reexamine as we study the emergence of Japanese management involve issues related to qualitative differences in management and production systems. It seems though that those qualitative differences were not sharp enough to arouse a great deal of interest, and in any case, they did not become the subject of such general debate that would have warranted the type of joint research described below. In contrast, although the subject of Japanese-style management in an international environment was first taken up as recently as about 15 years ago, the potential for its international transfer has already grown into a field arousing extensive interest and debate. Undoubtedly this stems from a strong impression that the issue concerns characteristics peculiar to the Japanese culture.

There may well be considerable protest against this attempt to forge a strong link between management theory and culture. Indeed it continues to be a matter of some debate even among the members of our own research group. It is only logical that the more we emphasize cultural factors, the more limited the potential for international transfer becomes. Conversely, the less emphasis on cultural factors, the greater that potential. However, culture is very complex, and depending upon the particular aspect one examines, and the way in which that aspect is related to management activities, the manner of evaluating the impact of cultural factors will vary greatly. If culture is only considered to be related to those characteristics peculiar to a given country and society, and therefore to have little significance to those types of human behavior, such as economic activity, which are common to all peoples, then international comparisons of culture are likely to be deemed of little value. In that case, it would be advisable to disregard such "irrational" country-specific factors as much as possible when examining the potential for the international application of a particular managerial system. Instead, attention would focus on a "scientific" method, which isolates and focuses upon those elements considered to be "universal."

Yet even if we perceive of culture fundamentally in terms of qualitative differences between distinct societies, that does not require treating it as an absolute and unchanging set of conditions. First, present systems and customs were formed over the course of history, and there is no reason to believe that they will not continue to change in the future. The important questions are whether such systems or behavioral tendencies that formed under the influence of specific historical and geographic conditions will only change with great difficulty, and whether significant differences between distinct cultures will remain despite such change. What we must remember is that there is a certain quality of timelessness to these cultural trends and that in different periods and under changing conditions they may lend themselves to a variety of expressions.[10]

Second, it is possible to isolate and express certain aspects of culture in terms of quantitative differences that may be compared internationally. The notion of "context," which was suggested by E. T. Hall is a particularly useful example.[11] K. Yasumuro utilizes this concept in a method that he proposes for comparing the international transferability of the Japanese and the American management systems.[12] "Context" expresses the aspect of culture concerned with human relations as a programming function that facilitates interpersonal communication. This enables us to treat different cultures in terms of, so to speak, degree of difference. According to this notion, Japan is a high-context society because its culture provides its members with a rich background of shared information that facilitates efficient interpersonal communication. On the other hand, the United States, where meticulously organized communication and conduct is necessary to maintain human relations, is a low-context society.

This aspect of culture suggests that when systems or methods of organization or behavior are transferred to a foreign social environment, their transfer will inevitably be accompanied by a certain amount of friction and that the systems and methods will undergo a certain amount of change or revision as a result. Of course, such a general observation does not suffice as a scientific analysis. The various elements and aspects constituting organizational and technological systems must be carefully examined both individually and as a whole. This must be followed by a thorough theoretical analysis of specifically which elements and aspects tend to change or be modified as a result of such international transfer and in precisely which way. This is particularly important in the case of international transfer from a high-context society, such as Japan, to a low-context society, because such a transfer will likely be accompanied by a greater degree of change or modification. Consequently, a viable theory of international transfer must, above all, identify which aspects of the system are most subject to change, and evaluate the degree of change that takes place.

The preliminary research reported in our previous publication was not received without some argument. The most noteworthy criticism was probably Koike's views concerning the international transfer of Japanese production technology. His views are important largely due to the fact that at one point they had a major influence on the construction of the theoretical framework we used for this joint research. His arguments are also notable because they differ from ours on some rather important points. In his review of our book, Koike was particularly critical of the above-mentioned culture-theory approach to examining the international transfer of Japanese management. Since most of Koike's work has been a critical reexamination of the theories that attribute special characteristics to Japanese unions or labor relations (in other words, stressing those characteristics that Japan has in common with Western countries, in contrast to a traditional, deep-rooted theory of Japanese backwardness), his criticisms were not unanticipated.

Although each of Koike's specific comments are referred to in later chapters, here we shall focus only upon the following points. First, Koike's own theory identified skill development at the shop floor level as the essential, core characteristic of the Japanese production system, and then carefully examined the international transferability of that characteristic. This is now virtually a classic proposition that research in our field can ill afford to disregard. Indeed, major parts of our own hypothesis were developed in accordance with this theory. Second, Koike stressed the essential compatibility of each country's production system and sharply criticized theories that attribute special qualities to Japan. It is this aspect of his theory with which we must take issue. His criticisms, based upon his own meticulous field research, demonstrated that superficial differences among organizations and systems of many countries actually concealed an extraordinarily high degree of similarity. As such, his discoveries were, needless to say, an effective rebuttal against arguments that tended to simply single out unique cultural characteristics, or late development due to backwardness, as the major factor behind different systems or organizations. But let us consider how these points relate to the idea that certain unique characteristics of Japanese society and culture are necessary conditions that produced and support the relative superiority (as well as the problems) of Japanese labor relations or management systems. If these conditions supported the development of a new production system and technology formation, and if they constituted an indispensable element in Japan's development to an economic superpower, and the resulting structural change of the world system, then isn't a theory that downplays the significance of such special characteristics apt to overlook an important dynamism in the development of the world economy? Furthermore, if we examine Japanese methods within such a "no-special-characteristics" context, then we are forced to impose a priori qualifications upon our interpretation of international compatibility. Granted, if the Japanese production system does establish a clear superiority over other systems, then within certain parameters, it will spread to other countries. However, the degree to which it permeates a given society will be governed by conditions existing in that society.[13]

In viewing Japanese methods as a system, and in examining the relationship between the structural elements of that system and Japanese culture or society, we have tried to specifically identify those conditions that limit, or determine, the potential for the international transfer of this system. Although focusing mainly upon the transfer of core elements, as Koike did in his research, is also a productive approach, we felt that a more rigorous analysis could be achieved by taking into account the extent to which the system as a whole, including its surrounding subsystem, was transferred, as well as the actual impact of the transfer upon production performance. Such an analysis of the costs and benefits resulting from international transfer is valuable because excessive costs may render the successful transfer of the core system meaningless or even counter-productive. Conversely, even where the core system has not been effectively transferred, the application of various subsystems may have contributed to keeping a plant competitive in the local market.

A theory such as Shimada's "humanware" offers some rather extreme views about cultural factors.[14] Shimada contends that the essential, humanistic elements of Japanese methods are both rational and universal, that it is precisely the irrational elements that consist of cultural factors, and that eliminating the latter is only a problem of refining the system and improving its cost-effectiveness. While we share the opinion that elements steeped in culture inevitably end up becoming modified, that does not mean that culture is only related to problematic areas and not to any rational parts of the system, nor that changing these elements is easy. Rather, as suggested above, it is precisely the core strengths of Japanese methods, together with accompanying problems, that are closely tied to the social and cultural environment. It is for precisely that reason that their international transfer, as well as modifications to suit a different domestic setting demands considerable expense and effort.[15]

This point is related to the "light and dark" theory of Japanese-style management. Kumazawa distinguished two aspects of Japanese corporations: the morale and software of production that inspires workers to show initiative in their work was characterized as "light"; and the semicoercion that resulted from the nature of group pressure was characterized as "dark."[16] From the perspective of international transfer, Kumazawa emphasized the need for modifying the "dark." This was necessary, he claimed, in consideration of the value attached to individualism in the West. Although this is a very sound proposal developed using methods introduced in our previous publication, the opposing relationship between these two aspects is not clarified, and there is virtually no attempt at explaining the costs of such modifications, or the effectiveness of the results.

Another important debate concerning the comparison of American and Japanese systems and methods, as a prerequisite for examining international transfer, is how to treat recent changes in the respective domestic systems of these two countries. Many researchers inside and outside of Japan, and particularly in Europe, put great emphasis upon such recent changes. As a result of their observations that the differences between systems in Japan and in other countries are shrinking, there is a tendency to place less emphasis upon the uniqueness of the Japanese system. One of the criticisms that Totsuka raised about our previous publication is that we did not sufficiently scrutinize such changes.[17] He suggested that rather than focus upon a Japan-U.S. comparison, we should examine contemporary capitalism and management in a more general, historical context.

As subsequent chapters explain in greater detail, there were in fact a number of salient changes taking place in various industries in the United States during the 1960s and 1970s. Some of these changes were clearly stimulated by the Japanese enterprises and involved the introduction of the labor-management cooperation style of management systems, as well the emergence of plants in which importance was placed upon "teamwork" as a method for work organization. In Japan, on the other hand, changes were occurring in employee consciousness partly as a result of the increase in the number of younger workers, and partly as a result of decreasing opportunities for promotion. There was therefore no lack of apparent evidence pointing to convergence between the management models of Japan and the United States. It is also a fact that to a certain extent, these changes made it easier for Japanese enterprises to operate plants in the United States. However, the results of our research and analysis to date do not indicate that the changes are sufficient to warrant any fundamental revision to our Japan-U.S. management system models (see Chapter 2). In other words, it is preferable to maintain separate models for the evaluation of the type and degree of these recent changes. Also, the clearest evidence of the considerable disparity in the efficiency of the two systems is the growing performance gap between Japanese and American plants. Moreover, these conclusions continue to be corroborated by results published by American researchers.[18]

As seen above, there is thriving debate on the international transferability of the Japanese management and production system, a fact which in itself alludes to the depth and scope of this issue. The Japanese management and production system is at the back of the "reluctant" Japanese multinational. If much of the system's relative superiority is related to Japanese society and culture, then it is unavoidable that the relationship between Japanese management and the social systems and customs in the U.S. local production environment will be strained. It has become necessary to expressly address the precise nature of the Japanese system's relative superiority. There is an urgent need to reexamine systematic and cultural factors in many areas, including MNE theory, relative superiority, corporate-specific factors, location-specific factors, and the related issue of internalization. This is the theoretical and methodological premise upon which the present research is based.

THEORETICAL FRAMEWORK AND RESEARCH METHODS

Before presenting the results of our research and analysis, we shall explain the theoretical framework and methodologies employed in the various tasks involved in the study, such as data collection, classification, and analysis.

Theoretical Framework

The theoretical framework of this research divides into two parts, namely the hypothesis, and the analytical framework for carrying out the survey and analysis. A general explanation of both follows, and a more detailed treatment of the analytical framework appears in Chapter 2.

Hypothesis

Our study focuses upon the overseas production activities of Japanese manufacturing firms, particularly in the United States. We believe it is possible to account for the managerial and productive superiority of the US plants of Japanese firms by applying an analysis that examines firm-specific factors (competitive superiority) and location-specific factors (localization) as posited by MNE theory. Furthermore, we intend to demonstrate how to most effectively exploit this potential for competitive superiority while meeting the demands posed by the local environment.

The most important factor accounting for the competitive superiority of Japanese manufacturing firms, particularly those in the assembly processing industries such as autos and electronics, is said to be the Japanese-style management system. The organization of human and material resources that emphasizes human factors at the shop floor, as well as certain characteristics of administrative operations, are responsible for the striking advantages in both efficiency of operations and quality of the resulting product. However, this management system relies to a considerable extent upon characteristically Japanese systems and customs. There are serious reservations about how effectively such systems can be transplanted to a society such as the United States, where the historical and cultural environment differs so radically. In other words, the U.S. plants of Japanese firms confront a dilemma: On the one hand, they attempt to introduce superior elements of their management and production system to the maximum extent possible ("application"), but on the other hand, they must modify those same systems in an effort to adapt to various local environmental conditions ("adaptation"). This is what we call the "Application-adaptation Dilemma Model." Through extensive surveys in the field, we have attempted to illustrate the type of "application-adaptation" trade-offs that are actually observed at the U.S. plants of Japanese firms.

One of the significant points of this hypothesis is the implied combination of the Western-style MNE model and Japanese-style management theory. In the case of the former, differences between factors of production and management resources that exist in a domestic or foreign environment are only quantitative. In the case of the latter, there are additional qualitative differences affecting technology and production systems that stem from human factors of management and labor. This has produced the view that there is a conflict between "application" and "adaptation." The reasoning that led to this view was explained in the first part of this chapter, and in Chapter 1 of the preceding publication. We see no reason to modify the basic hypothesis as introduced in the preliminary research. That is to say, the fundamental "Application-adaptation Model" has been very well received. Other prominent researchers have seen fit to use this model without modification, thus attesting to its support in academic circles. Business people have also frequently described the model as useful. However, aside from the somewhat technical problem of whether "dilemma" is an appropriate expression, preliminary research did reveal the necessity of examining the relationship between application and adaptation in greater detail. This was because the "Application-adaptation Analysis" produced a slightly different analytical perspective than was obtained from the above-mentioned "dilemma model." The brief explanation of the analytical framework that follows is intended to shed some additional light on this problem.

Analytical Framework

Theoretical and methodological aspects of the analytical framework will be discussed in detail in Chapter 2. The objective here is to explain the roles and characteristics of this framework as they relate to the research hypothesis. In accordance with the Application-adaptation Dilemma Model discussed above, the analytical framework produced two data-tabulating forms. The first is the survey standards form used to carry out the actual plant surveys, and the second is the assessment standards form used to process and analyze the data and information collected in the surveys ("Application-adaptation Evaluation Form" or "Hybrid Form").

In other words, this framework, based upon numerous field studies carried out at the plants of Japanese subsidiaries located in the United States, produces a model depicting basic elements related to the transfer of management and production system of Japanese auto and electronics plants overseas. Some of these elements are closely related to the fundamental strengths of the Japanese system. Others reflect conditions that typically exist at American domestic plants. In this case, the conventional model for U.S. plant analysis as described in the literature, observation of typical U.S. plants, and discussions with American members of the project team influenced the selection and description of the elements included in our model. For example, consideration was given to whether an element was significant to U.S. plants of U.S. firms, or whether a U.S. plant of a Japanese firm would have to adapt a particular element to the American system.

The resulting form is shown in Table 2–1 (Chapter 2). This form lists 23 elements (element 24 is of a slightly different nature) broadly classified into 6 groups. With the Japanese and U.S. plant models positioned at either extreme, each of the surveyed U.S. plants of Japanese firms, i.e. the "hybrids," was evaluated for each element on a scale of 1 to 5 according to where it was situated on a continuum between these two models.

Although this 5-point evaluation has no particular statistical significance, it was appropriate and useful for our purposes. If an element was found to be halfway between the U.S. and the Japanese models, it was assessed 3 points. If it was judged to be leaning closer to the Japanese model, then it received 4 points. Later, on the basis of comparisons between company records and the field study data described above, each of the five team members separately graded the elements for each subsidiary. Where these individual assessments failed to agree, the team members would readjust the assessment following careful debate. Consequently, although the figures themselves are no more than replacements for expressions such as "extremely," "somewhat," or "a little," they carry considerable conviction and cannot easily be changed. This is justified by the fact that in most cases, the assessments of the five team members were in agreement. There were also surprising similarities between the average assessments resulting from the first survey conducted in 1986 and the second survey conducted for the present research and between the team members' evaluations and company people's evaluations reflected in the questionnaire survey (see Ch. 4). Numerical evaluation brought out the strengths, and gradually made us gain a better appreciation of the merits of joint research. For example: 1) Expressing each member's assessment in terms of a number facilitated matching and adjusting the assessments. 2) A numerical evaluation reduced confusion during follow-up discussions between members. It also made it easier to present the results in the form of a graph or a table. 3) Numerical evaluations facilitated calculating averages and carrying out comparisons and correlation analyses between elements, groups, industries, and regions.

"Dilemma Model" and "Adaptation Analysis"
The analytical framework employed in the comprehensive research differed somewhat from the "Application-adaptation Analysis" of the preliminary research. That analysis divided the "23-Element, 6-Group" classification into two 3-group categories called "application groups" and "adaptation groups". Further analysis then investigated the possible existence of dependent or mutually supportive relations between groups or group elements.

While the "dilemma model" simply viewed the data in terms of a choice between the two contrasting alternatives of application and adaptation (Japanese and American-style systems, respectively), the "adaptation analysis" suggested the possibility of a more complex relationship, such as one where adaptation to certain aspects of the local American-style system might facilitate the application of other aspects of the Japanese-style system. This type of analysis implied a revision of the dilemma model. It is noteworthy for its potential to encourage a greater emphasis upon localization policies by Japanese companies at their U.S. plants.

The theoretical soundness of this point of view, and its indispensability for general MNE theory, have already been sufficiently emphasized by Abo (1984) and others. However, as a result of carrying the research through to this more comprehensive stage, problems that had remained unresolved following the preliminary research became increasingly evident. For example, it was discovered that adapting to the American system (i.e., adopting aspects of the U.S.-style management and production system) would only diminish the strengths of the Japanese system. This would be theoretically counterproductive, since our research proposed a model focusing on the transfer of those strengths of the Japanese system that stressed human factors at a local, plant level. A more technical problem was that, as a model for analysis, it was not possible to extract pairs of application and adaptation groups that were in a purely contrasting relationship. For these reasons, it was decided that it would be inappropriate to continue applying the same methods used in the preliminary study to the comprehensive research.

This research adopted the following solution to this problem: 1) The basic survey model follows the "dilemma" approach. According to that approach, the point assessment shows that a high degree of adaptation results from a low degree of application of Japanese-style elements (negative adaptation). This results in a limiting relationship that decreases production efficiency and quality levels. 2) At the same time, it was recognized that the following merits could be associated with adapting to the U.S.-style system: (1) Facilitation of the application of other elements of the Japanese-style system, (2) contribution to improved plant performance through cost-cutting and other measures, and (3) a generally positive effect upon the reception of Japanese-style management in the local environment. "Positive adaptation" thus serves to supplement the otherwise restrictive dilemma model. It also helps explain the phenomenon of "revised application" observed during the survey of Japanese plants in the United States (cf. Chapter 2).

"23-Element, 6-Group Evaluation" and "4-Perspective Evaluation"

The "4-Perspective Evaluation" provides the current research with a clearer analytical perspective for dealing with data that received only a cursory treatment in the preliminary study. The dilemma model considered the operating conditions existing at Japanese parent company plants as ideal, and established the "23-Element, 6-Group Evaluation" as a model for evaluating complete application. Accordingly, the degree of application for each element in this model measured the extent to which it was considered to have been successfully transplanted. However, more important than the mere numerical average of these figures is which aspects of these elements were transplanted and how these different elements were combined. In other words, what was necessary was not only a means of measuring the degree of application of the important structural elements, but also a way of evaluating these elements from different perspectives.

Such an evaluation is achieved by the 4-Perspective Evaluation. It distinguishes those elements that make a substantial and vital contribution to the transfer of the Japanese system to the local environment, from those which are merely beneficial to the operational performance of the local plants. It then rearranges those elements in the 23-Element, 6-Group Evaluation model. The "four perspectives" derive from classifying each element of the model as either "human" or "material," and distinguishing those elements that are introduced directly from Japan as "results" of the Japanese system, from those that are applied as "method" regarding how to make and operate the system. As we will examine in some detail below, however, one of the problems is that combinations of elements related to a more effective "method" of transplanting the Japanese system did not necessarily guarantee superior industrial performance. As a result, many companies did not always adopt these particular combinations of elements (cf. Chapter 2, Part 3).

Performance Evaluation

One of the important issues not adequately covered in the preliminary study is the performance evaluation of the surveyed plants. As explained above, the hybrid evaluation, and the adaptation analysis that supplements and reinforces it, illustrated average company profiles, industry types, and various pattern analyses. This made it possible to investigate how the application-adaptation conditions revealed by these analyses related to plant performance, namely, the efficiency of its operations and the quality of its products. Without such a performance analysis, the significance of any particular degree of hybrid evaluation would be unclear. Fully aware of the value of such a performance evaluation, we made careful theoretical and technical preparations based on advice from various industry specialists. We then accumulated extensive data through visits to plants in Japan and abroad. Since this was still insufficient, we requested further data from each of the plants involved in this study following completion of the actual survey. As discussed in Chapter 7, the response rate to our requests for data was far from satisfactory, no doubt reflecting the "wall of secrecy" that guards confidential company information. We were, however, able to gather the minimum amount of data we felt necessary, including data from key plants in this study.

Survey Methods

Upon completing the preliminary study, we were primarily engaged in field work in the form of daily plant observations and interviews. This was supplemented with interviews at head offices, the study of published papers and data, consultations with other researchers in related fields, and for the first time, a questionnaire. Our survey method consisted of 1-day plant observations and interviews (referred to below as "day observations"), which we carried out according to the general methods proposed by the companies where we conducted our surveys. Our options, particularly in the beginning, were limited, and our methods were simply a matter of complying with the conditions stipulated by those companies. As our observations accumulated, it became clear that this method was far more effective, and had a great deal more merit than we had at first imagined. Conventional methods for this type of survey research are questionnaire surveys and (periodic plant observation) case studies. Our "day observation" method was halfway between these two approaches. It may seem that this is a very simple, unprofessional method, and that the resulting data are sparse and unreliable. Although to a certain extent we are prepared to acknowledge these weakness, our method can also claim an important merit that is absent in the other two methods. We are convinced, therefore, that this method, depending upon how it is applied, can yield a number of advantages. A comparison with these alternative approaches will help illustrate the characteristics and advantages of our method.

A questionnaire can clearly target a much larger number of subjects than the "day observation" method can. However, the rate of response to questionnaire is a problem, and this becomes associated with other problems related to data and information reliability, as well as the quantity of data per element. With the "day observation" method, if one produces a theoretically and methodologically sound set of survey standards-survey chart (cf. Chapter 2 for details) as part of the analytical framework, then a checklist for the actual plant observation, as well as for the interviews that precede and follow the observation, can become very clear and detailed. By sending the checklist to the plant before the actual observation in the form of an agenda (list of questions to be used for the interview and the plant observation) and a question sheet (numerical data describing general plant operations to be obtained before the actual visit), it is possible to efficiently gather a considerable volume of information pertaining to the main points of interest on the day of observation, while simultaneously confirming this information through first-hand observation. Furthermore, if a number of team members conduct the observation, it is easy to verify the reliability of the information. Moreover, if there are several groups of team members, then it is possible to gather considerably more information than if visits are conducted by a single observer. Factory visits also provide additional opportunities for obtaining a variety of other pertinent information and materials. For these reasons, the "day observation" method compares very favorably with the questionnaire method. Also, in the case of questionnaire surveys, requesting a large amount of information reduces the response rate. However, when several groups of team members participate in "day observations," as in the case of our U.S. field survey conducted during the summer and fall of 1989 (nine Japanese and American members participating for 1.5 months), it was possible to visit approximately sixty locations, including almost all of the important Japanese plants, as well as some U.S. and Korean plants, in from four different industries, in addition to various state government and union offices.

Case studies represent the second type of typical survey method. According to this method, a researcher conducts observations at a single plant over a period of time and then individually gathers, checks, and confirms all of the data. This method is recognized as the ideal type of plant observation, and it has produced a number of seminal studies in the area of international plant comparisons. However, this type of study is clearly restricted to a single plant, or at best to a very limited number of plants. It is, however, difficult to select a single company or plant and then to judge the extent to which that single case is representative of a broader trend. This is particularly so in the case of the present research, where the surveyed plants had a relatively short history and where the resulting industry model is derived from a combination of different plant types. Finally, the most difficult obstacle for the case study would have been finding companies to cooperate with this type of intrusive survey. Such an attitude was particularly evident in the case of companies that utilize much advanced technology. Although "day observations" may have produced data that was inferior in terms of depth or reliability, the ability to target a large and diverse group of plants was an important advantage for producing an overall picture representative of a particular group of plants. For these reasons, and with respect to our specific research objectives, the "day observation" survey method was felt to be more appropriate than the case study.

The "day observation" survey method was clearly best suited to the purposes of the present research; it did not share the serious shortcomings yet was essentially able to provide the major advantages inherent in the other two methods. Of all important conditions mentioned above, the most critical, and the one which the "day observation" method was ideally suited to meet, was that of obtaining the cooperation of the companies whose plants we intended to survey. Another important factor was the contribution of teamwork. This was not only important because cooperation and burden-sharing was necessary for coping with such a large-scale research project. It was also important because it would have been very difficult to organize the complex and detailed customs and behavioral systems reflected in the analytical framework or in the preparation of the evaluation tables, into a single, cohesive framework, not to mention to construct a theoretical model to evaluate that framework, without the rich diversity of ideas and perspectives provided by the Japanese and American members of our team. Furthermore, since all three survey methods are clearly mutually supportive, we supplemented our "day observation" survey method with a questionnaire in order to ensure an even greater amount of data and to derive more objective evaluations from the company people's point of view.

The final matter to consider here is the way we processed, or in other words, arranged, evaluated, and analyzed the data. This is summed up as follows:

1. The first step was to generate detailed company records for Japanese parent companies located in Japan, as well as for their U.S. subsidiaries. These records were based mainly upon notes that team members took during the plant observation and interviews. Other sources of information included data related to general plant operations supplied on question sheets and obtained from the companies at the time of the observations, company documents obtained before and after the observations, as well as data gathered from newspapers, magazines, or other previously published sources. Since these data were fundamental to the parent-subsidiary comparison, in most cases they were cross-checked by team members as well as by some visiting researchers and then carefully and systematically recorded upon a special form.

2. The next step was to assign each plant a value of from 1 to 5 for each of the 23 elements in the hybrid evaluation on the basis of the application-adaptation evaluation. This stage also required the participation of every team member. Generally, there was unanimous agreement regarding the value to assign each element; however, in a number of cases, there were slight differences between individual evaluations, and it sometimes required lengthy debate to reach agreement on a single element.

3. Finally, this information was compiled in the form of an Application-adaptation Evaluation Table (Table 3–3), which shows average data for all four industries. The information shown in this table was fundamental to this research, and represents the point from which the analytical part of the research began in earnest.

2

Characteristics of the Japanese Production System and Its International Transfer Model

TETSUJI KAWAMURA

RESEARCH AND ANALYTICAL METHODS AND THE OPERATIONAL FRAMEWORK

Chapter 1 examined the theoretical framework underlying this research, as well as the analytical perspectives which derived from it. It also presented an outline of the analytical methods that were employed. The management and production system characteristic of Japanese enterprises in the target industries (automotive assembly, automotive parts, consumer electronics, and semiconductors) were put forward as a model. Survey items were created on the basis of that model and arranged in an analytical framework. Following the observation of each company and plant, the survey results were compiled as "company records" and then carefully reexamined using the model and the survey items. Next, the Hybrid Evaluation Model was developed in order to illustrate and analyze the relationship between "application" and "adaptation" discovered to exist at the local production plants. The final outcome is shown in the Hybrid Evaluation Table (Table 2–1). It illustrates the main characteristics of the Japanese management and production system, and arranges and analyzes every aspect of "application" in the management and production system model at the local production plants in the United States, in terms of 7-groups and 24-items.

The Hybrid Evaluation Model is the main framework for the application-adaptation analysis. Through a "degree of hybridization," it provides not only a qualitative but also a quantitative evaluation of the manner and extent to which the fundamental elements of the Japanese management and production system are applied or adapted to the local production. This method permits a comprehensive understanding of the actual management conditions obtaining at the local production plants. In order to perform a more multidimensional analysis, the "4-Perspective Evaluation" and the "pattern analysis" were also adopted. This chapter explains the characteristics and significance of this analytical method through a careful look at the underlying analytical framework and evaluation model.

Table 2–1. Application-Adaptation (Hybrid) Evaluation Form of "24-Item, 7 Group"

I Work Organization and Administration
   ① Job classification (JC)
   ② Wage system
   ③ Job rotation (JR)
   ④ Education and training
   ⑤ Promotion
   ⑥ First-line supervisors (or team leaders)
II Production control
   ⑦ Equipment
   ⑧ Quality control (QC)
   ⑨ Maintenance
   ⑩ Operations management
III Procurement
   ⑪ Local content
   ⑫ Suppliers
   ⑬ Procurement method
IV Group Consciousness
   ⑭ Small group activities
   ⑮ Information sharing
   ⑯ Sense of unity
V Labor Relations
   ⑰ Hiring policy
   ⑱ Job security
   ⑲ Labor unions
   ⑳ Grievance procedures
VI Parent-Subsidiary Relations
   ㉑ Ratio of japanese expatriates
   ㉒ Delegation of authority
   ㉓ Managerial position of americans
VII Community Relations
   ㉔ Donations and volunteer activity

Constraints on Local Production and Application, Adaptation

The application-adaptation analysis examines actual conditions at the U.S. pro-duction plants of the target companies in terms of the dynamic relationship between "application" and "adaptation". The basic concepts of application and adaptation can be summarized as follows: (1) Japanese companies in the United States attempt to apply their Japanese management and production system by transferring them to the U.S. managerial environment. (2) On the other hand, this application is often limited by a number of constraints emerging from the mana-gerial environment or other local conditions. The Japanese system may change its form, and in some cases may be clearly seen as "adapting" to those local conditions. The result may lead to a revised Japanese systems, or, in some aspects, to the out-right adoption of American-style systems. Consequently, local production systems of Japanese companies in the United States are considered as having developed through a dynamic interrelationship between application and adaptation.

Application and adaptation have an important bearing upon the "slow start," or the initial reticence with which Japanese companies approached local production overseas. It explains why, in the beginning, the companies had to be virtually compelled to adopt this approach to developing their offshore markets.

In Japan, each of these companies operates a flexible production system that is efficient and at the same time turns out high-quality products. This has been achieved by focusing primarily upon the human elements at the production plant, and at the same time, by developing the supportive managerial system. As typified by the "Toyota production system," this system has basically been established through the conscious effort of individual enterprises during and since the postwar era of rapid economic growth. As we shall explain later, these systems came to be referred to as the "Japanese-style," in comparison with the "American-style" management and production system. This was, in fact, a new paradigm that included certain common features among Japanese firms. Differences between industries notwithstanding, this became the basis of a general model describing the Japanese-style management and production system. Sometimes referred to as "human-ware," these systems utilized managerial and operating methods characterized by particular human elements that existed at the workplace.[1]

The competitive strength of Japanese companies in the marketplace can be attributed to this system. Since this system relies to such a large extent upon human factors, it contains a number of elements that are embedded in a Japanese cultural and sociological context. For this reason, the fundamental approach to developing offshore markets was exports, and for the same reason, the local production approach was so slow in starting. However, the success of the export approach aggravated trade friction. As a result, Japanese manufacturers were left with no choice but to advance into overseas production. One after another these industries began to shift some of their production abroad: Consumer electronics was first in the 1970s, followed by the automotive and semiconductor industries in the 1980s. The rapid yen appreciation in the fall of 1985 stimulated the move towards local production further still. Forced to uproot themselves from the Japanese soil and the domestic conditions that gave their system its strength, each firm found itself in a position where it was essentially *compelled* to develop local production in the United States in order to survive.

Once a company decides to embark upon local production, it attempts to apply the Japanese system that it recognizes as its source of strength. Operating in North America, the world's largest market, means not only competing against domestic U.S. firms, but against rival Japanese manufacturers as well. This reinforces its decision to apply the Japanese system. The most direct manifestation of this strategy is the transfer and application of the Japanese system, unchanged in any way. This is an "outright" application as opposed to "revised" application discussed below. However, since human factors play such an important role in this Japanese system, and since U.S. society, culture, and the "American way" differ markedly from those of Japan, the implementation of a different managerial system is likely to be burdened with limitations and to provoke discord. In such a case, it is impractical to directly apply the Japanese system under those conditions prevailing in the American managerial environment. This compels Japanese manufacturers to consider some form of adaptation.

Adaptation results in significant modifications to the management and production system. Conforming to local conditions and various aspects of local management is achieved by adopting many local operating procedures. Sometimes, parts of the Japanese system must be completely abandoned and replaced with local practices. In this case, adaptation is carried out only to the extent that application of the Japanese system fails. This is called "passive adaptation." In contrast, "active adaptation" results from attempts to duplicate totally the American system itself in the U.S. "Adaptation" does, however, greatly reduce the thoroughness and effectiveness of the Japanese system, with the possible consequence that the Japanese firm loses whatever strengths it hopes to gain. In that event, the Japanese manufacturer falls into a "dilemma."

The application-adaptation relationship, and consideration of the various local conditions, provide much insight into the character of a particular local production system. For example, the degree to which elements of the Japanese management and production system is manifested in local production varies according to the difficulty of their application. Conversely, aspects of the American system or other local conditions are mixed in with the Japanese system as reflected in the degree of adaptation. This results in a "hybrid" condition that reveals the distinctive character of a particular local production operation. The degree of "application" and the character of the adaptation, as seen from the application perspective, is determined by the Application-Adaptation Hybrid Evaluation. Table 2–1 shows the items and item-groups that constitute this evaluation method.

5-Point Evaluation of Application and Adaptation

A 5-point evaluation was used to provide a quantitative measure of this dynamic relationship. The 7 groups and 24 items shown in Table 2–1 represent, respectively, the elements and their related aspects considered necessary for the successful application of the overall Japanese management and production system (actually 6 groups and 23 items, since group 7, item 24 is of a different nature). On the basis of observations at the target plants, as well as other supporting research, we awarded 5 to an item which revealed the maximum degree of application and 1 to an item that was considered closest to the American system. Items that were regarded as situated between these two extremes were scored accordingly.

A focal point of this evaluation is the comparison of Japanese plants of Japanese companies, with American plants of American companies. For each constituent element and aspect of the Japanese management and production system, comparisons must be made between it and the opposite element or cultural counterpart in the American system. There are major cultural and historical differences that account for the polar-opposite character of the management and production systems between these two countries. By placing the Japanese and American systems at opposite ends of a continuum, we could determine the degree of application (or conversely of adaptation) accordingly. This method makes it possible to judge where a particular local production plant is to be located with respect to these two extremes and is based on the estimated hybrid (mix) between its application and adaptation.

Another focus is the comparison of local plants of different Japanese firms in the United States. Such comparisons may concern different companies in the same industry, different industries, or in some cases, different companies in different industries. Even though they are all Japanese companies, there is a strong possibility that differences between companies, or by industry, will appear as a result of different international expansion strategies, historical or developmental differences, or corporate cultures. A detailed explanation of evaluation standards and methods will be explained below. Table 2–2 lists the fundamental evaluation criteria.

The results from the observation of each target plant are compared with the criteria described in Table 2–2. For each target plant, and for each item listed in the table, a degree of application is determined and averaged for each group. This facilitates an unambiguous description of the overall degree of application of the Japanese management and production *system* established at each local plant. These company and plant evaluations provide a solid starting point for later analysis by industry or plant type.

Revised Application

The fundamental analytical perspective and method outlined above are insufficient as a means of describing the actual development of local production. The simple "hybrid" that results from a trade-off between Japanese and American systems is an inadequate analysis of the management and production system that actually exists at the local plants. For example, in the dilemma of the firm described above, one alternative is to implement a type of "revised application," and the other to pursue "active adaptation" to the American system. It is the former alternative that warrants our closer attention.

With respect to the trade-off between application and adaptation, the active adaptation suggested above implies actively implementing the American management and production system. Theoretically this is a feasible course of action. However, in this case, the Japanese enterprise must adjust to a system with which it has little experience and which may in fact prove difficult to become accustomed to. Also, if a Japanese company tries to implement an American management or production system, it will likely remain qualitatively different from a pure American system. Moreover, if the Japanese system makes the Japanese company more competitive in the market, and if it must compete against other Japanese firms in the same foreign market, then it is clearly unrealistic to attempt to come to terms with the local environment after sacrificing the advantage of its superior system. Active adaptation thus has some serious limitations.

According to the recent trends revealed in our surveys, there are few cases of Japanese firms still trying to actively apply the American-style system in every aspect of their management. Even in those cases where this was former policy, management is trying to change direction by applying numerous aspects of the Japanese system. This phenomenon is highly indicative of recent management trends at local

Table 2–2. Criteria for Application—Adaptation (Hybrid) Evaluation of "24-Item, 7 Group"

I Work Organization and Administration

① Job Classification (JC)
  5-Number of JC is: 2 or less
  4-   3 ~ 5
  3-   6 ~ 10
  2-   11 ~ 50
  1-   50 or more

② Wage System
  5-"Person-centered" wage determination main criterion is: length of service (Nenko); personal evaluation (PE) conducted by supervisors, closed to workers
  4-Wages determined mainly by length of service, and partly by objective PE that includes worker input and requires worker approval
  3-Simplified JC system is introduced; PE system determine wages
  2-Simplified JC determines wages; PE system does not determine wages.
  1-Rigid and detailed JC system determines wages

③ Job Rotation (JR)
  5-JR is carefully planned and frequently conducted within and beyond work teams. Its clear aim is training of multiskilled workers (e.g., training table kept by team leaders and supervisors)
  4-JR is planned and frequently conducted within but not beyond work teams
  3-JR is frequently conducted with work teams
  2-Rigid job assignment systems is moderated to some extent (job reassignment when product mix is changed; frequent product mix change, etc.)
  1-JR is nonexistent; job assignment is rigid

④ Education and Training
  5-1) On-the-job training (OJT) is the main system for training multiskilled workers, together with long-term systematic training, and
    2) There is a training system for team leaders and maintenance personnel through OJT and systematic training; sending trainees to Japan and bringing trainers from Japan with special training programs and facilities
  4-1) Workers trained through OJT and special preparations and arrangements are made to accommodate this
    2) Training of supervisors (team leaders) and maintenance personnel in Japan; special training programs and facilities (e.g., a training center)
  3-1) OJT is emphasized; team leaders have some responsibility for training workers; team leaders have assistants for task training
    2) Some training program for team leaders or maintenance personnel exists inside or outside the company
  2-1) OJT is not emphasized; some arrangements exist for outside training (e.g., reimbursement for school fees)
    2) Outside education and training is recognized as a job qualification
  1-1) OJT is not emphasized
    2) No special inside training program for team leaders or maintenance personnel

⑤ Promotion
  5-1) Worker promotion based on length of service (Nenkoh) and PE, which is conducted by direct supervisors
    2) Internal promotions to supervisor with recommendations by direct supervisor

continued

Table 2-2. (*continued*)

4-1) Based to some extent on length of service (Nenkoh)

2) Internal promotions to supervisor with recommendations by direct supervisor

3-1) Based on PE and specific qualification; seniority does not play a strong role; job posting

2) Supervisors internally promoted through job postings; corporate skills significant; seniority rule is not rigid.

2-1) Based on seniority and PE and conducted and utilize job posting

1-1) Based on seniority and utilize job posting

2) A high percentage of supervisors recruited from outside the company

⑥ First-line Supervisors (or Team Leaders)

5-Internally promoted and function as team leaders and have technical control of production process, including industrial engineering (IE) functions

4-Same as above (5 points) but to a lesser degree

3-Most supervisors internally promoted; weak team management and weak process control functions (e.g., no active role in job rotation or multiskill training; may have assistants for IE)

2-Some supervisors internally promoted; role is mainly labor management and discipline

1-Internal promotion is not a rule; role is exclusively that of labor management and discipline

II Production Control

⑦ Equipment

5-100 percent of equipment imported from Japan

4-75 percent

3-50 percent

2-25 percent

1-zero percent

⑧ Quality Control (QC)

5-Emphasis on QC conducted by workers during the actual process

4-QC conducted by workers during the process but there are insufficient accommodations for this (e.g. workers have no line-stop authority; QC or zero defect (ZD) circles are not very active)

3-QC conducted by specialists during each process; QC and quality checks by specialists from an independent QC section also emphasized (high proportion of such checks)

2-QC relies on checks by specialists from an independent QC section; relatively close checks are conducted during each process (number of QC specialists is relatively low)

1-Quality checks by QC sepcialists on completed products (post process and outgoing inspections) are emphasized

⑨ Maintenance

5-Shop-floor are internally trained and promoted to maintenance personnel (including inexperienced workers hired separately from ordinary workers); preventive maintenance is emphasized, shop floor workers have some maintenance roles

4-Same as above (5 points) but including some experienced workers hired separately from outside; preventive maintenance and shop floor workers' roles in maintenance are not stressed

3-Experienced workers hired separately but receive additional internal training before being promoted to maintenance personnel; shop floor workers do not have any commitment to maintenance.

2-Same as above (3 points) but experienced workers are sometimes hired directly as maintenance personnel

1-Maintenance personnel employed mainly from outside and maintenance by engineers is emphasized

⑩ Operations Management

5-Flexible setup and special arrangements to cope with line failures or defects (e.g., coordina-

Table 2–2. (*continued*)

tion and cooperation among first-line supervisor and team leaders, preventive maintenance, machine fail-safe devices (*Pokayoke*), production control signal board (*Andon*));
standard procedures and work manuals brought in from Japan and modified and
improved to accommodate local conditions (line balance adjustments etc.); high product
mix, frequent product changes; reduction of die change time is achieved to the same
extent as in Japan

4-Setup is less flexible than above (5 points); work manuals and maintenance know-how
obtained from Japan; local job improvement (kaizen) is achieved to a much lesser extent;
lots size is relatively small; die-change time is approximate, though slightly less than that
in Japan

3-Moderate product mix (relatively large lot size with some batch production, etc.) standard
procedures and work manuals brought in from Japan but only with slight modifications to
accommodate local conditions.

2-No specific provisions for coping with line fails or defects; operations control is engineering-
oriented; local IE specialists establish and modify standard procedures

1-Operations control is highly engineering-oriented (engineering section has dominant role in
machinery operation and maintenance; production based on large lot methods

III Procurement

⑪ Local Content
5-less than 20 %
4-(from 20 percent to 40 percent) 20 ~ less than 40%
3-   40 ~ less than 60%
2-   60 ~ less than 80%
1-more than 80%

⑫ Suppliers
5-Materials and parts mainly procured from Japan
4-Procured from sister plants or Japanese suppliers located overseas (U.S., Canada, S.E. Asia,
Mexico)
3-High proportion of procurement from Japanese suppliers in the U.S. and Canada
2-Procurement from Japanese suppliers in the U.S. and Canada, but the proportion of U.S.
suppliers is high
1-Most procurement from U.S. suppliers

⑬ Procurement Method
5-Japanese subcontracting system exists with local suppliers
4-To some extent the Japanese subcontracting system exists with local suppliers; technological
assistance and long-term contracts are applied to U.S. suppliers
3-Some arrangements are made to reduce parts inventory as much as possible; technological
assistance is attempted with U.S. suppliers
2-Local suppliers are held to strict observance of delivery times
1-Mainly spot trading with U.S. suppliers; parts inventories are relatively high in order to cope
with delayed delivery

IV Group Consciousness

⑭ Small Group Activities
5-All workers participate voluntarily and play significant roles
4-More than 50 percent of workers participate
3-20 percent to 50 percent of workers participate
2-Less than 20 percent of wokers participate, or only in special "model" cases; some emphasis
is placed on meetings and suggestions for quality and productivity
1-No small group activities

continued

Table 2-2. (*continued*)

⑮ Information Sharing

    5-Company-wide information sharing and communication actively practiced (e.g., meetings for all employees, president meets all employees in small groups, vigorous small group activities, open-style offices)

    4-Various provisions for information sharing exist but to a lesser degree than above (5 points)

    3-Attempts are made at information sharing at each level in the company through meeting and other means

    2-Meetings are held before work begins

    1-No special provisions for information sharing

⑯ Sense of Unity

    5-Various device and practices such as company uniforms for all employees, open parking, social events, morning ceremonies, etc.

    4-Many of the above devices and practices are implemented but to a lesser extent (e.g., uniforms are not compulsory)

    3-Only some of the above are practiced

    2-Only some social events are held

    1-There are no special practices

V Labor Relations

⑰ Hiring Policy

    5-Applicants are carefully, meticulously screened; plant site selected where there is a homogeneous work force

    4-Applicants are selected with care; plant site selected where there is a homogeneous work force

    3-Plant site selected where there is a homogeneous work force; if plant site is traditional industrial area, applicants are selected with care

    2-Special hiring considerations only if plant is located in a traditionally industrial area

    1-No special selection for hiring; plant is located in a traditionally industrial area

⑱ Job Security

    5-Explicit (written) no-layoff policy that seeks to avoid layoffs as much as possible; provisions for long-term employment

    4-Layoffs are avoided as much as possible but this policy is not explicit and there have been no layoffs; provisions for long-term employment

    3-Layoffs are avoided as much as possible but have occurred on rare occasion

    2-Layoffs are avoided as much as possible but have occurred many times

    1-Layoffs are prone to occur if at all likely

⑲ Labor Unions

    5-There is no union and labor relations are peaceful

    4-There is no union but some problems in labor relations (e.g., attempts at organizing a union); or there is a union but relations are very cooperative

    3-There is a union and a cooperative tendency with the union (e.g. Management-Labor consulting system exists); or there is no union and there have been organization drives

    2-Union exists but it has relatively low membership; there have been strikes but otherwise the union is not very active

    1-Union is 100 percent organized and there have been strikes

⑳ Grievance Procedures

    5-There is no union and grievances resolved mainly on shop floor and through managerial channels

    4-There is no union and personnel department intervenes in the process of resolving grievances; or there is a union and grievances are resolved mainly on shop floor

    3-There is a union, and official grievance procedures are formalized, but emphasis is on shop floor and through managerial channels

Table 2–2. (*continued*)

2-There is a union and official grievance procedures; grievances tend to be resolved on shop floor

1-There is a union and official grievance procedures; there are many grievances; grievance procedures include external arbitration

VI Parent-Subsidiary Relations

㉑ Ratio of Japanese Expatriates

For plants with 500 employees or more (with less than 500 employees: plus 1% to the following ratios):

5-Ratio of Japanese expatriates is 4% or more

4-	3 ~ less than 4%
3-	2 ~ less than 3%
2-	1 ~ less than 2%
1-	less than 1%

㉒ Delegation of Authority

5-Parent in Japan makes plans and decisions

4-Subsidiary submits suggested plans and parent decides

3-Subsidiary submits plans and parent evaluates and gives or withholds approval

2-Subsidiary makes plans for approval by parent

1-Subsidiary makes and approves its own plans

㉓ Managerial Position of Americans

5-Most important senior management positions, including president, are held by Japanese

4-President is Japanese and many important positions are held by Japanese

3-Japanese and Americans share management positions and important positions roughly equally

2-President is American and majority of important positions are held by Americans

1-President is American and all important positions are held by Americans

VII Community Relations

㉔ Donations and Volunteer Activities

5-Very little activity or intent to be good corporate citizens

4-Donations are made to some extent and Japanese management play a somewhat active role

3-There is a great deal of donation activity, employees are encouraged to participate in local volunteer activities

2-There is a section staffed by American specialists and there is an attempt to carry out the same type and degree of activities as other U.S. companies

1-There is a highly organized special section dedicated to community relations and have successfully achieved "good corporate citizenship"

plants. A more detailed understanding of conditions at these plants requires individual case studies or pattern analysis.

On the other hand, revised application exists when the local production operation faces difficulties in applying the Japanese system directly and it becomes necessary to fall back on local practices or systems as a vehicle for application. This may involve adopting a more acceptable local "form" in order to introduce the "spirit" of the Japanese system. For example, the characteristic Japanese education and training system that is usually carried out through a combination of job rotation and on-the-job training (OJT) and that functions as a powerful means of skill-formation was, in some cases, locally introduced through a more formal training program. Training manuals were meticulously prepared, a training center was created, and formal as well as practical training was carried out. In other cases, the application of Japanese-style personnel evaluation was carried out under the guise of the standard American-style performance evaluation. Although these borrowed forms may not always achieve the same degree of impact, there are many examples of this kind of application.

In these cases, actively utilizing local systems and customs facilitates application of the Japanese system. In this sense, adaptation carries a positive connotation. Sometimes certain practices take on a new form, quite apart from anything that already exists in America or in Japan.

From either perspective, revised application is a way of avoiding the application-adaptation dilemma. There are many cases where it is a very sensible approach for promoting the realistic development of local management. Moreover, there are cases where adaptation and application aspects are mixed in very complicated manners. "Revised application" will be examined in more detail in the section that deals with evaluation criteria for the application and adaptation of each item. For now, it must suffice to point out that since it includes a certain amount of adaptation to local conditions, revised application is judged as representing a lesser degree of application than outright application.

The Hybrid Analysis (Summary)

The 7 groups and 24 items listed in Table 2–1 summarize the elements of the Japanese management and production system that should be applied at local plants in the United States, as well as specific measures and practices that sustain those elements. They are applied at the local plants in the midst of the local managerial environment and the various related conditions such as general practices and customs. In that sense this is the "international transfer model" for the Japanese management and production system. It outlines the system model that the target companies should strive to apply at their local plants. It also functions as the fundamental analytical framework for organizing the research results obtained from surveys carried out at the local U.S. plants of the target Japanese companies.

In examining the local plants on the basis of this framework, it becomes clear that there is a dynamic interplay between two forces or tendencies: application of the Japanese system, and adaptation to local conditions. This is what makes our model a hybrid model. It enables us to judge the degree or quality of the application and therefore determine which aspects of the Japanese-style management and production system have been put into practice, and to what extent. It enables us to address such questions as whether and how the system has been revised, or what types of application result. Finally, it permits us to describe and to deal with the various management conditions and the problems that result.

Table 2–2 outlines the basic criteria employed in the hybrid evaluation. Since a detailed examination and explanation of this table would entail a very lengthy process, the following explanation will focus upon the essential meaning and significance of each item, as well as its fundamental evaluation criteria.[2]

ELEMENTS OF AND EVALUATIVE CRITERIA FOR JAPANESE STYLE MANAGEMENT AND PRODUCTION SYSTEMS

The Logic Behind Japanese Management and Production Systems

The hybrid model disregards interindustry or interfirm differences and concentrates instead upon those characteristics of the Japanese-style management and production system which Japanese firms attempt to apply at their local plants in the United States. Among these characteristics, the following can be identified as salient and central to the Japanese system.

First, there is a flexible organization of workers that is not governed by rigid job demarcations. This is based upon a versatile work force wherein individual workers have been highly trained in a broad variety of skills. Second, these workers constantly accumulate technical and production know-how by voluntarily and constantly improving their jobs or work methods. Third, there is a flexible and efficient production management system centering around its flexible work organization that is supported by this comprehensive technical and production know-how. Production technology and equipment are sophisticated as empodied in this shopfloor know-how. These production system characteristics are the keys to achieving high-quality and efficient production of a diverse product line. And fourth, workers, supervisors and managers, who function as agencies of the characteristic shopfloor system, actively take part in every level of managerial and operational functions of the workplace. This is vital for the smooth and successful functioning of the overall system.

These characteristics contrast with the traditional American-style system. In order to better understand these differences, it will be useful to take a closer look at the main characteristics and principles underlying the traditional American system.[3] For this purpose, we have to generalize them and synthesize a model.

The principles underlying work organization in the traditional American system can be described as follows: A group of engineers or IE specialists designs a "job" by breaking down into the smallest units or "job elements" the various work tasks constituting the entire production process for a specific product. These job elements are then reassembled into various job tasks. In accordance with a finely demarcated job classification system designed by the IE specialists, a worker is then rigidly assigned to a set of such job tasks, which constitutes a single "job". A "job" is thus designed based upon the principles of the "Taylor-system"; then workers are assigned jobs in a fixed and inflexible manner. The individual worker is expected to be single-skilled and is required to adhere strictly to the job manual prepared by the technical department. Work organization at the workplace corresponds to this job system, the smallest unit of which is the individual, single-skilled worker. The entire production process is thus organized around this rigid "job system".

In comparison, Japanese-style work organization is governed by a different principle. Its most salient characteristic is a flexible relationship between jobs and workers. In the Japanese system, job tasks are assigned to work teams. There is a notable absence of the fixed job concept that implies a single set of job tasks performed by a single worker.

Of course at any single point in time, the assignment of job tasks and duties carried out by the individual workers is quite clear. It is in compliance with the "Talor-system" principle. However, this differs from the American model in three important ways. First, the smallest unit of organization in the workplace is not the individual worker who is assigned a single, fixed job, but the work team. Moreover, flexibility extends to the relationship between a team and a particular job process, as well as to the workers that constitute a particular team. Second, the main regular supervisory function for this team-centered work organization is carried out by first-line supervisors including *hanchoh* (team leaders). Third, work analysis, or the determination of standard work procedures, as well as its improvement or reorganization, is carried out by the workers involved in these work procedures and by the first-line supervisors and not only by technical specialists. Much of the decision-making regarding job content and job assignment thus centers around the shop floor.

Such a system requires multiskilled workers who are capable of carrying out a variety of job tasks. The training and skill formation that results in such workers is a key to achieving this type of production system. In the Japanese system, the training and education of workers does not take place away from the workplace, in special training or educational facilities, or according to a formal schooling system. Rather, it is carried out at the actual workplace within the company, and in close proximity to the actual job operations that are the focus of the training. On-the-job training (OJT), with its emphasis on training and education at the workplace, is a special characteristic of the Japanese system. Together with regular job rotation, this practice facilitates workers' multiple skill formation. According to this system, workers develop into core personnel who have experienced a wide variety of job operations, within and away from their teams. Fostering "corporate-specific" multiskilledness of the work force through in-house training achieved by active job rotation and OJT is one of the fundamental characteristics of the Japanese production system.

The Japanese-style job assignment described above, in contrast to the American system, effectively removes the partitions separating the individual job tasks, thus greatly facilitating routine job rotation. At the same time, it promotes the accumulation of a wide variety of knowledge and skills that the overall production process requires and provides ample basis for *kaizen* (improvement activities). The multiskilled and well-trained work force that results makes it possible to implement a flexible system for job reassignment. This also facilitates the efficient versatile worker distribution necessary for coping with the results of Kaizen activities and frequent product changes, as well as responding to the changes in the marketplace.[4]

A weakening of the "job" concept[5] also means that it becomes impossible for the wage system to correspond closely to jobs. Other factors than the specific job content increasingly effect wage decisions. Labor management evaluation of "personal" factors (such as versatility, "depth" of knowledge of the work process, communication capability, and so on), play an important role in determining wages. Since the formation of a wide variety of "internal plant skills" depends upon job rotation and OJT, length of service, which supposedly corresponds to the accumulation of these skills, becomes an important determining factor.[6] This is in fact an important rationale for the seniority (*nenkoh*) wage system and the related employee assessment system. In contrast to the "job-centered" wage system, we may call this a "person-centered" wage system.

The accumulation of corporate-specific skills can also be seen as one of the fundamental reasons for a long-term employment policy, sometimes referred to as "life-time employment," which are characteristic of Japanese-style management.

An indispensable element in this type of production system is the voluntary and enthusiastic participation of all workers. Small-group activities play an important role in promoting a sense of involvement among workers and in encouraging them to contribute to ongoing job improvement, problem solving, and increased productivity. The lack of a rigid and fixed job assignment provides the basis for the activity. At the same time, a feeling of unity or of belonging to the company, fostered by policies such as long-term employment, helps to motivate workers to become involved in group work. In addition, having less rigid job demarcations makes it easier to switch job assignments or organize training programs. This gives the company greater flexibility in coping with surplus workers resulting from productivity gains achieved through the group improvement activities indicated above or from altered market conditions. It permits the company to avoid drastic measures such as layoffs in order to trim the work force.

In conjunction with such human resource management methods, special characteristics of the Japanese production system related to the management of production hardware such as machines and equipment also emerge. In the American system, innovations and improvements in manufacturing equipment or the development of production or manufacturing technology depends entirely upon specialized technical departments. In contrast, the accumulated worker know-how and the voluntary improvement activities that exist at the workplace in the Japanese system, are a source of constant feedback to the technical department. In this way, know-how and voluntary improvement activities help to complete or round out the overall production equipment system. The know-how accumulated at the workplace thus makes an important contribution to the entire production technology system.

Regular as well as preventive maintenance of production equipment and machinery is carried out by skilled maintenance workers who have been promoted after accumulating broad knowledge and experience on the workplace. The promotion of workers with high seniority and extensive knowledge of the workplace to positions of group leader or supervisor also facilitates the management of work places according with the actual conditions of the shop floor. That also helps to account for another characteristic of the Japanese production system, namely, smooth and uninterrupted plant operations despite frequent product changes or other negative operating conditions. Quality control is also based upon a thorough understanding of production processes and the accumulation of job skills by the production workers. This results in a system where the workers are themselves able to assure quality during the production process. It makes it possible to "build quality into the process" and to adhere to a principle of the Japanese production system that states "you mustn't pass defectives onto the next stage in the process." It makes it possible to simultaneously achieve high product quality, cultivate highly efficient workers, and produce a large variety of products.

These same characteristics of the shop floor are also the key to the "just-in-time" production flow management seen in the Japanese system. The Japanese-style procurement system is characterized by two important features: a just-in-time parts flow management that interlocks with the production of the parent factory and keeps parts inventory to a minimum by producing and procuring "only what is necessary and only when it is necessary"; and the long-term transaction relationship that exists between the parent company and its subcontractor through the vertical *keiretsu* (enterprise grouping) to which they belong.

Maintaining an efficient just-in-time parts supply system demands that the production lines of the supplier and the assembler are closely coordinated and that the supplier practices a similar type of quality and process control that can flexibly and efficiently provide frequent delivery of small lots of parts containing zero defectives. In order to achieve such a relationship, it is necessary for the parent company (assembly plant) to be involved in the production process system of the supplier and to provide ongoing guidance and cooperation. The closely interconnected vertical keiretsu play an important role in protecting and reinforcing this relationship. The Japanese production system cannot be limited to the conditions of the parent factory.

Examining the characteristics and fundamental principles of the Japanese-style production system in this way, the significance of the groups and items listed in the hybrid model (Table 2–1) becomes clear. Below, we shall examine each of these items in detail, while making reference to their 5-point evaluation criteria. For a detailed list of these criteria, the reader is referred to Table 2–2.

Work Organization and Administration

The group of items entitled "Work Organization and Administration" constitutes the core of the Japanese system responsible for simultaneously achieving high quality and high efficiency. Accordingly, this group includes six items: ① Job Classification, ② Wage System, ③ Job Rotation, ④ Education and Training, ⑤ Promotion, and ⑥ First-line Supervisors.

① *Job Classification*

The traditional American-style production system is typically characterized as having finely demarcated but inflexible job classifications. It is not unusual for there to be a total of over 100 different job classifications for operative workers. These classifications, which are situated within detailed job ladders and the internal promotion system, serve to raise the partitions between jobs. Based upon this type of job classification, labor unions established "seniority rule" and through collective bargaining they sought to protect jobs by restricting management's discretionary power to make arbitrary decisions on matters related to layoffs, promotion, or wages. With the development of "job control unionism," this trend has become all the more pronounced and the individual worker has consequently become locked into this rigid job classification system.

The introduction of a "group" work organization or "team" system and the creation of a Japanese-style flexible job organization based upon flexible job assignments and job descriptions requires significant changes to the existing American-style job classification system. Left unchanged, the introduction of job rotation or the Japanese system for the formation of versatile workers with multiple skills would be extremely difficult.

For this reason, evaluating application of the Japanese system with regard to this item involves judging the extent to which the job classification system is simplified. This entails counting the number of independent job classes or job descriptions. In order to determine how rigidly jobs are classified, we examine the extent to which different job classifications reflect different pay rates. This is because it is theoretically possible to switch job assignments where job classes are subject to the identical pay rate. However, when other data (job rotation, etc.) confirmed that job assignments remained inflexible despite equivalent pay rates, we resort to "number of job titles" as a means of determining the number of different job classes.

② *Wage System*

Simplifying the job classification system also necessitated altering the closely related wage system. In the traditional American system, different wages correspond to each of the different detailed job classes. Accordingly, pay raises are usually accompanied by a change to a higher job grade with a higher wage bracket. In this case, the degree of application of the Japanese system is judged by the extent to which this rigid job-based wage system is moderated.

The Japanese wage system adopts a "person-centered" as opposed to a "job-centered" approach. Wages are determined on the basis of length of service (*nenkoh*) as well as performance evaluations (*jinji kohka*), made primarily by the worker's immediate supervisor. Where such a wage system is found to exist, we award a 5 denoting the highest degree of application. Where wages are "job-centered" and conform to a detailed job classification system, we award a 1. Some U.S. plants employ a merit system for determining wages. This is based upon an objective performance evaluation form, the results of which are communicated to the worker being evaluated. Where this type of wage system is found to exist, we award a 4. In still other cases, notably the auto industry, job classifications have undergone radical simplification, sometimes resulting in only a single job class. Although wages remain determined by the job, this has resulted in a highly diluted "job" concept and consequently represents a significant departure from the American-style wage system. Since such wage systems do not even exist in Japan, we categorized this approach as "revised application" discussed earlier. In this case we awarded a 2 or a 3, representing some degree of application.

③ *Job Rotation*

Job rotation is a method for achieving the corporate-specific development of versatile, multiskilled workers, who are the backbone of the Japanese-style shop-floor work organization. We examine the extent to which job rotation is implemented. This also serves as another index for determining the extent to which a company introduces a flexible job classification and assignment system, or in other words, the Japanese-style "team" (*han*) work group. Consequently, this was a very important supplementary index for evaluating changes in the job classification and the related wage systems mentioned above.

In evaluating this item, we examine work groups or teams of about fifteen to twenty workers under the direct control of a first-line supervisor. We pay particular attention to job rotation coverage (does it extend beyond the work team?) and frequency (is it a daily, routine practice?). We also take into consideration whether the in-house training and development of versatile multiskilled workers is the overt objective for job rotation and if it is supported or supplemented by an explicit guide or planning system such as a supervisor's training chart.

④ *Education and Training*

An education and training system that develops workers with a broad range of skills, especially through intensive in-house training that emphasizes OJT, is a trademark of the Japanese system. Our primary criterion for evaluating this item is the extent to which such practices are utilized for the development of key production workers. In the Japanese system, such training is combined with extensive job rotation, which is premised upon long-term employment. This system also produces maintenance workers and supervisors who receive their entire training within the plant. Accordingly, a second criterion is the extent to which a system trains its own maintenance and supervisory personnel.

OJT is not a common practice in the United States. The introduction of the Japanese-style training system, especially for the training of maintenance and supervisory personnel, is therefore apt to result in a more formal training program. This type of "revised application" is considered similar to the Japanese system. Sending key personnel to Japan for training, or sending Japanese trainers to the U.S. plants, is also considered to enhance application of the Japanese system, because they utilize the Japanese training system itself or they are trying to transfer the system through trainers who embody it.

⑤ *Promotion*

The Japanese-style promotion system is based upon length of service (*nenkoh*) and recommendation through personal assessment (Jinji kohka) by an employee's immediate supervisor. Highly skilled and experienced, plant-trained employees who are promoted to the supervisory level from the production ranks are a key to the success of the Japanese-style production system. Our main criterion for evaluating this item is, therefore, whether a system for the internal promotion of supervisory personnel is firmly established. In this sense, a promotion system for rank workers among them is closely related to it. In contrast, a promotion system based exclusively upon job postings and seniority is considered to reflect the American system. However, if the strict seniority criterion is tempered with consideration of special in-house qualifications, this is judged to include some degree of application.

⑥ *First-line Supervisors*

In the Japanese plant, supervisors typically have two main functions. The first is managing the activities of the work team. This involves supervising job rotation through routine changes in job assignments, and organizing the skill training achieved through OJT. The second function is technical supervision related to the smooth operation of the production line. This includes IE functions such as setting up or revising standard practices, or making adjustments to the line balance through revisions or changes in job assignments. It also involves flexible trouble-shooting and coordination functions through cooperating with the maintenance or parts departments or with other supervisors as required by line breakdowns. By contrast, the primary function of supervisors in the American system is labor management and decipline. This reflects the principles underlying American-style shop-floor work organization. It means making sure that workers carry out their job assignments and adhere to the rules and procedures as specified in the job manuals or the process control and production plan established by the technical department. It is not necessary for such supervisors to be internally promoted. Where supervisors were observed to have only this type of disciplinary function, we awarded a 1.

Production Control

The items in this group measure the degree of application of Japanese-type production technology and process management systems. These items are ⑦ Equipment, ⑧ Quality Control, ⑨ Maintenance, and ⑩ Operations Management.

As explained above, in the Japanese-style production system, supervisors, maintenance workers, and production workers, develop a wide variety of skills and gain extensive knowledge concerning the production process through characteristic training and education practices as well as through the accumulation of practical know-how and experience in job improvement (*kaizen*) activities. These workers, working with production equipment that itself incorporates production know-how accumulated at the shop floor, result in a system that has the ability to "build quality into the process." At the same time, this creates efficient and flexible production control, which boasts smooth equipment operation despite frequent product changes or other operating problems. In this way, the "model" Japanese system is characterized by a flexible and efficient production control system that is capable of offering a diverse product lineup. The key to this system is flexible personnel assignment based on versatile production workers with multiple skills.

On the other hand, in the "model" American system, specialized technical departments look after the production technology and the manufacturing technology systems as well as related production and process control. Accordingly, the role and function of the ordinary production worker have no significance to manufacturing technology or production and process control systems. Rather, these workers are expected to carry out their detailed and fixed duties according to an operating manual prepared by the technical department. It is a system of single-skilled specialization. Process control and improvement in equipment operation takes place under the direction of the technical department, and productivity gains are largely a function of economies of scale. Quality control is also the responsibility of a specialized department and the procedure generally consists of inspecting for and scrapping defectives at the final stage of the production process. This system corresponds to the "mass production of a limited variety of products." Clearly, in this regard, the Japanese and American production systems are polar opposites.

In the long term, it is entirely conceivable that the Japanese system will be realized through revised application using local equipment, as well as local workers and managers. However, our survey indicates that at the present stage, the "ready-made" Japanese-style production technology and know-how systems, with some minor adjustments notwithstanding, are being applied to local production in their original form. This corresponds to directly bringing in the "results." At present, the application of the "methods" (as opposed to the results) is still only a distant goal, although efforts to achieve this goal are being made.

⑦ *Equipment*
Accordingly, the main criterion for determining a high degree of application regarding production equipment is "bringing-in" equipment directly from Japan. By contrast, local procurement is judged to decrease the degree of application. When there are local modifications to production equipment through improvement activities, and when there are firm feedback channels between production workers and the technical department, this is a considered to increase the degree of application.

⑧ *Quality Control*
Evaluating the application of quality control (QC) concerns searching for concrete measures or procedures through which production is able to "build quality into the process." Examples of consciousness-raising measures include QC and zero-defect (ZD) circles, as well as line-stop authority granted to production workers and the introduction of various fail-safe devices to help prevent careless mistakes (*poka-yoke*). On the other hand, emphasis upon inspection by an independent inspection or quality control department is judged an American practice.

Quality control carried out under the supervision of workers sent from Japan is also a type of quality control by specialists and therefore judged an American practice. However, if there is feedback from quality control to production workers, then this is considered a factor that increases application of the Japanese system. Finally, evaluating the quality control system also requires taking into consideration the actual level of quality that the system achieves.

⑨ *Maintenance*
Our main concern is whether maintenance workers were acquired by way of in-house training of experienced production workers. Emphasis upon preventative maintenance and the extent to which regular production workers or supervisors participate in maintenance are also important criteria. As modern production equipment relies increasingly upon advanced mechatronics, it is becoming increasingly necessary, even in Japan, to have personnel with specialized knowledge in this area. For this reason, the employment of technical high school graduates who have no former experience and receive in-house training as maintenance specialists, is also considered application of the Japanese system. On the other hand, maintenance carried out by a special technical department that obtains experienced workers from an external labor market, and in which there is little or no participation on the part of first-line supervisors and regular production workers, is considered to reflect the American system.

⑩ *Operations Management*

The final item for consideration under production control is management of general production operations. This is an overall assessment of how smoothly and successfully the local plant operates as a result of management based upon the Japanese-style production system. We examine the following points: Are standard work practices and procedures transferred directly from Japan or are they revised, and if so to what extent? Are these procedures revised locally and do they facilitate adjustments to the line balance? To what extent does the plant introduce measures and devices that help provide a flexible response to accidents [measures for the proper evaluation of and response to various conditions by production personnel, cooperation between supervisors, preventative maintenance methods, and *and on* systems (special signal boards) etc.]? Is there a high product mix and smaller production lots and are product changes carried out smoothly?

Efficient control over operations also requires a steady flow of parts and materials required by the different production processes. However, this depends not only upon parts receiving and inventory control but also upon arrangements for the procurement of parts and materials from outside suppliers.

Parts Procurement

This group consists of three items: ⑪ Local Content, ⑫ Suppliers, and ⑬ Procurement Method.

⑪ *Local Content*

So long as U.S.-Japan trade friction over the export of manufactured products remains the general backdrop to local production by Japanese firms, the strong pressure upon these local plants to increase local content (the proportion of parts locally produced and procured) will continue. This is one of the major problems facing local production by Japanese firms. Accordingly, the ratio of local content becomes an important criterion for evaluating a firm's degree of adaptation as an indication of its response to this pressure. At the same time, with knock-down assembly plants at one extreme and full-scale local production through the complete transfer of all major manufacturing processes at the other, this local content ratio is a direct measure of "localization." A low ratio reflects high application and results in a high evaluation in terms of our 5-point scale, and vice versa.

There may also be qualitative differences in local content that the local content ratio fails to pick up. Examples of qualitative factors include the source and the method of procurement. These items are described and evaluated below as ⑫ Suppliers and ⑬ Procurement Method.

In Japan the procurement system typically involves a special subcontractor or affiliated company relationship traditionally not seen in the United States between a "parent" company and various parts or processing companies. Through a special long-term transaction relationship, the "parent" company provides the subcontractors or affiliates with cooperation and guidance, even in the development and operation of manufacturing technologies and quality control techniques and processes. This type of procurement system, in combination with the characteristic internal production system of the larger "parent" company, constitutes an indispensable element of the overall Japanese production system.

The high quality and reliable delivery of parts and materials that result from this procurement method enable the "parent" company to minimize its parts and materials inventory and is a precondition for smooth and efficient control of the parent company's line operations. This is one of the most important factors in order for local plants to increase their product lines and achieve efficient production with a high product mix. The degree to which this procurement method can be transplanted to the United States is a key factor in determining whether local production in the United States can achieve the same level of quality and productivity that is achieved in Japan.

Japanese parts manufacturers are also establishing production facilities overseas. Procurement from such plants is an example of maintaining supplier relationships and constitutes importing or "bringing-in" the identical procurement method that exists in Japan. This is evaluated as a form of *result* application. When the parts supplier is a U.S. company but the same type of Japanese technical and managerial cooperation for quality control or production and delivery systems are established between the local production plant and the supplier, this is judged as application of *method*. However, the traditional relationship prevailing between U.S. assembly firms and parts suppliers is fundamentally different from the relationships that exist between similar companies in Japan. In America, delivery, price, and specifications are generally specified by contract, and spot transactions among multiple competing firms is the norm. Consequently, it is not very easy to establish the same type of "parent"-subcontractor relationship that exists in Japan. The degree of dependence upon U.S. parts suppliers is therefore an important indicator of degree of adaptation.

⑫ *Suppliers*

The varying degree to which local procurement systems have been established reveals another aspect of this issue, namely, the problems of nonlocal procurement. A low local content ratio signifies that much of the procurement comes from nonlocal sources resulting in a low degree of local adaptation. According to the analysis for this item, suppliers are grouped into three categories: Japan, Japanese firms operating in Mexico or in South-East Asia, and North America (i.e., Canada and the United States). A high proportion of procurement from Japan equates with "bringing-in" the Japanese-style procurement method and is accordingly judged as a high degree of application. Supply from North America includes Canada regardless of whether or not the supplier is a Japanese firm. The manufacture of components at the local plant, which in Japan would be procured from a subcontractor or a related firm, is considered a strategy for avoiding some kind of problem with local procurement, and for this reason is judged closer to application. Also, the supplier issue is closely connected with the developing international procurement system by Japanese firms related to factors such as labor costs and the yen appreciation.

⑬ *Procurement Method*

The local content ratio itself does not necessarily indicate whether a Japanese-style procurement system has been established. The procurement method offers better insight into this matter. The criteria for application evaluation listed under this section in Table 2–2 focus on relationships with American firms in an effort to determine the extent to which the Japanese procurement system has been established. These include guidance and cooperation in technical as well as quality control areas, and are based upon the strict observance of delivery times, such as multiple daily deliveries, the utilization of *kanban,* and the just-in-time delivery system.

The three groups described above, Work Organization and Administration, Production Control, and Procurement, represent the *core* constituent elements considered necessary for the target companies to successfully apply the Japanese-style production system. The three groups discussed below, namely Group Consciousness, Labor Relations, and Parent-Subsidiary Relations, constitute a subsystem or supplementary framework which, to varying degrees, supports and provides important preconditions for the effective application of the core elements.

Group Consciousness

As indicated earlier, voluntary and active employee involvement, especially on the part of production workers, is indispensable for the smooth functioning of the Japanese-style management and production system. Group IV will examine the items that help foster group consciousness. These items are ⑭ Small Group Activities, ⑮ Information Sharing, and ⑯ Sense of Unity. Of these, Small Group Activities is most closely connected to the production system.

⑭ *Small Group Activities*

We begin by examining employee involvement activities that are closely related to work organization at the shop-floor level. In Japan, such voluntary activity groups take the form of small group activities such as QC and ZD circles and *kaizen* teams. These small group activities perform two important and mutually supportive roles. The first is to supply feedback from the workplace, thus helping to accumulate valuable knowledge and know-how, such as for the improvement of production methods and work procedures. This is interrelated with various measures for workers to acquire a broad range of skills through education and training, such as OJT and job rotation. Through these small group activities, workers have an opportunity to learn from the experiences of workers in other areas of the plant, thus deepening their knowledge and understanding not only of their own operations but of those in other parts of the plant as well. This is a key to enabling workers to flexibly respond to breakdowns or other problems in the production operations. The second role is to provide production workers with channels for information sharing and opportunities for general communication, thus helping to promote a Japanese-style team spirit. This enhances employees' group consciousness and sense of unity with the company. In carrying out these two functions, small group activities constitute a general backdrop for other elements of the Japanese production system, such as management of work organization, in-house training and education practices, and the formation of Japanese process technology.

In view of the importance of these two roles of Small Group Activities, it might seem more appropriate to include this item with other core items in group I. However, the results of our study have revealed that at this stage in the development of local production, the second role takes precedence. In the future, the first role will take on the significance that it already has in Japan. Consequently, the voluntary participation of production workers in small group activities is included in the fourth group comprised of items that provide supportive conditions for the Japanese-style production system.

The rate of participation in QC circles is selected as the primary criterion for evaluation of degree of application of the Japanese system in regard to this element. At the same time, the actual content of the QC circle activities, the frequency with which they meet, and their functions are also taken into account. Specific considerations include whether or not activities are conducted during working hours, whether participation is voluntary or obligatory, how many times a week meetings are held, the rate of worker participation, and whether they play a significant role in contributing to job improvements, innovative production methods, and higher quality.

The very existence of the Japanese production system, as well as its various functions, including small group activities, is supported by the voluntary and active participation and involvement of production workers. This is unlike the U.S. production system. As a rule, such voluntary participation and involvement is simply not part of American corporate culture. In order for Japanese companies to establish the Japanese-style management and production system at their local production operations in the United States, they must make a conscious effort to create this type of corporate culture.

⑮ *Information Sharing and* ⑯ *Sense of Unity*

These items are used to evaluated efforts by the companies to try and create the kind of corporate culture rich in the qualities described above. In the absence of a supportive cultural and social environment, transferring this type of Japanese corporate culture to local production in the United States demands a deliberate, concentrated effort. This resulted in a tendency for revised application wherein features and practices that are informal in Japan, are formalized in the United States.⑮ Information Sharing, is evaluated by taking into consideration the communicative, information-sharing value of meetings and similar gatherings at all levels, including those at and above middle management, of small group activities, of open-style offices, and of other measures for communication within the company.⑯ Sense of Unity, is evaluated by examining a number of features that enhance employees' feeling of participation and membership in a group. These include: uniforms (are they prescribed and to what extent are they accepted by employees?); the absence of special parking privileges for staff, including upper management; open-style cafeteria; social events such as picnics, parties, or sports activities; and ritual gatherings at the start of the working day, such as a "morning ceremony."

Labor Relations

Labor relations vary significantly from country to country. They reflect historical differences in the socioeconomic development as well as different social and cultural norms and values. Various aspects of labor relations differ as a result, including labor practices and the legal system. As explained above, there are major differences between American and Japanese labor relations. The local application of the Japanese-style management and production system by Japanese companies in the United States faces a number of direct and indirect restrictions as a result. Local labor practices may pose serious restrictions on the application of the Japanese system, especially in regard to the core of the International Transfer Model, namely work organization and its administration at the local plant. Japanese companies attempting to apply the Japanese system overseas are forced to deal with various aspects of these restrictions. The following items, grouped under Labor relations, represent four such aspects: ⑰ Hiring Policy, ⑱ Job Security, ⑲ Labor Unions, and ⑳ Grievance Procedures.

⑰ *Hiring Policy*

One of the salient differences between the labor markets in Japan and in the United States is the relative homogeneity among employees in Japan. It is likely that a homogeneous work force facilitates integration and a sense of unity among employees. It may also make it easier to implement aspects of the Japanese-style production system such as flexible job assignments and work organization, as well as the underlying system for developing versatile employees through training in a multitude of skills. On the other hand, the heterogeneity and multicultural character of the U.S. labor market stands in sharp contrast to that of Japan, and this quite likely imposes significant restrictions upon the application of the Japanese system.

Hiring Policy is concerned with evaluating the hiring policies of Japanese local producers in the United States that reflect an attempt to cope with these restrictions. Some of these hiring policies are implemented through employee selection and/or plant site selection, in order to secure the type of human resources most suitable to the smooth functioning of the Japanese-style production and management system. Our primary criterion is the amount of emphasis that the company places upon employee selection.

A related consideration is the composition of the employee workforce as an indicator of the multiethnic and multicultural aspects of American society. This involves an analysis by social minority such as race or working women. We also consider the ratio of employees to the total number of local residents. If there is a high proportion of local residents, employee homogeneity is considered high regardless of differences between racial or ethnic groups. The hiring of minorities is also affected by legal affirmative action requirements, as well as by general hiring practices of American companies in the plant vicinity. These practices are influenced by plant location, and for this reason, such local conditions are considered to play an important role in decisions affecting initial site selection. Based on this type of managerial environment research data, we broadly categorized each of the target plants as belonging to one of three regions, namely the East and Midwest, the South (including Texas), and the West Coast. An additional consideration is whether the plant is located in a traditional industrial region or in a predominantly rural one.

⑱ *Job Security*

A well-established practice that serves as a general basis for Japanese-style management in Japan, is long-term, or "life-time" employment, and the related seniority system (*nenkoh*). This item attempts to evaluate the application of this long-term employment policy in local production. As seen above, the in-house training and education of versatile and multiskilled employees is a key factor in the successful operation of the Japanese-style production and management system. It results in internally promoted, skilled and experienced maintenance and supervisory personnel who are highly familiar with and knowledgeable about their plant. This in turn helps achieve smooth and efficient operations that are characterized by a flexible shop-floor work organization and the ability to cope with various problems that might arise during production operations.

In fact, this accumulation of in-house training and the resulting internal promotion system are produced through the so-called structured internal labor market, which is based upon long-term employment. Also, the general foundation for these practices is the sense of unity that shop floor and other employees have with the company, and the active, voluntary participation that results. Consequently, if Japanese companies wish to establish the Japanese-style production and management system at their local production operations, then they must pursue policies that ensure long-term, stable employment.

In contrast, the American-style production system is based upon a finely demarcated and rigid job classification system, and it relies upon technological advances, skill specialization, and mass production economies of scale to realize efficiency gains. It constitutes a simple mass production system. This is why adjustments in production to meet changes in market demand must take the form of employment adjustments through layoffs. It is one of the reasons that American industrial labor unions have pursued "job control unionism," which incorporates job designations and adherence to the seniority rule in their collective labor agreements. Accordingly, the emphasis that Japanese local producers place upon long-term employment and job security is evaluated in terms of their approach to layoffs as a means of adjusting production.

Specifically, this is judged in terms of whether a company has an unambiguous "no layoff" job security policy, or if not, how often it has resorted to layoffs in the past. Other measures to promote long-term employment are also considered. However, the American practice of a seniority-based layoff system is not necessarily inconsistent with the notion of employment stability for experienced key personnel. Consequently it is possible for a Japanese company to make use of layoffs as a way of adjusting local production. For this reason, it is less vital for local Japanese plants to observe the rigid no-layoff policy. However, in general, a layoff has a negative effect upon an employee's sense of unity with the company. In this respect, job security must remain a fundamental precondition for the application of the Japanese system.

⑲ *Labor Unions*

Labor practices and labor relations in the United States are inseparable from unionism. The main features of these practices are contained in the labor contracts. The type of labor relations that typically results is dominated by traditional "job control unionism" and produces a finely demarcated and inflexible job classification system and a corresponding wage system. These conditions are likely to impose significant restrictions on the application of Japanese-style work organization and management. For example, in the U.S. system, there is a sharp distinction between labor and management, which imposes restrictions upon the term-type relationship between supervisors and shop floor workers. There are union regulations that restrict changes to work rules; seniority regulations affect internal promotion. Another salient difference between unions in Japan and in the United States is that in Japan they are mainly enterprise unions, while in America industrial unions, and many variations thereof, are the norm.

A necessary condition for the application of a Japanese-style system is therefore either a cooperative relationship between management and the labor union, or a nonunion plant. The first point that should be taken into consideration in evaluating this item is whether or not the plant is unionized. If it is, then the organization rate and a history of strikes or other form of labor disputes are studied in order to determine the actual state of labor-management relations. If the plant is not unionized, then a closer look should be taken at practices to promote a cooperative labor-management relationship, and whether or not there have been any attempts at forming a union, and if so, the employee reaction to such attempts. Differences among industries are also taken into account.

⑳ *Grievance Procedures*

Labor relations in U.S. plants, and particularly where there is a union, have developed a formal, multistage grievance procedure. This is intended to deal with various grievances that may arise over interpretation of the detailed, comprehensive labor contract, which is the result of collective bargaining. This is an indispensable element of American union-style labor relations that have developed over the years. Rather than settling grievances through the existing work organization and administration system, the purpose of these grievance procedures is to resolve labor disputes through a process that involves a formal procedure and route that is separate and independent from the administration of the workplace.

By contrast, in Japan, disputes are mainly resolved at the workplace. Although there are a number of variations, the general procedure is for the supervisor, who is in daily contact with the employees concerned, to personally help resolve problems concerning job assignment or promotion. In some cases a labor-management conference system is established. In examining this item, a procedure for resolving grievances at the shop floor and carried out through the existing work organization is evaluated as application of the Japanese system. On the other hand, the "open door" approach in which the personnel department plays an active role in resolving disputes or complaints that arise on the job, is also observed in the United States, particularly in nonunion shops. However, the most typical example of the American-style approach is judged to be that where a formal, multistage grievance procedure is specified in the collective agreement, based upon a detailed union contract.

Parent-Subsidiary Relations

In examining parent-subsidiary relations, the focus is on the managerial relationship between Japanese parent companies and the local subsidiaries in the United States, and in particular, on the local subsidiaries' degree of managerial independence. This degree of independence is related to the manner in which application of the Japanese system is carried out; whether it is introduced quickly under the guidance of the parent company, or whether it is gradually transplanted while simultaneously adapting to local conditions. This is also intimately connected with the parent company's corporate strategy. This suggest patterns of application that are not unique to a particular industry. There may also be differences in the kinds of application ultimately achieved depending upon whether this task is delegated to Japanese personnel dispatched from Japan and to whom the important managerial posts have been assigned, or whether this process is entrusted to local managers. The items included in this group are ㉑ Ratio of Japanese Expatriates, ㉒ Delegation of Authority, and ㉓ Managerial Position of Americans.

㉑ *Ratio of Japanese Expatriates*

The ratio of Japanese personnel transferred directly from Japan, to the total number of employees at the local production plant, is considered a direct index of application. The general practice for firms engaged in local production is to post American nationals in positions ranging from senior management to lower supervisory levels, and in areas including finance, personnel, production control, and engineering. At the same time, personnel transferred from Japan are also assigned to key posts in various important departments. These Japanese personnel are highly familiar with the Japanese system and their presence functioned as an important channel for the application of the Japanese-style management system. At the same time, they are able to assist management in those areas where application of the Japanese system remained inadequate. This vital role of helping to maintain smooth operations contains, in itself, an aspect of result application. The ratio of Japanese personnel is therefore chosen as the criterion for the application of this item (Table 2–2).

This ratio tends to rise in cases where a relatively small scale plant operates with relatively few employees. It is therefore necessary to take into consideration variations in the standard scale of operations typical for different industries. Accordingly, where the total number of employees is 500 or less, we deduct one percentage point from the ratio of Japanese expatriates. However, if the total number of permanent Japanese employees is 100 or more, this is considered high by any standard, and a percentage point is added. Also, some companies temporarily dispatch extra employees from Japan to local operations during plant startup or at periodic intervals for consulting or training purposes. If there is a large number of such temporary certain percentage points are also added.

㉒ *Delegation of Authority*

This item deals with the extent to which the local subsidiary is independent from the parent company with respect to all types of decision making affecting local management. In particular, this concerns the delegation of responsibility for aspects of decision making, such as making preliminary proposals or granting final approval, in areas including production and sales planning, investment, procurement method, and local personnel. In cases where most major decisions are made in Japan, with little input from the local subsidiary, this is evaluated as application.

However, most of the target companies are strictly plant operations, and in some cases there is another local controlling or parent company between the local plant and the Japanese parent. In such cases, the relationship among all three companies, as well as differences among their respective international business strategies, also has to be taken into account. Where the local operation has formed a joint venture with an American partner, the influence of this relationship upon decision-making at the local plant is also an important matter for consideration.

㉓ *Managerial Position of Americans*

This is concerned with evaluating the managerial position and function of American employees in relation to that of their Japanese counterparts with respect to the local management organization. In particular, attention is focused on the extent to which Americans fill positions such as president, director, and general manager. The studies revealed that, in general, senior positions responsible for personnel are filled by Americans, while senior responsibility in areas such as manufacturing, finance, or production engineering, is assigned to Japanese. An index for application is established by determining how far a particular local operation deviates from this standard pattern. Finally, in order to evaluate the true role of American managerial personnel, it is also necessary to take into account the posting of Japanese managerial personnel, as well as assistants (coordinators, advisors) at every level of management.

Finally, a few points are in order concerning group VII, Community Relations. With the recent increasing scale of Japanese local production in the United States, several areas of friction with local communities have begun to appear. Although this study focuses primarily on the production and management system existing inside the local plants, as well as relations between these plants and their parts suppliers, the relationship between local production and its local social environment, particularly in terms of management's "adaptation" to local society, must not be overlooked.

American enterprises place great importance upon community relations, and to that end they implement a number of local programs, including the practice of making many donations. Japanese companies, in comparison, have made little effort to develop this type of corporate behavior. However, in order to promote smooth local production, the Japanese manufacturers have in recent years also been willing to place greater emphasis upon this aspect of their activities. They are now willing to actively accommodate American corporate customs and culture in order to become good corporate citizens. This is especially so insofar as trade friction has played a major role in stimulating local production in the first place. Aggressively dealing with this problem is probably in the best interests of long-term stability of local production. Maintaining amicable relations with local communities is also in the interest of successfully transplanting the Japanese management and production system onto foreign soil. In this respect, Community Relations differs from the other elements in that its primary motivation is not application of the Japanese system, but rather adaptation to the local community. The Japanese local production enterprises must learn from the behavior of the American firms and aggressively carry out the same type of activities. It is therefore questionable whether this type of activity can be usefully examined from the perspective of the application-adaptation analysis. The only item selected for this group is ㉔ Donations and volunteer activities. It is treated as an "extra" element and utilized only for certain references as deemed necessary.

The evaluation of this item involved considering the degree of donation or volunteer activity. It is important to account for the ongoing nature of such activities, as opposed to single, isolated events. Company support for such employee activities, types of contributions to the community, or whether the company created a special committee or position to look after these matters, are the important points for consideration.[7]

THE FOCUS OF THE HYBRID-MODEL ANALYSIS

4-Perspective Evaluation: Internationalization and Transfer of the Japanese Model

The groups and items which appear in the application-adaptation analysis summarized above are shown in Table 2–1. This is the 23-item, 6-group analysis of the internationalization of Japanese-style management and production system. With particular emphasis upon group I, Work Organization and Administration, the groups and items in this analysis represent the elements and their related aspects considered necessary for the successful application of the Japanese production and management system by the firms and plants under investigation (group VII, Community Relations, is of a different nature). Based upon our plant surveys and the study of related material, the results of this analysis are expressed as "degrees of hybridization" for the application and adaptation of each item. This information made it possible to grasp the extent to which these plants have applied the Japanese-style management and production system at their local operations, or adapted to various conditions existing in the local environment. This constitutes the most fundamental method of analysis employed in the present research.

As mentioned in Chapter 1, there is an additional tool for analyzing the conditions existing among the target firms and plants in even greater detail. This is the 4-Perspective Evaluation (Table 2–3), which focuses upon the "results" and "method" application of "human" and "material" elements.

In this case, the "material-results" and "human-results" aspects refer to directly bringing-in sets of production equipment, as well as production know-how accumulated in Japan, or directly dispatching trained employees from Japan to the local production operations in the United States. Such employees would be expected to play various supplementary roles in local plant management. In contrast, "material-method" and "human-method" refer to the application of the material and human management methods which are themselves characteristic of the Japanese-style management and production system.

The significance of the 4-Perspective Evaluation lies in its ability to distinguish between whether a firm puts priority upon transplanting the methods of the Japanese management and production system, thereby bringing about an independent

Table 2–3. Items of 4-Perspective Evaluation

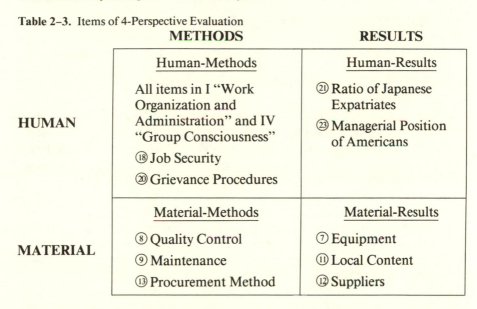

	METHODS	**RESULTS**
	<u>Human-Methods</u>	<u>Human-Results</u>
HUMAN	All items in I "Work Organization and Administration" and IV "Group Consciousness" ⑱ Job Security ⑳ Grievance Procedures	㉑ Ratio of Japanese Expatriates ㉓ Managerial Position of Americans
	<u>Material-Methods</u>	<u>Material-Results</u>
MATERIAL	⑧ Quality Control ⑨ Maintenance ⑬ Procurement Method	⑦ Equipment ⑪ Local Content ⑫ Suppliers

and self-reliant local operation, or whether the priority is on transferring the results of the system in order to realize mother-plant operations, and a comparable degree of performance, in local production and management anyway. Although both cases are equally representative of application of the Japanese system, they result in major differences in local management conditions.

To varying degrees, each of the plants investigated above brought in their "tried and true" production equipment from Japan, and procured many of their important components and materials from Japan or from Japanese firms situated abroad. Likewise, these companies dispatched employees from the Japanese parent company to take control of various managerial and production functions at various levels of the local plant operations. This is an attempt to achieve plant operations at the local overseas plants that are similar to those at the Japanese plant by bringing-in "ready-made" production technology as well as the human resources that embodied the relevant know-how.

Conversely, this "bringing-in" can be interpreted as an attempt to directly supplement those areas where transplanting Japanese methods is weakest, such as continuous improvement activities, accumulation of production know-how, and the creation of skilled human resource, and so on. It supplements those parts of the Japanese system that are difficult to apply locally or that face numerous restrictions. Sending key employees such as upper management, as well as shop-floor or maintenance employees, to Japan for special training and education fulfills a similar function. The greater this type of application of results, the more that local management relies upon Japan, and the less independent is its management and production system.

The 4-Perspective Evaluation highlights these different types of application. In fact, the 23-item, 6-group international transfer model is itself constructed by arranging items in terms of whether they reflect application of the Japanese system according to their degree of impact upon efficient operations management. The 4-Perspective Evaluation can be seen as a way of categorizing items in groups in order to clearly reflect these two types of application, namely transplanting the "method" and bringing-in "ready-made" parts (results) of the system. This is one practical application of the hybrid analysis.

Table 2–3 illustrates these relationships. It categorizes Ratio of Japanese Expatriates (item 21), and Managerial Position of Americans (item 23), as "human-results" because they indicate the extent to which personnel are transferred from Japan, and conversely, the extent to which local human resources are employed. Secondly, Equipment (item 7), Local Content (item 11), and Suppliers (item 12), are classified as "material-results." They show the extent to which production equipment and components are brought in from Japan. On the other hand, Quality Control (item 8), Maintenance (item 9), and Procurement Method (item 13), are listed as "material-method." Those three items represented use of Japanese methods for plant operations and production control. Finally, all items in group I Work Organization and Administration, and group IV, Group Consciousness, as well as Job Security (item 18) and Grievance Procedures (item 20) from group V, are categorized as "human-method." Those items described the methods of personnel management at the local plant. This 4-Perspective Evaluation makes it possible to observe the extent to which each of the target plants implements the different types of application—in other words, the extent to which a plant brings in "ready-made" results of the Japanese system, and the extent to which it transplants the "method" itself.

Pattern Analysis: Application Patterns of Local Production

Different types of management conditions existing in the local plants are identified through the application-adaptation analysis and through a coordinate axis that reflects the different aspects of application represented in the 4-Perspective Evaluation. The results of this analysis revealed various differences in local plant management and production operations among the various plants and industries investigated. These differences amounted to much more than the variation that would be expected to exist among a number of different plants. In fact, this description of Japanese local production in the United States revealed a variety of management patterns that can provide valuable suggestions for the future development of local production. The pattern analysis undertaken in this book is a synopsis of the research, as well as an attempt to illustrate those different patterns.

The pattern analysis follows the international transfer model and is based upon systematic correlation between application items. It attempts to identify patterns in the management and production systems shared by a number of different local production operations. By comparing the business results or performance of these different operations, it is possible to determine present and future trends in the management or production systems implemented by Japanese local production in the United States. To a certain extent it is also possible to predict the type of structural development necessary to ensure the long-term stability of these operations.

The evaluation of local production operations in accordance with the application-adaptation model revealed numerous patterns that varied according to industry, company, or plant. These patterns differed in terms of which items, and which corresponding aspects of the management and production system, are applied, as well as the type of application (out right or revised; results or methods), the degree of application, and the combination of items involved. The "model" Japanese-style management and production system itself does not exist among the local plants. Analyzing these different patterns makes it possible to observe which aspects of Japanese management and production system are applied, in which manner, and to what extent. It makes it possible to determine if a hybrid system that differs from the Japanese model, or a system that is in fact closer to the American model has been formed.

Finally, analyzing these "patterns" using the 4-Perspective Evaluation makes it possible to portray the local plants in greater detail still. It permits the identification of various pattern characteristics of local plant management, such as which aspects of the Japanese system are typically transplanted as "method" and to what degree human or material "results" (resources) are brought in directly from Japan. These patterns are analyzed in detail in Chapter 6.

3

The Typical Japanese Overseas Factory

KUNIO KAMIYAMA

OUTLINE OF THE SURVEYED FACTORIES

Local plant observations were carried out in the United States, Canada, and Mexico, over a period of approximately 1.5 months from the middle of August to the end of September, 1989. A total of forty-nine American, Japanese, and Korean plants from the auto assembly, auto parts, consumer electronics, and semiconductor industries was investigated. Table 3–1 provides the outline of forty-one Japanese plants included in this total. Since the principal objective of this research is to study conditions pertaining to the transfer of the Japanese-style management and production system to the United States, the study focuses upon conditions obtaining among thirty-four Japanese plants located mainly in the United States. Three of these are located in Canada, but since management conditions affecting these plants are judged to be essentially the same as those in the United States, they are evaluated according to the same criteria as the plants located in the United States.

This study includes nine auto assembly plants identified as plants AA to AI. The oldest of these is plant AA, which began producing automobiles in 1982 (motorcycles in 1979), followed by plants AB and AC, which also began production in the first half of the 1980s. The other six plants had a history of less than 2 years and in some cases had only just come on stream when the study was carried out. The nine auto parts plants were established over virtually the same period of time, reflecting the relatively short history of the expansion into the United States by the Japanese auto industry as a whole.

In contrast, the nine consumer electronics (mainly color television) plants, identified as plants EA to EI, have a longer history. Six of these plants started operating in the 1970s, and the 1982 start-up of plant EG is the last of such operations carried out by a major color television producer. Also, plant EI, which was established in 1986 as a joint venture with a major U.S. consumer electronics manufacturer (the joint ventured is now dissolved), has the same Japanese parent as plant ED, and is that company's first attempt at producing color CRTs in the United States. Likewise, plant EH was the second local operation by a company that had already established a plant in California in 1977.

The advance into local U.S. production by the Japanese semiconductor industry occurred approximately midway between that of the auto and consumer electronics industries. With the exception of plant SA, the four plants SB to SE all started production between the late 1970s and the early 1980s. Plant SF was launched a little later than the rest, but its parent company had already established a local subsidiary and carried out experimental production at a local test plant in 1983. Also, plant SG was newly established as a wafer fabrication plant affiliated with plant SE which carried out an assembly and testing process. Plant SA, which started up in 1971, has the longest history of all and can therefore be considered a pioneer among these local operations. However, as will be explained below, there are fundamental differences between plant SA and the other plants established by major semiconductor firms.

In addition to the above, we visited a further seven plants located in Mexico. These seven plants, referred to as "other plants visited", included two auto assembly plants (AS and AT), one auto parts plant (AU), and four consumer electronics plants (EJ to EM). The last five of these plants are *maquiladoras* plants, which are established under a system for manufacturing goods for export by utilizing low-cost Mexican labor and taking advantage of special privileges, including the duty-free import of parts and equipment. Since the management conditions at the Mexican plants are judged to be significantly different from those at U.S. (and Canadian) plants, the results of their analyses are not directly incorporated into the main body of this study. However, including the Mexican plants in the overall study has greater significance than merely that of providing a broader field for comparison, which can be helpful in analyzing Japanese production in the United States. The Mexican plants helped provide a clearer understanding of the interrelationships among U.S. plants, such as parts supply or process specialization. For these reasons, the present research contains a distinctly "continental North American" perspective.

In short, this study is remarkably comprehensive in its coverage of Japanese local production in these four industries. Apart from a very few exceptions, the survey has managed to target every Japanese auto assembly, color television, and semiconductor plant, as well as the major Japanese auto parts plants located in North America. This has been achieved in the midst of highly diverse and rapidly expanding Japanese investment in North America, including the construction of secondary plants in the United States and the *maquiladoras* plants in Mexico.

In order to provide an even greater basis for comparison between Japanese and non-Japanese local plants, we also visited a Korean plant (AZ) as well as several U.S. plants of American companies (Table 3–2). The U.S. plants are four auto plants (including each of the U.S. Big Three auto manufacturers) and three semiconductor plants. The Korean plant is an auto assembly plant located in Canada. This study, therefore, surveyed a total of forty-nine plants, including thirty-four Japanese plants located in the United States and Canada, seven Japanese plants located in Mexico, and eight non-Japanese (U.S. and Korean) plants.

THE TYPICAL JAPANESE OVERSEAS FACTORY

Table 3–3 (a hybrid evaluation table) presents an aggregate and an industry average hybrid evaluation for all of the thirty-four Japanese target plants located in the

Table 3–1. List of Surveyed Japanese Plants

			A. Target Plants	
Industry and Plants	Start of Operation	Number of Employees	Location	Main Products
Auto assembly				
AA*	Nov. 1982	6,500	Ohio	Passenger car, motorcycle, motorcycle and auto engines
AB*	June 1983	3,294	Tennessee	Passenger car, pickup truck
AC*	Dec. 1984	2,800	California	Passenger car
AD	Sep. 1987	3,477	Michigan	Passenger car
AE	May 1988	2,950	Kentucky	Passenger car, power train
AF	Sep. 1988	2,300	Illinois	Passenger car
AG	Nov. 1988	710	Canada	Passenger car
AH	Apr. 1989	997	Canada	Multi-purpose four wheel drive vehicle, passenger car
AI	Sep. 1989	864	Indiana	Passenger car, pickup truck
Auto parts				
AJ*	Feb. 1984	663	Tennessee	Air conditioner, evaporator, etc.
AK*	Dec. 1985	411	Tennessee	Instrument panel, lid cluster, etc.
AL	Feb. 1986	82	Kentucky	Wiper-related products, control devices
AM	July 1986	800	Michigan	Car heater, car radiator, etc.
AN	June 1987	210	Michigan	Pressed metal and sub-assembly, metal stamping dies and assembly fixtures
AO	May 1988	138	Kentucky	Automotive Brakes
AP	Aug 1988	243	Illinois	Stamping parts
AQ	Sep. 1988	140	Michigan	Seat for motor vehicle
AR	Apr. 1989	90	Canada	Seat for motor vehicle
Consumer electronics				
EA	July 1972	1,700	California	CRT for CTV, CTV
EB*	May 1974	567	Illinois	CTV
EC*	Jan. 1977	650	Arkansas	CTV
ED*	Aug. 1978	700	Tennessee	CTV, microwave oven

	Date	Number of employees	Location	Products
EE	Apr. 1979	290	California	CTV, VCR
EF*	Oct. 1979	744	Tennessee	CTV, microwave oven
EG	June 1982	250	New Jersey	CTV
EH	Sep. 1986	644	Georgia	CTV
EI	Nov. 1986	1,242	New York	CRT for CTV
Semiconductor				
SA	July 1971	577	California	Integrated circuit
SB*	Nov. 1978	750	California	256KDRAM, ASIC, microcomputor
SC	May 1979	318	Texas	256KDRAM, 1MDRAM, 64SRAM, etc.
SD*	Apr. 1980	209	California	1MDRAM, ASIC
SE*	May 1981	314	California	256KDRAM, 1MDRAM, EPROM, ECL
SF	1986	over 400	North Carolina	256KDRAM, 1MDRAM, ASIC, etc.
SG	Nov. 1988	355	Oregon	ASIC, wafer process for 256KDRAM

B. Other visited plants (in Mexico)

	Date	Number of employees	Location	Products
Auto assembly				
AS	July 1966	4,860	Mexico	Passenger car, commercial vehicle
AT	Nov. 1982	1,092	Mexico	Engine and transaxle for motor vehicle
Auto parts				
AU	June 1983	1,700	Ciudad Juarez	Wireharness for motor vehicle
Consumer electronics				
EJ	Jan. 1980	1,900	Tijuana	CTV, chassis for CTV
EK	May 1987	1,100	Tijuana	CTV, chassis for CTV
EL*	Sep. 1987	250	Tijuana	Transformer for microwave oven, etc.
EM	Nov. 1987	706	Ciudad Juarez	Chassis for CTV

Number of employees reflects the figures current at the time of our research from August to September, 1989. * represents thirteen target plants in the 1986 study. At that time, Plant EL was located in Tennessee.

Table 3–2. Non-Japanese Plants Visited

Plants	Location	Main Products
AV	Michigan	Passenger car
AW	Michigan	Passenger car
AX	Illinois	Passenger car
AY	Michigan	Stamping parts
AZ	Canada	Passenger car
SH	Arizona	Integrated circuit
SI	Texas	Integrated circuit
SJ	California	Integrated circuit

United States and Canada, based on the 5-point application-adaptation evaluation described in the previous chapter. The seven Mexican plants have also been evaluated, but because of different evaluation criteria, their results are not included in Table 3–3. Ratings for the five *maquiladoras* plants are provided for reference purposes only. The other two Mexican plants that are not *maquiladoras,* along with American plants (located in the United States) and a Korean plant (located in Canada) that are not evaluated, are excluded from the table. Also, for reasons explained in Chapter 2, the evaluation for group VII, Community Relations, item 24, Donations and Volunteer Activities is provided for reference only and displayed separately from the main table. The ratings for this group are not calculated into the overall average. The resulting table condenses the results of the analysis covering all aspects of the local managerial and production system in terms of the six groups and twenty-three items and for the thirty-four Japanese target plants located in the United States and Canada. The data presented in this hybrid evaluation table constitute the fundamental results of this study. These results will be applied towards gaining a better understanding of the average local operating conditions among the four industries and thirty-four plants representing Japanese production in the United States.

As Table 3–3 clearly shows, the overall average degree of application for all plants and all items is 3.3. This is slightly closer to the application end of the 5-point application-adaptation continuum. This average is surprisingly close to the 3.2 average produced by the 1986 study. In fact, a comparison of averages between the two studies for each industry and for each group shows that the maximum difference is only 0.2 and that most of these average evaluations are within plus or minus 0.1 points. In view of changes to group contents, revisions in the evaluation criteria, and changes in the number and in the scale of plants investigated, the similarity in the results is too great to be passed off as coincidence. Rather, in spite of the rapid changes within the local Japanese plants and their environment over the 3 intervening years, these results suggest that there have been no major changes in the management and operation of the local plants, and that the assumptions of and evaluations produced by this analytical model are fundamentally valid. They indicate that Japanese companies undertaking local production in the United States, where the management environment differs radically from that in Japan, continue to favor the application of the Japanese-style management and production system. However, due to the need for adapting to local conditions in the United States, they

Table 3–3. Hybrid (Degree of Application) Evaluation of "23-Item, 6 Group" in the 4 Industries

	Auto Assembly	Auto Parts	Consumer Electronics	Semiconductor	Average of 4 Industries	Maquiladoras (ref.)
I Work Organization and Administration	3.3	3.1	2.4	2.9	2.9	2.3
①Job classification	4.8	4.2	2.8	2.7	3.7	2.2
②Wage system	2.1	2.6	2.0	3.1	2.4	2.8
③Job rotation	3.2	2.7	2.1	2.6	2.6	1.4
④Education and training	3.4	2.9	2.2	3.0	2.9	2.6
⑤Promotion	3.2	3.3	2.7	3.1	3.1	2.8
⑥Firstline supervisors	3.1	3.0	2.6	2.7	2.9	2.2
II Production Control	3.4	3.6	3.1	3.1	3.3	3.4
⑦Production equipment	3.9	4.8	4.0	4.6	4.3	4.8
⑧Quality control	4.0	3.9	3.0	2.4	3.4	2.8
⑨Maintenance	2.9	2.8	2.1	2.6	2.6	3.0
⑩Operations management	2.9	3.0	3.3	2.9	3.0	3.2
III Procurement	3.0	3.0	2.6	3.5	3.0	3.1
⑪Local content	2.3	2.7	2.0	3.7	2.7	3.5
⑫Suppliers	3.8	3.7	3.6	4.4	3.9	3.3
⑬Procurement method	3.0	2.6	2.1	2.3	2.5	2.5
IV Group Consciousness	3.9	3.8	2.3	2.9	3.2	2.9
⑭Small group activities	2.7	2.9	2.2	2.4	2.5	1.8
⑮Information sharing	4.4	4.1	2.4	3.3	3.6	2.8
⑯Sense of unity	4.6	4.4	2.1	2.9	3.5	4.2
V Labor relations	4.2	4.1	2.7	3.5	3.6	3.7
⑰Hiring policy	4.3	3.8	2.4	3.1	3.4	3.0
⑱Job security	4.9	3.8	2.2	2.3	3.4	2.8
⑲Labor unions	4.2	5.0	3.4	5.0	4.4	4.8
⑳Grievance procedures	3.2	3.9	2.8	3.6	3.3	4.0
VI Parent-Subsidiary Relations	3.5	4.2	3.0	3.9	3.6	2.9
㉑Ratio of Japanese expatriates	3.8	4.6	2.6	3.9	3.7	1.6
㉒Delegation of authority	3.3	4.0	3.2	4.0	3.6	3.8
㉓Managerial position of Americans	3.3	4.0	3.2	3.9	3.6	3.4
Average of 23 items	3.5	3.6	2.7	3.2	3.3	3.0
VII Community Relations	1.8	2.0	2.7	2.8	2.3	4.0
㉔Donations and volunteer activities	1.8	2.0	2.7	2.8	2.3	4.0

implement a type of hybrid system that differs from that of U.S. companies, as well as from that of their own parent companies in Japan.

Of course it must be remembered that this 3.3 point rating for degree of application is an average for all plants and all items. The isolation of any one particular item or group is bound to reveal considerably different results.

23-Item, 6-Group Evaluation

6-Group Evaluation

Figure 3–1 is a graphical representation of the average degree of application of each group for each industry separately, and for the four industries as a whole. In each diagram (industry), the distance from the center to the point at which the vertex (group) intersects with the hexagon, represents the average degree of application for that respective industry and group. As these diagrams show, those groups that, according to the 4-Perspective Evaluation, represent the "Human-Results" or "Material-Results" aspects of application, namely group V, Labor Relations, group VI, Parent-Subsidiary Relations, and group II, Production Control, exhibit relatively high degrees of application. The lowest degree of application is seen in group I, Work Organization and Administration, which represents the "Human-Method" core of the Japanese system, followed by group III, Procurement, which represents the "Material-Results" aspect. Group IV, Group Consciousness, which as a sort of subsystem represents the "Human-Method" aspect of application, com-

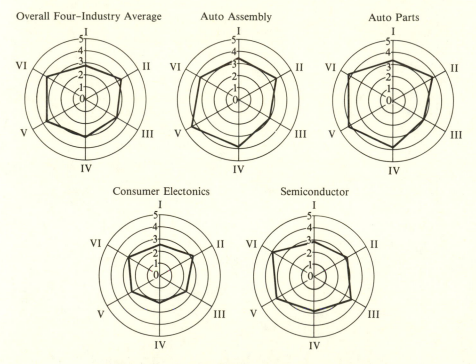

Figure 3–1 Degree of Application for Each Group

pensates for these lower scores with a higher degree of application. The following discussion examines the average degree of application for each group and for the four industries as a whole in greater detail.

Groups V and VI reveal the highest degrees of application. This is the result of Japanese companies' attempts to achieve stable and efficient local plant operations by strengthening external conditions. The high rating of 3.6 points for group V, Labor Relations, reflects the fact that the Japanese-style management and production system rests upon labor stability. For this reason Japanese companies do their utmost to secure peaceful labor relations by carefully selecting beneficial environmental conditions and by implementing constructive policies. Similarly, a high 3.6 for group VI, Parent-Subsidiary Relations, comes about as a result of the vital role that employees dispatched from Japan play in plant management and operations. It also results from the considerable authority that the Japanese parent company reserves for itself in regard to decision making that effects the local plant. In other words, at present, Japanese companies engaged in production in the United States continue to place much emphasis upon the "result" application of "human" elements. This type of leadership supplied by Japanese personnel thus remains an important characteristic of local production.

Group II, Production Control, is one of the core-system groups in this analytical framework, along with Work Organization and Administration. Its average degree of application is evaluated at 3.3, which is equal to the overall average for all items and industries. This suggests that companies are succeeding in bringing-in the production control core of the Japanese production system. However, as will be explained in greater detail below, this is in fact largely sustained by importing "materials" such as production equipment, and does not necessarily justify the conclusion that the "method" of the Japanese production system itself is being sufficiently applied in the United States.

The degree of application for group I, Work Organization and Administration, is conspicuously low in these diagrams. This is because group I is closely related to the human element existing on the shop floor, which is the nucleus of the Japanese production system. It is anticipated that the application of this type of Japanese method to workers not accustomed to such organization and administration will be difficult. For this reason, the low rating of 2.9 is below average and is in fact the lowest among all six groups. This figure is however high enough to suggest that, to some extent, the Japanese method of work organization and administration is being systematically introduced.

Group III, Procurement, receives a rating of 3 for degree of application, which is also below average. Evaluating this group involves judging the extent to which parts are directly imported from Japan, and the extent to which the procurement methods implemented overseas reflect the Japanese system. With regard to the procurement source, although the plants are strongly inclined to procure parts directly from Japan, they did place greater emphasis upon local procurement. Also, concerning the method of procurement, a low degree of application for introducing the Japanese procurement system reflects the difficulty of implementing Japanese methods in a managerial environment that differs considerably from that in Japan.

Finally, group IV, Group Consciousness, receives an application rating of 3.2, which is just slightly below average. This showed that there are fairly strong efforts to create an atmosphere conducive to promoting the application of the Japanese core system. However, certain restrictions in the local environment hampered these efforts.

Examining the group application ratings for all industries combined reveals that the degree of application for the core groups (groups I, II, and III) is relatively low in comparison with group IV, which represents the subsystem, and groups V and VI. In particular, there are high degrees of application for Labor Relations and for Parent-Subsidiary Relations. Also, the overall level of application is supported by the high degree of application in the area of production control, particularly concerning production equipment, as well as the high degree of application for suppliers and their function in local procurement method.

When results for each of these industries are compared, certain differences emerge. Looking at the hexagons shown in Figure 3-1, it is clear that in the auto assembly industry, the points of the hexagon representing groups IV and V protrude much more than in the other industries. Group I is also higher than the other industries. As emphasized below, this high degree of application in group I, Work Organization and Administration, and in group IV, Group Consciousness, reflects the major application characteristic of the auto assembly industry, namely, the "Human-Method" aspect of application. The high degree of application in group V, Labor Relations, is all the more notable for the fact that the target plants included those organized by the United Auto Workers (UAW). In the auto parts industry, the points representing groups IV and V also protrude in the same way as in the auto assembly industry. A more notable characteristic of this industry is that the points of the hexagon representing groups II and VI protrude farther than in the other industries. In the case of group II, Production Control, the high degree of application results from the high rating given to Equipment. The high degree of application in group VI, Parent-Subsidiary Relations, reflects the considerable guidance provided by Japanese employees. In the consumer electronics industry, the hexagon points for five groups, with the single exception of group II, are all closer to the center of the diagram. In this case, group II approaches the same rating as in the other industries because of the continued high reliance upon equipment from Japan. A high degree of application in Operations Management, another item in group II, seems to reflect the longer history of local U.S. production for this industry. The most notable feature about the semiconductor industry is that the hexagon point representing group III protrudes further than in the case of the other industries. This reflects a characteristically high degree of dependence upon Japan for technology and parts.

Hybrid Evaluation of the 23 Items

Figure 3-2 illustrates the average degree of application of each of the 23 items examined in this study, for all of the target plants. It is clear from this diagram that there is considerable variation in the degree of application among the different items. Item 19, Labor Unions, receives the highest rating of 4.4 points. This item best represents the major characteristic of group V, which as explained above, is the intention of Japanese local plants in the United States to achieve stable labor relations.

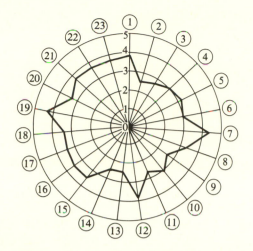

Figure 3–2 Degree of Application by Item (Average of All Plants)

The next highest rating of 4.3 points is given to item 7, Equipment, which represents the "Material-Result" aspect of application. Among the 6 items in group I, item 1, Job Classification, stands out from the rest with a relatively high 3.7. Similarly, group III, item 12, Suppliers is conspicuous with a high rating of 3.9. On the other hand, conspicuously low areas of the diagram are found for item 2, Wage System, which receives only 2.4 points, and items 13 and 14, Procurement Method and Small Group Activities, respectively, which receive only 2.5 points each. The high degree of application for Job Classification indicates that the Japanese plants in the United States have, to a large extent, succeeded in replacing the traditional American finely demarcated job classification system. However, that they have not been nearly so successful in abolishing the base rates for job classes, which are closely related to the traditional job classifications, is evident from the low degree of application for Wage System. The high degree of application for item 12, Suppliers, contrasts with the low scores for the other items in group III, namely, 2.7 for item 11, Local Content, and 2.5 for item 13, Procurement Method. This shows that as Japanese plants in the United States increase local content (decreasing application), and as they discover that it is difficult to implement Japanese methods such as JIT with U.S. suppliers (decreasing "method" application), they cannot help but strengthen their dependence upon Japanese subsidiary local suppliers (increasing application of Suppliers). The low degree of application for Small Group Activities reflects the difficulty of applying the "Human-Method" aspect of the subsystem.

Degrees of Application by Plant

Examining the average degree of application for each plant, it is apparent that there is a great deal of deviation from the average 3.3 rating that is calculated for all plants. The plant ratings vary from a high of 3.9 for those plants strongly committed to applying the Japanese management and production system, to a low of 2.0 for those plants that went to great lengths to adapt to local American conditions. It is

Table 3–4. Number of Plants by the Degree of Application

	Total	Auto Assembly	Auto Parts	Consumer Electronics	Semiconductor
3.6 ~ 3.9	8	5	3	0	0
3.2 ~ 3.5	15	4	6	1	4
2.8 ~ 3.1	6	0	0	3	3
2.4 ~ 2.7	2	0	0	2	0
2.0 ~ 2.3	3	0	0	3	0

not surprising that the differences in degree of application that are found among these plants reflect characteristics of their respective industry. Table 3–4 compares the number of plants in each industry according to degree of application. Comparing the average degree of application per plant by industry, a high average of 3.6 points for the auto parts industry, closely followed by 3.5 points for the auto assembly industry, reflects the strong commitment of the auto industry as a whole towards application of the Japanese system. The semiconductor industry is next with an average of 3.3 points, and the lowest average of 2.7 points is in the consumer electronics industry. These figures correspond closely to the results obtained in the earlier study, which showed average application scores for the auto, semiconductor, and consumer electronics industries of 3.6, 3.3, and 2.8 points, respectively.

4-Perspective Evaluation

Until now, emphasis has been upon characteristics revealed by the 6-group, 23-item hybrid evaluation of the thirty-four target plants. The following analysis examines these thirty-four plants on the basis of the 4-Perspective Evaluation. The five diagrams in Figure 3–3 illustrate the 4-Perspective Evaluation for each of the four industries separately and an average evaluation for all four industries. These diagrams represent the "result" application of "human" and "material" aspects of the Japanese system on the vertical axes, and the "method" application of these aspects on the horizontal axes. In each diagram, the vertical dimension of the figure described within the concentric circles is greater than the horizontal dimension. This illustrates the relative emphasis that Japanese plants in the United States place upon the "result" application of the "human" and "material" aspects of their management and production system. The lesser horizontal dimension, especially for "material," signifies less transfer of the "method" underlying the Japanese management and production system. Chapter 5 deals with the overall, and individual industry characteristics revealed by this analysis. This chapter focuses mainly upon the characteristics of application revealed by this 4-Perspective Evaluation through an analysis at the group-item level.

"Human-Method" Aspect at the Core of the System: Relatively Low Application of the Japanese Method to Work Organization at the Shop-floor Level

Group I, Work Organization and Administration, is comprised of the core elements of the "Human-Method" aspect of application. The average degree of application

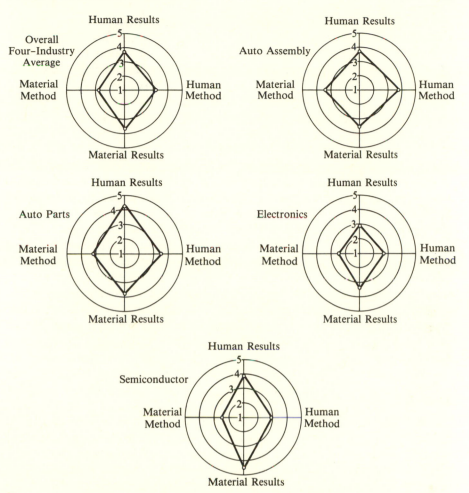

Figure 3–3 Four-Perspective Evaluation of the 4 Industries

in this group is 2.9 points, which is the lowest among all six groups. This group concerns elements of the system that are closely linked to human factors at the shop-floor level. A number of restrictions emerge as a result. It is difficult to apply the Japanese system to American workers who have different attitudes from Japanese workers and who are accustomed to American labor practices. These difficulties account for the low degree of application found in this group. Although differences according to industry do appear, if a company intends to recreate the Japanese system at a local plant in the United States, it cannot allow this core group to adapt to the American system. There must be a strong determination to apply Japanese-style work organization at the shop-floor level.

This is most clearly reflected in the high degree of application for Job Classification, which receives a rating of 3.7 points. According to the evaluation criteria, this rating corresponds to the existence of about seven or eight different job classifications at the shop-floor level. In contrast, the traditional American job classification system frequently consists of anywhere from many tens to several hundreds of job classifications. The existence of a mere seven or eight classifications is evidence that the company has succeeded in laying the foundation for the Japanese production system by implementing a flexible work organization based upon workers with multiple skills. This has been particularly successful in the case of the auto assembly industry, which receives an extremely high 4.8 points for degree of application. Although the auto parts industry does not score as high as auto assembly, it too receives a high rating of 4.2 points. In comparison, the consumer electronics industry, whose expansion into local production predates that of the auto industries, rates only 2.8, and the semiconductor industry is slightly behind with 2.7 points. In evaluating the differences in the degrees of application among industries, it is important to take into account the variation among plants. Accordingly, Job Classification ratings have standard deviations of 1.03 for the consumer electronics and semiconductor industries, indicating that although the average is low, some plants in these two industries are energetically simplifying their classification system. In fact, since the previous 1986 study, a number of plants in the consumer electronics and semiconductor industries have begun attempting to simplify their job classification systems. Although a 1.23 standard deviation over all target plants indicates even greater variation, the average 3.7 degree of application for this item shows that, to a certain extent, simplification of the job classification system is being successfully accomplished. Wage System, which is closely connected to job classification according to traditional American labor practices, receives an even lower 2.4 points for degree of application. This is because even in those cases where simplification is well underway, wages paid to blue-collar employees are still closely tied to the job classification system. Interestingly, the auto assembly industry, which receives the highest application rating for Job Classification, receives the second lowest rating of 2.1 for degree of application in Wage System (consumer electronics scored lowest with 2.0). Conversely, the semiconductor industry, which receives the lowest rating for Job Classification, receives the highest rating of 3.1 for Wage System. Perhaps this shows that, compared with the high-tech semiconductor industry that is pursuing an entirely new form of labor relations, the auto assembly industry is unable to shed the American-style hourly wage system based upon job classifications. Or perhaps it reveals the difficulty of applying the Japanese-style merit system. Moreover, a very low 0.31 standard deviation among auto assembly plants would seem to discount any significant influence of the UAW. Although these observations clearly indicate that it is difficult to apply the Japanese-style wage system in the United States, many Japanese firms operating in the United States are making gradual headway through the introduction of performance evaluations and the Japanese-style bonus system.

Finally, the degree of application for Job Rotation is also low at 2.6 points, indicating that it is not easy to introduce the Japanese practice of multiple skill formation. According to the evaluation criteria, a rating of 2.6 is approximately midway between a situation where the traditional American fixed job assignment system is sufficiently relaxed in order to, for example, allow flexibility in job assignment during machine changes, and a situation where job rotation is frequently carried out within job teams. Thus, although fixed job assignment is relaxed to a certain extent, job rotation is judged insufficient by Japanese standards. Full application of the Japanese system would require scheduled job rotation on a routine, daily basis. In the auto assembly industry, where the nature of the production line necessitates this type of flexible work organization, the degree of application for Job Rotation is evaluated at a fairly high 3.2 points. This is another illustration of the auto assembly industry's strong commitment to the application of "method". In the other industries, application for this item remains at the 2-point level, indicating that many plants still utilize a fixed job assignment system. Of course in some cases, such as the consumer electronics industry which receives a score of only 2.1 for Job Rotation, there may be relatively little need for applying this element of the Japanese system. In this industry, even without multiple skill formation, efficiency gains can be realized by increasing the training for relatively simple tasks in order to speed up production. Furthermore, in the semiconductor industry, a high 1.29 standard deviation for this item reveals a great deal of variation among plants.

The degree of application for Education and Training receives an average rating of 2.9 points. The essential element of Japanese-style education and training is broad skill formation achieved through OJT. Therefore, a major factor that restrains application of Education and Training is the restriction upon OJT that results from insufficient job rotation at U.S. plants. However, almost all plants emphasize the importance of OJT, and particularly in the case of the auto assembly industry, some plants intend to implement the type of long-term, systematic education and training programs practiced in Japan. In addition, many plants energetically pursue programs that include sending employees to Japan for training. Some plants, particularly in the auto assembly industry, have also established training centers for long-term programs that emphasis an extremely thorough and systematic approach to education and training. For these reasons, the degree of application for Education and Training is higher than for Job Rotation.

Application for First-line Supervisors is evaluated at 2.9, but especially noteworthy is the low 0.49 standard deviation for this score over all the plants in the survey. In other words, most of the Japanese plants operating in the United States exhibited about the same degree of application for this element of the Japanese system. The average scores per industry are distributed over a narrow 3.1 to 2.6 range, with the auto assembly industry at 3.1, auto parts at 3.0, semiconductors at 2.7, and consumer electronics as 2.6 points.

According to the evaluation criteria, a 3 reflects a situation where supervisors are primarily acquired from inside the plant but where their operational function in relation to the work team, as well as their technical grasp of the production process is weak. Many Japanese expatriates complained that the function of supervisors constituted a major difference between most plants in the U.S. and those in Japan. Most plants make an effort to bring the level of supervisors closer to the Japanese model and emphasize the internal promotion of employees to the rank of supervisor. Those plants that have no choice but to hire supervisors from the outside because of a lack of suitable candidates available internally receive a lower evaluation. Even at those plants that obtain supervisors internally, U.S. labor practices are frequently reflected in the use of job postings, as well as in the priority placed on seniority as a criterion for making a selection from among a number of qualified candidates. On balance, the role of the supervisor in the U.S. plants tends to be one of labor management, and the stronger this tendency, the lower the degree of application of the Japanese system.

In contrast, a rating of 3.1 for degree of application of Promotion is slightly above average for this group. Moreover, there is a large discrepancy between the rating for Promotion (3.1) and Wage System (2.4), although both items are directly concerned with the treatment of employees. Reasons that Promotion leans closer towards application include the observations that, as mentioned above, many plants make an effort to promote their own employees to the rank of supervisor, and that a significant number of plants attempt to take ability as well as seniority into account when making promotions. Taking a look at each industry, it is notable that the three industries excluding consumer electronics are fairly uniform in their application of this item. Consumer electronics receives a somewhat lower 2.7 points, because a number of these plants place a greater emphasis upon seniority, thus reflecting the influence of traditional American labor practices.

Having examined the six items in Work Organization and Its Administration, it is clear that although Job Classification reveals the extent of efforts to apply the Japanese system, the entire group only averages 2.9 points. The main reason seems to be that this group is closely concerned with the "human aspect" of work organization at the shop-floor level and that it is ultimately difficult to introduce Japanese methods to workers who are accustomed to American labor practices. However, on a positive note, the Japanese plants can be considered fairly successful in achieving this degree of application in such a difficult application environment. We may conclude that, to a certain extent, the Japanese companies have succeeded in bringing-in the "human aspect" of their system. Precisely how substantial this transfer has actually been is a question this book hopes to answer.

"Human-Method" Application at the Subsystem: The Effort to Promote Group Consciousness and Its Limitations

The degree of application for group I, which represents the core of the "human-method" aspect of application, is relatively low. This underscores the importance of creating an atmosphere that will increase employees' sense of belonging to the group and encourage their voluntary and enthusiastic participation in plant activities. Such an atmosphere promotes application among the group elements of the core system and thus facilitates the introduction of the Japanese system. The three items of group IV, Group Consciousness, constitute a subsystem of elements that provides precisely such support for the core system. The average degree of application for this group is 3.2 points, which, although less than the overall average, is more than group I. Moreover, the items Information Sharing (3.6 points) and Sense of Identity (3.5 points) receive particularly high ratings, thus providing evidence of the Japanese companies' strong intentions to promote application in the area of Group Consciousness.

In Japan, information sharing and mutual understanding are to a large extent governed by informal interaction among employees. In this survey, Information Sharing evaluates the efforts of plants to establish formal systems that promote these aspects of group behavior. The auto assembly and auto parts industries, both of which show relatively high degrees of application for the core system, also receive high scores of 4.4 and 4.1 points respectively for this item. Conversely, the consumer electronics industry, which receives a low score for degree of application for the core system, is closer towards adaptation with a score of only 2.4 points.

The same is true of Sense of Unity, although the discrepancy between the industries is notably larger. For this item, the auto assembly and auto parts industries score 4.6 and 4.4 points, respectively, and the consumer electronics only scores 2.1 points. In other words, the auto industry as a whole places greater importance upon cultivating a sense of belonging to the company or unity among the employees. This is achieved by actively implementing practices such as open and nonreserved parking, an open-style cafeteria, and company uniforms, and holding social events such as picnics or parties. These measures are not without cost and meet with a certain amount of resistance from white-collar employees.

Both of these items show conspicuously high scores for degree of application averaged over the four industries. They also both have high standard deviations (Information Sharing, 1.10, Sense of Unity, 1.24). For example, while the wearing of company uniforms is a standard, accepted practice in Japan, there is much variation concerning this policy among the Japanese plants located in the United States. Some plants make the wearing of uniforms mandatory, while others are not particularly strict about enforcing this practice. It is also interesting to note that some of these plants implement practices of "excessive application" that are not even observed in Japan. Such practices include opportunities for any employee to have a personal interview with the president, extreme open-style offices, or the nonreserved, open parking mentioned above.

In contrast, Small Group Activities only receives 2.5 points in its degree of application. This low score reflects an average rate of participation in these activities of only around 30 to 40 percent. Scores for each of the four industries are at the 2-point level, ranging from a high of 2.9 for auto parts to a low of 2.2 for consumer electronics. Although a slightly high 0.8 standard deviation indicates that several plants have higher rates of participation, the overall impression is that it remains difficult to attract the degree of participation that results in the sort of constant improvement activities that exist in Japan. Some plants have abandoned previously established small group activities and only have a system for collecting suggestions from employees, while other plants have even given up on a suggestion system. On the other hand, some plants make a strenuous effort to implement small group activities. It is notable that in some of these cases, plants have given up on the kind of voluntary participation found in Japan, and instead establish participation activities that are an integral part of the job. Although stimulating interest and voluntary participation in small group activities from the bottom up is desirable, these companies realize that the labor environment in the United States is not conducive to such an arrangement. Mandatory participation is intended to bring about improved quality and productivity through organized group activities imposed on all employees from the top down.

As seen above, Japanese companies operating in the United States actively try to promote group consciousness mainly as a means of supporting application of the core Japanese production and management system. However, as the limited achievements in the area of small group activities demonstrates, there are limitations to the extent that such measures are able to support the "Human-Method" aspect of application in the U.S. environment.

Low Application for "Materials-Method": Difficulty in Applying the "Method" of Production Control and Procurement Method

The lowest degree of application within the 4-Perspective Evaluation is found in the "Material-Method" aspect. Items that belong to this aspect of application are Quality Control and Maintenance (group II, Production Control), and Procurement Method (group III, Procurement). Of these, Maintenance and Procurement Method are the factors that decrease the average degree of application for this aspect.

At 3.4 points, the degree of application for Quality Control is slightly above the overall average. The auto assembly industry with 4.0 points and the auto parts industry with 3.9 points are particularly avid in their application of Japanese-style quality control. However, although many plants succeed in introducing the critical element of the Japanese quality control system, namely, the shop-floor workers' own efforts to "build in the quality" during the production process, an important characteristic is still missing: Shop-floor workers do not seem to have the same quality consciousness of their counterparts in Japan. They still rely heavily upon quality inspectors inside and outside the production lines, and there are even instances where Japanese employees are involved in the inspection for defective products. Lower scores for degree of application are recorded for the semiconductor industry (3.0) and the consumer electronics industry (2.4). In these cases, it is even difficult to apply the outward form of Japanese quality control. It must also be remembered that the degree of application is slightly higher for these items because Japanese plants operating in the United States all exert maximum effort at quality control in order to maintain the same levels of quality that they achieve in Japan.

While Quality Control has a higher than average degree of application, Maintenance is considerably lower at 2.6 points. Each of the industries is evaluated between 2 and 3 points with auto assembly at 2.9, auto parts at 2.8, semiconductors at 2.6, and consumer electronics at 2.1 points. According to the evaluation criteria, a 3 represents a situation where ordinary shop-floor workers are not involved in maintenance, but where experienced shop-floor workers are separately organized and given special training. The auto industry comes closest to implementing such a system, while the semiconductor and consumer electronics industries have a high rate of dependence upon externally acquired maintenance workers.

The U.S. industrial environment places a very significant restriction upon the application of this item. In other words, the rigid job classification system makes it very difficult for regular shop-floor workers to do maintenance. There are many cases where regular production workers are not permitted to adjust or touch the machinery because "they will damage something". In recognition of job classification boundaries, many plants in the auto industry therefore established a separate framework for the organization and in-house training of special maintenance workers. The most application-oriented plants have established a systematic training program for the in-house cultivation of maintenance workers over the long term.

Procurement method, which evaluates methods and systems used for procurement between Japanese local producers and local parts suppliers, also has a low 2.5 points for degree of application. Moreover, even the auto assembly industry, which is locally accompanied by a large number of parts suppliers in comparison with the other industries, only scored 3.0 for this item. Of course, some of the Japanese plants are making an effort to pursue long-term reliable supplier relationships with local American companies, but most of those relationships seemed to be burdened with quality and delivery problems. Even when the Japanese companies maintain a supplier relationship by setting up local U.S. operations together, it is difficult to establish Japanese-style procurement systems such as JIT because of the limited transaction volumes involved.

Measures and Conditions that Promote Application of "Method": Aiming for Cooperative Labor Relations

Although applying the Japanese system overseas is apparently no easy task, it is equally clear that most of the local plants are very determined to achieve some measure of success in the attempt. Although such application is, to a certain extent, supplemented by internal factors such as employee group consciousness, external conditions also play an important role. For this reason, Japanese companies locating in the United States attempt to choose a plant site that provides relatively advantageous conditions for the application of the Japanese system. An element which receives priority consideration in this respect is labor relations. Most Japanese companies want to cultivate an atmosphere of cooperation and harmony between labor and management and seek to avoid traditional American labor relations as much as possible. The items in group V, Labor Relations, reflect these types of measures and considerations. This group scores a high 3.6 points for degree of application. The first item in this group, Hiring Policy, receives a degree of application score of 3.4 points. According to the evaluation criteria, this level reflects preference for a site location, which is ethnically homogeneous, and if the plant is located in a traditional industrial zone, then it reflects a tendency to pay careful attention to the selection of employees. A great deal of variation among the different plants must, however, be taken into consideration on account of the high 1.06 standard deviation for these scores. Comparing the degree of application by industry also reveals a large variation in scores: auto assembly has 4.3, auto parts has 3.8, semiconductor has 3.1, and consumer electronics has 2.4 points.

The degree of application for Job Security is also 3.4 points. This corresponds to the following situation: layoffs are avoided as much as possible; a no-layoff clause is not included in the contract; there have been occasions in the past where plants laid off workers; many plants offer some long-term employment incentives. There is, however, a great deal of variation among plants as reflected in an extremely high 1.43 standard deviation. The auto assembly industry has the highest score of 4.9 for degree of application, as well as a low 0.31 standard deviation. In this case almost all of the auto assembly plants promise to avoid layoffs as much as possible and include an express provision to that effect in the contract or in the employee handbook. They also adopt various measures to promote long-term employment. However, in the low application semiconductor and consumer electronics industries, a number of plants have laid off employees on several occasions.

The highest degree of application in this group is the 4.4 points for Labor Unions.

Among Japanese plants in Canada and the United States, a total of 9 plants, 4 in the auto assembly industry and 5 in the consumer electronics industry, are union shops. In other words, over 70 percent of the plants are nonunion. Where unions do exist, such as in the auto industry, they often accept labor practices that differ significantly from the traditional American practices.

On the other hand, the lowest degree of application for an item in this group is 3.3 points for Grievance Procedures. The system that exists in the United States is fundamentally different from the one in Japan, where grievances are settled informally and through the existing channels of the workplace. In the United States, such business is typically handled through a separate and formally established procedure. The relatively low degree of application for this item probably reflects the difficulties that the plants experience in dealing with these procedures. Moreover, the Japanese plants consider the grievance procedure system as having highly significant consequences for the stability of labor-management relations, and therefore they make the utmost attempt to implement the same type of workplace settlement system that exists in Japan. Consequently, in the auto parts and semiconductor industries where there are no unions, the score for the degree of application is 3.9 and 3.6 points, respectively. In the partially unionized auto assembly and consumer electronics industries, the scores are somewhat lower at 3.2 and 2.8, respectively. Variation among industry or plant is relatively low.

Among the four items in this group, Job Security and Grievance Procedure belong to the "Human-Method" aspect of application, as shown in the 4-Perspective Evaluation. The degree of application for these two items is higher than all the items in group I (except Job Classification) and higher than Small Group Activities in group IV. The Japanese companies believe it is desirable to bring in the "method" of their system as much as possible, although the U.S. industrial environment restricts the degree to which they can influence application. The group V items, namely Job Security and Grievance Procedure, as well as Information Sharing and Sense of Unity from group IV, have the potential to increase application, depending upon the specific measures that the plants introduce.

As explained above, the high degree of application for this group is mainly the result of careful attention to overall labor relations, and efforts to create cooperative labor relations, especially on the part of local plants in the auto industry. However, this does not justify the blanket conclusion that Japanese companies have succeeded in transferring Japanese-style labor relations to their local operations in the United States. It must be remembered that in other respects, traditional American labor practices impose major restrictions on the application of the Japanese-style management and production system. For example, even though Japanese companies have succeeded in bringing about stable long-term employment practices at their local U.S. operations, many complications related to the seniority system, which is deeply rooted in traditional American labor practices, can arise in those cases where there is a lack of flexibility in job assignments. Also, a strict "no layoff" policy may be difficult to maintain over the long term, especially as there is no subcontracting system in the United States to serve as an important safety valve for coping with extreme fluctuations in business cycles. Perhaps, as a number of plants in the consumer electronics and semiconductor industries have shown in the past, the active use of layoffs, to which there is little resistance in American labor practices, is after all the wisest policy.

Strong Inclination Towards "Human-Result": Application Guided by Japanese Expatriates

So far, discussion has focused upon application of the human and material aspects of the Japanese method. Many conditions existing in the American environment seem to impose significant restrictions on this type of application. Japanese plants have consequently implemented measures related to group consciousness or to labor relations, in order to promote the application of method. However, in order to transfer their competitive advantage to the local plants as expediently as possible, these plants have also relied upon bringing-in the results of the human and material aspects of the Japanese system.

The human aspect of results transfer ("Human-Results") is shown in group VI, Parent-Subsidiary Relations and particularly in two of its items, namely, Ratio of Japanese Expatriates, and Managerial Position of Americans. The following discussion will consider the roles of Japanese expatriates and the authority of the parent company in Japan in regard to the management and operation of the local plants.

The degree of application for Ratio of Japanese Expatriates is rated at a high 3.7 points. This reflects a situation where more than 4 percent of the employees at the local plant are Japanese expatriates. However, a great deal of variation among the plants (standard deviation 1.39) reflects diverse business strategies. Among the 34 plants investigated, the proportion of Japanese expatriates ranges from a low of 0.6 percent to a high of 14 percent. There is a total of 16 plants with more than 4 percent Japanese expatriates, including one plant with as many as 350 regular and 200 temporary Japanese personnel. There is also much variation among the industries, with the highest rating given to auto assembly (4.6) and the lowest to consumer electronics (2.6). In general, the large role of Japanese expatriates deserves to be strongly emphasized.

Delegation of Authority also receives a high 3.6 rating for degree of application. This corresponds to a situation where plans and proposals affecting all manner of managerial decision-making originate at the local plant, but where the final decision to accept or reject such plans or proposals is made in Japan. It is noteworthy that the auto parts and semiconductor industries both receive high 4.0 point ratings for this item. A contributing factor in both cases is the relatively small scale of plant operations, as well as the fact that the auto parts industry has a very short history as a local producer, and the semiconductor industry is particularly dependent upon its Japanese parent company for technology. Moreover, even the consumer electronics industry, the most adaptation-oriented industry investigated, receives a rating of 3.2 points, which is equal to that of the auto assembly industry. This suggests that, overall, the Japanese parent companies retain considerable authority over their local plants in the United States.

Degree of application for Managerial Position of Americans also receives 3.6 points. This rating denotes that more than half of the local managerial posts, including the more important positions, are held by Japanese. The existence of some auto assembly and consumer electronics plants, which are very active in filling managerial posts with American personnel, accounts for much of the variation among plants and has the effect of lowering the average degree of application for this item. On balance, the rating for degree of application indicates that Japanese expatriates continue to play a very important role at the local plants.

The overall degree of application for this group receives a high rating of 3.6 points. Large variation among the industries, ranging from 4.2 points for auto parts to 3.0 points for consumer electronics, reflects the different length of their respective histories as local producers, as well as special characteristics of each industry. The picture that emerges from these observations is that the Japanese companies have been carrying out local production based upon the Japanese-style management and production system through the guidance of numerous Japanese expatriate personnel. In other words, local plant management and operation is supported by the human-results aspect of application, which offsets the restrictions that the American environment imposes upon the application of method.

Slight Inclination towards "Material-Results": The Different Characteristics of Production Equipment and Parts

The "Material-Results" aspect of application includes three items, Equipment from group II, and Local Content and Suppliers from group III. The average degree of application for these three items is a high 3.6 points. This is the same as the items that represent the "Human-Results" aspect of application, and helps compensate for the low application of method. In examining the application of these items it will be necessary to pay close attention to the large difference between the characteristics of production equipment and parts.

In this analysis, Equipment represents material that are made in Japan and brought in to the United States. This evaluation is a straightforward matter of observing the ratio of equipment brought over from Japan. The degree of application for this item is rated at an extremely high 4.3 points and helps increase the average degree of application for group II. This rating corresponds to a level of at least 80 percent Japanese equipment. Although there is a certain amount of variation according to industry, the degree of application is high throughout. It is the result of a determination to rapidly achieve quality and productivity levels comparable to those achieved in Japan, by utilizing production equipment that is developed, produced, and through practical shop-floor experience, improved and perfected in Japan. An additional factor that makes the bringing over of this familiar production equipment an attractive course of action is that it allows the plants to exercise more of their extensive, equipment-related production know-how.

Bringing over from Japan the various parts that local plants must procure for their manufacturing process constitutes another element of the material-results aspect of application. There are, however, significant differences between bringing over parts and bringing over production equipment. The parts-related items are Local Content and Suppliers, both of which belong to group III, Procurement. The degree of application for the Local Content is a low rating of 2.7 points, while that for Suppliers is 3.9 points. The latter is not as high as for Equipment but fairly high nevertheless. The contrast between the degree of application for these two items is noteworthy. When local plants import parts directly from Japan, they cannot expect the "just-in-time" delivery they would receive in Japan, but they can be certain about quality. The resulting stability of their production operations make these plants strongly inclined to rely on imports as much as possible for the most important parts required in their manufacturing process. However, while bringing-in production equipment is a once-only event that takes place when the local plant first becomes established, procurement method is an ongoing activity that must keep up with daily operations. Moreover, it is also necessary to consider trade friction in the light of strong pressure from American parts manufacturers. For this reason there is a common understanding among Japanese local producers to increase local content (decrease the degree of application). Finally, the appreciation of the yen after 1985 made it too costly to import parts from Japan, and this also promoted local procurement. For these reasons, the degree of application for Local Content receives a low rating of 2.7 points. By industry, the consumer electronics and auto assembly industries are particularly low at 2.0 and 2.3 points, respectively. According to the evaluation criteria, a rating of 2.7 indicates approximately 65 percent local content. But as suggested above, this adaptation-oriented position does not mean that the Japanese companies are enthusiastically adapting to local conditions. In fact, the plants are almost unanimous in complaining that there are major problems with the quality of American parts. In view of the need to respond to the threat of friction with local parts manufacturers, they have no choice but to increase the local content ratio.

However, since Local Content includes procurement from American parts manufacturers as well as from Japanese parts manufacturers that have established their own local operations, the local content ratio does not by itself provide an accurate description of procurement method. Moreover, imported (nonlocal) parts might also originate from Asia, Mexico, or Japan. The item Suppliers addresses this shortcoming by focusing upon the origin of the suppliers and their relation to Japanese companies. Accordingly, the degree of application for Suppliers is rated at a very high 3.9 points, effectively the reverse of Local Content. By industry, semiconductors is highest at 4.4 points, since it continues to import many of its parts directly from Japan, followed by auto assembly (3.8), auto parts (3.7), and consumer electronics (3.6 points). The high ratings for each industry result from the fact that although parts imported directly from Japan are limited to high-value added parts, such as ICs and important functional components, the consumer electronics plants import a high percentage of their parts from their own subsidiaries in Asia or Mexico, and the auto assembly plants procure many of their parts from the Japanese auto parts plants that have also established local plants in the United States.

In sum, the Japanese local plants prefer to exercise material-results application, but in order to avoid friction with local manufacturers, they have decreased the extent of such direct application, particularly regarding procurement method. Here also, the different orientation of Local Content and Suppliers is characteristic of "Material-Results" application.

Merging with American Society

Finally, an aspect of local production that becomes important as the Japanese local plants prepare for continued production in the United States over the long term, is that of smoothly integrating with American society. This aspect of local production is examined and classified as group VII, Community Relations, which contains a single item, Donations and Volunteer Activities. Other elements that could have been included in this group, for example, "minorities," are not a part of the current study because of insufficient data.

Donations and Volunteer Activities receives a low 2.3 points for degree of application. This suggests that in general Japanese companies have an awareness of the American social environment and are making fairly diligent efforts to cultivate good relations with rural society. Several factors including site location, plant scale, and predisposition of the company affect the plant's activities in regard to this item, and consequently there is considerable variation among plants, as revealed by the somewhat high 0.94 standard deviation for this rating. Moreover, due to their inexperience in dealing with rural society, most plants have experienced some difficulties in trying to establish good relations. In order to rectify this problem, some plants endeavor to provide the person in charge with the requisite education, and other plants employ special American staff.

In order to gain acceptance by rural society as a "good corporate citizen," most plants rely primarily upon the act of giving donations. There are many cases of plants actively responding to requests for donations. Specific examples include providing half the cost of an indoor gymnasium, and purchasing video equipment for a local library, or medical equipment for a hospital. Donations to America's largest charity and volunteer organization, United Way, are a matter of course. On the other hand, some plants report that there are more donation requests than they can handle. A variety of approaches to deal with this situation are observed. In some cases, the person in charge will decide about each request as it arises, or a department manager will create a special committee to deal with donation requests. In still other cases, a fixed set of criteria for responding to donation requests will be established.

Local plants attempt to create a harmonious relationship with rural society in several ways in addition to financial donations. They open facilities such as athletic grounds to the public, regularly invite teachers to take a trip to Japan, invite children on plant tours, contribute to blood donation campaigns, and otherwise encourage their employees to become actively involved in a variety of volunteer activities. In recent years, the idea that good community relations is an important concern is also gaining currency in Japan. In this way, experience gained overseas can have a valuable impact upon Japanese society.

SUMMARY

The preceding analysis has dealt primarily with the target plants as a group and has provided insight into the conditions obtaining at the average local Japanese plant in the United States. It may be useful to summarize these findings.

First, Japanese companies engaged in local production in the United States have an average degree of application of 3.3 points. This indicates that these companies view the application of the Japanese management and production system as an important objective, and that to a certain extent, they have succeeded in transferring this system to their local plants. However, if the evaluation standard is the Japanese parent factory, then the degree to which the Japanese system has been successfully transferred is only slightly over 50 percent. Another problem concerns the fact that not all aspects of the system have been transferred to the same extent. Particularly noteworthy in that regard is the relatively low degree of application for the "Human-Method" and "Material-Method" aspects of the system as revealed by the 4-Perspective Evaluation. This shows the extent to which the Japanese-style method has failed to effectively take root in the United States. It also reveals the important role played by the direct transfer of system elements ("results") from Japan. For "material" elements this is represented by the import of production equipment from Japan, and for the "human" element, it takes the form of dispatching Japanese employees overseas to serve at the local plants. The "Human-Results" and "Material-Results" aspects thus become important factors raising the degree of application.

At present, most of the Japanese companies pursue local production by emphasizing the application of the Japanese-style management and production system. In choosing the site location for their plants, they select local conditions within the diverse American environment that are most advantageous for their purposes. But in the future, in order to deal with the possibility of increasing investment friction, the plants will probably put greater emphasis upon localization and integration with local society. Many issues remain to be resolved as Japanese plants search for the best path towards a long-term presence in the United States.

4

Questionnaire and Survey

DUANE KUJAWA
HIROSHI KUMON

UTILIZATION OF THE QUESTIONNAIRE SURVEY

To help offset the limited number of plants wherein we were able to conduct on-site interviews, and to facilitate comparisons with plants besides those from our four main targeted industries, we carried out a survey based on questionnaires (see pp. 99–105). First, we attempted specific analyses of the response we received regarding the following seven key items in the application of the Japanese style manufacturing system to North America: (1) job classifications (Q1), (2) wage systems (Q2), (3) job rotation (Q3), (4) education and training (Q6), (5) quality control (Q7), (6) layoff policy (Q10), and (7) small group activities (Q11). We then proceeded to select twelve questions and apply the application-adaptation ratings to them in the same way as we did to the plants actually visited. In fact, we obtained results that were surprisingly similar to those obtained from the field investigation. The application-adaptation ratings based on our questions give further credence to those given to the 23 items in our field investigation and provide them with a greater degree of objectivity.

Field Conditions and an Outline of Surveyed Factories

Here, then, is a brief explanation of how we carried out our questionnaire survey and an overview of the target industries. From August through September, 1989, we mailed our questionnaires to 450 Japanese-related manufacturing companies located in North America (the United States and Canada) and received 88 valid responses, a response rate of 19.6 percent. The information from these 88 plants was distributed among seven industrial categories, namely auto assembly (7 plants), auto parts (15 plants), electronics (21 plants), metalworking (11 plants), chemicals (13 plants), other machinery (8 plants), and other manufacturing (13 plants). Since only two semiconductor plants responded to our questionnaires, we included these two plants with electronics.

Next, we sorted out the 88 companies according to the following five points: (1) overlap with plants already visited, (2) plant size, in terms of number of employees, (3) start-up period, (4) type of ownership, and (5) presence or absence of a labor union. Roughly, an average plant would be one that started operation in the 1980s, is middle sized in terms of number of personnel, advanced into North America on its own initiative, and does not have a labor union. Now let us look at this more closely. First, among the 88 plants that responded, 14 (15.9 percent) also returned our questionnaires. Of these, we visited all seven plants that returned our questionnaires in the auto assembly industry, and three of the 15 plants that returned our questionnaires in the auto parts industry. We visited four of the 21 electrical equipment plants that returned our questionnaires, and this included the two above-mentioned semiconductor plants. We were not able to visit the plants of the other respondents. In short, we recovered questionnaires from all the plants we visited in the auto assembly industry, whereas there were many plants among our respondents in the auto parts and electrical equipment industries that we did not visit, and we did not visit the plants of respondents in the other industries at all. Therefore, through this survey we are able to compare a broad range of plants.

Second, in terms of size, eight plants had 1,000 or more employees, eleven had from 999 to 500, forty-one had from 499 to 100, and twenty-seven had ninety-nine or less. Thus, most prevalent are those plants with between 499 and 100 employees (46.6 percent), followed by those with ninety-nine or less (30.7 percent). Nineteen plants had 500 or more employees. It can be seen that most responding plants were middle or small-sized operations. Seen by industry, all seven auto assembly plants had more than 500 employees. Plants in other industries were mostly middle or small in size, although the electrical equipment, metalworking, and chemical industries each had one plant with 1,000 or more employees.

Third, regarding the start-up period, twenty-three plants started in 1979 or earlier, twenty-four between 1980 and 1984, and thirty-nine between 1985 and 1989. In the case of two plants, the start-up period was unclear. Seventy percent of the total started their operation in the 1980s. It was during the 1980s that Japanese manufacturers made major inroads into the American market in order to overcome the effects of trade friction and the appreciation of the yen. We see this same trend reflected in those plants that responded to our questionnaire. By industry, whereas plants belonging to electrical equipment and "other machinery" and to "other industries" are scattered throughout three different periods, auto assembly and auto parts plants are concentrated in the second half of the 1980s.

As for the fourth point, type of ownership, overwhelmingly dominant are those plants that are 100 percent owned by a Japanese firm (fifty-seven plants, or 64.8 percent). In second place are Japanese-American joint ventures (seventeen plants, or 19.3 percent), followed by joint ventures between Japanese firms (ten plants, or 11.4 percent).

With regard to the fifth point, labor unions, seventy-two plants (81.8 percent) had no union and sixteen plants had unions (18.2 percent). Eight plants out of ten, then, did not have a union. However, since plants with unions usually had 1,000 or more employees, the rate of unionization could be higher than the number of unionized plants would lead us to believe. By industry, three auto assembly, one auto parts, two electronics, five metalworking, one chemical, and four "other" manufacturing plants had unions.

Utilization

Next, let us look at some of the items on the questionnaires. Due to limited space, we will confine our discussion to the local application of the Japanese manufacturing system, particularly the seven items concerned with people's work and management, even though there are seventeen items in all. These seven items are: job classifications, wage system, job rotation, quality control, education and training, layoff policy, and small group activity. The tendency toward application of the Japanese system can best be seen in job classifications, job rotation, education and training, and layoff policy. The application of the Japanese wage system can be found more on the side of adaptation, and the application of quality control and small group activity was found not to have been carried out in a consistent manner.

Job Classifications

In America, one's job description dictates one's basic wage rate and shows, albeit rather abstractly, the actual content of one's work. Related jobs are grouped together into job "ladders" through which one progresses based on seniority. In Japan, on the other hand, one's work, wages, and promotion are not directly related to each other, and the actual content of the work is different than the content of the work in America, although in job title, two jobs may appear to be the same. Thus, we asked for the number of job classifications to serve as an index to show more precisely the organization of work. A high number of job classifications can be seen as a prerequisite for the existence of the traditional American style work organization, whereas a small number of job classifications would indicate an attempt to use a new work organization or, indeed, the traditional Japanese work organization.

In passing, we may note that our research in America and at local Japanese-owned plants indicates two main approaches to job descriptions or job duties. The first approach, as taken by the automobile manufacturing industry, for example, is to define job duty groups and then individual job duties within these groups. Related jobs within the same process or work area make up the job duty group. Individual job descriptions within these groups indicate wage rates. In this case, different job descriptions show the work, basic wage rate, and the application of seniority. Thus, two jobs can be differentiated by means of their job descriptions, even though both have the same wage rate. The second approach, as exemplified by the electronic industries, is to establish wage levels first and then to define job descriptions or job titles within the specific wage levels. This approach is dedicated to showing wage levels.

As a result, it becomes important to know which approach the surveyed corporations were using when they answered our questionnaires about the number of job classifications. If they were taking the first approach, their job classifications indicate work, although abstractly. Thus the wage rate may be the same and the work different, with two jobs indicated by two job descriptions. On the other hand, if they were taking the second approach, different jobs indicate different wage levels. Here the same wage level means the same work duties. When we visited Japanese-owned plants and asked about job descriptions, they often answered the questions assuming that job descriptions meant wage descriptions. Thus, it is necessary to understand whether a plant based its answer to the number of job descriptions on wage rates or wage levels.

As Table 4–1 shows, there are 30 plants who said they had 3 to 5 job classifications. This was the most common answer (34.1 percent). Sixteen plants answered "2 or less." Although not many, it is significant that, as we suspected, a certain number of plants (13) answered "11 to 50" or "51 or more," which is comparable to the number of wage ranks in American corporations. American corporations had more than 10 wage levels and between 50 and 100 job classifications. Compared to this, Japanese-owned plants not only had fewer job classifications, but are attempting to further reduce this number.

If we compare one industry to another, the automobile assembly and automobile parts industries were most likely to answer "2 or less," which shows they are trying to simplify their job classifications. In the other industries, the most common answer was "3 to 5," followed by either "6 to 10" or "11 to 50". They have not carried the process of simplification of job classifications as far as the automobile industry. We found similar differences concerning job classifications among the industries in our field survey.

Next, let us take a look at whether there is a correlation between the existence of a union and the number of job classifications. There is no correlation in the automobile assembly industry, but there is a certain correlation in other industries. As stated earlier, there are 16 plants with a union. Three of the automobile assembly plants had a union, and all these plants had simplified the number of job classifications to 2, 3, or 4. No correlation could be seen between the existence of a union and the number of job classifications here. In other industries, however, a certain correlation could be observed; in other words, one automobile parts plant had a union and the number of job classifications was 20. Likewise, one electronics plant had a union and the number of the job classifications was 18. In the case of industries other than these, 5 metal plants had a union, and the number of job classifications was 32, 12, 5, 3, and 1 unknown, respectively. One chemical plant had a union and the number of job classifications was 20. In "other industries," four plants had unions and the job classifications numbers there were 150, 10, and unknown in the case of two of the plants. Thus, except for auto assembly, a certain

Table 4–1. Job Classifications on the Shop Floor

	Auto Assembly	Auto Parts	Electronics	Metalworking	Chemicals	Other Machinery	Other Manufacturing	Total	(%)
2 or less	5	6	3	0	1	1	0	16	(18.2)
3 to 5	2	3	7	7	6	2	3	30	(34.1)
6 to 10	0	2	5	1	1	3	1	13	(14.8)
11 to 50	0	2	2	2	1	2	3	12	(13.6)
51 or more	0	0	0	0	0	0	1	1	(1.1)
N.A.	0	2	4	1	4	0	5	16	(18.2)
Total	7	15	21	11	13	8	13	88	(100.0)

correlation can be seen between the existence of a union and the high number of job classifications.

Wage System

In America, wages are based on job grades; however, in Japan wages are not based on job descriptions but are determined mainly by seniority and merit. It is typical for a Japanese plant to apply a performance evaluation system to production workers. More than half of the Japanese-related plants have simplified job classifications. But how about wages? We asked multiple choice questions in regard to this question. As Table 4–2 shows, wages are basically adapted to the American system and 61 plants (69.3%) are using job grades (4). Nevertheless, 33 plants (37.5%) are using a merit system (1) and 23 plants (26.1%) are using a seniority system (2). Thus, although many plants have adapted the American wage system, some plants use a Japanese-style merit system or a continuous service wage system. Twenty-one plants (23.9%) use a bonus system.

Looking at each industry individually, we find a job grade system used in all industries, but its most thorough application is in the auto assembly industry. None of the respondents from auto assembly plants were using any form of a merit system, whereas many respondents in auto parts, electronics, chemical, and "other industries" answered that they used a merit system in addition to the job grade system. The overwhelming majority said they used the orthodox merit system alongside some other form of wage system.

Thus, it is not unusual to determine wages primarily on the basis of a job grade system while simultaneously attempting to use the Japanese system. If we juxtapose the effects of this with the effects of job descriptions, we find an interesting contrast wherein job classifications are simplified so that the Japanese work organization can be introduced while simultaneously adapting it to the American style wage system. This contrast is most apparent in the automobile assembly plants but can also be seen to some degree in other industries.

We asked about the origin of the "methods" in regard to ten of the items in the questionnaire and presented the following seven choices: (A) "Practice typically followed by U.S. plants in this industry," (B) "Japanese parent company required this practice," (C) "Japanese expatriates at the plant initiated it on their own judgment," (D) "American managers at the plant initiated it by their own judgment,"

Table 4–2. Wages for Blue Collar Workers

	Auto Assembly	Auto Parts	Elec- tronics	Metal- working	Chem- ical	Other Machinery	Other Manufac- turing	Total	(%)
①Merit	0	6	9	3	6	4	5	33	(37.5)
②Seniority	1	1	6	3	3	4	5	23	(26.1)
③Bonus	2	1	4	5	4	3	2	21	(23.9)
④Job grades	6	7	17	8	10	6	7	61	(69.3)
⑤Others	1	2	0	0	0	1	0	4	(4.5)
Total	10	17	36	19	23	18	19	142	(161.4)

(E) "Outside consultants recommended the practice, which was then initiated," (F) "Union contract defined this practice originally," and (G) "Others."

Table 4–3 indicates the results and these will be analyzed here. As the total column shows, the most common answer was Japanese expatriates at 36.4%, followed by American managers with 27.5%, Traditional practice at 15.6%, and Parent company at 9.6%. All four figures combined total 89%. In general, the most common source of the practice was the recommendation of Japanese expatriates, followed by the recommendation of American managers. However, the analysis of the wage system produced different results. There the top-ranking reasons were American managers and Traditional practice, both with 28.7% or 57.4% combined. The wages are on the side of adaptation, suggesting that American management is strongly inclined to follow the American system. Japanese expatriates comes third, at 23.4%. The answers Japanese expatriates and Parent company would point to initiatives from the Japanese side, but this does not always mean that the Japanese methods are practiced. Sometimes the Japanese managers consider it inappropriate to adopt Japanese methods, and either a compromise between the local system and the Japanese system is attempted or they opt for adaptation to the local system. Similarly, the answer "American managers" indicates the initiative has come from American management, but it does not necessarily mean the adoption of the American system. Given these considerations, the results of our inquiry as to the source of the wage system matches the fact that wages are on the adaptation side.

Job Rotation

Under the traditional American mass production system, it is normal that the job duties of an individual worker are fixed, and work is subdivided and specialized. On the other hand, in Japan there is no notion of a fixed job that establishes specific work tasks and the wage. And in order to train the multiskilled worker and prevent

Table 4–3. Source of Practice

	Q1 Job Classifications	Q2 Wage Systems	Q3 Job Rotation	Q6 Training	Q7 Quality Control	Q10 Layoff Policy	Q11 Small Group Activities	Total	(%)
(A) Traditional practice	17	27	13	12	17	10	6	102	(15.6)
(B) Parent company	7	4	4	21	10	9	8	63	(9.6)
(C) Japanese expatriates	31	22	37	43	41	31	33	238	(36.4)
(D) American managers	23	27	28	30	24	26	22	180	(27.5)
(E) Outside consultants	1	2	1	2	0	1	0	7	(1.1)
(F) Union contract	7	7	7	1	0	6	1	29	(4.4)
(G) Others	6	5	7	3	5	5	4	35	(5.4)
Total	92	94	97	112	97	88	74	654	(100.0)

work from becoming monotonous, job rotation is practiced. Job rotation is done within a production team or beyond the team. In America, a shop worker sometimes initiates job trading in order to prevent monotonous work, but it is not done consciously and systematically to make a versatile worker. In question 3, we asked the status of the job rotation practice. In Table 4–4 the answers indicate that quite a few corporations practice job rotation in some form.

The most common answer is ② "It is required of all employees within a work group," chosen by 29 plants (33.0%), followed by ③ "It is conducted across different work groups for selected employees capable of handling a variety of work assignments," chosen by 19 plants (21.6%). In addition, ① "It is conducted across different work groups for all employees systematically," indicating extremely active participation, was chosen by 7 manufacturers (8.0%). The total of the 3 figures amounts to 57.9%. ④ "It is conducted within a work group for selected employees capable of handling a variety of assignments," which indicates that job rotation within the team is done among particular employees, was chosen by 12 plants (12.6%). Thus, 70.5% of plants practice some form of job rotation. On the other hand, only 20 percent had negative answers. ⑥ "It is hardly ever implemented" was chosen by 12 plants (12.6%), and ⑤ "It is implemented only to fill temporary job vacancies" by 7 plants (8.0%).

Thus it is obvious that approximately 70 percent of plants practice some method of job rotation. But 52 plants (59.1%) answered "different" and 10 plants (11.4%) answered "same" to the question whether the practice is the same or different than Japanese plants. They practice job rotation here, but it can be surmised that they are not practicing job rotation in the same way that their Japanese parent company does. Job rotation at the respondants is likely less pervasive and less intensive.

Table 4–4. Job Rotation on the Shop Floor

	Auto Assembly	Auto Parts	Elec-tronics	Metal-working	Chem-ical	Other Machinery	Other Manufac-turing	Total	(%)
① Across work group	0	3	1	1	1	0	1	7	(8.0)
② Within work group	5	6	6	3	6	1	2	29	(33.0)
③ Across work group partly	2	3	4	2	3	2	3	19	(21.6)
④ Within work group partly	0	2	4	2	0	2	2	12	(12.6)
⑤ Fill temporary	0	0	2	1	0	2	2	7	(8.0)
⑥ No	0	1	4	0	4	0	3	12	(13.6)
⑦ Others	1	0	3	2	0	1	2	9	(10.2)
Total	8	15	24	11	14	8	15	95	(108.0)

Training for Engineers and Plant Workers

Question 6 asks the method of employee training. It is necessary to train employees to help them apply the Japanese work organization to the local plant. There are two levels of training. One level is to develop the technical capability and work practices with regard to operating and setting up machinery. Another one is to develop not only the skills of direct operation but also of quality control, the ability to perform easy maintenance, group consciousness, and the practice of improvement activities.

In this way, the Japanese system requires an employee not only to repeat a given task but also to carry out an operation precisely, to be mindful of what is happening around the task, and to develop a sense of togetherness (group consciousness) toward the work. It is necessary to train local employees, who are brought up by the scientific management method, about these other aspects that relate to Japanese management.

We requested multiple answers. The number of possible answers was 204 and they are displayed on Table 4–5. Among them, ③ "The parent company sends Japanese trainers to the United States and has them train local employees there" was the most common answer, chosen by 57 plants (64.8%). The next most common answer was ② "OJT (on-the-job-training)," and 54 plants (61.4%) chose this. With respect to the most costly method, which is to send employees to Japan for training, 20 plants (22.7%) send ① "Both engineers and general workers to Japan," and 32 plants (36.4%) send only engineers to Japan and trained general workers in America. A total of 52 plants send local employees to Japan. Among the 88 plants, 52 plants (59%) send local employees to Japan, and very often, in 57 of the plants, they also send Japanese to America. Few plants (15 plants, 17.0%) use their own corporation training center. There were 24 plants (27.3%) who use ⑥ outside schools or institutions in accordance with the American style.

Thus, we can summarize that the main training method by a Japanese-owned plant is to send Japanese to a local plant or to send local employees to Japan or both

Table 4–5. Training for Engineers and Factory Workers

	Auto Assembly	Auto Parts	Electronics	Metalworking	Chemical	Other Machinery	Other Manufacturing	Total	(%)
① Send engineer and worker	7	5	3	1	0	1	3	20	(22.7)
② Send worker	1	6	9	3	7	4	2	32	(36.4)
③ Japanese trainers to the U.S.	7	11	11	8	7	4	9	57	(64.8)
④ OJT	4	10	11	8	10	3	8	54	(61.4)
⑤ Training center	6	2	3	2	0	2	0	15	(17.0)
⑥ Outside school or institution	3	4	4	2	4	2	5	24	(27.3)
⑦ Others	0	0	1	1	0	0	0	2	(2.3)
Total	28	38	42	25	28	16	27	204	(231.8)

and, at the same time, to practice OJT. OJT is essential to transfer skills that local employees have acquired in Japan or which are known by expatriate Japanese to other employees.

In addition, it is interesting to note that training is usually carried out at the request of the parent company in Japan, as can be seen in Table 4–3. In other words, answer (B) at the request of the parent company in Japan ranked fourth with 9.6% of the total. But here it ranks third (21 plants, 18.8%). As we expected, more than the average (36.4%) percentage of respondents chose (C) on the advice of Japanese expatriates, with 43 plants (38.4%) choosing this answer. The fact that these two answers were selected by a relatively high number of plants shows the emphasis placed on education and training by the Japanese corporations, including parent companies of local operations overseas.

Quality Control

The strength of the Japanese manufacturing corporation is the efficient production of high quality products. The creation of a manufacturing management system capable of efficiently producing high-quality products supports the strong international competitiveness of Japanese corporations. A key to realizing this high standard of quality lies in the fact that the "quality is built-in as the manufacturing process proceeds." Quality control is not considered merely the specialized job of a quality control section but rather the responsibility of the production workers. It is necessary that workers actually engaged in the manufacturing process accurately apply their power of attention and decision, that they cooperate with other workers at the local plant in avoiding defects by sending back defective products to the source of the defects in the previous manufacturing process. Naturally, we can presume that employees will be asked to engage in this "quality build-up" process at local plants. Question 7 is concerned with a method of quality control at a local plant, and the rather subtle results are shown in Table 4–6—that is to say, the results are somewhat complex. Although emphasis is put on "quality build-up," it is not a thorough implementation of this process, and very often inspectors are assigned according to the American style.

In fact, the local workers at the Japanese plants we visited had the same sense of responsibility for maintaining quality, and there were two approaches to quality inspection. In one, an inspector makes spot checks throughout the manufacturing

Table 4–6. To Secure Quality of Product

	Auto Assembly	Auto Parts	Elec-tronics	Metal-working	Chem-ical	Other Machinery	Other Manufac-turing	Total	(%)
① Workers without inspectors	2	6	3	1	4	2	4	22	(25.0)
② Workers with inspectors	5	7	11	5	4	4	5	41	(46.6)
③ Inspectors	2	3	8	4	3	2	4	26	(29.5)
④ Others	1	0	0	1	2	0	1	5	(5.7)
Total	10	16	22	11	13	8	14	94	(106.8)

process and local workers are responsible for the quality. In the other, both an inspector and a production worker check quality in the manufacturing process. In addition, Japanese-owned plants in America also request quality control of the production workers, but how they assign the department of inspection or the department of quality control at local plants differs. Here we can also observe similar results. The most common answer, chosen by 41 plants (46.6%), was ②, "workers take care of quality but quality control inspectors are assigned in the line and are part of the production organization." This most common answer can be interpreted to mean that the plants adopt a local quality control method by making workers responsible for quality, and at the same time assign inspectors in order to secure quality. And 26 plants (29.5%) chose ③, "We assign quality control inspectors in the line who are in a QC control section," whereas 22 plants (25.0%) chose ①, "Workers take care of quality without the assistance of quality control inspectors." So approximately 50% use inspectors to check quality and 50% use a system of responsibility that involves the production workers themselves. Interestingly, when the question was amplified by asking whether or not the method of quality control is the same as that found in a Japanese plant, 31 plants (35.2%) answered that it was the same, but 30 plants (34.1%) answered that it was different, and 27 plants (30.7%) did not answer at all. This can be interpreted to mean that the plants did not know whether it was the same or different. In conclusion, approximately 30 percent are identical, and approximately 70 percent are using a method that is not the same but that nevertheless cannot be said to be totally different than the method used by Japanese plants.

Layoff Policy

There are clear differences concerning employment customs and policies between Japanese and American corporations. American corporations lay off people as a result of production fluctuations, but Japanese corporations do not. It is very interesting to find out whether Japanese-owned plants in America follow Japanese employment customs or the American method. Question 10 addresses layoff policy and practice.

According to Table 4–7 approximately 80 percent said either that they do not

Table 4–7. Layoff Policy

	Auto Assembly	Auto Parts	Elec-tronics	Metal-working	Chem-ical	Other Machinery	Other Manufac-turing	Total	(%)
(1A) No layoffs, written	0	0	2	1	0	1	3	7	(8.0)
(1B) No layoffs, unwritten	1	2	2	1	1	1	0	8	(9.1)
(2A) Avoid it, written	4	4	2	1	0	1	1	13	(14.8)
(2B) Avoid it, unwritten	1	7	10	5	11	2	2	38	(43.2)
(3) Resort to it, if necessary	1	2	4	3	1	3	7	21	(23.9)
Total	7	15	21	11	13	8	13	88	(100.0)

practice layoffs or that they try to prevent them, and 21 plants (23.9%) answered (3), "We will resort to layoffs if necessary," which is the American method. Thus, the policy to avoid layoffs is the predominant policy among the Japanese-owned corporations. Thirty-eight of these plants (43.2%) chose (2B), the most common answer, namely, "We have a policy to avoid layoffs as long as possible. Policy is unwritten." Following this, 13 plants (14.8%) said that if possible they avoid layoffs and the policy is written. Fifteen plants answered flatly, no layoffs. As we stated earlier, many middle and small size plants answered our questionnaires, and their operation was most likely to be affected by fluctuations in production, but we can see that they, too, try to maintain employment continuity as much as possible.

Table 4–8 shows that 23 plants (26.1%) answered "yes", they had done it, and 51 plants (53.0%) answered "no", they had not done it. So 26% practiced layoffs, a number that slightly exceeds the 21 plants who answered the policy question with "if necessary they lay off." Fourteen plants (15.9%) did not answer (N.R., for "no response"). We presume that among these there are some plants who have already practiced layoffs. Thus, we see a slight gap between policy and practice. By industry, only auto assembly has not practiced layoffs, but in all the other industries some plants have done so. Among the electronics and "other industries," 9 and 7 plants, respectively, have practiced layoffs and this number exceeds the number that answered "no." On the other hand, in the auto parts, metal, and chemical industries, only one or two plants answered "yes," an unexpectedly small number. So layoffs were more prevalent in the electronics and "other industries." In the electronics industry, the gulf between policy and practice is quite apparent, for in spite of the fact that 4 plants said their policy was "to lay off if necessary" 9 plants answered, "Yes, they have done it."

Small Group Activities

One of the characteristics of the Japanese production system is that employees feel a sense of togetherness to their work and participate voluntarily in activities that improve their work. This is one of the important factors that make it possible to simultaneously realize high quality and high efficiency. Small group activities are known in Japan as work group-based volunteer activities. In fact, it includes both cultivation of group consciousness, or sense of participation, and improvement activities. Everyone usually participates. Question 11, then, addresses the subject of these small group activities, a vital part of the Japanese production system. Here we asked whether or not the plant engaged in small group activities and, if so, the

Table 4–8. Layoff Practice

	Auto Assembly	Auto Parts	Elec-tronics	Metal-working	Chem-ical	Other Machinery	Other Manufac-turing	Total	(%)
Yes	0	2	9	1	1	3	7	23	(26.1)
No	5	12	8	8	10	4	4	51	(58.0)
N.R.	2	1	4	2	2	1	2	14	(15.9)
Total	7	15	21	11	13	8	13	88	(100.0)

Table 4–9. Small Group Activities

	Auto Assembly	Auto Parts	Elec-tronics	Metal-working	Chem-ical	Other Machinery	Other Manufac-turing	Total	(%)
① Full attendance	0	3	2	2	1	1	3	12	(13.6)
② Over 50%	5	2	1	2	0	2	0	12	(13.6)
③ 20% to 50%	1	1	2	0	2	0	2	8	(9.1)
④ Below 20%	0	1	3	1	0	0	4	9	(10.2)
⑤ None	0	5	11	5	10	5	3	39	(44.3)
⑥ Others	1	1	0	0	0	0	0	2	(2.3)
N.A.	0	2	2	1	0	0	1	6	(6.8)
Total	7	15	21	11	13	8	13	88	(100.0)

participation rate. For the items that we have been examining so far, even though the wage system may be adapted to the local situation and quality control may have some slightly subtle nuances in its application, in these cases the application of the Japanese method still constitutes the pivotal focus. However, nearly half the plants do not practice small group activities and even when they do, the participation rate is not as high as in Japan. This result suggests that small group activities are not easy to implement.

As shown in Table 4–9, 39 plants (44.3%) chose ⑤, "We don't implement small group activities," the most common answer. Among plants we visited, many plants practiced some form of small group activities. The results obtained through our questionnaire may indeed better reflect the reality. By industry, auto assembly did not chose selection ⑤ at all, whereas the other industries selected ⑤ most often. The electronics, chemical, and other industries chose ⑤ often, numbering 11, 10, and 5, respectively. As such, many plants do not practice small group activities in the first place, and even if they do the participation rate is not as high as in Japan. The reason may be that American workers do not easily accept the practice of spending their nonworking hours participating in such group activities. As we expected, American individualism constitutes a barrier to the full implementation of these so indelibly Japanese small group activities. In fact, one of the electronics plants we visited practiced small group activities once a month, but only during working hours while they had stopped their production line. Their participation rate was unusually high, but still not 100 percent.

HYBRID EVALUATION BY QUESTIONNAIRE

Comparison of the Evaluated Degree of Application and Adaptation

The design of the questionnaire, that is, the questions and available choices, was based on our experiences in visiting plants in Japan and America and on the analytical framework of our research for the purpose of determining the degree of application of Japanese elements, and to determine and confirm the preconditions for the existence of such elements. From among the questions, we selected the 12 items most appropriate for scoring the degree of application-adaptation. To score the degree of application-adaptation, we referred to the 23 items of the evaluation as our standard whenever possible. (Please refer to the appendix.) But, the scores for the 23 items are based on a combination of the key evaluation criteria together with other items of consideration, whereas the questionnaires were scored solely on the basis of the key evaluation criteria; that is, the answers were ranked on a scale of one to five. Consequently, the scores are sometimes the same and sometimes not necessarily the same as those based on the 23 items. Here, "not necessarily the same" means that there exist only available choices for the scoring standard. It does not mean that it is completely different.

The selected 12 questionnaire items were: job classifications (Question 1), wage system (Question 2), job rotation (Question 3), foreman (Question 4), maintenance (Question 5), quality control (Question 7), plant equipment (Question 8), local content (Question 9), job security (Question 10), small group activities (Question 11), status of local managers (Questions 15 and 16), and ratio of Japanese expatriates (data-base item). Obviously, these points are all critical in determining the state of application-adaptation. Scoring for the 4 items, job classifications, local content, small group activities, and ratio of Japanese expatriates, was based on the same standard key criteria as the 23 items, and the other 8 items were scored based on the scores for each available answer.

The first of three conclusions that we were able to determine was that the average scores for the 12 items based on field research were about the same as those of the questionnaires, and that the questionnaire survey also confirms the tendency of local plants to incline toward application in dealing with the Japanese management-production system. Next, in auto assembly, auto parts, and electronics, the relative position indicated in the scores is exactly the same regardless of whether it has been determined through our field research or the questionnaire survey. In other words, the degree of application is high in the auto parts and assembly industries and relatively low in the electronics industry. Third, according to the results of the questionnaire survey, the degree of application is the highest in auto parts and the lowest in electronics. So it would appear that our field research covered industries that ranged from those with the highest degree of application to those with the lowest.

Table 4–10 compares the degree of application-adaptation between the 12 items

Table 4–10. Comparison of the Rate of Application

	12 Items from Field Research	12 Items from Questionnaire
Auto assembly	3.5	3.6
Auto parts	3.4	3.5
Semiconductors	3.1	—
Metalworking	—	3.1
Other machinery	—	3.1
Other manufacturing	—	3.1
Chemicals	—	2.9
Electronics	2.6	2.9
Total	3.1	3.1

from the questionnaire with the 12 items from the 23 items of our field research. The 23 items compared the four industries of auto assembly, auto parts, semiconductors, and electronics; in addition to these, the questionnaire compares the metalworking, chemical, other machinery, and other manufacturing industries. As mentioned above, it is natural to have different scores between the questionnaires and the 23 items even for the same items, because, except for four items, we did not use identical standards of evaluation. But the overall application-adaptation rate for all 12 items shows a surprising similarity in the scores and relative positioning of each industry.

To begin with, the overall average score for the degree of application-adaptation for the 12 items is 3.1 whether based on field research or the questionnaires. As mentioned before, the overall average of the 23 items was 3.3. Even though the average for the 12 items is slightly lower, here again it shows that, in America, Japanese-owned corporations operate their plants based on an application of the Japanese management-production system. And we can see that the rate of application for the 12 items is about the same among the three industries. That is, auto parts scored 3.5 based on field research and 3.6 based on the questionnaires; auto assembly scored 3.4 and 3.5 and electronics scored 2.6 and 2.9, respectively. The scores based on the questionnaires are only slightly higher.

Second, when we look at the relative position of each industry, we find that auto parts and auto assembly are high and electronics is low. In other words, according to the scores from the questionnaires, the application rate is the highest, 3.6 in auto parts and auto assembly follows with a mere 0.1 point difference. Electronics scores the lowest at 2.9 in the application rate. We visited all seven auto assembly plants that returned our questionnaires, but this overlap did not occur often in plants of the auto parts and electronics industries. Despite this fact, the results show that overall scores based on the 12 items from the field research, and those based on the 12 items from the questionnaires, had about the same relative position in these three industries. Thus, here too we find confirmation of the difference between the high application type in auto parts and auto assembly and the adaptation type in electronics.

Third, when we look at the scores in the seven industries based on the questionnaires, auto assembly and auto parts (3.6 and 3.5) may be seen as forming one group and the remaining industries (3.1 and 2.9) another group. Thus, based on what we see here, among the manufacturing industries the application rate is extremely high in auto parts and auto assembly. Among the relatively low application rate group, metalworking, other machinery and other manufacturing (3.1) can be distinguished from the chemical and the electronics industries (2.9). It is regrettable that because only two semiconductor plants returned our questionnaires, we were not able to deal with semiconductors as a separate industry. But it is interesting that all five industries from metalworking on have only a 0.2 point difference. According to the scores of the field research, auto parts and auto assembly are classified as application types, home electronics as an adaptation type, and semiconductors as being between the two, but closer to the application type. According to the scores based on the questionnaires, auto parts, auto assembly, and electronics share the same position, but metalworking, other machinery, and other manufacturing are located between the two types, although closer to the application side.

Degree of Application and Adaptation for 12 items

Now let us turn to an explanation of the 12 items taken from the questionnaire while looking at Table 4–11, which shows the scores of the application-adaptation rate based on the questionnaire's 12 items.

Overall, the items can be seen as belonging to the application type, but when we look at each item individually, we can distinguish items that tend toward application and those that tend toward adaptation. If 3.0 is used as the application rate standard, the 6 items with higher numbers and thus a greater tendency toward application are: job rotation, foreman, plant equipment, job security, status of local managers, and ratio of Japanese expatriates. On the other hand, the items whose scores are below 3.0 and are therefore to be regarded as belonging to the side of adaptation (or incomplete application) are: wage system, maintenance, quality control, and small group activities. Local content scored 2.1 and is adaptive.

As in our previous analysis, job classifications, job rotation, education and training, and layoff policy came through on the application side. In contrast, the wage system was adaptive, and the application of quality control and small group activities was subtle and inconsistent. Thus, the results of our analysis based on the 7 items and the results of the calculated scores of the application rate closely agree.

Among application items some have a high application rate and some a relatively low one. Status of local managers (3.9), foreman (3.9), ratio of Japanese expatriates (3.8), and job classification (3.7) all showed a high degree of application. Preconditions for applying the Japanese system are to simplify the job classifications, to have a high ratio of Japanese expatriate employees, and to put less emphasis on the

Table 4–11. Rate of Application from Questionnaire

	Auto Assembly	Auto Parts	Elec-tronics	Metal-working	Chem-icals	Other Machinery	Other Manufac-turing	Average
(Q1) Job classification	4.7	4.0	3.6	3.5	3.8	3.3	2.8	3.7
(Q2) Wage	1.8	2.5	2.5	2.5	2.5	2.8	2.8	2.5
(Q3) Job rotation	3.7	3.7	2.9	3.4	3.0	2.9	2.7	3.1
(Q4) Foreman	4.0	3.8	3.7	3.9	4.0	3.4	4.2	3.9
(Q5) Maintenance	3.1	3.2	2.9	3.2	2.5	2.9	2.2	2.8
(Q7) Quality control	3.0	3.4	2.5	2.4	3.2	3.0	3.0	2.9
(Q8) Plant equipment	3.3	3.8	2.8	2.8	2.6	3.1	3.0	3.0
(Q9) Local content	2.3	2.5	2.3	1.8	1.1	2.6	1.6	2.1
(Q10) Job security	3.7	3.4	2.6	2.3	3.3	2.8	2.3	3.0
(Q11) Small group activities	3.8	2.8	1.9	2.5	1.6	2.3	2.7	2.3
(Q15,16) Local managers	4.6	4.5	3.8	3.6	2.8	3.4	4.5	3.9
Japanese expatriates	4.0	4.3	3.0	2.9	3.8	4.6	4.3	3.8

role of local managers (in scoring this translates into high marks) when applying the Japanese method. All of these together underscore the big responsibilities shouldered by the Japanese managers. On the other hand, job rotation (3.1), plant equipment (3.0), and job security (3.0) although applicable are inconsistent.

Inter-industry Comparisons by the 4-Perspective Evaluation

Next, let us look at the characteristics of each individual industry in terms of the 4-perspective evaluation. The 4-perspective evaluation from the questionnaires lead to basically the same results as it did when applied to our field research. To begin with, let us compare overall averages. First, when we compare the 19 items that have been picked out and calculated from the 23 items on the basis of the 4-perspective evaluation, based on the field research with the 12 items observed here, we have essentially the same scores on any calculated items (human methods, etc.) with a maximum difference of 0.2. In short, even with a different number of items, each score and the relationship of the balances of the 4-perspective evaluation remains essentially the same. What are the results, then, of comparing the 4-perspective evaluation based on the field research (calculated from the 12 items) with that based on the questionnaire survey? As it is obvious from Tables 4–12 and 4–13, in the case of three aspects, "human-methods," "material-methods," and "human-results," the results are essentially the same with differences ranging from 0.1 to 0.2. However, "material-results" based on the field research scores was 3.5, whereas that based on the questionnaire scores was 2.6, a significant difference. This is due to the fact that the scores based on the field research are higher for plant equipment and local content, the constituents of the material method, with a big difference for plant equipment in particular. That is, the field research-based score was 4.3, whereas the score from the questionnaire was 3.0. This can be attributed to the greater role played by the chemicals, metalworking, and other manufacturing industries in the questionnaire research, all industries with a relatively low application rate for plant equipment.

Second, industry-specific characteristics based on the 23 items for auto assembly, auto parts, and electronics once again emerged. Because we cannot single out the semiconductor industry as a similar case, we will confine our comments to these three industries. First, we see that the results of Table 4–12 and the sum total of the 19 items based on our field research collected under the 4-perspective evaluation

Table 4–12. 4-Perspective Evaluation of Hybrid Model from Field Research

	Auto Assembly	Auto Parts	Electronics	Semiconductors	Average
Human methods	3.5	3.2	2.3	2.6	2.9
Material methods	3.5	3.4	2.6	2.5	3.0
Human results	3.6	4.3	2.9	3.9	3.7
Material results	3.1	3.8	3.0	4.2	3.5
Methods	3.5	3.2	2.4	2.6	2.9
Results	3.3	4.0	3.0	4.0	3.6

Table 4–13. 4-Perspective Evaluation of Hybrid Model from Questionnaire

	Auto Assembly	Auto Parts	Elec-tronics	Metal-working	Chem-icals	Other Machinery	Other Manufac-turing	Average
Human methods	3.6	3.4	2.8	3.2	3.0	2.9	2.8	3.0
Material methods	3.0	3.3	2.8	2.9	2.7	2.9	2.5	2.9
Human results	4.4	4.6	3.6	3.4	3.1	3.7	4.4	3.9
Material results	2.9	3.2	2.5	2.3	2.0	2.9	2.3	2.6
Methods	3.4	3.3	2.8	3.1	2.9	2.9	2.7	3.0
Results	3.8	4.1	3.2	3.1	2.8	3.5	3.8	3.5

are essentially the same. In other words, the industry-specific characteristics of the summed 4-perspective evaluation of the 19 items is that auto assembly is classified as a high application and methods application type, auto parts is classified as a high application and human-material-results application type, and the electronics industry is classified as the adaptive type. The results of Table 4–12, which are calculated from the 12 items that have been taken from the 23 items, are essentially the same. Then, looking at the results of the 4-perspective evaluation based on the questionnaire (Table 4-13) with this fact in mind, we see that all three industries are marked by the same characteristics. Auto assembly is classified as a method application type, auto parts as a human-material results direct application type, and the electronics industry as an adaptation type with a "material"-centered application. In concrete terms, the application rate of human-methods and methods for auto assembly is 3.6 and 3.4, the highest in the seven industries, clearly showing that this industry is to be classified as a "methods" application type. The application of human-results, material-results, and material-methods by the auto parts industry ranks highest, scoring 4.6, 3.2, and 3.3, respectively. It is different on Table 4–13, which shows the application of material-methods for auto parts is higher than it is for auto assembly.

Third, we would like to point out that the average impression portrayed by the overall average of the questionnaires is rather similar to that of the auto parts industry. Auto parts shows a relatively similar score distribution and slightly higher scores when its scores for the 12 items (Table 4–11) and the 4-perspective evaluation (Tables 4–12 and 4–13) are viewed against the total average as the reference. The reason for this is not obvious. The average impression of the plants that were studied by means of the questionnaire survey was "an average plant would be one that started operation in the 1980s, is middle-sized in terms of number of personnel, advanced into North America on its own initiative, and does not have a labor union." This coincides well with the average impression of the auto parts industry and may be the reason that the two have the same scores distribution.

QUESTIONNAIRE

Company name:

Please provide the following information for the plant only.

Start of operation:

Cumulative Investment:

Number of employees:

Number of Japanese employees:

Main products:

Annual production: ($ Amount)   (Volume: by products, by units—estimates)

Labor union (production workers): Yes①   No②

For each of the following 17 questions, please circle the appropriate number, or numbers, or fill in the correct numbers in the parentheses ( ) where requested. For many of the questions, the source of the practice is requested. In those cases, circle the most appropriate letter in accordance with the following key:

(A) Practice typically followed by U.S. plants in this industry.

(B) Japanese parent company required this practice.

(C) Japanese expatriates at the plant initiated it by their own judgment.

(D) American managers at the plant initiated it by their own judgment.

(E) Outside consultants recommended the practice which was then initiated.

(F) Union contract defined this practice originally.

(G) Others (   ).

Q 1. Job classifications on the shop floor.
   a. The number of job classifications for factory workers are ( ).
   b. Fill in the number of employees in the following job categories.
      (1) Production workers (   ).
      (2) Maintenance (   ).
      (3) Quality Control (   ).
   c. Source of the practice (A B C D E F G)

continued

Q 2. Wages for blue-collar workers.
    a.   Determination of wage. (You may choose more than one.)
        (1) There is a merit system involving personal performance evaluation.
        (2) Wage increases due to seniority, which is determined by length of service
        (3) There is a bonus system or profit sharing.
            [Approximately ( ) months for yearly income].
        (4) Wage is determined by job classifications or labor grades.
        (5) Others (   ).
    b.   Source of the practice (A B C D E F G)

Q 3. Job rotation on the shop floor.
    a.   Practice (Check here _____ if practice is the same as at the parent company in Japan, or, check here _____ if the practice is different from that at the parent company in Japan.)
        (1) It is conducted across different work groups for all employees systematically.
        (2) It is required of all employees within a work group.
        (3) It is conducted across different work groups for selected employees capable of handling a variety of work assignments.
        (4) It is conducted within a work group for selected employees capable of handling a variety of assignments.
        (5) It is implemented only to fill temporary job vacancies.
        (6) It is hardly ever implemented.
        (7) Others (   ).
    b.   Source of the practice (A B C D E F G)

Q 4. Promotion or hiring of first-line supervisors.
    a.   Practice
        (1) They are selected from production workers by considering ability.
        (2) Candidates (inexperienced) are hired separately from production workers and are trained.
        (3) We mix both (1) and (2).
        (4) We hire persons experienced as supervisors in other companies.
        (5) We mix both (1) or (2) and (4).
        (6) Others (   ).
    b.   Source of the practice (A B C D E F G)

Q 5. Maintenance of machines and equipment.
    a.   Practice (Check here _____ if practice is the same as at the parent company in Japan, or, check here _____ if the practice is different from that at the parent company in Japan.)

    (1) Not only professional maintenance workers but also ordinary workers engage in it.

    (2) Mainly professional maintenance workers engage in it.

    (3) Others (   ).

  b. Hiring and training for maintenance workers.

    (1) Ordinary workers are promoted to become maintenance workers by considering ability and desire.

    (2) We hire candidates (inexperienced), separately from ordinary workers, and train them.

    (3) We mix both (1) and (2).

    (4) We hire experienced persons.

    (5) We mix (1) or (2) and (4).

    (6) Others (   ).

  c. Source of the practice (A B C D E F G)

Q 6. Training for engineers and factory workers. (You may choose more than one item in this question.)

  a. Practice

    (1) We send engineers and/or technicians and relatively many factory workers to Japan and train them there.

    (2) We send engineers and/or technicians to Japan but train factory workers in the United States.

    (3) The parent company sends Japanese trainers to the United States and has them train local employees (both engineers and/or factory workers) here.

    (4) Mainly we use OJT (on-the-job-training).

    (5) We use a training department or center within the company.

    (6) We use outside schools and training institutions.

    (7) Others (   ).

  b. Source of practice (A B C D E F G)

Q 7. To secure quality of products.

  a. Practice (Check here _____ if practice is the same as at the parent company in Japan, or, check here _____ if the practice is different from that at the parent company in Japan.)

    (1) Workers take care of quality without the assistance of quality control inspectors.

    (2) Workers take care of quality but quality control inspectors are assigned in the line and are part of the production organization.

    (3) We assign quality control inspectors in the line who are in a QC control section (separate from the production organization).

    (4) Others (   ).

  b. Source of the practice (A B C D E F G)

continued

Q 8. Main machines of your plant.
      (1) We install machines that were first *used* in our factory
          operating in Japan.
      (2) We install machines that were first *tried out* in Japan.
      (3) We install the same machines as in Japan without a trial
          operation.
      (4) We install basically the same machines as in Japan, but
          make some modifications to them for their use in the
          United States.
      (5) We install machines that were used in the Japanese
          plant, as well as machines that are unique to the U.S.
          plant.
      (6) We install machines which are unique to the US plant.
      (7) Others (   ).

Q 9. Procurement of materials and parts.
    a. Our level of local content (by dollar value) in the shipment
       of products is ( ) % (including the added value at your
       plant).
    b. Distribution of parts procurement.

	Brought from Japanese-owned companies	Bought from non-Japanese-owned companies
Japan	About ( ) %	
USA	About ( ) %	About ( ) %
Asia	About ( ) %	About ( ) %
Others	About ( ) %	About ( ) %
USA	About ( ) %	About ( ) %
Total		100 %

    c. We give technical support and guidance in the case of
       procurement from companies in the United States that are
       Japanese-owned (check _____ Yes or _____ No) and that are
       locally (non-Japanese) owned (check _____ Yes or _____ No).

Q 10. Layoffs.
    a. Policy
      (1) We have a policy of no layoffs or we provide permanent
          job security.
          *Please circle A or B
        (A) Policy is written. (B) Policy is unwritten.
      (2) We have a policy to avoid layoffs as long as possible.
          *Please circle A or B.
        (A) Policy is written. (B) Policy is unwritten.
      (3) We will resort to layoffs is necessary.
      (4) Others (   ).
    b. Practice. We have experienced layoffs already.
       Check _____ Yes or _____ No.
    c. Source of the policy (A B C D E F G)

Q 11. Small group activities. (Please give an example
here: (   )
    a. Practice
        (1) We have a policy of full attendance by all workers in
the plant.
        (2) Participation in it is voluntary and exceeds 50% of all
workers.
        (3) Participation in it is voluntary and ranges from 20% to
50% of all workers.
        (4) Participation in it is voluntary and fewer than 20% of
all workers participate.
        (5) We don't implement small group activities.
        (6) Others (   ).
    b. Source of the practice (A B C D E F G)

Q 12. Turnover ratio of our company is ( ) % per year or ( ) % per
month.

Q 13. Grievance procedure.
    a. Practice
        (1) The procedure is defined in the collective labor
agreement with the union and _____ includes, or
_____ does not include finishing arbitration.
        (2) We have a special written procedure (that is, not in a
union contract) to handle grievances, in which, for
example, (A) grievance committee or (B) other
(   ) plays an important role.
        (3) We have an unwritten procedure for handling
grievances, in which, for example, [(A) supervisors or
(B) others (   )] play an important role.
        (4) Others (   ).
    b. Source of the practice (A B C D E F G)

Q 14. Ownership of the local affiliated company.
        (1) Wholly-owned by Japanese parent company and/or the
Japanese parent and its other U.S. or foreign
subsidiaries or sister-companies in Japan.
        (2) Joint venture between several different Japanese
companies.
        (3) Joint venture between a Japanese company and an
American company.
        (4) Joint venture between several different Japanese
companies and American companies.
        (5) Others (   ).

Q 15. The most senior executive at this plant is
        (1) Japanese
        (2) American
        (3) Other

continued

Q 16.

(1) Please fill in the following matrix, as appropriate to your plant.

	Most Senior Executive for this Function is: (check one for each function		Number of Other Managerial Position for this Function Staffed by ____. (enter appropriate numbers)		Number of Nonmanagerial Technical Positions for this Function Staffed by ____. (enter appropriate number)	
	Japanese Expatriate	American or Other	Japanese Expatriate	American or Other	Japanese Expatriate	American or Other
Product engineering						
Process engineering						
Manufacturing/ production						
Quality control						
Accounting/ finance						
Procurement						
Sales/ marketing						
Management information systems/(CIS)						
Human Resources/ personnel						
Public relations						

(2) Please make a statement on your company's purpose and philosophy regarding the use of Japanese expatriates. In other words, what do Japanese expatriates do or

accomplish? (Respond for expatriates in both managerial and technical positions.)

Q 17. Regarding the board of director for the U.S. subsidiary that operates this plant.
    a. Which national occupies the following position? (Please circle the answer)
        Chairman of the board [(A) American   (B) Japanese]
        President [(A) American   (B) Japanese]
    b. How many nationals are on the board of directors that are American (   ), Japanese (   ), or other nationalities (   )?

5

Correlation Analysis Between Structural Elements of the Hybrid Model

HIROSHI ITAGAKI

This chapter examines correlation among the data obtained for each of the target plants. Specifically, attention will focus upon correlation among the degrees of application for the 23 items composing the hybrid analysis, and between the degree of application for each item and the managerial environment in which the target plants exist.

The first step in carrying out this type of analysis is to determine the difference between the item correlation that is expected for the successful international transfer of Japanese management, and the actual item correlation found among the various elements at the local plants. Second, this gap between expected and actual relationships will provide clues for determining which items constitute a bottleneck or hindrance for the transfer of the Japanese system. Third, the same gap will provide material for reexamining and verifying the hybrid model and its underlying assumptions. And fourth, while focusing on the degree of application correlation, it will be possible to define standards for industry and company descriptions, by which to obtain a clearer understanding of the types of enterprises that become established overseas.

GROUP CORRELATIONS

Before examining item correlation, it will be helpful to briefly consider the overall relationships among groups that link similar items. As Table 5–1 clearly illustrates, there is fairly close correlation among groups I, Work Organization and Administration, II, Production Control, IV, Group Consciousness, and V, Labor Relations. Correlation exists among the human and functional core systems (groups I and II), their supporting subsystem (group IV), and labor relations (group V), which has a strong overall influence upon plant management. There is also a clear correlation between group III, Procurement, and group VI, Parent-Subsidiary Relations. This is probably on account of a parallel relationship between the high degree of dependence upon the parent company for the supply of parts, and the degree of depen-

Table 5–1. Group Correlation Coefficients
(Unit: Simple Correlation Coefficients)

	I Work Organization and Administration	II Production Control	III Procurement	IV Group Consciousness	V Labor Relations	VI Parent-Subsidiary Relations	VII Community Relations
I Work organization	X						
II Production control	0.52**	X					
III Procurement	0.32	0.02	X				
IV Group consciousness	0.62**	0.48**	0.34*	X			
V Labor relation	0.61**	0.48**	0.36*	0.70**	X		
VI Parent-subsidiary relations	0.32	0.22	0.47**	0.31	0.46**	X	
VII Community relations	−0.18	−0.32	0.09	−0.34	−0.24	0.15	X

Notes:
*Indicates signifcant at the .05 level
**Indicates significant at the .01 level

dence on the parent company from a human or authority standpoint. In contrast, the absence of a clear correlation between group VII, Community Relations, and any of the other groups is itself interesting because it shows that there is no meaningful relation between the method used to judge a company's response to its social or community environment and the application-adaptation approach used to assess issues related to plant management.

ITEM CORRELATIONS

The brief analysis presented above confirms that correlation does exist among the major element groups constituting the Japanese production system. The following more detailed analysis will pinpoint this correlation in terms of the individual items involved. Table 5–2 shows, in the form of a matrix, correlation coefficients between degrees of application at all target plants and for each item in the hybrid evaluation. By examining this table we can readily discover those items between which there is significant correlation (or conversely, where there is none) and begin to explore the implications.

Work Organization and Administration

To begin, it is notable that there is a close relationship among those functions and systems constituting the broad skill formation and flexible work organization core (including the number of jobs and job classes, job rotation, the training system, and methods for developing supervisors but excluding the wage system and promotion). In those plants where boundaries separating jobs are blurred, there is a greater possibility for the vigorous job rotation and OJT that lie at the heart of the broad range of shop floor skill formation. In addition, supervisory personnel (including team leaders) who gain their knowledge and experience in such plant systems have the requisite skills for performing a wide variety of functions. Conversely, for those plants that have a low degree of application for some of these items, there is a clear tendency for a low degree of application for the other items as well.

In particular, the number of different job classifications is correlated not only with other group I elements, but also with production control elements such as quality control and maintenance, the method of parts procurement, various measures aimed at increasing mutual understanding or a sense of unity among employees, and adherence to strict hiring guidelines and a no-layoff policy. Job Classifications is thus correlated with application of the core production system, and with the application of important subsystems. This item is thus highly symbolic of the Japanese management and production system, and in particular, of the stance adopted by those firms attempting to vigorously and systematically transfer their human and material resource management methods to their overseas plants.

Item correlation for Education and Training is largely similar to those for Job Classification. Both of these items also show a strong correlation with the average degree of application for all 23 items. This is not unexpected, since fewer barriers between jobs is an important precondition for shop floor-centered, broad-ranged skill formation, and since the existence of such skills is a key point of the Japanese production system.

However, a notable difference between these two items is that while there is a clear correlation between Education and Training and Labor Unions, there is no similar correlation between Job Classification and Labor Unions. In other words, although the existence of unions or the type of labor relations may influence the extent to which the Japanese education and training system is transferred to the local plant, these factors do not seem to have a determining effect on job demarcations or the number of job classifications. This relationship between the existence of labor unions and job classifications is examined further under the following section, Labor Relations.

Correlation found between Job Rotation and other items are similar to those for Job Classification, except that the degrees of correlation, including those with the First-line Supervisors and Maintenance, are generally lower in the case of Job Rotation. This seems to suggest that, at least at the present stage of development, the role of job rotation in skill formation remains relatively limited.

Strong correlation with items outside the group is not limited to Job Classification, but is also evident for Job Rotation, Education and Training, and First-line Supervisors. For example, these items are positively correlated with items classified under group IV, Group Consciousness, such as Sense of Unity, or under group V, Labor Relations, such as Job Security. If a plant makes an effort to eliminate job boundaries or to achieve the formation of a broad range of shop floor skills, or to introduce flexible work organization, then it will also tend to establish a no-layoff policy, or to energetically introduce measures designed to cultivate a sense of unity, such as open-style cafeterias. In other words, elements related to human management methods (human-method) are able to influence each other by transcending their core system, subsystem, or labor relations domain.

First-line Supervisors and Maintenance are similarly correlated. While supervisors and maintenance workers are both skilled and essential shop-floor workers, their roles and character differ greatly. Nevertheless, there is a distinct correlation between these items at plants that acquire and train these types of employees in similar ways. For example, those companies that emphasize in-plant training and promotion of shop-floor workers to the supervisor rank tend to do likewise for the training and promotion of maintenance workers, and vice-versa.

On the other hand, although they are both concerned with treatment of workers, and are both related to the human-method aspect of the system, Promotion, and especially Wage System, are subject to rather different conditions. The determining factors of the wage system or promotions are governed to a considerable extent by historical and social conditions of the environment into which transfer is being attempted. Difficulties accompanying the transfer of a system into different cultural settings are therefore predictable. According to this study, the average degree of application for Wage System, which receives only 2.4 points, is the lowest among all 23 items surveyed. This demonstrates the difficulty of transferring this element. For the same reason, there is a notable absence of significant correlation between Wage System and any other element other than Labor Unions. In Japan, both the wage system and the promotion system are largely responsible for helping to main-

Table 5–2. Item Correlation Coefficients (Unit: Simple Correlation Coefficients)

	① Job Classification	② Wage System	③ Job Rotation	④ Education and Training	⑤ Promotion	⑥ Supervisor	⑦ Equipment	⑧ Quality Control	⑨ Maintenance	⑩ Operations Management	⑪ Local Content
① Job Classification	X										
② Wage System	0.04	X									
③ Job Rotation	0.62**	0.00	X								
④ Education and Training	0.62**	0.12	0.60**	X							
⑤ Promotion	0.36*	0.15	0.33	0.47**	X						
⑥ Supervisor	0.55**	0.15	0.45**	0.56**	0.67**	X					
⑦ Equipment	-0.05	0.26	-0.08	-0.07	0.20	0.03	X				
⑧ Quality Control	0.72**	-0.24	0.34*	0.36*	0.28	0.38*	0.01	X			
⑨ Maintenance	0.57**	0.19	0.40*	0.66**	0.66**	0.60**	0.01	0.41*	X		
⑩ Operations Management	-0.02	-0.14	0.20	-0.04	0.05	0.30	-0.01	0.12	0.18	X	
⑪ Local Content	-0.11	0.09	0.14	0.22	0.15	-0.06	0.26	-0.33	-0.06	-0.29	X
⑫ Suppliers	-0.05	0.09	0.13	0.21	0.31	0.17	0.51**	-0.25	0.00	-0.13	0.73**
⑬ Procurement method	0.53**	-0.06	0.45**	0.49**	0.11	0.34*	-0.31	0.47**	0.42*	-0.03	-0.13
⑭ Small group activities	0.20	0.20	0.42*	0.05	0.35*	0.41*	-0.01	0.05	0.34	0.24	-0.12
⑮ Information sharing	0.46**	0.09	0.33	0.33	0.30	0.35*	0.20	0.36*	0.42*	-0.05	0.21
⑯ Sense of unity	0.71**	0.16	0.38*	0.45**	0.30	0.37*	0.27	0.62**	0.39*	-0.16	0.12
⑰ Employment	0.51**	-0.17	0.38*	0.44**	0.15	0.24	0.02	0.51**	0.33	-0.08	0.26
⑱ Job security	0.65**	0.00	0.32	0.50**	0.34*	0.53**	0.19	0.60**	0.50**	0.07	-0.12
⑲ Labor union	0.16	0.45**	0.22	0.47**	0.25	0.22	0.28	-0.04	0.42*	-0.18	0.32
⑳ Grievance procedures	0.06	0.18	0.08	0.40*	0.27	0.05	0.18	0.10	0.35*	-0.28	0.20
㉑ Ratio of Japanese expatriates	0.34	0.06	0.16	0.26	0.29	-0.03	0.28	0.23	0.20	-0.17	0.40*
㉒ Delegation	0.16	0.30	0.18	0.43*	0.25	0.09	0.34*	0.05	0.04	-0.28	0.47**
㉓ Local Manager	0.07	0.16	-0.04	0.29	0.18	0.00	0.40*	0.02	0.07	-0.11	0.26
Average	0.71**	0.24	0.58**	0.72**	0.58**	0.58**	0.34**	0.51**	0.65**	-0.01	0.31

	(12) Suppliers	(13) Procurement Method	(14) Small Group Activities	(15) Information Sharing	(16) Sense of Unity	(17) Employment	(18) Job Security	(19) Labor Union	(20) Grievance Procedures	(21) Ratio of Japanese Expatriates	(22) Delegation	(23) Local Manager
(1) Job Classification												
(2) Wage System												
(3) Job Rotation												
(4) Education and Training												
(5) Promotion												
(6) Supervisor												
(7) Equipment												
(8) Quality Control												
(9) Maintenance												
(10) Operations Management												
(11) Local Content												
(12) Suppliers	X											
(13) Procurement method	-0.35*	X										
(14) Small group activities	0.03	0.24	X									
(15) Information sharing	0.36*	0.33	0.42*	X								
(16) Sense of unity	0.17	0.39*	0.16	0.68**	X							
(17) Employment	0.15	0.53**	0.10	0.56**	0.65**	X						
(18) Job security	0.07	0.44**	0.19	0.61**	0.70**	0.55**	X					
(19) Labor union	0.18	0.16	0.24	0.34	0.38*	0.27	0.22	X				
(20) Grievance procedures	-0.02	0.32	0.01	0.10	0.25	0.21	0.09	0.69**	X			
(21) Ratio of Japanese expatriates	0.20	0.09	-0.03	0.27	0.56**	0.28	0.28	0.36**	0.43*	X		
(22) Delegation	0.48**	-0.10	-0.25	-0.02	0.29	0.10	0.04	0.38*	0.37*	0.40*	X	
(23) Local Manager	0.28	0.00	-0.03	0.13	0.28	0.14	0.15	0.32	0.35*	0.43*	0.53*	X
Average	0.36*	0.44**	0.33	0.69**	0.83**	0.64**	0.71**	0.60**	0.43*	0.58**	0.43*	0.41*

Notes:
*Indicates significant at the .05 level
**Indicates significant at the .01 level

tain long-term employment and are important devices for encouraging the formation of a broad range of skills. If these elements become difficult to transfer, and become poorly connected to the core elements of work organization or human resources formation, then it may be a significant limiting factor for the application of the Japanese system.

Although the auto manufacturing industry, as we will examine more closely in Chapter 6, shows a strong overall application tendency for group I, Work Organization and Administration, the rating for Wage System is anomalously low. In fact, the auto assembly industry's degree of application for this element conforms more to an adaptive pattern such as seen in the consumer electronics industry. This contributes to the absence of a strong correlation between the wage system and other elements. It remains to be seen whether in the future, this element of the Japanese system will meet continued shop-floor resistance by the American system, or whether a change in the wage system will gradually come about. This is an interesting area for future research.

Promotion also concerns the treatment of employees, but although correlation for this item is not as strong nor as extensive as in the case of most other group I items, it is more widespread than in the case of Wage System. In particular, there is a notably strong positive correlation between Promotion and items related to skill formation such as Education and Training, First-line Supervisors, and Maintenance. Moreover, compared to Wage System, the application rating for Promotion is a relatively high 3.1 points and fairly consistent among the four industries. The Japanese promotion system is easier to transfer as it is not as strongly resisted as the wage system. Plants that nurture their supervisors from within, or that select relatively inexperienced shop floor workers to train in the specific maintenance skills required at their plant, also tend to apply promotion criteria that focus on the individual worker, such as individual employee performance evaluations.

Production Control

There is a clear correlation between Equipment and Suppliers. Those plants that utilize production equipment similar to the type used in Japan and that therefore have a high degree of dependence upon Japan, tend to procure parts from their parent companies or from other suppliers in Japan. Even where these plants procure parts from suppliers located in the United States or in a third country, a large proportion of those suppliers are either sister companies or Japanese affiliated parts suppliers. In other words, there is a strong correlation between the degree of dependence upon Japan for material-results elements such as production equipment and parts, both of which would be brought into the local production ready-made.

Correlation also exists between the degrees of application for Equipment and Delegation of Authority or Managerial Position of Americans. A high degree of application for Delegation of Authority means that most of the authority remains vested in the parent company, and a high degree of application for Managerial Position of Americans indicates that Japanese expatriate employees in the managerial ranks have a higher status (hold a greater number of important positions) than their American coworkers. A correlation between these items and Equipment reveals that those plants whose parent companies retain much authority, or at which Japanese expatriate personnel have a relatively high status, also tend to be highly dependent upon Japan for production equipment. Conversely, those plants that are strongly "localized" in terms of management and personnel tend to procure their production equipment from purely local sources.

No correlation was discovered between the degree of application for Equipment and plant management methods such as skill formation or type of work organization. In other words, there is no indication of a connection between a tendency to apply various plant management methods and the degree of dependence upon Japan for production equipment.

There is a natural relationship between quality control and those elements that represent skill formation or work organization, such as job classification, job rotation, education or training, supervisors, and maintenance. However, with the single exception of Job Classification, there is a not so strong correlation between the degrees of application for these respective items and Quality Control. This may reflect the fact that quality control, in the sense of "building quality into the process," has yet to fully penetrate the production system. There is, however, a relation between efforts to implement a variety of measures for improving quality, and vigorous attempts at promoting a sense of belonging to the company, the careful selection of employees at the time of hiring, and adherence to a no-layoff policy. This is supported by the strong correlation between Quality Control and Sense of Unity, Hiring Policy, and Job Security. This suggests that, at the present stage, Japanese local producers put priority upon the application of worker participation and labor relations aspects of quality control. There is also a definite correlation between the degree of application of Quality Control and that of Procurement Method. A partial explanation may be that both items reflect the material-method aspect of application.

There is strong correlation between Maintenance and most of the work organization (group I) elements. There is also some correlation between this and the items that belong to Group Consciousness or to Labor Relations. The correlation pattern is very similar to that for Education and Training and First-line Supervisors. That Maintenance should be related to these human-method elements follows from the fact that maintenance is closely connected with skill formation. It must, however, be remembered that this reflects one of our criteria for evaluating degree of application of Maintenance, namely the in-house training and development of maintenance workers, as opposed to their acquisition from an external labor market.

There is no evidence of a correlation between Operations Management and any other item. This suggests that the introduction of flexible work organization, or of the systems dedicated to the formation of a broad range of job skills, have yet to reach the point where they can bring about the higher-order, efficient, overall plant operation system capable of turning out an ever-changing, small-lot product mix, or of encouraging the regular shop-floor worker's active involvement in job improvement or preventive maintenance. Consequently, the only way to evaluate the degree of application of Operations Management is in terms of whether plant operations are stable and smooth, rather than at what level the Japanese system functions.

Some slight correlation between Operations Management and other elements do appear when industries are examined individually. For example, in the auto industry,[1] Operations Management is positively correlated to Small Group Activities, but negatively correlated to Delegation of Authority. Although this can be interpreted as indicating that smoothly operating plants tend to invest a great deal of effort in small group activities, there is no equally convincing explanation for the negative correlation between operations and delegation of authority to local plants. As discussed below under Item and Managerial Environment Correlation, there is a correlation between operating period and the degree of application of Operations Management in the auto industry. Accordingly, those plants that have been operating for a longer period of time also tend to have greater managerial authority and smoother plant operations. However, since there is no clear correlation between length of operating period and local plant autonomy, it is difficult to lend broad support to this explanation.

For the electronics industry,[1] there is a correlation between attention to quality control and stable operations. In regard to the managerial environment, a correlation also exists between the number of employees and the degree of application of operations management. A possible explanation for this is that management at large-scale plants (i.e., plants with many employees) tends to make a more earnest, concerted effort, and this results in more stable operations.

Parts Procurement

There is a distinct correlation between Local Content and both Suppliers and Delegation of Authority. There is also a correlation, although not as strong, between Local Content and Ratio of Japanese Expatriates. The connection between Local Content and Suppliers is not surprising. It is also easy to understand how a high (low) degree of local content would correspond to strong (weak) local plant authority and a low (high) ratio of Japanese expatriate employees (it is important to remember that a "high" degree of local content or "strong" local authority reflects a "low" degree of application). In other words, there is a parallel relationship between the localization (local adaptation) of material elements such as parts, and the localization of human- or management-related elements. Moreover, as can be seen from Table 5–3, there is no correlation between length of period of operation, and degree of local content or local plant authority. It would therefore be reasonable to conclude that the type of application correlation referred to above is not the product of length of operating experience, but reflects special characteristics of the respective plants.

Suppliers and Local Content show similar correlation patterns. A notable difference, however, is that while there is a significant correlation between Suppliers and Equipment, none exists between Local Content and Equipment. This shows that the degree of reliance upon Japan for production equipment is not simply a matter of the local procurement ratio but of whether the supplier is a Japanese company, be it situated in Japan, North America, or Southeast Asia. Also, apart from a slight correlation between Suppliers and Information Sharing, neither Local Content nor Suppliers provides evidence of a clear correlation with any of elements in the

Table 5–3. Item and Managerial Environment Correlation

	All Plants						Automobile		Electronics	
	Period of Operation	Number of Employees		Plant Location Average			Period of Operation	Number of Employees	Period of Operation	Number of Employees
	Correlation Coefficient	Correlation Coefficient	Correlation Ratio	West Coast	Midwest Northeast	South	Correlation Coefficient	Correlation Coefficient	Correlation Coefficient	Correlation Coefficient
① Job classification	−0.17	0.33	0.10	3.1	4.1	3.5	−0.42	0.16	0.25	0.22
② Wage system	0.34*	−0.13	0.23*	3.1	2.3	2.1	0.07	−0.27	0.36	0.02
③ Job rotation	0.09	0.35*	0.02	2.9	2.6	2.6	0.20	0.45	0.29	0.08
④ Education and training	0.04	0.20	0.05	3.0	3.0	2.6	−0.34	0.14	0.30	−0.01
⑤ Promotion	−0.14	0.02	0.01	3.0	3.1	3.1	−0.18	−0.10	0.00	−0.12
⑥ Supervisor	−0.08	0.26	0.00	2.9	2.9	2.8	0.00	0.13	0.14	0.26
⑦ Equipment	−0.49**	−0.16	0.04	4.1	4.5	4.1	−0.15	−0.24	−0.66**	−0.19
⑧ Quality control	−0.28	0.35*	0.30**	2.6	3.6	3.6	−0.15	0.16	0.05	0.38
⑨ Maintenance	−0.05	0.19	0.05	2.5	2.8	2.4	−0.04	0.06	0.17	0.19
⑩ Operations management	0.03	0.36**	0.00	3.0	3.0	3.1	0.66**	0.46	−0.10	0.57**
⑪ Local content	−0.17	−0.36*	0.05	3.0	2.6	2.4	−0.40	−0.40	−0.29	−0.49
⑫ Suppliers	−0.45**	−0.18	0.01	4.0	3.8	3.8	−0.28	−0.20	−0.64**	−0.22
⑬ Procurement method	0.25	0.35*	0.09	2.4	2.7	2.3	−0.17	0.31	0.83**	0.00
⑭ Small group activities	0.08	0.20	0.04	2.8	2.4	2.6	0.44	0.18	0.22	0.14
⑮ Information sharing	−0.37*	0.36*	0.06	3.0	3.7	3.6	0.20	0.34	−0.29	−0.16
⑯ Sense of unity	−0.41*	0.30	0.09	2.9	3.8	3.6	−0.13	0.11	−0.19	−0.24
⑰ Hiring policy	−0.30	0.27	0.09	2.9	3.6	3.6	0.01	0.13	−0.11	−0.10
⑱ Job security	−0.49**	0.45**	0.21*	2.4	4.0	3.1	0.02	0.60**	−0.42	−0.25
⑲ Labor union	0.02	−0.11	0.07	4.9	4.3	4.1	0.21	−0.34	0.13	−0.17
⑳ Grievance procedures	0.07	−0.20	0.00	3.4	3.3	3.3	−0.21	−0.52*	0.27	−0.24
㉑ Ratio of Japanese expatriates	−0.33	−0.17	0.12	3.3	4.2	3.2	−0.48*	−0.37	−0.25	−0.49
㉒ Delegation of authority	−0.02	−0.43*	0.02	3.8	3.5	3.7	−0.42	−0.61**	0.08	−0.29
㉓ Local Manager	−0.04	−0.29	0.00	3.6	3.6	3.5	−0.23	−0.33	0.02	−0.72**
Average	−0.30	0.18	0.05	3.1	3.4	3.2	−0.30	−0.08	−0.04	−0.06

human-method groups of Work Organization and Administration or Labor Relations. This is also interesting because, as in the case of Equipment, it demonstrates that local procurement of materials, or dependence upon Japan for materials, is unrelated to the intention to apply Japanese methods to the management of human resources.

It is not surprising that there is a correlation between Procurement Methods and Suppliers. More notable is the fact that, unlike Local Content or Suppliers, there is correlation between "Procurement Methods" and various human-aspect items in Work Organization and Administration and Labor Relations. In particular, correlation exists with Job Classification, Job Rotation, Education and Training, First-line Supervisors, Hiring Policy, and Job Security. This shows that plants that vigorously introduce elements of the Japanese system governing relations with parts suppliers, such as cooperation with technological guidance and quality control systems, or the "just-in-time", as well as less extreme delivery systems, also tend to implement flexible work organization, establish training programs for the formation of a broad range of shop-floor skills, and attempt to maintain cooperative labor relations through careful employee screening and a no-layoff policy. The correlation pattern for Quality Control, which is a type of materials management, is similar to that of Procurement Method. Moreover, the clear correlation between Quality Control and Procurement Method suggests strong similarities between the materials-method and human-method orientations of application that cannot be ignored. However, the overall average degree of application of Procurement Method only receives a rating of 2.5, which is second lowest after Wage System. It is necessary to give sufficient consideration to this aspect of the difficulty in applying the Japanese management and production system to local production.

Group Consciousness

The average degree of application for Small Group Activities (2.5 points) is equal to that for Procurement Method, and second lowest overall following Wage System. In other words, Japanese companies perceive difficulty, at least at the present stage, in transferring to the local U.S. plants the small group activities system for encouraging employees to be actively involved in production management. Consequently, a significant correlation with Small Group Activities is only observed with Job Rotation, Promotion, First-line Supervisors, and Information Sharing. Once again, it is notable that these four items belong to groups that represent work organization or group consciousness.

It is a little surprising to find no correlation between Small Group Activities and Sense of Unity, despite the fact that both items belong to the same group. Moreover, in contrast to Small Group Activities, the degree of application of Sense of Unity is clearly correlated with that of many items, including Job Classification and Education and Training that represent human-core elements, Hiring Policy and Job Security, which belong to the labor relations group, and Quality Control and Ratio of Japanese Expatriates. Sense of unity is achieved through a wide variety of systems and devices designed to promote a sense of belonging to the group or of equality among employees. These include open parking, uniforms, open-style cafeterias, or picnics and other social events. Because of the relatively high degree of application of this item, as well as the positive correlation between it and many other items, it is probably fair to conclude that these various systems and devices themselves constitute the core of the Group Consciousness group. If these Japanese-style measures for maintaining a homogeneous workforce and promoting a sense of belonging to the group play a significant role in preparing the soil for the transfer of a flexible work organization and the formation of a broad range of skills, then the media may not have been far off the mark in reporting this as the main characteristic of Japanese-style management.

The strong tendency for plants with a high degree of application of Sense of Unity to have an explicit no-layoff policy Job Security is explained in part by the employees' sense of belonging to the group, which is characteristic of both items. There is a similar tendency for such plants to adopt a cautious approach to plant location and employee selection (Hiring Policy). The strong positive correlation between Sense of Unity and both of these items is clearly due in part to the fact that a common attribute is their concern with the employee values and homogeneity.

Information sharing is achieved through measures such as various levels of meetings that are held in order to promote mutual understanding among employees. The correlation pattern and underlying rationale for this item is very similar to that for Sense of Unity, so it is probably unnecessary to reiterate those points. However, it should be noted that in the case of Information Sharing, the degree of correlation and the number of correlated items is more restricted.

Labor Relations

A no-layoff policy (Job Security), along with the various measures and devices used to promote a sense of unity, is frequently cited as a typical characteristic of Japanese enterprises located abroad. Moreover, as discussed above, both items share the attribute of increasing employees' sense of belonging to the group. For this reason, there is likely to be a strong positive correlation between these two items, and a good deal of similarity in the overall correlation pattern with other items, such as Job Classification, Education and Training, and Information Sharing.

The only significant difference between these correlation patterns is that First-line Supervisors and Maintenance are more strongly correlated with Job Security than they are with Sense of Unity. In other words, the no-layoff policy is not simply a reflection of attempting to foster employees' sense of belonging to the group, but reveals the intention to cultivate important core personnel within the plant and over the long term.

A positive correlation between Hiring Policy and Job Security is also to be expected. This is because employment policies, which include taking into consideration location-specific conditions such as employee turnover or long-term residence intentions, as well as the type of employee selection to implement in view of such conditions, are closely related to employees' sense of belonging to the group and their willingness to stay with the company for a long time. Therefore, it is also not surprising that the correlation pattern for Hiring Policy should closely resemble that for Job Security.

In contrast to the items discussed above, Labor Unions has little correlation with other items. Moreover, the only core-system items to which it is positively correlated are Wage System, Education and Training, and Maintenance. Where employees are unionized and where American-style labor relations are in effect, the wage system tends to link wages with jobs. Conversely, where there is no union, or where there is a high degree of labor-management cooperation in spite of the existence of a union, other elements of the Japanese system become more important wage determining factors. This relationship is understandable in view of the type of "job-control unionism" widely encountered in the United States.

Correlation between the degree of application of Labor unions and Education and Training or Maintenance probably arises because a unionized plant imposes constraints upon the Japanese system for broad-ranged, shop-floor skill formation. Other than that, there is little evidence that the presence or absence of a union has a significant influence upon the plant management system.

This is illustrated by the fact that the existence of a union seems to have little effect upon the number of job classifications. This may seem strange in view of the historical chain of events through which the American-style "job-control unionism" led to the finely demarcated and rigid job classification system. Nevertheless, there is no correlation between degrees of application of Labor unions and Job Classification in either the automotive or electronics industries. Although this analysis is pursued in greater detail in Chapter 5, the results can be summarized as follows. To begin with, in the auto assembly industry, the number of job classifications underwent a considerable reduction in all plants regardless of union organization. In the auto parts and semiconductor industries, there is considerable variation in the degree of rigidity of the job classification system in spite of the fact that none of the surveyed plants are union shops. In the case of consumer electronics, there is great variety among plants regarding the degree of simplification of the job classification system and the existence of unions or the degree of labor-management cooperation. Nevertheless, there is no significant determining relationship between the existence of a union and the number of job classifications.

Of course we cannot generalize that, as a result, American labor unions do not restrict the transfer of the Japanese management system. That is to say, many plants in the auto assembly industry exert great effort to remain nonunion, and even at unionized plants, efforts to create a flexible management system often entail time-consuming and otherwise costly negotiations with or countermeasures against the unions. In the auto parts industry, efforts to remain nonunion are carried out even more strenuously than in the auto assembly industry. We must not, therefore, forget that the weak correlation between Labor Unions and work organization elements such as Job Classification is partly the result of precisely such costs and considerations.

The correlation pattern for Grievance Procedures is similar to that for Labor Unions. The only notable difference, in fact, is the correlation with Wage System. Also, in the case of unionized plants, there is a very natural tendency for employee grievance procedures at the unionized plants to follow the route normally established by American unions.

Parent-Subsidiary Relations

The three items included in this group, namely Ratio of Japanese Expatriates, Delegation of Authority, and Managerial Position of Americans, are positively correlated, and moreover, their correlation patterns with other items are also similar. As explained above, a high degree of application for these items signifies a high degree of dependence, in terms of authority or human resources, upon Japan in general, or upon the parent company in particular. Conversely, a low degree of application indicates advanced localization in these areas.

It is very interesting that, with the exception of the relationship between Delegation of Authority and Education and Training, there is no significant correlation between any of these items and the human aspect of the core system. Similarly, aside from the obvious correlation between Ratio of Japanese Expatriates and Sense of Unity, there is no significant correlation between either of these three items and any items of group IV, Group Consciousness. Finally, there is a notable absence of a correlation between these items and either Hiring Policy or Job Security, both of which are strongly correlated with items in group I, Work Organization and Administration, or group IV, Group Consciousness. This shows that just because a plant is highly dependent upon Japan for authority or human resources does not necessarily mean that it has a high degree of application in the area of human management methods.

On the other hand, group VI items are positively correlated with Labor Unions and Grievance Procedures, both of which are only very weakly correlated with items in groups I and IV. Plants that are highly dependent upon Japanese employees for managerial support thus tend either to be nonunion plants or, if they are unionized, to have very cooperative labor-management relations. Conversely, plants that are more locally oriented show a strong tendency to be unionized.

It was also mentioned above that plants that tend to look to Japan for support in the area of management or human resources are also highly dependent upon Japan in the material-results aspect, such as production equipment and parts. This means that the degree of dependence upon Japan (or the parent company) for managerial personnel or for decision making (or conversely, the degree of localized management) is more strongly related to the materials aspect (equipment and parts) or labor relations (presence or absence of a union) than to human systems or functions existing at the local plant.

Labor relations, the ratio of Japanese expatriates, or the delegation of authority are all elements that exert a broad, overall effect upon local production. This implies that whether the local U.S. plants of Japanese companies targeted in this study lean towards an application or an adaptation model, is not directly determined by this managerial framework that governs production at the local plants.

CORRELATION BETWEEN ITEMS AND THE BUSINESS ENVIRONMENT

Correlation between elements of the managerial environment and the 24 items in the hybrid analysis were investigated and appear in Table 4–3. The three elements of the managerial environment that are referred to in this table are Period of Operation, Number of Employees, and Plant Location.[2]

Period of Operations

Examining the data for target plants, we can see that the only item that is positively correlated with the period of operations is Wage System. On the other hand, negative correlation is observed for Equipment, Suppliers, Information Sharing, Sense of Unity, and Job Security (see Table 5–3). However, when each of these industry groups are examined in isolation, no correlation (positive or negative) with period of operations is found for either Wage System, Information Sharing, Sense of Unity, or Job Security. These results suggest that the characteristics of the electrical industries, whose advance into the United States took place in the 1970s, and of the automotive industries, which did not launch the main thrust of their overseas expansion until the latter part of the 1980s, are reflected in terms of their length of operations.

The remaining items that displayed significant correlation in the aggregate data, namely Equipment and Suppliers, both continued to show a negative correlation with period of operations in the case of the electronics industries alone. However, they did not show any significant correlation in the case of the automotive industries. Moreover, among the plants in the semiconductor industry, with one single exception, there is little difference in the degrees of application according to period of operations for either of these two items. Consequently, consumer electronics plants, with their long experience and early advance into overseas production, show signs of greater independence from Japan, directly and indirectly, in terms of the local procurement of production equipment or parts suppliers.

Number of Employees

This study represents plant scale in terms of number of employees. This approach facilitates scale comparisons among plants of different industries. Positive correlation with the number of employees exists for Job Rotation, Quality Control, Operations Management, Procurement Method, Information Sharing, and Job Security. Negative correlation exists for Local Content and Delegation of Authority. Turning first to the positively correlated items, it is interesting to note that they are all related to the method aspect of human or materials management. However, each of these item correlations must be carefully qualified. With the exception of Operations Management and Job Security, none of the other items listed above show any significant correlation with number of employees in either the automotive or electronics industries alone. Job Security shows a positive correlation with number of employees in the case of the automotive industries, but this is a clear reflection of the explicit no-layoff policy established by the larger auto assembly plants. Operations Management is positively correlated with number of employees in the electronics industry, while in the automotive industry it correlates with the period of operations. Negative correlation with number of employees in the case of Local Content or Delegation of Authority means that plants with a large (small) number of employees have a high (low) rate of local parts procurement, and are inclined to rely more (less) on local management.

Factory Location

A thorough analysis of the effect of plant location requires examining ethnic composition and degree of mobility for each region. However, this study did not obtain such details for each target plant. Rather, the approach consisted of identifying three major regions (the traditional industrial region in the Midwest and Northeast, the West Coast region consisting of California and Oregon, and the Southern region of Texas and Kentucky), and then searching for cross-industrial characteristics that might emerge for each item. However, only examining the average application ratings for the plants in each region is not very meaningful. This is because even if a regional difference between the average degrees of application for a specific item is detected, large variation among the plants in that region means that the results cannot be interpreted as a true regional characteristic. For this reason, a correlation ratio has been calculated between plant location and each item. The items of special interest then are those for which there is high correlation ratio resulting from a small variation within a particular region, but a large variation among the different regions (Table 5–3).

Significant correlations with location were only found for three items, Wage System, Quality Control, and Job Security. In the case of Wage System, the average degree of application is clearly higher in the West Coast region. The main factor is that the majority of high-application semiconductor plants are located in this region. However, many of the consumer electronic plants located in this region also have a high degree of application of Wage System. The auto assembly plant notwithstanding, it seems that the West Coast region, with its majority of high-tech plants, offers little resistance to the transfer of the Japanese-style wage system.

Conversely, the average degree of application of Quality Control is lower in the West Coast region than in other regions. This is also attributable to the presence of many semiconductor plants at which the Japanese-style control methods have only penetrated to a low degree.

In contrast, the degree of application for Job Security is highest in the traditional industrial regions of the Midwest and Northeast. This reflects a strict no-layoff policy maintained by the auto assembly plants and some of the auto parts plants. However, since consumer electronics plants in the same region have never established such a policy, and have in fact already laid off employees, it is difficult to claim that this is a cross-industrial, regional characteristic. Nevertheless, this region has a history of periodic layoffs and much of its industry is hollowed out. Employees in this area thus seem particularly receptive to the promise of job security. If the no-layoff policies enforced by the Japanese auto plants appeal to this type of employee consciousness, then although it clearly does not extend to all industries in the region, it would not be an exaggeration to claim that it did reflect a certain regional characteristic.

As a result, although it is impossible to assert that there are definitely no cross-industrial characteristics based on location-specific conditions, it does seem that industry-specific characteristics have a greater impact on the degree of application of the Japanese system elements.

SUMMARY

The first point that deserves special emphasis is the strong correlation that exists among the various systems and functions that result in flexible work organization and broad-ranged, shop-floor skill formation. Moreover, these elements are also clearly correlated with a no-layoff policy and a variety of other devices that foster a feeling of equality and unity among employees. In short, there is clear correlation among human-method items within the core system, between human-method items in the core system and those in the subsystems, and between human-method core or subsystem items and items that represent elements of Labor Relations.

Human-method items are also correlated with items that represent methods for materials management, such as Quality Control or Procurement Method. In other words, the degree of application of human-method and materials-method items are positively correlated; a high (low) degree of application in the one tends to be matched by a high (low) degree of application in the other. There is also correlation among the core "materials-method" items of Maintenance, Quality Control, and Procurement Method themselves.

Human-results items, such as Ratio of Japanese Expatriates and Managerial Position of Americans, are correlated with materials-results items, such as Local Content and Equipment that reflect the extent to which completed, ready-made materials are introduced into the production system. There is also correlation among the materials-results items such as equipment and parts, and among the human-results items themselves. However, there is little correlation between human-method items and human-results items, just as there is none between materials-method and materials-results items.

It is interesting that method items, or results items, tend to be correlated among themselves regardless of whether they are human or material but that there is no similarly significant correlation between pairs of items that are both human or both material but of which one is results and the other method.

Also, not only are the degrees of application of Wage System and Small Group Activities very low, there is little correlation between the degrees of application for these and any other items. This suggests that it may be rather difficult to introduce elements of the Japanese system that are closely related to historical or social factors, or "Japanese" elements linked to patterns of human behavior or set ways of thinking.

Finally, the present study did not reveal any evidence of a significant correlation between the degrees of application of those elements reflecting plant production conditions, and the managerial environment characterized by elements such as parent-subsidiary relations, period of operations, and number of employees.

6

Industrial Analysis by Industry Types

HIROSHI KUMON
KUNIO KAMIYAMA
HIROSHI ITAGAKI
TETSUJI KAWAMURA

In this chapter, we will examine characteristics of the hybridism of application-adaptation in each of the four industries: auto assembly, auto parts, consumer electronics, and semiconductors. In Chapter 4 and 5 we have been describing the general characteristics of Japanese factories engaged in local production in the United States, but clearly, as we have suggested more than once, there are rather major differences in the concrete heterogeneous conditions of the four industries. We are able to study the actual conditions of transplants in America from various angles by examining specific features of application-adaptation within each industry.

AUTOMOTIVE ASSEMBLY

Outline of Surveyed Factories: High Application, System Application

Out of eleven Japanese automotive plants operating in North America, we were able to visit all but the one in Canada. In the previous investigation, we were limited to the three plants that were then in operation. Because we were able to visit ten plants this time, we feel we have conducted a thorough investigation of the auto assembly industry of North America. We were also able to visit the Big Three's plants, the UAW (United Auto Workers) International and one of its locals, as well as a Korean auto assembly transplant. Although the current study uses only the information on the Japanese transplants we visited in the United States and Canada for its assessment and analysis, the visits to the other factories and the UAW facilities allowed us to obtain information for a comparison, and to more fully understand the subject.

Let us present an overview of the Japanese automotive transplants targeted in our study. We have space here to discuss only these four points: (1) entry form, (2) plant size and composition of its facilities, (3) start of operation, and (4) site location (see Table 6–1).

First, in terms of the entry form, seven plants made their advance on their own, three as a joint venture with an American firm, and one as a joint venture with several Japanese companies. In the case of the three American joint venture plants, it should be noted that a leadership conflict with the American partner that might present an obstacle to the application of Japanese-style management does not exist. This is because, in all three cases, the American company relies on its Japanese partner for production models and manufacturing technology for the purpose of learning Japanese-style management. Thus the Japanese are responsible for managing the plants.

Second, all the plants except one joint venture have been newly constructed with fully integrated processes for automobile manufacturing, including the stamping, welding, painting and assembly processes. They are full-scale operations with production capacities of 200,000 units or more a year, and personnel of around 3,000.

Third, putting Mexico aside, these plants moved into the United States and Canada in two periods, namely, during the first and the second halves of the 1980s. Three plants, AA, AB, and AC, started their operation in the first half of the 1980s. All the others began production in the very late 1980s. All the plants except AA and AB reluctantly moved into America as a means of countering the voluntary restriction on exports to America that was in some sense forced upon them by the uneasy trade situation. Nevertheless, those who made inroads in the first half of the 1980s have been able to build additional facilities because of the market share that they had previously acquired through exports to America and also because of their superior quality.

Fourth, for site location, the Japanese automobile transplants typically choose rural areas in the U.S. Midwest and South. A variety of factors were taken into account in the process of site selection. One of the most important was the work ethic and behavior of the local workers. Transplants in Canada are also located in rural areas. We will omit the Mexican plant, although its experience in dealing with complex problems is of special significance, because it is located outside the area covered in our study.

Why High Application, System Application?

It is characteristic of the auto assembly industry to rate high in application in general and high in application of methods in particular. Let us first look at the application rating in general. The average application rating for the auto assembly industry is 3.5. This is second to the 3.6 of the auto parts industry, and exceeds the 3.3 average for all industries. Looking at application ratings by group, we see that among the four industries, auto assembly showed the highest ratings in work organization and its administration, group consciousness, and labor relations. According to the 4-Perspective Evaluation, the application rating is highest for the human-method (3.6) and material-method (3.3), the aspects that show the Japanese system in such areas as job classification, job security, and quality control. In comparison with the other industries, the application rating for human-result and material-result, that is, with bringing-in ready-made things from Japan, was not as high as for method. The score for method in auto assembly was highest at 3.5, compared to the overall average of 3.0. The score for result in auto assembly was 3.4, which placed it in third position, the overall average being 3.6 (see Figure 6–1). Nevertheless, according to the figure, the human-result factor still weighs heavily for certain items, as is indicated by the convergence of human-result in auto assembly with the industry-wide average. How this lends support to the high application of method will be discussed later on.

Next, let us examine three basic reasons why we call this industry "high application and method application". The first is that to actually apply the relative advantage of being a Japanese automobile enterprise on foreign soil, it is necessary to apply the "soft" side, the management methods developed in Japan, together with the "hard" side, the equipment. That is, both Japanese-style human resources management method and production control method (the Toyota production system) that are successful in achieving high quality and efficiency have been applied. Second, the auto assembly companies' strategy to enter America consisted of building full-sized and fully equipped assembly facilities from the outset, and for this reason they have actively applied the Japanese system. As for scale, all U.S. transplants have an annual production capacity exceeding 200,000 units. Such an annual production capacity allows operation rates to be maintained at a high level by introducing automated machines as well as two shifts. Each transplant consists of the four basic processes: stamping, welding, painting, and assembly. The fact that they build their own fully-integrated and complete, rather than partial, process lines differentiates this industry from, for example, color TV transplant operations, where the final assembly process was brought in. The third factor is that, due to operational characteristics of the auto assembly plant, there is a strong need to apply Japanese-style production methods in order to achieve high quality and efficiency. Speaking of manufacturing processes and operations common to any plant, a certain level of skill and power of concentration is required to operate the equipment in the four processes, stamping, welding, painting, and assembly. Of these processes, the assembly process is basically a manual operation, requiring some skill and the ability to pay attention to what one is doing. Skills are also needed to operate the increasingly automated stamping, welding, and painting equipment. Furthermore, compared with a consumer electronics plant, although not with a steel mill, relatively large-sized machinery is used in the automated process, and requires a similar level of attentiveness and power of concentration. Because car bodies move automatically on the conveyor and large machinery is operated, there are many relatively hazardous operations that demand such attentiveness.

Item Analysis

In this section let us examine characteristics of the auto assembly industry by item. First, because of the industry's characteristically high application rating for human methods, we will examine work organization and administration and group consciousness, since these are composed of items concerning human management methods, and then look at the application rating of material management methods according to production control and procurement method. There is not much dif-

Table 6–1. Profile of Japanese-Owned Automotive Assembly Plants in North America

Plant	AA	AB	AC	AD	AE
Site location	Ohio	Tennessee	California	Michigan	Kentucky
Start of operation	Nov. 1982	Jun. 1983	Dec. 1984	Sept. 1987	May 1988
Mode of entry	Wholly-owned, new	Wholly-owned, new	Joint venture, renovated	Wholly-owned, new	Wholly-owned, new
Investment (mil. U.S.$)	1,846	775	500	550	1,100
Employees	6,500	3,294	2,800	3,477	2,950
Japanese expatriates	350	20	34	150	72
Product	Passenger car, motorcycle, engine	Passenger car, truck, engine	Passenger car	Passenger car	Passenger car
Annual capacity (ten thousand)	36	26.5	20	24	20
Processes	Stamping, welding, painting, assembly, plastics, engine	Stamping, welding, painting, assembly, plastics, engine	Stamping, welding, painting, assembly	Stamping, welding, painting, assembly, plastics	Stamping, welding, painting, assembly, plastics, engine

Sources: Interview at each plant. Nissan Motor Co., Ltd. *Handbook of Automobile Industry,* August, 1989. Kinokuniya-Shoten (in Japanese).

Notes: (1) Data obtained during the 1989 survey.

(2) For AA. Motorcycle production commenced in September, 1979. A second plant came on-stream in 1989. The same engine plant is currently being expanded. At full capacity, total output will reach 510,000 units, and for the engine plant, 500,000 units.

(3) For AB. Production of trucks began in 1983, and passenger cars in March, 1985. The passenger car assembly line is currently being extended. Capacity output in 1992 is expected to reach 440,000 units.

(4) For AC. This is a joint venture with a U.S. company. Approximately 60 percent of the production will be delivered to the U.S. company. The production line was extended in 1991 to include production of trucks.

(5) For AD. Approximately 60 percent of the production is delivered to the U.S. company that has capital participation in the parent company in Japan. The U.S. company will join in capital of AD in 1992.

ference in the way these two items with their high application ratings for method are handled from one plant to another, whereas labor relations and parent-subsidiary relations become the framework for applying aspects of the Japanese system to a plant. Of them, the parent-subsidiary relations group includes items that are clearly handled differently from one Japanese auto assembly transplant to another. Such differences are indicated by the high standard deviation in these two groups, parent-subsidiary relations and labor relations, as shown in Table 6–2.

In the case of the auto assembly industry, the overall application rating is high, and all the companies show nearly the same scores. However, in the group parent-

AF	AG	AH	AI	AS	aa
Illinois	Canada	Canada	Indiana	Mexico	Canada
Sept. 1988	Nov. 1988	Apr. 1989	Sept. 1989	May 1966	Dec. 1988
Joint venture, new	Wholly-owned, new	Joint venture, new	Joint venture, new	Wholly-owned, new	Wholly-owned, new
650	400 CA$	500	500	103 bil. peso	266 CA$
2,800	710	997	1,800	4,860	800
50	31	61	121	17	
Passenger car	Passenger car	Passenger car, truck	Passenger car, truck	Passenger car, truck, engine	Passenger car
24	5	20	24	12	8
Stamping, welding, painting, assembly, plastics	Stamping, welding, painting, assembly	Stamping, welding, painting, assembly	Stamping, welding, painting, assembly	Stamping, welding, painting, assembly, engine	Stamping, welding, painting, assembly

(6) For AE. Power train plant under construction.

(7) For AF. Joint venture with U.S. company. Approximately 50 percent of products shipped to the U.S. company. The U.S. company sold equity of AF in 1991, so it becomes wholly Japanese-owned.

(8) For AG. Two shifts in the fall of 1989. Full operation in 1990.

(9) For AH. Joint venture with Canadian company that has head office in the U.S. Seventy percent of production goes to the partner. Planned production for third year of operations in 200,000 units.

(10) For AI. This is a joint venture between two Japanese companies. This plant produced both trucks and passenger cars from the start. In the first period of operations production capacity was 120,000 units, and in its second period it will be 240,000 units.

(11) For AS. Passenger cars are produced in plant number 1, truck in plant number 2, and engine in plant number 3.

(12) Plant aa was not visited.

(13) Number of Japanese expatriates does not include short-term dispatched employees.

subsidiary relations, the application rating is slightly below the overall average, and the deviation is high at 0.83. In like manner, the application rating of labor relations exceeds the overall average, and the deviation is relatively high at 0.43. These different approaches and the high standard deviation in parent-subsidiary relations stem from the different plant management strategies chosen by individual companies for their advance into America. The different approaches to labor relations taken by the various plants is primarily due to the different forms of the venture and the subsequent presence or absence of a union based on those forms.

Furthermore, let us mention some differences in the score that resulted from our

Four Perspective Evaluations of
Auto Assembly Industry

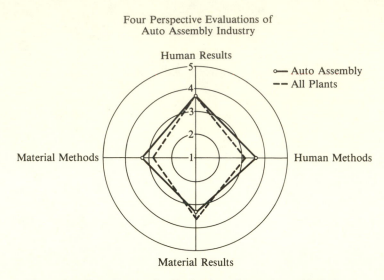

Figure 6–1 Four-Perspective Evaluation of Auto Assembly Industry

previous study. There was no fundamental change in overall average application rating, 3.6 previously, 3.5 in the current study. At the time of the previous study, the automotive industry as a whole had just started local production, there were fewer target transplants, and the distinction between auto assembly plants and auto parts plants was not made. Three assembly plants and two parts plants were combined. If we separate the assembly plants from the parts plants, the application rating average of the three assembly plants would become 3.5, the same as the application rating in the current study. The two parts plants had relatively high application ratings, bringing up the average to 3.6. In terms of the specific groups, these three had higher ratings in the previous study: Work organization and administration (previously 3.7), production control (previously 3.5), and procurement method (previously 3.3). In two groups, group consciousness (previously 3.5) and labor relations (previously 4.1), ratings were lower in the previous study. There was no change in parent-subsidiary relations.

The basic reasons for change can be found in the increased number of transplants that had just started operations at the time of our current study. That is, first, lack of operating experience is reflected in less application of the Japanese system. Therefore, the application ratings dropped in work organization and administration and production control. Second, the higher ratings for group consciousness and labor relations, especially the rise of the former by 0.4 point, are interesting and probably are due to the great importance given to these areas by newly started plants. In contrast to the early starters where the transfer of manufacturing technology was regarded as the most important, the late arrivals appear to be attempting to apply the Japanese system in toto, including the group consciousness. This indicates that from the very beginning the top executives have become active in the

Table 6–2. Hybrid Evaluation in the Auto Assembly Industry

	Auto Assembly (A)	Average of 4 Industries (B)	(A) − (B)	Standard Deviation
I. Work organization and administration	3.3	2.9	0.4	0.16
① Job classification	4.8	3.7	1.1	0.42
② Wage system	2.1	2.4	−0.3	0.31
③ Job rotation	3.2	2.6	0.6	0.63
④ Education and training	3.4	2.9	0.5	0.50
⑤ Promotion	3.2	3.1	0.1	0.42
⑥ First line supervisors	3.1	2.9	0.2	0.31
II. Production control	3.4	3.3	0.1	0.31
⑦ Equipment	3.9	4.3	−0.4	0.88
⑧ Quality control	4.0	3.4	0.6	0.00
⑨ Maintenance	2.9	2.6	0.3	0.31
⑩ Operations management	2.9	3.0	−0.1	1.10
III Procurement	3.0	3.0	0.0	0.22
⑪ Local content	2.3	2.6	−0.3	0.47
⑫ Suppliers	3.8	3.8	0.0	0.42
⑬ Procurement method	3.0	2.5	0.5	0.00
IV. Group consciousness	3.9	3.2	0.7	0.20
⑭ Small group activities	2.7	2.5	0.2	0.47
⑮ Information sharing	4.4	3.6	0.8	0.50
⑯ Sense of unity	4.6	3.5	1.1	0.50
V. Labor relations	4.2	3.6	0.6	0.43
⑰ Hiring policy	4.3	3.4	0.9	0.82
⑱ Job security	4.9	3.4	1.5	0.31
⑲ Labor union	4.2	4.4	−0.2	0.92
⑳ Grievance procedures	3.2	3.3	−0.1	0.42
VI. Parent-subsidiary relations	3.5	3.6	−0.1	0.83
㉑ Ratio of Japanese expatriates	3.8	3.7	0.1	1.47
㉒ Delegation of authority	3.3	3.6	−0.3	0.67
㉓ Managerial position of Americans	3.3	3.6	−0.3	0.94
Average	3.5	3.3	0.2	0.19
VII. Community relations				
㉔ Donations and volunteer activity	1.8	2.3	−0.5	1.07

application of the Japanese system, reflecting the overseas experiences gained by corporate Japan and the rise of international esteem for Japanese-style management. Third, the fact that adaptation increased by 0.3 points in procurement method is due to efforts made by Japanese companies to procure parts locally.

Work Organization and Group Consciousness: Team System and Flexibility

Let us start with an outline of the main points in regard to work organization and administration. To achieve the possibility of a Japanese-style team system and the development of multi-skilled workers, there is a very strong inclination toward application in job classification. By way of contrast, the wage system shows the effect of adaptation to American methods. The other items in the group, job rotation, education and training, promotion, and first-line supervisors, are a mixture of Japanese and American elements, although they lean slightly toward application.

As shown in Table 6–2, the application rating of job classification is 4.8, exceeding the industry-wide average by 1.1 points. The wage system is 2.1, lower than the industry-wide average by 0.3 points. Other items are: Job rotation, 3.2, education and training, 3.4, promotion, 3.2, and first-line supervisors, 3.1. All are a little above the industry-wide averages and in general their standard deviations are not high. Compared to the other industries, particularly consumer electronics and semiconductors, whose standard deviation in job classification, in wages, and in job rotation is roughly 1.0, the low standard deviation of the auto assembly industry stands out. This means that the auto assembly transplants have very similar systems for job classification and wages. However, the standard deviation is somewhat high in job rotation and education and training. A high standard deviation of 0.63 for job rotation shows the obvious difference between the plants that have been operating for a while and those that have just started operations.

At the time of our previous study, three transplants had already begun operations and had greatly simplified the traditional American system of job classification. We were especially interested to see how the new Japanese transplants would handle this. We found that all the auto assembly transplants in the United States and Canada had simplified job classification in the same way as the three early companies.

Since this is a critical point, let us cite the number of hourly job classifications for each plant: AA had 2, AB 4, AC 3, AD 2, AE 3, AF 2, AG 2, AH 2, and AI 2. These include maintenance, which means skilled trades, and except at plant AB, there is only one category for production workers.

At AB, aside from maintenance, there are three job categories. In the Big Three plants, usually composed of three processes—welding, painting, and assembly—there are somewhere between eighty and ninety job categories, even excluding the skilled trades that are called maintenance by the Japanese transplants. If the skilled trades were included the number would be closer to 100. If we also include the jobs belonging to the stamping plants (generally built as separate units), as is done in the Japanese plants, then there would dozens of additional job titles. The Big Three, especially GM, are attempting to reform their segmented job classification system and reduce the number of categories, but, because it is not easy to do this in existing plants, the practice is not yet widespread. In contrast, all Japanese transplants in the United States and Canada, without exception, have simplified job classification. Job classification is simplified to create the preconditions necessary for the introduction of the system of work organization and its administration developed in Japan by reforming the American traditionally segmented job classification and pulling down the premise of American style work organization. In short, based on such preconditions, a production team system can be adopted, multiskilled workers brought in, and improvement of working methods based on the workers themselves made possible. The Japanese automobile industry built a work organization that fosters the ability to carry out improvements (*kaizen*) and the ability to handle a wide variety of problems. Such a work organization and its administration is also suited to a flexible production system. These two aspects are so intimately interconnected that it is difficult to determine a cause-and-effect relationship between them. On the other hand, the traditional segmented job classification in America premised on wages that correspond to job titles, fixed job assignments, and boss-type supervisors whose job consists mainly of labor management, has been developed hand in hand with the American style mass production system. The Japanese work organization and its administration and the production system are deeply connected to each other, and it was difficult for Japanese companies to separate them and to introduce only one of them to their transplants. In short, the Japanese-style work organization could not be separated from the flexible production system.

A brief explanation is in order here on production teams and the control organization to unify them. A production team is composed of five to twenty members and a team leader who controls it. There is also a group leader in charge of several teams. The team leaders and team members are hourly workers. So if a plant is unionized, they could be union members. The responsibility to allocate jobs falls to the group leaders who are salaried workers. In practice, however, job allocation and changes in the allocation within a team are carried out by the team leader. In actuality, then, a team leader acts partly on behalf of the group leader in job allocation. Job scope and work load for each of the team members are predetermined, but within a team, there is job rotation and improvement of working methods. But in some cases, there is a division of labor between the team leader and the unit leader, with the one in control of operations and the other in control of labor.

Wages are basically adapted to the American system, based on the nature of one's duties. The Japanese-style wage system where wages are based on seniority, one's ability and qualifications, and the performance evaluation system have not been adopted. First, wages are based on the nature of one's duties, but the meaning of job correspondence here has changed. As mentioned earlier, job classification has been simplified, and therefore, there are no such wage differences corresponding to segmented job classification. Wages for production workers are all the same, markedly different than the job correspondence type American wage system. Second, with the presence of the UAW or CAW locals the wage level is of course union scale, but, even without any union, wages are at or close to the level of the UAW or CAW. So even though these transplants are mostly located in rural areas across the Midwest and throughout the South, their wage levels are not related to the wage level of their respective local labor market, but adapted to the level of the automobile industry. Naturally, such a high wage level is a key factor in being able to attract good workers. Third, contrary to the practice in Japan, there is a clear-cut difference in wages between production workers and maintenance workers. The wage level of maintenance workers is similar to that found in the skilled trades categories of the automobile industry. As long as the labor markets for production workers and for maintenance workers are different, no choice remains but to go along with this.

Consequently, both the wage system and the wage levels are basically adapted. However, due to the simplification of the job classification, wage differences are reduced to the equivalent number of job titles. For those with the same job title, the wage is the same for all. The only difference is found between production workers and maintenance workers. Thus, Japanese-style wages based on one's ability and qualifications, length of service, and the performance evaluation have not been adopted. An exception to this is the performance evaluation data that AE is employing as criteria for a small part of the biannual bonus. Rejection of the performance evaluation may be because the union has not been very receptive to the idea of ability-based wage differences, fearing it might lead to favoritism on the part of management. So far it has been possible to reward the improvement of individual ability with promotions but, with a future that holds the prospects of the stagnation of promotional opportunities and of the necessity for longer years of service to get them, it might be necessary to provide certain other incentives. This necessity will intensify if wages are to parallel the production worker's ability to become multi-skilled and make improvements. On the other hand, the criteria and means for installing the corresponding differences in wages would be a problem. The management would be forced to make a delicate choice, that is, whether to maintain egalitarianism in wages, or to introduce a system based on ability in one form or another.

Job rotation is actively carried out within a team by regularly switching jobs either every 2.5 hours or every day. However, we heard top management complain, saying, "It is carried out according to the workers' taste, and skills are not systematically accumulated". Also, it is interesting that although it is rare that job rotation requires crossing the team boundary, it is not easy to transfer an employee when this does happen. The rating for education and training is 3.4, which is higher than those for promotion and first-line supervisors, and close to the industry-wide average. This is precisely because the auto assembly industry attaches such great importance to this aspect. In other words, these companies send more than 100 of their American employees to Japan, and at the same time dispatch Japanese employees to their transplants for training in manufacturing technology and the team system. The fact that they regard this expensive, albeit reliable, human-result factor of education and training as so important, is characteristic of the auto assembly industry. Nevertheless, on the other side, there is some attempt to carry out the education and training program, not only for maintenance workers but also for production workers, by opening in-house education and training facilities. The application rating for first-line supervisors is slightly over 3. The reason is that, although first-line supervisors are doing as good a job as they can under the circumstances, in some cases because the transplant had been in operation only a short time or because of the speed of its rapid expansion, they were simply not able to develop the requisite abilities to function properly in their role, not as a boss, but as a facilitator or leader of improvement projects.

Next, let us turn our attention to group consciousness. The application rating of 3.9 was high, and particularly high were the ratings of information sharing and sense of unity at 4.4 and 4.6 respectively, whereas small group activities, at 2.7, was almost the same as the industry-wide average. Any comparison of American auto manufacturers with Japanese transplants reveals a striking difference in the treatment of production workers. In Japanese transplants, a number of measures are used to treat all employees on an equal basis without setting up distinctions, such as a common term for all employees (associate, for example), communication between top management and production workers, with the former making frequent tours of shop floors and talking with the latter, and cafeterias shared in common by all. These measures for treating all employees equally could be said to actually exceed those in plants in Japan. This is quite different than the management method used in American automobile plants, where production workers and management, hourly workers and salary workers, are clearly separated, not only by the wage system, but also in various other ways, and is something the Japanese companies are deliberately trying to avoid in their transplants by using measures that, through the equal treatment of all employees, in essence serve to promote a sense of unity with the company and a group consciousness. This egalitarianism may constitute a factor of success in the management of hourly employees but, in the management of salaried employees on the contrary, it presents the problem of how to handle the feeling of discontent generated by the very absence of the kind of differential treatment between the two classes that exists in the plants of the Big Three. Add to this slow promotions, and the salary workers' discontent can be further exacerbated. The low level of the application rating for small group activities is due to the fact that, unlike in Japan, employees do not "all participate voluntarily" and carry out a high level of improvement activities. It would seem that it will be difficult to achieve parity with Japan in this area. All the transplants are opting for a voluntary participation system, but the average participation rate holds at around 25 percent.

The Application and Metamorphosis of Japanese Production Control and Procurement Systems

The Japanese automobile industry built up a flexible production system wherein waste was scrupulously eliminated, and is attempting to apply this system to its transplants.[1] Although application has been somewhat successful within the transplants, it has not been sufficiently applied in the case of outside parts vendors. And the method of not maintaining a parts inventory was brought in only in a modified form.

The "production control" application rating was 3.4. The breakdown by item (see Table 6–2) is: production equipment, 3.9; quality control, 4.0; maintenance, 2.9; and operations management 2.9. The standard deviation is especially high in production equipment and operations management at 0.88 and 1.10, respectively. This indicates that the ratings for the other items differ little from one transplant to another. But there is a great disparity among transplants in the method of handling these two items. The newly built plants have been equipped with the most up-to-date production equipment, but the application rating is unusually lower than in other industries. This can be seen by the high standard deviation for production equipment, and is due to the fact that although in many cases the equipment is brought in from Japan, there are also cases in which some of equipment has been locally supplied. Take the case of AB, for example. Its stamping and welding lines are equipped with Japanese-made machinery, while the painting and assembly lines are composed mainly of American-made equipment. Quality control is universally regarded as important by Japanese transplants, and their approach is based on the idea of an incremental buildup of quality by paying attention to it in each manufacturing process. However, the actual method of doing this differs somewhat from one plant to another. For example, AI is attempting to do something that even their parent factory in Japan has yet to fully develop. That is, they are carrying out a system called "guaranteeing one's own process" that is applied simultaneously to all production processes, and which the plant in Japan is developing only gradually, and which is taking a long time to become established there. Specifically, in this system quality is guaranteed by quality inspectors who have been assigned to each individual production department from stamping to shipping, although in dealing with anything outside the company, quality control is still the responsibility of the QC department.

At 2.9, the rating for maintenance is not so high. This is because they have not yet reached the point where they are able to develop skilled technicians within the company who are able to cover all aspects of preventive maintenance. As we will see, when you touch on this subject in the section dedicated to the different patterns of transplants, every transplant has its own way of handling the hiring and training of maintenance workers. Nevertheless, they all share a common objective: to perform this training within the company from now on, and it will be interesting to see how well they achieve this. The rating for operations management, like maintenance, is not so high, and it reflects major differences among the transplants. Those transplants that started up in the first half of the 1980s have stable operating conditions and have already experienced full model changes. Whereas, those that started operations in the second half of the 1980s, with a few exceptions, were still in the process of completing their transition to full two-shift production at the time of our survey.

The so-called JIT production system, that is, to keep in-house inventory to a minimum by means of hourly parts deliveries, has been altered somewhat because of problems of quality and the delivery of parts in America. That is, the plant is provided with hourly parts deliveries just like in Japan from some of the Japanese-owned parts vendors, but receives only daily deliveries from American parts vendors. Even in the case of Japanese-owned parts vendors, the JIT system is not always smoothly applied. Because, unlike Japan, the parts vendors have problems maintaining the quality of parts and delivering them on time and because they are also importing functional parts from Japan, they maintain a certain level of inventory within the assembly facilities. Therefore, to the extent that deliveries come from some of the Japanese-owned parts vendors and their in-house, in-process inventories, the Japanese system is applied but, in other cases, circumstances peculiar to the local area are taken into consideration. The rating for local content is 2.3, indicating a fair degree of localization. However, this is based on a domestic sourcing rate that has already factored in the value added in the plant. Thus, further pressure to improve this can be expected in the future, and then the key will be in the local production or local sourcing of engines.

Guaranteed Employment and Cooperation Between Labor and Management

The application rating of labor relations is quite high at 4.2 and, as Table 6–2 shows, the rating for three items in the group exceeds 4 points. Note that the application rating for job security (4.9) is nearly 5.0, and at the same time its standard deviation is low at 0.31. All the transplants, once they have reserved the right to lay off, have declared themselves on the side of job security within the company. In fact, while cutting production, AC retained their entire work force, whereas an American company faced with a similar situation would have resorted to a layoff. We heard company officials say that this builds the employees' trust in the company. Of course, job security in this case implies some premise of work sharing with the plants in Japan, whereby exports from Japan are regulated so that continued employment at the U.S. transplant is given priority. Be that as it may, the important point is that their policy differs from that of the Big Three, where employment management is conducted upon the premise of a layoff.

Hiring policies and labor unions also have high application ratings of over 4 points, but at the same time, their standard deviations are high, 0.82 and 0.92, respectively, indicating a disparity in how these areas are handled from one plant to another. The presence or absence of labor unions, is determined by the distance from the American Big Three. Those who have the UAW or CAW locals are the three plants with joint ventures with American firms, namely, AC, AF, and AH, and one plant, AD, that made the advance into America on its own, but whose parent company has a financial tie-in with an American firm. Since the union had organized on the side of their American partner, the Japanese side was unable to refuse unionization. Among the transplants without a union, there are those that experienced a union offensive but drove it back, and those who have not yet been the object of such an offensive. Naturally, even in the case where there is no union, these plants consider any attempt to unionize their employees by the union very carefully. More than anything else, they see to it that their wages are comparable to the level of the UAW and CAW. Therefore, even though the existence of the union influences all Japanese transplants, so far, the distance from the Big Three has dictated their response to unionization.

The distance from the Big Three somewhat influences site selection and recruitment as well. This accounts for the high standard deviation for hiring policies and labor unions. However, whenever they are able to select the site themselves, they discreetly choose a rural location; in addition, they are very careful in the way they recruit new employees. This raises the application rating for hiring policies. Even when faced with an organized union, these transplants try to treat it as if it were a Japanese company-differentiated union.

That is why the rating for labor unions is high. First, they schedule talks with the union on a regular basis under the aegis of a labor-management consultation system that provides a channel for negotiation separate from collective bargaining. Second, although they can resort to external arbitration, they follow the policy of solving workplace issues within the same workplace as far as possible, especially through talks between the active front-line supervisor on the shop floor and workers. The third point is that under the traditional system of American labor relations, when a satisfactory solution to an issue regarding production standards, health, and safety cannot be found through use of the internal company procedure for handling grievances, the union has the right to resort to a strike even while its current contract is still in effect. However, in the case of Japanese transplants, it is specifically stipulated in the labor contract that a strike is not allowed. Therefore, in these areas also, labor relations are molded on the premise of finding solutions within the company.

Parent-Subsidiary Relations: Diverging Approaches

The first thing that strikes us about this group is the high ratio of Japanese expatriates, and the next thing is the great number of individual variations found at item level, which can be attributed to differences in the original strategy used by the respective parent companies in their advance into America. Looking only at the ratio of Japanese expatriates, we find an application rating of 3.8, higher than the industry-wide average, and an exceptionally high standard deviation of 1.47. (See Table 6–2.) The auto assembly industry has a high application rating for method. This, together with the Japanese expatriate element, or what we call human-result, can be viewed as a set, and each company has its own way of dealing with this set.

Among those matters that require definite decisions by the parent companies are how many Japanese employees will be dispatched to the transplant, and the method of promoting local workers. Strictly from the standpoint of application of method, in view of the superior familiarity that Japanese managers possess in management and problem handling "in the manner of '*genba*ism' " that they acquired in Japan, it would be more dependable and safer to dispatch many Japanese expatriates and to entrust them with the management of the plant. On the other hand, sending many Japanese means increasing the labor cost burden and incurring the risk of adversely affecting the morale of local workers due to the corresponding reduction in their promotional opportunities. The parent company bears such a dilemma. Also, the question of how many Japanese expatriate shop-floor coaches are needed depends on the plant administration strategy of the parent company. Here we find significant differences in approach from one transplant to another.

Among the auto assembly plants, these approaches can be grouped into three categories. The first is the AA, AD, and AI plant type. Here a definite transfer of technology and business management methods is expected by dispatching more than 100 Japanese for long-term assignments. Second, there is the AB plant type that places a severe limit on the number of Japanese employees by entrusting the management of the plant to local managers. The third type falls in between these two extremes, dispatching in the neighborhood of 50 Japanese employees. Most plants belong to this group. Except the four plants mentioned above, joint venture plants and plants that established themselves independently fall into this group. Two plants in Canada, AG and AH, would be included in the first group according to the ratio of Japanese expatriate employees found at the time of the survey, but they can be expected to become part of the third group as soon as they go into full operation. The general tendency of transplant management in the auto assembly industry is to use the approaches of the first and third group, in which Japanese expatriate employees play a large role. At present, AB would constitute the single exception.

Summary

Let us sum up the characteristics of the auto assembly industry in the application-adaptation of Japanese-style management under the following three points. First, there is the high application and method application type, that is supported by human-result factors in critical areas. High application and method application conforms with the industry's strategy of advancing into America. And that was accompanied by the high application of such human-result factors as having a high ratio of Japanese expatriates and educating and training local workers in Japan. This implies that to actively apply the peculiar methods developed in Japan, the Japanese transplants in America had to depend on human-result factors. This is made even more necessary by the fact that the degree of implementation of method application is often insufficient for critical items. Second, we noticed an interesting contrast of items with high application ratings and those with low ratings in terms of the contents of hybrid. So although a transplant achieved the simplification of job classification that is indispensable for the application of the Japanese-style work organization and its administration, the wage system was an adaptation to the American approach. Group consciousness received a high overall application rating, but within this group, small group activities alone had a low rating. These facts suggest the existence of a nearly insurmountable wall in the process of the application of Japanese methods. Therefore, items for which higher application ratings can be expected as more and more experience is accumulated, and items for which such higher ratings cannot be expected appear to coexist next to each other. The third point concerns adaptation. In the case of auto assembly, the degree of adaptation or localization has not always been high. The question is how far the transplants can go in localization in the future, including faster promotion and more authority for local managers and a further increase in the rate of local sourcing of parts, and so on. Most importantly, in the final analysis, the key to the success of a transition from method application that is supported by human-result factors in the critical areas to a method that is firmly rooted in the local soil will depend on the degree to which the local managers and workers can grow accustomed to the Japanese system and absorb it. Since auto assembly transplants are quite high in method application rating, such a transition may require more vigilance in mutual Japanese-American exchanges and more emphasis on the accumulation of experience in plant operations from now on.

Finally, let us acknowledge the role that Japanese cars occupy in the American passenger car market. The Japanese car share, including imports and local production, had been around 20 percent until 1986; then, from 1987, it began to grow rapidly. As the production of transplants increased, so did the market share. The share of locally manufactured cars in overall sales increased from 4.7 percent in

1987, to 5.6 percent in 1988, and then to 8.0 percent in 1989. And in 1990 it approached the so-called danger zone of 30 percent. That is, Japanese cars made up 27.9 percent of all passenger cars sales, with imports at 16.5 percent and sales from local transplants at 11.4 percent.[2] The growth in market share reflects the overall strength of product development, manufacturing, and sales, but more directly indicates that local production is increasingly replacing imports. Also, it undoubtedly shows the effects of applying the Japanese-style management and production system to the transplants.

In this chapter, we have explained the auto assembly industry's characteristics according to the hybrid evaluation. In the next chapter, we would like to analyze patterns pertaining to individual plants, based on the characteristic of the industry thus presented. Our principle approach will be to clarify these patterns by way of the different business strategies used by Japanese parent companies in their advance into America. At the same time, this should reveal how individual plants are dealing with the dilemma of the application of the Japanese-style management system and its adaptation to local business environments, the subject of our study.

AUTOMOTIVE PARTS

Outline of the Surveyed Factories

For our study this time we visited a total of ten Japanese auto parts transplants in North America—eight in the United States, one in Canada, and one maquiladora in Mexico. Of those, we retained nine plants located in the United States and Canada for our analysis. Let us review them briefly from the overview perspective of Table 6–3.

In the auto parts industry, in contrast to the other three industries, there is a large variety of product items from one plant to another, and production processes, too, differ from plant to plant. Thus, it is difficult to grasp the overall characteristics of the industry. A closer look at the product lines of each plant reveals that AJ and AM make heater and air conditioner-related products and radiators, AN and AP stamping parts, and AQ and AR seats; these pairs are of the same product line, but the remaining target plants all manufacture different products. However, there is a common denominator to them all: Each is deeply linked to a particular assembly maker or makers, and each supplies parts for mounting onto cars. Therefore, it should be noted that a certain similarity in characteristics arises from the need to meet production control parameters required by assembly makers regarding certain terms of delivery, quality control, and so forth.

AU started up early, in 1983, and the other plants followed, one in 1984, one in 1985, two in 1986, and in the 3 years from 1987, the remaining five plants opened. Thirty-five-member companies of the Japan Automobile Parts Manufacturers Association invested in production operations in America in the period from 1961 to 1985. This jumped to thirteen in 1986, twenty-six in 1987, forty-four in 1988, and thirty-three in 1989. (*Monthly Auto Parts* (in Japanese), February, 1991). While the American production of the auto manufacturers expanded in the 1980s, the advance of the parts makers into America was concentrated on the second half of the 1980s, peaking in 1988. We can fairly assume that our target plants are representative of the general tendency of these Japanese automobile parts manufacturers in their advance into America. Compared with the other three industries of our study, the history of this industry's venture into America is short.

Many said their move was motivated by a response to the auto manufacturers' move, and also several of them cited concern about the "hollowing out" of industries in Japan. Parent companies of six of the ten plants are affiliated with a specific auto assembly maker, and the other four plants belong to independent manufacturers that are not affiliated with a specific auto manufacturer. Please refer to Table 6–3 for details.

We are confident that the ten plants that we targeted for our study provide an adequate basis to describe the overall status of the Japanese auto parts manufacturers' local production in America, because these plants include those affiliated with auto manufacturers as well as those that are independent operations, manufacture a wide variety of products, and geographically, they cover mainly the United States but also Canada and Mexico. In the following sections, we will describe characteristics of the local production operations of the nine plants that we selected as the main target for analysis in the current study.

Tendency Toward High Application

The application ratings of the nine transplants are found somewhere between 3.9 and 3.2 with the average at 3.6, highest of all four industries. The most striking characteristic of the auto parts transplants, then, is a stronger inclination toward application of the Japanese-style management and production system than is found in the other industries. However, it differs only slightly with the auto assembly industry, which also has a high rating of 3.5, and this strong inclination toward application probably is a characteristic common to the automotive industry. So then, we will focus our analysis on identifying common points and points of difference with the auto assembly transplants.

Although the auto parts industry generally has a high inclination toward application, it has not scored high application ratings in every aspect of the management and operation of the transplants. As is clearly shown in Table 6–4, application ratings of the main groups range from the highest rating, VI, Parent-Subsidiary Relations at 4.2; followed closely by V, Labor Relations, at 4.1; IV, Group Consciousness, at 3.8; and II, Production Control, at 3.6. There is then a fair-sized gap between these and the remaining groups: I, Work Organization and Administration, at 3.1, and III, Procurement Method, at 3.0.

The auto parts industry showed ratings higher than the three other industries, in II, Production Control, and VI, Parent-Subsidiary Relations. On the other hand, three groups—I, Work organization and Administration, IV, Group Consciousness, and V, Labor Relations—rated lower than the same groups in auto assembly. III, Procurement, was below semiconductors and at par with auto assembly. In other words, it is in Production Control and Parent-Subsidiary Relations where the

Table 6–3. Profile of Japanese-Owned Auto Parts Plants Visited in North America

Plant	AJ	AK	AL	AM
Location	Tennessee	Tennessee	Kentucky	Michigan
Start of operation	February 1984	February 1985	February 1986	July 1986
Ownership	Wholly-owned (joint-venture by 2 local subsidiaries)	Wholly-owned by parent co. in Japan	Wholly-owned by parent co. in Japan	Wholly-owned by local subsidiary
Number of employees	663	411	82	800
Sales	$138m.	$46m.	$14m.	$288m.
Affiliation	AB	AB	AB	AC,AE
Customer	AB,AI,AD, U.S. companies	AB	AB,AA	Local Japanese companies except AB, U.S. companies
Main products	Air conditioning system, condenser, evaporator, radiator, etc.	Instrument panel, lid cluster, etc.	Wiper-related products, control devices	Car heater, car radiator, car cooling units, condenser, evaporator, etc.

inclination toward high application of the auto parts transplants is most prominent, while the ratings of the other four groups are in second place among the four industries.

The same thing can be said when we look at the level of the 23 items. Out of 23 items, the auto parts industry scored highest in eight items, namely Promotion, Production Equipment, Small Group Activities, Labor Unions, Grievance Procedures, Ratio of Japanese Expatriates, Delegation of Authority, and Managerial Position of American Employees. Except for two of the remaining 15 items, application ratings were in second position among the four industries. These two exceptions were Education and Training and Procurement Method that both placed second from

AN	AO	AP	AQ	AR	AU
Michigan June 1987	Kentucky May 1988	Illinois August 1988	Michigan September 1988	Canada April 1989	Tijuana June 1983
Joint-venture by parent co. (85%), a bank and a general merchant in Japan	Joint-venture with an American company (50–50)	Wholly-owned by parent co. in Japan. Parent co. is a joint-venture by 16 companies	Wholly-owned by parent company in Japan	Joint-venture by a Japanese company (65%) and an American company (35%)	Wholly-owned by a local subsidiary in the U.S.
210	138	243	140	90	1,700
$102m.	$15m.	$17m.	$36m.	C$8m.	—
Independent U.S. companies	Independent U.S. companies, AA,AI	AF AF	AD AD	Independent AH	Independent Local Japanese companies, U.S. companies
Pressed metal and sub-assembly, metal stamping dies and assembly fixtures	Automotive brakes	Stamping parts	Seat for motor vehicle	Seat for motor vehicle	Wireharness for motor vehicle

Sources: Based on the interviews at local plants. Regarding sales, the data were obtained by additional question-naires to parent companies in Japan.

Note: Affiliation shows the relationship between Japanese parent cos. and auto assembly makers.

the bottom. (Incidentally, the application rating for Donation and Volunteer Activity was also second from the bottom.) These facts indicate, first of all, that the high application inclination of the auto parts industry extends across the entire management and operation of the transplants. But at the same time, they show that application ratings of the auto parts industry do not always exceed in all aspects the other industries; in particular, they do not exceed those in the auto assembly industry. In the following, we will clarify the actual situation of the auto parts industry in its local production in America by studying the areas that are inclined toward high application and those that lean toward relatively low application by means of some concrete examples.

Table 6–4. Hybrid Evaluation in the Auto Parts Industry

	Auto Parts (A)	Auto Assembly	Average of 4 Industries (B)	(A) − (B)	Standard Deviation
I Work organization and administration	3.1	3.3	2.9	0.4	0.39
① Job classification	4.2	4.8	3.7	0.5	0.79
② Wage system	2.6	2.1	2.4	0.2	0.50
③ Job rotation	2.7	3.2	2.6	0.1	0.67
④ Education and training	2.9	3.4	2.9	0.0	0.57
⑤ Promotion	3.3	3.2	3.1	0.2	0.82
⑥ Firstline supervisors	3.0	3.1	2.9	0.1	0.47
II Production control	3.6	3.4	3.3	0.3	0.34
⑦ Production equipment	4.8	3.9	4.3	0.5	0.42
⑧ Quality control	3.9	4.0	3.4	0.5	0.31
⑨ Maintenance	2.8	2.9	2.6	0.2	0.79
⑩ Operations management	3.0	2.9	3.0	0.0	0.47
III Procurement	3.0	3.0	3.0	0.0	0.62
⑪ Local content	2.7	2.3	2.7	0.0	1.05
⑫ Suppliers	3.7	3.8	3.9	−0.2	0.67
⑬ Procurement method	2.6	3.0	2.5	0.1	0.68
IV Group consciousness	3.8	3.9	3.2	0.6	0.48
⑭ Small group activities	2.9	2.7	2.5	0.4	0.79
⑮ Information sharing	4.1	4.4	3.6	0.5	0.78
⑯ Sence of unity	4.4	4.6	3.5	0.9	0.68
V Labor relations	4.1	4.2	3.6	0.5	0.22
⑰ Hiring policy	3.8	4.3	3.4	0.4	0.63
⑱ Job security	3.8	4.9	3.4	0.4	0.79
⑲ Labor unions	5.0	4.2	4.4	0.6	0.00
⑳ Grievance procedures	3.9	3.2	3.3	0.6	0.35
VI Parent-subsidiary relations	4.2	3.5	3.6	0.6	0.39
㉑ Ratio of Japanese expatriates	4.6	3.8	3.7	0.9	0.96
㉒ Delegation of authority	4.0	3.3	3.6	0.4	0.67
㉓ Managerial position of Americans	4.0	3.3	3.6	0.4	0.47
Average of 23 items	3.6	3.5	3.3	0.3	0.21
VII Community relations					
㉔ Donations and volunteer activity	2.0	1.8	2.3	−0.3	0.63

Reliance upon Japanese Equipment and Personnel

First, let us examine those areas where high application is most apparent. As mentioned above, application ratings of the auto parts industry were higher than the other industries in two groups, Production Control and Parent-Subsidiary Relations. All three items under Parent-Subsidiary Relations have a rating higher than the other industries, showing incontestably the inclination of auto parts for high application in this area. Whereas, although its application rating for Production Control as a group is the highest among individual items, only Production Equipment has the highest rating, and the other three items are all in second place, with Quality Control and Maintenance lower than in auto assembly, and Operations Management lower than in consumer electronics. In short, the high application rating of Production Equipment accounts for the high application rating of this group. Therefore, the high application orientation of the auto parts industry can be represented by production equipment and three items of the Parent-Subsidiary Relations group. Incidentally, according to the 4-Perspective Evaluation, Production Equipment represents the "result" bringing-in of ready-made "materials" from Japan. And, in the Parent-Subsidiary Relations group, Ratio of Japanese Expatriates and Managerial Position of American Employees indicate the "human-result" aspect where Japanese expatriate employees take part in the management of local business. "Human-result" and "material-result" are more apparent in the auto parts industry than anywhere else and clearly show its inclination toward application.

Now let us examine the substance of the high application in these four items individually. Although the other industries also scored high marks here, the 4.8 rating for production equipment demonstrated a striking inclination toward application in the auto parts industry. Indeed, this industry is almost entirely dependent on Japan for equipment. Moreover, we noticed two or three plants were bringing-in new machines after trials had been conducted in Japan. Also, there were few cases where equipment was modified or orders placed with American machine manufacturers, partly because in general they have not been in business many years. Therefore, auto parts found itself constantly drawn toward the side of application, in comparison with auto assembly, whose 3.9 rating shows that it is making some effort toward domestic sourcing of equipment. By way of explanation, we can point out the underlying circumstances in which car models that Japanese auto manufacturers have been manufacturing in America were first developed in Japan and the parts supplied by auto parts transplants had been developed by their respective parent companies in Japan after many years of effort and after having passed through a number of changes in design. So the equipment that produces these parts incorporates a great deal of know-how that was generated in Japan, and would have been indeed difficult to find in America. Basically, then, there was no choice but to bring it in from Japan.

All three items under group VI, Parent-Subsidiary Relations, have an application rating of 4.0 or higher. Ratio of Japanese Expatriates, especially, is much higher, at 4.6, than in other industries. However, its standard deviation is a high 0.96, indicating a great disparity among individual plants. Some have, for the auto parts industry, an exceptionally low rate of 2.2 percent (9 out of 411 workers), or 3.3 percent (22 out of 663 personnel). But the rates of the remaining seven plants are somewhere between 4.3 and 12.9 percent. As a whole, then, the auto parts industry has relatively more Japanese employees than the other industries, and these dispatched Japanese expatriates are playing active roles in the management of the local business.

The 4.0 rating for Delegation of Authority is also high. At 0.67, its standard deviation is not so high. In contrast with AJ, with its rather considerable amount of operation experience compared to the other eight plants and its conscious effort on behalf of localization, or with AR, whose status as a joint venture places it along with AJ more or less on the side of adaptation, there are two or three plants that are strongly application-oriented, and this causes the overall balance to lean toward the application side. For instance, the annual business plan at one plant is determined by the board of directors of the parent company in Japan, and its shipping prices are decided between the parent company and the auto manufacturer. As such, given the short history of local production in the auto parts industry, in general the degree of localization of the delegation of authority at the local company appears to be quite limited. The item "managerial position of American employees" is also 4.0. Here, too, AR tends somewhat toward adaptation by virtue of its status as a joint-venture and possibly because of the effects of Canadian legislation. Nevertheless, the industry as a whole is marked by the strong authority wielded by Japanese executives.

So the auto parts transplants in America are currently striving to achieve the same level of quality and efficiency as Japan, while Japanese employees are actively involved in operating the local plant, and using equipment brought in from Japan, under the strong control of the main office in Japan. Such an inclination for material and human result application is, to a certain extent, characteristic of the Japanese transplants in America but, in the case of the auto parts industry, this trait is especially pronounced.

Inferior Core System Compared with Automobile Assembly

The next group to examine is I, work organization and administration, which we have placed at the core of our analytical framework of the Japanese-style production system and which represents the human-method aspect in the 4-Perspective Evaluation. However, its application rating was 3.1, lower than the 3.3 of auto assembly, and below the 23-item average rating for the auto parts industry. In terms of the individual items, we notice that out of six items, only Promotion had the highest rating for auto parts, whereas four of auto assembly's items rated highest. This could be explained by the general characteristic of the auto assembly industry toward a stronger inclination to application of methods regarding work organization than is found in the auto parts industry.

Let us look at this more closely. The application rating of Job Classification was 4.2 for auto parts, in comparison with 4.8 for auto assembly. The disparity is due to the fact that whereas the auto assembly industry almost completely achieved the simplification of job classification, the auto parts industry has two or three plants that lag behind the auto assembly industry. At one plant, for example, there are four grades, the fourth being the equivalent of a leadman, but there are seven job categories for grades one through three. Moreover, even within the same grade a job category change must be posted. At another plant, there are eight different wage grades for production workers, and each of them corresponds to a different job category. However, we should take note that the auto parts industry greatly exceeded the application ratings of consumer electronics and semiconductors, probably because it made its advance only after the auto assembly industry had torn down the wall of the traditional American system of job classification, in addition to belonging to the high application automotive industry in general.

In Job Rotation also, the auto parts industry rated low at 2.7 by comparison with the 3.2 of auto assembly. The primary reason for this is the lack of success in simplifying job classifications and the many restrictions this imposes on carrying out job rotation. Some of the plants went so far as to assert that "basically no job rotation is possible between individuals whose wage levels are different". But in no plant did anyone fully deny the necessity or significance of job rotation. Some of the transplants are at the stage where "It is done upon individual consent. It is virtually impossible to get everyone to go along. There is not sufficient leeway to do it." This accounts for the low rating. Of course, on the contrary, some plants showed a fairly motivated approach to job rotation, as seen in the case of AO, where all the members of a team rotate every month under the instruction of their team leader, and where a job training board has been set up to help develop versatile, multiskilled workers. This brought the rating up above those of the consumer electronics and semiconductor industries.

The application rating of Education and Training was 2.9, below auto assembly, and even lower than semiconductors, indeed ranking second from the bottom. In this industry most of the transplants are generally at the stage of producing a limited line of products with a comparatively small number of workers. So, in comparison with auto assembly, where many workers are placed on the final assembly line and for which ensuring the flexibility of its work organization is important, and also in comparison with the semiconductor industry, where process technology is highly advanced and complex, the auto parts industry seems to have less need for education and training. Therefore, there was less job rotation than in auto assembly and less education and training of maintenance technicians and engineers than in semiconductors, resulting in a correspondingly low application rating.

The application rating of First-line Supervisors was 3.0, also below auto assembly, although the difference was an insignificant 0.1 point. Since the auto assembly and auto parts industries, probably because both are part of the automotive industry, attached such great importance to in-house development and training they took almost the same attitude toward supervisors, namely to develop them not only as the persons in charge of labor management, but also as persons with a thorough understanding of floor conditions who could assume the key role in the operation of teams. This is why its rating was higher than those of consumer electronics and semiconductors. Nevertheless, even among auto parts, those plants, the products of which carry traits of the electrical industry, occasionally relied on outside recruitment. This brought down the application rating to slightly below that of auto assembly, and was one factor in lowering the overall application rating.

In contrast to these four items, the application rating for Promotion was 3.3, the highest of the four industries. This is due to the attitude, common throughout the automotive industry, of attaching great importance to internal promotion and to the immunity that the auto parts industry at least has had to the influence of traditional American labor relations. The application ratings for AO, AJ, and AM, in particular, were especially high. It is noteworthy that although AO is a joint venture with the largest American auto manufacturer, it showed the highest application rating among all nine auto parts companies. Here, performance evaluation has an actual effect on promotions. But then, it is necessary to acknowledge that, should a line worker have doubts, these are to be resolved through mutual understanding brought about by discussions with the team leader, and that this is different from the performance evaluation practiced in Japan. In the case of AJ, recommendation of the supervisor is taken into account for promotion to leadman, and at AM, the performance evaluation is reflected in the promotion. These factors elevated the application ratings of the two plants. Again, among the auto parts transplants also, there are a few cases of the adaptation-type relatively common in America, namely, when an opening occurs, post it, then fill the position on the basis of individual skills and experience and everything else being equal, give precedence to seniority. This factor lowered the overall application rating slightly.

Wage System was low in application rating at 2.6, but still higher than the auto assembly's Wage System with its low rating of 2.1, and below the 3.1 for the semiconductor industry that has labor relations of a high-tech type. To begin with, for blue-collar workers, the system of "wages based on the nature of one's duties" and paid on a hourly basis in correspondence with segmented job classification is firmly rooted in traditional American labor-management practice. So among the Japanese transplants, in consumer electronics and auto assembly that are still partly under the influence of that tradition, the application rating is low. Semiconductors, however, succeeded to some degree in bringing-in the Japanese-style performance evaluation, with some reward for years of service, and in borrowing the form of the American performance evaluation. However, the auto parts industry, as a member of the automotive industry, has taken a more discreet position toward the application of the performance evaluation in particular, and thus the lower application rating. Therefore, while its application rating for Promotion, which also refers to personnel treatment, was the highest among the four industries, that for Wage System rated behind semiconductors.

Likewise, in group II, Production Control, those aspects of method that form another component of the core system in the auto parts industry rank below those of auto assembly. As mentioned earlier, in the average application rating by group, the auto parts industry ranks highest among the four industries. However, when looked at by individual items, its strong inclination toward application is most obvious in Production Equipment. On the other hand, Quality Control and Maintenance, those aspects that represent the method side of material control in the 4-Perspective Evaluation, ranked lower in their application ratings than they did in auto assembly, although in both cases the 0.1 difference is hardly significant. At any rate, the fact that the auto parts industry was also behind the auto assembly industry in application ratings for material-method, just as for human-method, bears investigation as possibly showing the weakness of auto parts in method application in comparison with auto assembly's inclination for it.

The application rating of Control of Operations fell behind consumer electronics with its long operating experience because many of the plants have not been operating very long and have been rapidly increasing production, and are still in the stage of trying first of all to stabilize their operations. However, it was higher than that of auto assembly, if only by a mere 0.1 point. This is due to the fact that under actual running conditions operations in the auto parts plants were seen as proceeding smoothly, since their processing setup was simpler than that required by auto assembly.

Notable Adaptation for Parts Procurement

The application rating for III, Procurement, was 3.0, in line with auto assembly, and almost midway between semiconductors at 3.5 and consumer electronics at 2.6. Procurement is the only group with an average on a par with the industry-wide average in contrast to the other auto parts groups that are generally strongly application-oriented. However, at the individual item level, a different significance emerges. Although all the three items are means for judging the procurement aspect, in terms of the 4-Perspective Evaluation, Local Content and Suppliers represent material-result because they indicate the extent to which ready-made parts are brought in, whereas procurement method represents material-method because it concerns methods by which parts are procured. Therefore, they are of a different nature.

Thus, let us examine individual items. Local Content rated low at 2.7, which is in line with the average for the four industries. For this item, auto assembly also had a low score of 2.3, even lower than auto parts, indicating the high local sourcing rate of the automotive industry. All the auto parts transplants, concerned as they are about friction with American parts manufacturers, share the same attitude toward increasing the local sourcing rate. However, in addition to the insufficiency of inroads on the part of their related parts vendors (subcontractors), as is the case with the auto assembly transplants, there are many variations in the ways of dealing with this matter from one firm to another, as the high standard deviation of 1.05 suggests, and this pushed up the application rating slightly.

The next item, Suppliers, was high at 3.7, yet it is below the four-industry average by 0.2 points. The application rating of this item is high for all four industries, and this is particularly true for the semiconductor industry, which is still dependent on Japan for most of its key components. In auto parts also, there is a strong desire to use Japan-made components if possible but, in fact, out of the fear of friction resulting from their advance, a great deal of effort is spent to raise the domestic sourcing rate, and this has been translated into the current rating. However, many plants point out that under present circumstances in procuring parts from American vendors they must struggle for higher quality and lower costs, and since nearly all of their imported parts are from Japan, the application rating is high. Even for resources that can be relatively easily procured in America, although there is AK that uses 100 percent American resources, we heard other opinions, such as, "Special steels cannot be made here" (AQ), or "Parts, like rubber products, that require a tight tolerance to function properly come from Japan" (AL). For these reasons, at the time of our survey, we got the impression that any plant that "locally procures 80 percent of its resources and 25 percent of its parts" would be quite representative of the average procurement situation.

In contrast to this, the application rating for procurement method was low at 2.6, although it exceeded the four-industry average by only 0.1 point. Specifically, in regard to delivery, for example, it was common to hear such sentiments as these: "We tried the Japanese system of eliminating inventory, but it didn't work out. We were forced to handle the situation by maintaining an inventory" (AQ), or "Parts suppliers don't care if they fail to make a delivery on time, so we have no other choice than to order surplus amounts" (AR). In regard to quality, most plants are in the same situation as described by AL: "We are still struggling, and under present conditions we have no choice but just to reject the bad parts after the fact." Of course we saw many attempts to build up a Japanese-style procurement system in these plants, but so far these efforts have been futile.

As we have seen above, this group is the only one where the average application rating was not above the industry-wide average, but the import of its rating level differs for each item. Local Content and Suppliers both help us judge the extent that material-result is brought in from Japan, but whereas the former has a low application rating due to consciousness of localization, the latter, being still strongly dependent on Japan, remains at a high level. They are in striking contrast. By comparison, procurement method, which is of the nature of material-method, has a low application rating, in the same way as other items that reveal method.

High Application for "Group Consciousness"

The application rating for Group Consciousness was 3.8, and as a group it was considerably higher here than in consumer electronics and semiconductors, and a little lower in auto assembly. However, the gap between auto assembly and auto parts is only 0.1, which is not necessarily significant.

The rating for Small Group Activities is 2.9, not a very high level, indicating that it is next to impossible to carry out unmodified Japanese-style small group activities in America. Nevertheless, since some plants like AJ and AK showed a willingness to implement small group activities, and the number of cases opposing the implementation of small group activities were few, the Small Group Activities rating was higher here than in other industries. At AJ, QC-circle and TQC activities have been carried out on an "everyone must join" basis since about 3 years ago. AK was carrying out small group activities on a voluntary basis, and the participation rate was 50 percent or higher. Even where there was no small group activities and no suggestion system, some plants, such as AL, had begun to take steps to provide classes for all workers to learn QC statistical control techniques.

By way of contrast, Information Sharing and Sense of Unity had high ratings of 4.1 and 4.4, respectively, yet these were still lower than the auto assembly industry. As for information sharing, although the case of AM, where the president has meeting with all the workers twice a year, can be considered rather an exception, many plants are organizing active meetings at different levels, and the open-style office system is being used virtually without exception. Company uniforms, first-come-first-serve parking lots, and events promoting mutual friendship, as measures to foster a sense of unity, are also eagerly implemented, with most plants following auto assembly in this regard. However, its standard deviation was higher than for auto assembly because a few plants paid little heed to such measures, and the rating was subsequently lowered.

Thus, for the three items comprising Group Consciousness, part of human-method in the 4-Perspective Evaluation, the rating of Small Group Activities was slightly high because of the greater eagerness of a few plants to engage in this than was the case in auto assembly, whereas in the case of Information Sharing and Sense of Unity, the passive attitude of a few plants brought about an opposite result. In general, then, in regard to measures concerning this group, a common attitude can be seen among many plants in both auto assembly and auto parts. Although this group is a subsystem to promote application of the core system, it is noteworthy that in contrast with the weakness in the auto parts industry in method application in the core system, on this subsystem side, the inclination for human-method application was readily apparent.

Labor Relations Stressing Nonunionism

Labor Relations application rating was high at 4.1, and like Group Consciousness, its difference with auto assembly was a mere 0.1 point. However, at the individual item level, this group has characteristics differing greatly from auto assembly. That is, its application ratings for Hiring Policies and Job Security are substantially lower than auto assembly, whereas those for Labor Unions and Grievance Procedures are, on the contrary, considerably higher.

To understand Labor Relations in the auto parts industry, more than anything one must understand the approach taken toward labor unions. The application rating for this item scored highest, 5.0, in line with semiconductors. Unlike the semiconductor industry, in which unionization is partial even among American firms, in the automotive industry, to be an American company means to be under the strong influence of the UAW. Despite being part of that industry, all nine plants targeted for the current study had no union, and yet their labor relations were stable; these facts gave rise to this high rating. Even those auto assembly manufacturers that accepted a relationship with the UAW succeeded in negotiating a considerable degree of flexibility into their contracts. However, lacking such power to negotiate, auto parts manufacturers attempt to avoid the union if at all possible. Also, we heard it said that some plants that are, for example, joint ventures or have close dealings with American auto manufacturers received instruction from the Big Three "not to let unionization occur." In general, then, the auto parts manufacturers faced unionization attempts with a careful, discreet posture, and while increasing the scale of production in America, they avoided expanding the scale of the workforce at a single plant. There was even a case in which a company resorted to building second and third production facilities by splitting its original plant.

The high 3.9 rating for Grievance Procedures provides an interesting point in relation with nonunion policy. In auto assembly, they also are very conscious of their way of dealing with the Grievance Procedures, but due to the presence of the union, they are unable to escape completely from the traditional American Grievance Procedures framework, and as a result their application rating remained at 3.2, behind semiconductors. The auto parts industry, on the other hand, not only was able to avoid the traditional framework because of the absence of a union, but also worked out more active measures on behalf of its Grievance Procedures as a defense against possible union offensives. This accounts for its rating of 3.6, higher than semiconductors. Let us turn now to specific cases. AL, for example, has no special system for handling complaints, partly because of the small size of its operation. Complaints are brought in to "one's direct superior or a manager, someone easy to talk to." In general, as can be seen in the case of AO, the trend is toward an open-door policy, fairly common in America, and to issue directions such as, "It is best to talk to your team leader."

Hiring Policies and Job Security both had the same rating, 3.8, exceeding the industry-wide average, but falling short of auto assembly. As large-scale operations, auto assembly manufacturers carefully considered site location and hiring policies, and clearly expressed their position to avoid layoffs as much as possible, while auto parts, small of scale and with limited financial resources, followed suit but only to a much lesser degree, hence the lower rating.

Summary

It has became clear that the auto parts industry has an inclination toward high application in its local production in America. We can cite such reasons as the limited number of years of operation, the relatively small scale of operations, and so forth. But it would also appear to be related to the inclination toward application that is so characteristic throughout the automotive industry, of which it is a part. In particular, it is necessary that auto parts plants accept the production control system required by the auto manufacturers in regard to the delivery system and to quality control. Also, it seems likely that at the time they were studying their future advance into America, they were influenced by the feasibility studies of auto manufacturers. For one reason or another, a number of features common to both auto assembly and auto parts can be seen. On the other hand, a fairly important difference between the two also became increasingly clear. That is, auto assembly, as we have often pointed out, has a tendency to hope to achieve through method application the formation of a flexible work organization that can function as the core of the Japanese production system in America. In the final analysis this would seem to be the prime objective in America, although it is also striving diligently for localization in other areas. Auto parts, on the other hand, as is symbolized by the high application ratings for group II, Production Control, and VI, Parent-Subsidiary Relations, is currently marked by the tendency to "directly" bringing-in human and material from Japan. In other words, in contrast to the development of local production by the auto assembly industry wherein great importance is given to method, the auto parts industry characteristically attaches great importance to the direct bringing-in of ready-made elements from Japan, with less concern for the application of method.

Let us examine it from the viewpoint of the 4-Perspective Evaluation. Figure 6–2 illustrates the 4-Perspective Evaluation for auto parts in comparison with all four

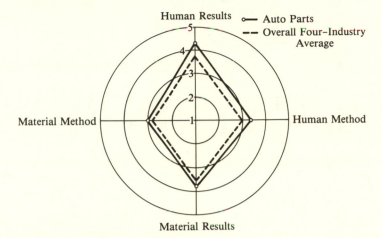

Figure 6–2 Four-Perspective Evaluation of Auto Parts Industry

industries. As shown in the figure, the rectangular shape of auto parts falls every-where outside of the four industries, showing a strong overall inclination toward application, and the high application rating for human-result is especially obvious. In short, the chief feature of the auto parts industry is its overall pronounced incli-nation toward application, with the direct bringing-in of ready-made elements from Japan, rather than bringing-in the Japanese method unmodified, in which it leans in the direction of the human side of result application rather than the "material" side. (Semiconductors is chiefly characterized by the emphasis it places on the direct, bringing-in of material. Refer to the industrial analysis for the semiconduc-tor industry for details.)

CONSUMER ELECTRONICS

Outline of the Surveyed Factories

The nine consumer electronics plants that were targeted for this survey (EA through EI), as shown in Table 6–5, produce mainly color television sets, picture tubes, and microwave ovens. In this section, we will focus our analysis on color television sets.

First, we would like to mention a few general characteristics of the consumer elec-tronics industry's American production, that dictate the conditions of application and adaptation for its transplants. Since in the color TV field, U.S.-Japan trade fric-tion intensified earlier than for the semiconductor or automobile industry, most of the major manufacturers put their local production on track in the 1970s, and now-adays, with the exception of a few models, nearly all products are being made locally. Therefore, the first characteristic of the color TV industry is that it started local production in America relatively early compared to the other Japanese man-ufacturing industries, and that Japanese products sold in America are mostly sup-plied by the American transplant, not by imports from Japan.

Table 6–5. Profile of Japanese-Owned Consumer Electronics Plants in the United States

	EA	EB	EC	ED	EE	EF	EG	EH	EI
Location	California	Illinois	Arkansas	Tennessee	California	Tennessee	New Jersey	Georgia	New York
Start of operation	July, 1972	May, 1974	Jan., 1977	Aug., 1978	April, 1979	Oct., 1979	June, 1982	Sept., 1986	Nov., 1986
Form of establishment	Startup	Acquisition	Acquisition	Startup	Startup	Startup	Startup	Startup	Used plant
Mode of entry Number of employees	100% 1,700	100% 570	Joint → 100% 650	100% 700	100% 250	100% 740	100% 250	100% 640	Joint → 100% 1,240
No. of Japanese expatriates	45	12	9	12	12	21	8	7	8
Products	Color TVs CRTs display monitors	Color TVs projection TVs	Color TVs	Color TVs microwave ovens	Color TVs VCRs	Color TVs microwave ovens personal computers	Color TVs	Color TVs mobile telephones	CRTs
Production volume (thousand units)	CTV:640 CRT:1,600	CTV:450	CTV:800	CTV:1,100 Oven:450	CTV:120 VCR:90	CTV:1,000 Oven:900	CTV:450	CTV:540 Telephone:200	CRT:1,600

Sources: Interview at each plant.

As the second general characteristic, we would like to bring up the fact that, although it is called local production of color TVs, only the final assembly stage of the entire manufacturing process is done on American soil. The other processes, mounting components onto a printed board or assembling the chassis, for example, are performed either at the maquiladoras in Mexico or affiliated plants in Asia. Although the transplants in America are also called Japanese-owned overseas color TV plants, when compared with those in Taiwan or Malaysia, their process is far simpler, and the size of their workforce is generally smaller. In other words, in actuality Japanese color TV plants in the United States are operating rather technically limited processes with a workforce that is not very large. As described later, this fact greatly influences the state of application-adaptation in consumer electronics transplants in America.

Next, let us examine the average picture of the consumer electronics industry that emerges through our hybrid evaluation (Table 6–6). The most striking characteristic is without a doubt the 2.7 industry application rating average, the lowest among the industries targeted in this study. (Industry-wide average is 3.3, auto assembly 3.5, auto parts 3.6, semiconductors 3.2). Furthermore, it should be noted that not only the average for all 23 items, but also for every single one of groups I through VI, are lower than those of the other industries, and that three out of the nine plants had an all-item average application rating of 2.0 at most, which is very low. (i.e., the consumer electronics industry has a strong inclination toward adaptation).

So, we would like to get a rough idea of the contents of the low application ratings, while using the 4-Perspective Evaluation as a source of clues (Figure 6–3). In the 4-Perspective Evaluation, those elements that stand out with low application ratings are related to human-method and material-method. In regard to human-method, VI, group consciousness, has conspicuously low ratings (consumer electronics average 2.3, industry-wide average 3.2), and two groups, V, Labor Relations (consumer electronics average 2.7, industry-wide average 3.6), and I, Work Organization and Administration (consumer electronics average 2.4, industry-wide average 2.9), both show fairly large disparities with the industry-wide average. As a result, it is also natural that the application rating for material-method in such items as quality control and maintenance would also be low.

On the contrary, for material-result, which indicates the bringing-in of ready-made equipment and parts or both, the application rating has the smallest disparity with the industry-wide average, and there is little difference among plants. We may infer that for the consumer electronics industry also, the dependence on Japan in such areas as production equipment and parts is critical to the maintenance of quality and efficiency in American transplants.

It is not that the level of the application ratings itself is extremely low, but that human-result items such as the ratio of Japanese expatriates show large disparities with the industry-wide averages. This contrasts somewhat with the image of the typical Japanese transplants in America, where plant management is supported by a relatively high number of Japanese expatriate employees. Of course, in consumer electronics transplants also, Japanese expatriate employees play critical roles, but the lower ratio of Japanese expatriates and the relatively higher importance given

Table 6–6. Hybrid Evaluation in the Consumer Electronics Industry

	Consumer Electronics (A)	Average of 4 Industries (B)	(A) − (B)	Standard Deviation
I Work organization and administration	2.4	2.9	−0.5	0.63
① Job classification	2.8	3.7	−0.9	1.03
② Wage system	2.0	2.4	−0.4	1.15
③ Job rotation	2.1	2.6	−0.5	0.87
④ Education and training	2.2	2.9	−0.7	0.79
⑤ Promotion	2.7	3.1	−0.4	0.47
⑥ First-line supervisor	2.6	2.9	−0.3	0.50
II Production control	3.1	3.3	−0.2	0.58
⑦ Equipment	4.0	4.3	−0.3	0.94
⑧ Quality control	3.0	3.4	−0.4	0.67
⑨ Maintenance	2.1	2.6	−0.5	0.74
⑩ Operations management	3.3	3.0	0.3	0.82
III Procurement	2.6	3.0	−0.4	0.22
⑪ Local content	2.0	2.7	−0.7	0.00
⑫ Suppliers	3.6	3.9	−0.3	0.50
⑬ Procurement method	2.1	2.5	−0.4	0.31
IV Group consciousness	2.3	3.2	−0.9	0.68
⑭ Small group activities	2.2	2.5	−0.3	0.92
⑮ Information sharing	2.4	3.6	−1.2	0.83
⑯ Sense of unity	2.1	3.5	−1.4	0.57
V Labor relations	2.7	3.6	−0.9	0.71
⑰ Hiring policy	2.4	3.4	−1.0	0.83
⑱ Job security	2.2	3.4	−1.2	1.31
⑲ Labor union	3.4	4.4	−1.0	1.34
⑳ Grievance system	2.8	3.3	−0.5	0.79
VI Parent-subsidiary relations	3.0	3.3	−0.6	0.61
㉑ Ratio of Japanese expatriates	2.6	3.7	−1.1	0.83
㉒ Delegation of authority	3.2	3.6	−0.4	0.63
㉓ Managerial position of Americans	3.2	3.6	−0.4	0.92
Average	2.7	3.3	−0.6	0.45
VII Community relations				
㉔ Donation, volunteer activities	2.7	2.3	0.4	0.94

to the roles of local executives could be seen to indicate that this industry is a step ahead of the others in the localization of management because of its length of operational experience.

Next, let us consider how these average characteristics of the consumer electronics have arisen by examining individual items one by one.

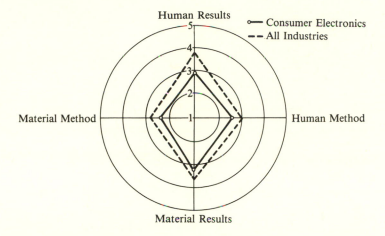

Figure 6–3 Four-Perspective Evaluation of Consumer Electronics Industry

Low Application for Work Organization and its Factors

The application rating for I, Work Organization and Administration (consumer electronics average 2.4, industry wide average 2.9), indicate the low extent to which the Japanese-style system has been brought in to the core region that is associated with the human elements in the production system of the consumer electronics industry. However, it should be pointed out that the presence of three plants with extremely low application ratings of less than 2 (no plants in other industries had a group I average rating below 2), resulted in further accentuating the low average application rating of the consumer electronics.

No plant in this industry so severely reduced the number of job titles as did the auto assembly transplants. Nevertheless, the disparity is fairly large, ranging from EB plant, which inherited the existing system from its previous owner with 100 job titles divided into 14 job grades, to EG plant, which has a simplified system wherein there are only two classifications, production workers and maintenance crew. (Standard deviation of this item is 1.03). EG can be called somewhat of an extreme exception. EA and EI, which have about four levels for general through maintenance workers, may be more typical examples of those that have opted for a rough classification of jobs in the consumer electronics industry.

EB is typical of the old type American factories. An American working in personnel affairs in a different transplant told us that in a major American electrical plant where he had worked before, the job titles likewise numbered 100, and the job grades ranged from 12 to 14. Job classification at EA or EI seems to be almost the same as the system observed in the new, nonunion type electrical plants. (This, too, is according to the same American executive.) Between these two groups are found plants with approximately 20 job titles and somewhere in the neighborhood of 10 job grades.

At any rate, as we mentioned in the correlative analysis in Chapter 5, job classification is closely correlated to the degree of the bringing-in of Japanese methods, primarily personnel management methods. Therefore, with job classification as it should be, this item in consumer electronics can be said to indicate symbolically the degree and diversity of the orientation toward application of the whole industry.

The application rating for wage system, although below the industry-wide average, is almost identical with auto assembly (auto assembly 2.1, consumer electronics 2.0). However, unlike auto assembly, where the wage system based on the nature of one's duties is adopted in almost all cases, in consumer electronics there are large disparities between plants (standard deviation 1.15). On the one hand, four of the nine plants use a traditional American-type system in which wage rates correspond one-to-one with segmented jobs; on the other hand, some have introduced a system wherein wages reflect such things as somewhat longer years of service and a performance evaluation.

These plants differ in the extent to which elements that deal directly with individuals, such as years of service and the performance evaluation, are reflected in wages. The most extreme case could be that of EG. Here, among those working on the shop floor, from assembly to adjustment to inspection, there are no differences in wage levels. They receive pay raises according to individual's years of service. Moreover, no cap has yet been placed on the number of years. Although they have a performance evaluation system, it has very little effect on wages. For all intents and purposes it is a wage system based totally on the length of one's service. Nevertheless, there is a separate wage structure for the class of technicians who perform product repair and maintenance. This, too, can be said to reflect the nature of the American labor market, a market divided and separated by job categories and job classes. In EA, the system is set up so that within roughly divided job grades, wages reflect years of service with a cap of 7 years as well as the results of the performance evaluation. In the case of EI, as long as one stays in the same job grade, the pay raises stop in 3.5 years, and the frequency at which one is given a raise varies depending on the performance evaluation.

Both extremes can also be seen in consumer electronics plants that have a union. The cause, then, cannot be simply attributed to the presence or absence of a union in the case of this industry. Unlike the automobile industry, the labor union's industry-wide controlling power is quite weak. The tendency toward fixed jobs, where specific workers repeatedly perform specific, fixed jobs, is generally more pronounced than in auto assembly. The three plants with low application ratings in particular can be said to be of the totally fixed-job type. Three plants carry out job rotations within the area of control of the first-line supervisors, but all the others follow a system in which designated workers perform fixed operations until a model changeover occurs.

Consequently, the Japanese method of developing multiskilled workers that consists of the accumulation of a broad range of experience by attaching great importance to OJT has not penetrated deeply. Furthermore, with one or two exceptions, such measures that we find in auto assembly, such as training shop floor personnel by sending them in large groups to Japan or, in reverse, sending skilled workers en masse into American facilities for coaching, are virtually nonexistent here.

All these transplants opted for a job-posting system in promoting production workers. Selection is based on the worker's abilities or qualifications coupled with seniority—that is, either the individuals' abilities or qualifications are checked first and seniority is used to break a tie or, contrariwise, candidates are interviewed in order of seniority and then their abilities are checked. These are the usual methods, but there is one plant that gives to seniority the overruling priority, and two plants appoint whomever they feel is best qualified, regardless of seniority.

Many of the transplants replied that they attach great importance to promotion from within the company for the recruitment of supervisors. Even so, they have the alternative of hiring someone from outside if no qualified person is found. Even in the case of internal promotion, the width and depth of the on-site operational experience that a new supervisor is likely to have will be limited because of the limited means available for developing skills mentioned earlier and how much the more in the case of a supervisor hired from outside. It is only natural to assume a considerable gap in the actual experience of hands-on coaching and job improvement activities with comparable supervisors in a Japanese plant. It would be unreasonable to assume that supervisors of a transplant could take on various concurrent roles as do their counterparts in Japan. It is inevitable that their role becomes primarily centered around tasks connected to labor management.

An interesting antidote to this limitation is being tried at two or three plants. In these plants, the supervisors, while primarily performing tasks related to labor management, is supported by experienced workers with hands-on skills and extensive knowledge of the production process, thus helping to make up for a lack of shop-floor experience. This could be called a system of, so to speak, "two performing as one" where the duties of a Japanese-style supervisor are shared by two workers.

Next, let us investigate the cause for such a low application rating on the side of personnel management method, mainly focusing our attention on the work organization and its administration in consumer electronics, while comparing characteristics of the transplants with factories in Japan.

The workforce of the shop floor of a typical color TV or VCR plant in Japan is composed of, roughly speaking, two groups: One is female workers performing relatively simple tasks in the final assembly process, and the other is male workers with higher skills whose duties are mainly maintenance-related. In the case of female workers, even in the Japanese plants, the scheduled job rotation is not necessarily carried out actively or over a broad range, whereas for male technicians, job rotation is actively carried out with the objective of developing a wide range of skills. Job rotation spans a wide range from the final assembly to the insertion of parts into printed boards, so that the whole production process of TVs or VCRs can be learned. The more capable the worker, the more frequent will be that worker's job rotation across a broad range. And it is not rare that such a person even gains experience in several plants within a corporation.

Such a male technician, with full experience in hands-on operation and extensive knowledge of the whole production process, is promoted to first-line supervisor after having served the company for 10 to 20 years. He is management at its most extended point, an all-around player on the shop floor, who is not only capable of

actually teaching jobs to workers, but also of assuming responsibility for and holding authority over all the duties involved on the shop floor, such as assigning jobs,
quality control, setting of standard processing times, operation improvement, performance evaluations, and so forth. This is our supervisor, whose existence, it is no
exaggeration to say, is the key support for the shop floors of Japanese domestic
plants.

How about the local assembly plants in America? First, the skilled workers of this
type are limited due to the scale of the plant. Furthermore, all these plants do not
operate the insertion of components to printed board process within their facilities,
and are totally dependent on maquiladora plants in Mexico or affiliate companies
in Southeast Asia for chassis (printed board sets with components mounted). Naturally, this provides another reason for reducing the class of skilled workers. There
is a great difference in length of experience service. Although the color TV business
in local production began earlier than the automobile and semiconductors industries, even the plant with the longest history of local operation has less than 20 years.
Just by simply counting the number of years, we can see that only those who have
been continuously working at that plant since its startup could be regarded as having finally accumulated enough experience to become eligible for promotion to
first-line supervisor were it in Japan.

Moreover, the large gap in the degree of personnel stability between Japan and
the United States is well known. Furthermore, it is not simply a question of the
overall turnover, but rather the turnover of key personnel with accumulated skills.
It is not rare to see skilled key workers job-hopping with a personal history of
employment at a Japanese-owned plant in their background. This more or less
forces the industry to look outside for talented people even though they have no
experience in color TV production. Internal promotion is hampered by the problem of developing skills, as mentioned earlier, and from this standpoint also, the
industry has no alternative but to rely on a workforce with limited experience. It is
against such a background that the system of placing veteran workers with hands-
on experience as assistants to supervisors has been employed.

On the one hand, the process in these plants in America is limited to the final
assembly of color TVs. In comparison with the process of inserting components
into printed boards, the equipment is far simpler. The degree to which it must rely
on the skills of production workers for quality and efficiency is much lower than it
is in auto assembly, for example. Even though the class of key personnel is so limited, both for supervisors and maintenance technicians, it is possible to achieve
quality and operational efficiency that rivals plants in Japan as long as the equipment is securely set up and the personnel management is carried out properly with
the areas of individual responsibility clearly defined. Given such a situation, we
have to say the transplants are not greatly motivated to bring in the Japanese-style
work organization by breaking the labor-job practices of job control unionism so
deeply rooted in America, and knowing this entails the danger of triggering friction
with their employees. Naturally, in order to respond with flexibility to a wide range
of changes, such as model changeovers and fluctuation in the production volume
of color TVs and other products, it would be better to keep barriers between different job categories as low as possible. In fact, some plants are looking in this direction

with a fairly open mind, but there is still a large gap compared to the automobile industry, for example.

In addition, we should not forget that the local production of color TVs started at a comparatively early time. We suspect that, in what was the early stage of local production in America for the Japanese manufacturing industry as a whole, there was probably no choice but to be very discreet in the application of Japanese-style plant operation methods. This tendency is especially pronounced in those transplants that got their start by buying out an existing enterprise. It seems reasonable to assert that it was a combination of these factors that served to lower the average application ratings for the items in I, Work Organization and Administration, in the color TV industry.

Low System Application and Reliance upon Japanese Technology for Production Control and Parts Procurement

The application rating for II, Production Control approximates both the industry-wide average and the auto assembly industry average. (Consumer electronics average 3.1, industry-wide average 3.3, auto assembly average 3.4). This can be attributed to the following.

First, the high dependence on Japan for production equipment is also evident in the field of color TVs. In most of the plants, minor adjustments at the local site aside, the production equipment is essentially the same as that of their respective counterparts in Japan. But we find nothing here that corresponds to the auto assembly industry and to some of the auto parts transplants that even have trial runs performed in Japan prior to bringing-in machinery to their local facilities. Some TV transplants have introduced local machinery to a certain extent, and there is little doubt that this industry's localization in equipment is ahead of semiconductors and auto parts. In spite of this, the basic equipment is essentially the same as in the plants in Japan.

Second, the fact that this industry has had a longer experience than the others and has accumulated a great deal of expertise plays an important part in its ability to build up a stable production system particular to each of the plants operating under local conditions. The in-line rejection rate approaches closely that of Japanese plants, when rejection stemming from some defect in components is excluded. Although there is a weakness in maintenance capability, since the equipment is simple, equipment down time is also nearly that of the Japanese plant. However, as far as the productivity in the sense of operational efficiency is concerned, partly due to the restrictions imposed on the work organization mentioned above, the overall average could run as much as 20 percent lower than plants in Japan. But in terms of productivity, leaving the future out of it, at this point in time the consumer electronics industry as a whole is not inferior to the other industries that have more flexible plant operations.

The difference with Japan is not small, however, on the side of material-method, in such areas as maintenance and quality control. Many reported that what they call "quality buildup," according to which production workers perform their job by paying careful attention to quality, including the quality in the previous production stage, is not on par with that in Japan. It seems there is disparity with the plants in Japan in the feedback system as well. The question is whether or not to inform a supervisor immediately when a problem occurs in production. To one extent or another almost all the plants depend on experienced people from outside for the recruitment of maintenance personnel. In regard to the relationship of production workers with maintenance work, it is more than an issue of the "infringement of professional territory," and management at more than a few plants have given directions to leave it alone. Generally, in the plants in America, there is a tendency to ensure quality and to maintain and control equipment, while simultaneously clearly defining individual job territory and the allotment of responsibility.

But, as far as the final assembly process for color TVs is concerned, it is necessary to pay heed to the fact that there is no extreme disparity with the plants in Japan for the quality control or maintenance systems in themselves in the sense of the involvement of production workers. First, for quality control, the method of placing dedicated inspectors at the end of a production process or at key areas, and the number of inspectors employed in general, does not differ greatly with plants in Japan, although two transplants have inspectors who, in a way different than in Japan, belong to the quality control department but who are posted on the line. This is true for maintenance also, as mentioned earlier, for, in the plants in Japan also, there is a tendency to dichotomize employees into production workers and maintenance personnel.

Because of these factors, the disparity of the application ratings with other industries is smaller in production control than in the other groups.

Group III, Procurement, it should be noted, has a higher local content here than it does in the other industries. For the consumer electronics industry, where variations between plants are quite conspicuous, there is no significant disparity in the level of local content. The domestic sourcing of picture tubes contributes to the high local content rating. As is widely known, picture tubes are subject to a high import duty rate of 15 percent. Therefore, with a few exceptions, the transplants are forced to procure them either from American vendors or from Japanese-owned local plants. Among main items besides picture tubes that are procured locally are cabinets, which are bulky and also have no significant impact on function.

The most interesting thing on the side of suppliers is that the transplants are utterly divided into two groups for their procurement source of chassis: One from maquiladora plants in Mexico, another from Southeast Asian plants. The choice of source seems, with one exception, to have something to do with the difference in attitude at individual plants, as is demonstrated in their application ratings. Those that procure their chassis from maquiladora plants are EA, EB, EC, and ED. All four plants, excluding EA, have extremely low application ratings. The remaining transplants receive chassis from their sister plants in Malaysia, Taiwan, or Singapore, and these expressed rather skeptical opinions on the use of a maquiladora.

The following are the disadvantages of maquiladora plants in Mexico according to these skeptical opinions: (1) The worker stability rate is poor because workers move around to whoever offers better wages. (2) This poor worker stability affects quality. (3) The biggest problem is a shortage of human resources for middle management. (4) You cannot procure all the parts in the local markets, and will be forced to go to Japan or Southeast Asia anyway. In fact, at one plant that utilizes a maquiladora plant, the product rejection rate fluctuates greatly, with a particularly big surge in rejections at the beginning of the year. When we asked about this we received the reply, "At the maquiladora plant, many of the employees who have left for home at the year-end holidays do not report back, so the plant has no choice but to hire new people to fill in. This is why the quality of chassis from Mexico drops sharply." This businesslike approach to securing quality of the final product by rejecting defects at the final inspection stage, even if chassis quality has been inconsistent all along, may have something in common with how the American facilities of companies with low application ratings are run.

On the other hand, at some of those plants utilizing the maquiladora system, we heard the opinions expressed that the start-up period aside, once a certain amount of experience has been accumulated, stable quality can be ensured by utilizing a core workforce, in part comprised of veteran employees with longer years of service. But more than anything else, low processing and freight costs to the United States are the main attractions of Mexico. The comparison between maquiladora and Southeast Asia plants is an extremely interesting subject unto itself that would require much more investigation to do it justice.

It is common to procure those parts that greatly effect functionality, such as the yoke, tuner, and speaker, from Southeast Asia, Mexico, or Japan. It is not necessarily true that all these parts are supplied by sister plants or by Japanese-owned parts factories, but even when a third party is the vendor, it appears that "many of them are operating under the technical assistance of some Japanese companies." This is according to ED. Faced with the appreciation of the yen, "How to cut off ties with the yen (Japan)" (ED) is a question for any transplant. On the contrary, it is also true that "it is unlikely that there will be no procurement from Japan, which is the most advanced source in the world" (EB). We estimate that procurement from Japan, which primarily consists of critical high precision parts such as ICs and chips, represents 15 to 16 percent of the total cost of parts.

Japanese methods of procurement, such as the kanban-system and multi- or frequent delivery, are rarely used. Some plants are very active in supplying technical assistance to their parts suppliers, and some do almost nothing, and we found considerable variations among the plants in how they handled this.

In short, in material control, including maintenance and quality control, the degree of penetration of Japanese methods is not high. However, on the side of material-results, for example, production equipment and critical parts, including product design, a subject that we have not discussed here, both direct and indirect dependence on Japan is high. Without a doubt material-results application constitutes one of the important sources of competitiveness in the American market for color TVs' transplants.

Tendency Towards Adaptation

Let us start examining IV, Group Consciousness, the group with the lowest application rating. To begin with, small group activities ranks lowest among the 23 items, not only in consumer electronics but also in all the target industries. Nevertheless, the rating of this aspect is again conspicuously lower than in the other industries. We found three plants among all the transplants of the current study that have no small group activities at all. Two of these are color TV plants (EC and ED), and the third, SF, a semiconductor plant, is the most recent, having just started operation. The activities of those that do carry out small group activities such as QC-circles are extremely limited in terms of the percentage of participating employees, frequency of activities, and objectives, with one exception, EF, which is unusually active in such activities.

As for Sense of Unity, the low application rating or, put another way, the posture of adaptation to the American environment, is even more apparent. Uniforms can be seen at two or three plants, but they are not mandatory. Only a few plants stick to an open style office for white collar workers. Regarding the common cafeteria for all personnel, although it may be because of the scale of the workforce, even if it does exist, it does not look as good as those in auto assembly plants. Events to promote mutual friendship, such as summer picnics and Christmas parties, are organized in some of the plants. But the company sports festival of EC plant that occupied the mass media for a while has ceased. Activities such as these, along with a no-layoff policy, are often cited as typical measure that represent the most "Japanese"-like aspect of "Japanese-style management," and the weakness in application found here can be regarded as a major characteristic of the consumer electronics industry. A statement like "We do not do anything as Japanese-like as radio exercises but behave as a normal American company," sounds somewhat extreme, yet may indeed symbolize the general tendency of the consumer electronics industry.

On the side of V, Labor Relations, adaptation to the American environment is also very apparent. First, in hiring production workers, there is nothing to match the extremely careful selection of the auto assembly plants. As for job security, three out of nine plants have already carried out layoffs. Only two plants have come out clearly, either in written form or verbally for a no-layoff policy, that is the intention to avoid layoffs as much as possible.

Also, in the case of the consumer electronics industry, as suggested by the fact that as many as five of the plants are unionized, a position is taken that is somewhat different than the strong position to prevent the union from being organized that is considered almost de rigueur for Japanese enterprises. As we stated in the passage on the wage system, one of the reasons is that the central organizations of the labor unions of the electric industry are, unlike the UAW or USW, strongly imbued with job control unionism, and not strongly disposed to provide nationwide control or direction regarding wages and jobs. For example, even at the head office of the IUE (International Union of Electric), which is considered fairly aggressive among electric and electronic unions, in response to our interview, officials said that the tendency of Japanese companies to simplify job classifications and to have wages or promotions reflect the results of the performance evaluation are no problem as long as it does not lead to a drop in wages or an increase in the workload.

However, strictly speaking, this means that the head office does not interfere as long as a local does not raise the issue and does not rule out a type of wage system that is totally based on the nature of one's duties or the firm application of the seniority rule in the case of promotions for individual plants. Also, among the American general managers of personnel who work for Japanese companies, many criticize the union in fairly strong terms, saying "The labor unions care only about the interests of their organizations; the employees' welfare would actually improve without a union". Regardless whether or not their assessment is to the point, the fact that they have accepted the existence of unions in spite of such an attitude also indicates the strong tendency of consumer electronics toward local adaptation.

In our current investigation, we got the impression that there are signs of change in the old traditional type unions. A new direction for labor relations may be appearing there, although it is not yet fully developed. A good example of this may be EC, but we will discuss this subject in the next chapter when we discuss patterns.

Such a marked inclination to adaptation on the side of group consciousness and labor relations may be closely connected with the low application ratings for I, Work Organization and Administration. This is because a weak orientation toward application in the core part of the production system obviates the need to increase the intensity of application on the side of the subsystem that supports the core. Actually, as we described in Chapter 5, a fairly high correlation can be observed between these groups.

However, even in the case of EA, EG, and EI with average application ratings for I, Work Organization and Administration, at 3 or slightly more and, for that matter, with virtually the same score for this group as auto assembly plants, the average application ratings for IV, Group Consciousness, and V, labor relations are considerably lower than those in the auto assembly. In other words, in the consumer electronics industry, the low application ratings of these two groups may not just be simply reduced to the question of a low rating for I, Work Organization and Administration. In comparison with the core system part, group consciousness and labor relations, as a matter of course, have stronger ties with social and cultural factors such as behavioral modes and values than with the technical elements of production. So we can assume that in these areas, the attitude that accepts the local environment without clinging to the Japanese style is revealing itself more clearly.

The fact that the rating for VI, Parent-Subsidiary Relations, is on the adaptation side, stems first from the considerably lower rate of Japanese expatriate employees here than in the other industries. This is probably due to its head start in accumulating experience in local production. Therefore, both the autonomy of local transplants in regard to their parent companies and the position of top American executives within the plants are relatively high compared in the auto parts and semiconductor industries. However, when the Japanese expatriate employees rate is excluded from consideration, no major difference with the auto assembly industry is to be seen.

EF is making steady and persistent contributions to the local community. Donations, including those on behalf of United Way, are made at the rate of 1 percent of pretax profit, and there is a person at the level of general manager dedicated to the job of selecting recipients. So far, the plant has been carrying out the program on its own, but they have a plan to develop better planned activities in conjunction with their North America sales company, whose volunteer activities include support for thirteen different regional organizations. In addition, employees provide various services to local schools.

Nevertheless, except in these cases, we have the impression that despite its long experience in local production and also its high application ratings in a variety of areas, the consumer electronics industry in general, at the individual plant level, is not as active as the auto assembly industry in local community activities. There could be two explanations for this. The first is that friction within the various fields of the industry have been practically resolved. The second is that the scale of these plants is not particularly large. However, since it is inevitable that the presence of Japanese enterprises in American society will increase further, there will be pressure in the future to deal with these matters from a broader perspective, free of the limitations imposed by the circumstances of an individual company or of individual industry.[2]

Summary

Let us restate the characteristics of the consumer electronics industry that we have been discussing above. First, its low application ratings are below the industrywide averages in all groups.

Moreover, the low ratings are most apparent in the areas of human-related control method, such as work organization and its administration, group consciousness, and labor relations. Underlying the reasons for this is the fact that, with the exception of two picture tube factories, all the transplants have production processes that have been reduced to the final assembly stage, a process fairly limited in both scale and the technology involved. The first reason, then, is that the skills of the production workers have relatively little impact on product quality and operational efficiency. Second, not only is the level of expertise required for technicians such as the maintenance crew not very high, but a large contingent of people for this class is not needed. The third reason naturally follows; there is no strong motive to forcibly introduce job practices and systems of a different nature that might trigger friction with local personnel or cause other problems. The industry's posture of adaptation to the local environment is particularly apparent in such elements as group consciousness and labor relations, areas not necessarily directly connected to the purely technical side of production, but which directly reflect the morphology of consciousness of the people involved, their behavioral patterns, or their sense of social values. At the same time, its long experience operating in America is reflected in the low ratio of Japanese expatriate employees (i.e., the human-results application rating is low), and the relatively high degree of autonomy of the local company.

Although the application ratings on the human-related side are low regardless of whether they belong to method or results the transplants are achieving fairly good results in product quality and operational efficiency. The reason is that, in addition to the above-mentioned factors, the direct and indirect dependence on Japan has a strong impact on the material side, in such areas as product design, production equipment, and functionally critical components. In other words, although the application ratings are strikingly low on the human sides, with limited production process and dependence on Japan for elements from the material side, consumer electronics has been able to achieve good product quality and stable, efficient operations. This may be the average image of consumer electronics.

Finally, let us ascertain what position the Japanese consumer electronics industry, as it expands its local production, plays in the U.S. market. Since the data sources vary, figures are not accurate, but we can assume that at the time of our investigation the local production by Japanese companies of color TVs in America made up approximately 50% of all American domestic production. The remaining 50% would be shared, then, by an American, a French, a Dutch, and a minor Korean company. As for the American market share by brand including imports (imports make up about 40% of the American market), American, French, and Dutch companies hold approximately 40%, Japanese companies 30%, miscellaneous brands primarily of giant retailers 25%, and Korean and Taiwanese companies 5%, respectively. Nevertheless, and this goes without saying in the case of the giant retailers, the local color TV manufacturers, too, are being supplied on an OEM basis with custom brands by the Japanese and Korean companies. Thus, the market share by brand mentioned above does not actually reflect the real situation. If we add all the imports from maquiladoras, and plants in Malaysia, Singapore, and Japan to the local production by Japanese transplants in America, we would estimate that products of "Japanese companies," including OEMs, comprise well over 40% of the market.[3]

Incidentally, regarding the microwave oven that once overwhelmed the American market with a market share reaching as high as 90%, partly because the American market is focused on low value-added products with few features, Japanese companies have been forced into tight competition with the influx of products from NIES, including Korea. Some Japanese transplants produce microwave ovens along with color TVs. One of these has ceased production, and another one has announced plans to withdraw from the field.

SEMICONDUCTORS

Outline of the Surveyed Factories

Among the Japanese firms that moved into America and are operating local production of semiconductors, we targeted six firms with seven plants for our current study. We also surveyed three major American firms for comparison purposes. Compared to the 1986 study, we have increased the number of target firms and were able to cover most of the Japanese semiconductor firms that have made inroads into America. This enabled us to conduct our analysis from a wider range of viewpoints. Three transplants, SB, SD, and SE, were the target of both studies. To these we added three transplants, SA, SC, and SF, of three additional firms and a new plant, SG, of a firm previously studied.

First, let us survey the local production of these targeted semiconductor firms by means of Table 6–7. The transplants of these firms, with the exception of SA, a middle-sized firm that moved into Silicon Valley in 1971, all belong to major manufacturers that advanced into America immediately before or at the very beginning of the period when Japanese-U.S. semiconductor friction was starting to make itself felt. These plants started up roughly in two periods; SC, SD, and SE started in the period between the end of the 1970s and the beginning of the 1980s. SF and SG

Table 6–7. Profile of Japanese-Owned Semiconductor Plants in the United States

Plant	SA	SB	SC	SD	SE	SF	SG
Location	California	California	Texas	California	California	North Carolina	Oregon
Start of Operation	April, 1971	Dec., 1978[a]	May, 1979	April, 1980	May, 1981	1986	Nov., 1988
Mode of entry	Wholly-owned/ GF	Wholly-owned/ GF	Wholly-owned/ GF	Wholly-owned/ AQ	Wholly-owned/ GF	Wholly-owned/ GF	Wholly-owned/ GF
Investment ($m.)	N.A.	120	22	N.A.	55	150	25
Employees	577	750	318	205	314	500[c]	355[d]
Products	ASIC various ICs	256KDRAM, 256KSRAM, ASIC, Logic	256K· 1MDRAM 64K· 256KSRAM[b] Logic	1MDRAM, ASIC (sample), 16K· 64K· 256K, SRAM, Logic	1MDRAM, 256K· 512KEPROM, 4K· 16KECL, Hybrid IC	256K· 1MDRAM, Memori-modules, ASIC	256KDRAM, 1MDRAM (in preparation), ASIC
Processes	Pre-process	Pre-process and assembly	Pre-process and assembly	1MDRAM: Assembly ASIC: Pre-process and assembly	Assembly	Memori and ASIC: Pre-process and assembly	Memori:Pre-process and assembly ASIC: latter part of pre-process and assembly
Capacity (m. units)	$50m(value)	60	N.A.	12.6	About 20	35	—**e

Notes: As of 1989 summer. Based on various data from interviews and other resources furnished by each firm. GF:Greenfield AQ: Acquisition
[a] Acquisition of a U.S. firm. Construction of SB began Oct., 1982. Operation started in 1984.
[b] Integrated production of SRAM began at May, 1989. Assembly only for 1MDRAM.
[c] Includes 90 part-timers.
[d] Includes 35 part-timers. Plants were in set-up.
[e] No single indicators.

began operations in mid-1980. However, SB's parent company achieved its inroads through the acquisition of an American enterprise at the end of the 1970s, so it has a relatively long experience in local semiconductor production. SA and SD are located in Silicon Valley. SB is located in California, comparatively close to Silicon Valley, while SE is further south. All the rest are far away from Silicon Valley; SD is in Texas, SF in North Carolina, and SG in Oregon.

All these plants are 100 percent owned by their respective parent companies in Japan either directly or indirectly (ownership via a local sales company, etc.). This is characteristic of the semiconductor industry. In terms of employees, SD is the smallest in scale with approximately 200 employees. SB is the largest, with a workforce of approximately 750, and when SB's 4M DRAM plant starts up, another 400 or so will be added. The size of the workforce in the other plants is somewhere between 300 and 400, which is about average. At any rate, these plants are smaller in scale than there counterparts in Japan.

The Japanese companies hold an edge over the American manufacturers in memory chips. The position in the market held by Japanese and American firms was reversed when the switch was made from 64K to 256K chips, and by the time of the 1 megabit chips, the Japanese position had become unassailable. In recent years, American firms have withdrawn from the memory business one after another. At the same time, Japanese firms are expanding into the Application Specific IC (ASIC), the CPU and logic IC business, considered the strongholds of American firms. Reflecting this situation, the main product line of transplants, generally centered on memory chips in the mass-production of which Japanese firms have the technological edge, is in the process of shifting from the 256K DRAM to the current 1M DRAM. And some transplants also manufacture SRAM, and EPROM and logic IC, or both. There are already two companies that plan to start production of 4M DRAM in the near future, and SB had a new plant under construction at the time of our survey. We see signs that the production of ASIC is increasing, which appear to be a growing recent trend, although at present the relative weight of ASIC in the total production volume is rather small compared to memory chips.

With the exception of SA, the production lines of these transplants mainly consist of the downstream process, that is, the assembly process. There is a move underway to shift the preprocess, wherein silicon wafers are fabricated into semiconductor chips, to local facilities. SB especially has been the earliest to carry out the full integration of production processes. SD and SF also are partially operating preprocesses. SG, which has the same parent company as SE, was newly built with the express purpose of running the preprocess in North America. It started partial operations in the fall of 1988, and at the time of our investigation, it was at the stage where the test production was already underway and preparations for mass production were in progress. On the other hand, since from the beginning SA advanced into Silicon Valley, with the acquisition of American semiconductor manufacturing technology as one of objectives, it operates the preprocess in America, and the downstream process (assembly) in Japan and Southeast Asia (parent company and affiliates). In this, it follows the same pattern as the American semiconductor manufacturers. SB also relies on a plant in Singapore for three-fifths of its assembly work, then ships it all back to America again. Operations at the other transplants are primarily based on the downstream process.

None of the transplants have a union, and this is characteristic of labor relations in semiconductor transplants in comparison with the other industries. This parallels the lack of a union in virtually all American semiconductor firms.

General Characteristics: Predetermined Adaptation

In the application-adaptation relationship, the semiconductor industry has the characteristic of "result bringing-in and method-adaptation". The overall average application-adaptation rating of the semiconductor transplants is 3.2, which falls almost in the middle between auto parts (3.6) and auto assembly (3.5) on the application side, and consumer electronics (2.7) on the adaptation side. It is below the industrywide average by only 0.1 point. Thus, in the semiconductor industry, application and adaptation nearly balance each other, with a slight edge toward the adaptation side.

The group average application ratings are higher than in other industries for III, Procurement, and VI, Parent-Subsidiary Relations, and equal to or slightly below the industry-wide averages for the other groups. Especially, for Procurement, the semiconductor industry average is 3.5, higher by 0.5 than the industrywide average of 3.0. (See Table 6–8.) This contrasts with the low 2.6 of consumer electronics, and is one of the striking characteristics of semiconductors. Auto assembly and auto parts have almost the same ratings as the industrywide average for this group. Also, Parent-Subsidiary Relations at 3.9 exceeds the industrywide average by 0.3 point. I, Work Organization and Administration, is at the same level as the industry-wide average, and the other ratings are below the industrywide averages. The negative disparity is largest (-0.3) for IV, Group Consciousness, in particular, although this is not quite as large as in the case of consumer electronics. Group II, Production Control, comes next (-0.2 point), which places it at the same level as consumer electronics. The averages of group II are above the industry-wide average for both auto assembly and auto parts. However, there is little disparity among industries for this group. (see Figure 3–1).

Examination from a different angle using the human-results, material-results, human-method, and material-method of the 4-Perspective Evaluation reveals that the result bringing-in and method-adaptation type is a general characteristic of semiconductors. That is, on the one hand, ready-made production technology cultivated under the Japanese system is brought in as well as production equipment and components that embody Japanese expertise. Human talent that has incorporated the Japanese way of doing business is also brought in and by means of these, the prowess of individual companies is shown off in the new local environment. On the other hand but simultaneous with this, on the human and material-related control and operation side, local methods are assimilated. Features that appeared in the average ratings by groups are in close relation with these points.

The characteristic of the semiconductor industry from the perspective of the 4-Perspective Evaluation is that in comparison with the other industries, the material-results side has pushed up the application rating to the highest point, and that this industry, along with consumer electronics, is the most adaptive on the material

Table 6–8. Hybrid Evaluation in the Semiconductor Industry

	Semiconductor Average (A)	Average of 4 Industries (B)	(A) − (B)	Standard Deviation
I Work organization and administration				
① Job classification (JC)	2.7	3.7	1.0	1.03
② Wage system	3.1	2.4	−0.7	0.46
③ Job rotation (JR)	2.6	2.6	0.0	1.29
④ Education and training	3.0	2.9	−0.1	0.76
⑤ Promotion	3.1	3.1	0.0	0.64
⑥ First-line supervisors (or team leaders)	2.7	2.9	0.2	0.45
Average	2.9	2.9	0.0	0.52
II Production control				
⑦ Equipment	4.6	4.3	−0.3	1.05
⑧ Quality control (QC)	2.4	3.4	1.0	0.49
⑨ Maintenance	2.6	2.6	0.0	0.49
⑩ Operations management	2.9	3.0	0.1	0.64
Average	3.1	3.3	0.2	0.32
III Procurement				
⑪ Local content	3.7	2.6	−1.1	0.88
⑫ Suppliers	4.4	3.8	−0.6	1.05
⑬ Procurement method	2.3	2.5	0.2	0.70
Average	3.5	3.0	−0.5	0.43
IV Group consciousness				
⑭ Small group activities	2.4	2.5	0.1	0.90
⑮ Information sharing	3.3	3.6	0.3	0.88
⑯ Sense of unity	2.9	3.5	0.6	0.83
Average	2.9	3.2	0.3	0.59
V Labor relations				
⑰ Hiring policies	3.1	3.4	0.3	0.83
⑱ Job security	2.3	3.4	1.1	0.88
⑲ Labor unions	5.0	4.4	−0.6	0.00
⑳ Grievance procedures	3.6	3.3	−0.3	0.49
Average	3.5	3.6	0.1	0.35
VI Parent-subsidiary relations				
㉑ Ratio of Japanese expatriates	3.9	3.7	−0.2	1.36
㉒ Delegation of authority	4.0	3.6	−0.4	0.53
㉓ Managerial position of Americans	3.9	3.6	−0.3	0.35
Average	3.9	3.6	−0.3	0.73
VII Community relations				
㉔ Donations and volunteer activity	2.8	2.3	−0.5	0.40
Average	2.8	2.3	−0.5	
General average	3.2	3.3	0.1	0.29

method side. (See Figure 6–4.) These firms, like semiconductor manufacturing in general, tend to be highly dependent on equipment and manufacturing technology. It would seem that because of this dependence, these transplants bring in to their local sites the production technology built up in Japan, and the manufacturing equipment that embodies such technology, then try to display their prowess by relying on these. To manage this "hard" side, on the other hand, they opt for American-style management methods. Likewise, this can be observed in the "human" areas. The high application ratings there rank next to the auto parts industry. This means Japanese expatriate employees who have acquired Japanese methods play critical roles in a variety of stages in the operation and administration of the transplants. In the human-method, on the other hand, semiconductors leans slightly more to the side of application than does consumer electronics, but compared with the auto assembly and auto parts it is still on the side of adaptation. So it is closer to the local way in the methods of management concerning local human elements.

Reliance upon Japanese Manufacturing Technology: Overseas Transfer of Components and Equipment

Let us develop the "result bringing-in and method-adaptation type" characteristics of the semiconductor industry that have emerged in the above discussion even further, into clearer and multidimensional images, by means of the items of the "hybrid model."

First, the characteristics of "result bringing-in" from Japan may have to do with the fact that while developing local production that consists mainly of the secondary production process for standard memory products, the industry is simultaneously carrying forward the transfer of the preprocess.

The major manufacturers procure 70 to 90 percent of their parts and materials from Japan. Since wafer chips from Japan make up a considerable portion of the cost of the final product, when the proportion of the downstream process is high,

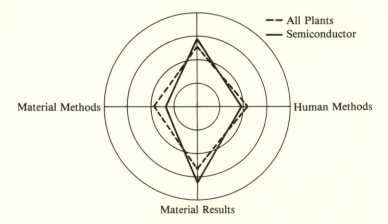

Figure 6–4 Four-Perspective Evaluation of Semiconductor Industry

the local content figure is low. On the other hand, it appears that most general supplies and machined products are procured locally. In many cases the gases and chemical products for the preprocess are locally supplied. There is a certain amount of procurement of wafers from American vendors, but the relative amount purchased from Japanese-owned local vendors is growing. Nevertheless, when still in the early phase, not long after start-up, for the preprocess also it is common to depend mostly on procurement from Japan. However, SA, as the exception (explained in 6D), uses local vendors for 70 percent of its procurement, and 70 percent of that is from American vendors. On the other hand, it is pursuing the application of Japanese-style methods in its procurement. So it is going in a direction opposite to that of the other major manufacturers.

The competitive edge of Japanese companies in the memory chip business resides in their superiority in mass production technology based on a superiority in the miniaturization technology. Moreover, in contrast to American semiconductor manufacturers that moved the highly labor-intensive downstream process overseas to achieve cheaper labor costs, the manufacturers in Japan have responded by promoting automation. Such automated machinery that incorporates their own expertise proves to be very powerful in operating the downstream process in the United States. It appears that major Japanese semiconductor manufacturers are attempting to maintain their predominance in manufacturing technology by bringing-in the production equipment, which itself is the embodiment of that very manufacturing technology.

Furthermore, in semiconductor manufacturing, the parameter setting and maintenance of equipment have particularly important effects on the yield. Even compared with the chassis assembly of the consumer electronics, in the downstream process there are more minute and precise working and inspection processes, and naturally there are a great deal more than in auto assembly or auto parts. In the operation of automated machines, the self-acquired know-how of individual plants based on hands-on operational experience greatly influences yield and productivity. In the wafer process (preprocess), this is particularly obvious, since the working tolerance in today's semiconductor manufacturing is reaching the submicron level, and the whole process consists of the accumulation 200 to 300 processes piled one on the other that require control at the atomic level. The "semiconductor-agriculture theory" that contends that semiconductor manufacturing is like agriculture, in that you cannot tell how it will come out until it is done, was emphasized at some of the companies that we covered in the current survey. Because of this particularity of the manufacturing technology, there is a keenly felt need to bring-in the system of manufacturing equipment for which the know-how has been well-established in Japan. Due to moves to shift the preprocess to the United States, and to upgrade products, the "result bringing-in" tendency can grow only stronger in the near future.

On the other side, due to this particularity of the industry, the ability to set equipment parameters at each working process and to find "abnormalities" in equipment operating conditions by local production workers has a extremely significant effect on yield, and the role of maintaining this manufacturing equipment, too, must increase in importance. We have seen "bringing-in" on the "hard" side, but to what extent is the Japanese way implemented on the side of management of the "hard" side at the local site? In fact, introduction of Japanese methods in this area is somewhat weak.

Adaptation Basis for Management of Personnel and Materials and Equipment

Materials and Equipment Management

According to the 4-Perspective Evaluation, the industry tends rather toward adaptation in the areas of "material" method. For the item ⑨ Maintenance, the semiconductor industry average is higher than consumer electronics, 2.1, but equal to the industry-wide average of 2.6. Little commitment of the production workers and a built-in structure that promotes reliance on the technicians of the technical department is the general pattern. Furthermore, generally the transplants are dependent on the outside labor market for their maintenance crew, and they are hired and treated in a way quite different than production workers. The industry average of ⑧ Quality Control is 2.4, which is the lowest both in absolute value and relative to the other industries. There is not much participation from floor workers. Since this industry is the technology-led type with its characteristically strong dependence on manufacturing devices and equipment, the role of the production workers in the manufacturing process is relatively minor compared to the other industries. According to the evaluation criteria of the hybrid model, it is a peculiarity of the material-related management side of the semiconductor industry to be construed as the adaptive type in the first place.

However, in actuality, the issues involved are not confined to these alone. As a matter of fact, several companies pointed out that the gaps between Japanese and American workers in their quality consciousness, perception of equipment problems, and intersection cooperation all effect product quality, yield, and productivity. And in reality, on the "hard" management side, in such areas as quality control, for example, Japanese expatriate employees take on the role of supplementing the weaknesses of the local system, directly and indirectly, and in this regard, dependence on Japan is very strong.

For the semiconductor industry, the average rating of VI, Parent-Subsidiary Relations, is second only to that of III, Procurement, in the amount it exceeds the industry-wide average, and ranks second to the auto parts industry. By individual items, the average rating for delegation of authority (4.0) is the highest, on a par with auto parts. There is a tendency for important management decisions, such as capital investments, decisions on products and markets, and personnel matters, to take place at the parent company in Japan. ㉓ Managerial Position of Americans is in second place (differing 0.1 point from its average in auto parts), and ㉑ Ratio of Japanese Expatriate Employees is also slightly behind auto parts, but higher than that of auto assembly (by 0.1 point).

With such close relations with Japan on the side of managerial organization, and so intimately dependent on Japan for components, materials, and manufacturing equipment, the extent to which localization has penetrated business decision making and managerial organization is also small. In the semiconductor industry, dependence on Japan is high on both the human and the material side, although it dependence on Japan is high on both the human and the material side, although it naturally differs from one firm to another. The ratings of SA, SB, and SE are below the industry-wide average. All of them started local production fairly early, and have accumulated experience doing business in the local environment. This would seem to have something to do with the low ratings. In fact, even with the same parent company, the recently built SG plant has high ratings. Nevertheless, SC, with an equally long operating experience, is highly dependent on Japan. How to interpret this point remains a question. This company is working on ways to revise and restructure its local production. We need to take into consideration the connections that exist with this kind of corporate strategy. From one point of view, the scale of SA's parent company and the significance of its local production in corporate strategy are different than the other major manufacturers. This may be the reason for it. These points fall under a more detailed analysis of types and categories; here we are just pointing them out.

Personnel Management

In the semiconductor industry, the application rating is not necessarily high on the side of human-related management. The rating for I, Work organization and Administration, that is, the centerpiece of the Japanese-style management and production system, is lower than the industry-wide average by a mere 0.1 point, but there are clear distinctions at the individual item level.

First, the rating for ① Job Classification has the lowest rating relative to the industry-wide average (see Table 6-8), and the job classification system is of the American type. In general, within the realm of specificities, work is classified by jobs within each individual process, which are then divided into several levels of job grades. Job rotation is not so actively practiced, and tendency to maintain fixed jobs is strong. A team system like the use of job teams in Japan is generally weak. This is fairly obvious at SB, SE, and SF, but also can be observed in other plants to various degrees.

Second, ② Wage System, has the highest rating relative to the other industries, and approximates the Japanese type. This is just the opposite of the automobile industry, which has simplified job classifications and at the same time retains the wage system based on the nature of one's duties, and this is the characteristic of the semiconductor industry. (Actually, deviations by individual plants are great.)

All the plants without exception opted for a system of personnel performance evaluation or personnel assessment for use in determining wages. In any case, the form resembles the "performance evaluations" found in nonunion American companies, and in fact that is precisely what they are called at the transplants. The system uses a form that clearly indicates the objective criteria. The results of the evaluation are open to those evaluated in the sense that they are asked to put their own signature on them, and this is different than the way of handling the personnel performance evaluation in Japan. However, it is utilized for the determination of wages in every company, and to mention just those that we were able to check, SA, SC, and SG have adopted the range rate for each wage grade. Those ranges overlap. Thus, by the introduction of the performance evaluation, the human element is included in wage determination.

Furthermore, we notice among these wage-determining factors such expressions as "degree of difficulty of duties and years of service" (SA), "experience, knowledge, assessment of skills and ability" (SC), "experience and annual results (evaluation)" (SD), "job classification, experience and review" (SE), and "nature of duties and assessment" (SF). So in the determination of wages, experience or years of service has considerable importance attached to it. Instead of a simple wage system corresponding to the nature of duties, the semiconductor manufacturers, while having a fairly common system of job classifications in which a relatively detailed segmentation with high barriers between jobs is the norm, still opt for a method of wage determination that somewhat responds to the human aspect, including placing substantial importance on experience or years of service, through the performance evaluation.

Opinions may be divided as to whether or not such a wage system can be considered to be of the Japanese type or should be thought of as a pattern common to what are called American nonunion, high-tech firms, but for the moment we would like to consider it as being closer to Japan. To generalize about the semiconductor industry, we see that compared to the other industries, one of its characteristics is to have a job classification of the American type, and a wage system more like the Japanese type. Although the degree differs from plant to plant, when compared with auto assembly and auto parts where the wage system is overwhelmingly on the side of adaptation, semiconductor plants share a common tendency toward application. The job classification at SA and the wages at SF both are exceptions. On the other hand, SD has at once job classifications with low "barriers" between jobs, and a more or less Japanese type wage system, which are both on the application side.

Third, item ⑥, First-Line Supervisors, the center of control and operation of the Japanese system on the production floor, is slightly on the adaptation side reflecting the American character of the work organization and its administration. The semiconductor industry average is higher than consumer electronics but lower than auto assembly and auto parts, and -0.2 points below the industrywide average. In the work organization and its administration on the shop floor, the team system is not always adopted. In this regard, the supervisor's Japanese type function is weak. The function of a Japanese type supervisor is split into a leadman, who is supposed to be a veteran with hands-on experience of the jobs of the shop floor and who has primarily been trained within the company, and a supervisor who is a salary worker. Since a supervisor is not necessarily someone who has been promoted internally, the supervisor will usually have little hands-on experience of the job, and will function mostly on the side of personnel management. The function of technical control of the process also, in many cases, is entrusted to specialists, of industrial engineering (IE), for example. But, in those cases in which the barriers between job classifications are low and the development of multiskilled workers is attempted by means of limited job rotation, at SA, for example, more than half of the jobs are filled from promotions within the company, and the company is planning to further expand its internal promotion capability in the future. In the case of SD, internal promotion is mostly used to select leadmen from operators, and supervisors from leadmen. On the other hand, at SC, recruitment for the preprocess is from those with a college degree who have worked for another IC manufacturer, and for the downstream process, 70 percent are hired from outside.

So it is that "teams" that could act as a force to bind together workers' groups on the shop floor are ineffectual in this industry. And in fact, measures to promote voluntary participation among shop-floor workers are not much applied. The 2.9 industry average of IV, Group Consciousness, is the lowest relative to the industry-wide average. This is higher than the consumer electronics average by 0.6, but somewhat lower than the auto parts by 0.9. At the individual item level, this is due to the low rating of ⑭ Small Group Activities. However, this item is low for the other industries as well, all at around 2.0. The characteristic of semiconductors is to be found rather in low application ratings for ⑯ Sense of Unity and ⑮ Information Sharing (although it is still higher than consumer electronics). Overall, compared with auto assembly and auto parts, the application of measures to promote the group consciousness of employees is not actively pursued. Is this due to semiconductors particular tendency to be a technology-led type industry, or is it due to reasons related to American culture and society, or both?

At this point, only SA is carrying out small group activities. Here, too, these activities are carried out within normal working hours, and the rate of participation is 30 to 40 percent. Moreover, they are mainly under the initiative of the technical department, and said to be marked with a top-down character. Also, there are cases in which some activities used to be conducted but failed. In the case of SD, in spite a previous failure, certain activities were reinstated in March, 1989, and have been carried out since then with full participation. In operation since the spring of 1980, SD has many years of actual operation. It has exhausted, they say, its source for introducing technology from Japan, and the increases in yield have already been pushed to the limit. Therefore, out of the need to somehow increase the yield, again the decision was made to restart small group activities. This is probably because there are still some elements in semiconductor manufacturing that cannot be fully handled by the technology alone, and thus it was necessary to improve the quality consciousness and problem solving ability of the workers. In fact, although it is not an absolute rule, it appears that the longer the operational experience of a transplant that is supposed to be fairly progressive in the transfer of technological aspects from Japan, the stronger the willingness to introduce these activities. SB is seeking to enhance problem-solving ability through "horizontal connections" problem-solving teams, while SC, although with no ongoing activity at present, is showing its willingness to engage in such programs. SE has demonstrated interest in reopening the program, based on its experience of failure in the past. On the other side, at SF and SG, no small group activities currently exist, and at present there is no indication that any will be adopted.

It seems to be a given reality that Japanese-style small group activities are difficult to bring about despite a willingness to do so. Whether or not the reason for this can be found in the cultural and social characteristics of the workers in America will need further reflection, as stability is gained in the other industries. At any rate, for semiconductors, it is at least certain that this issue corresponds to the weakness of the "team system" in the shop-floor work organization and its administration.

There are many cases in which a suggestion system is introduced instead. Also, information sharing through meetings at various levels tends to be widely practiced. Measures to foster a sense of unity, such as open-style offices and events promoting friendship, have been introduced to some degree, with objectives that include heightening the group consciousness and sense of unity, and listening to opinions from the shop floor so that they may be taken into consideration in labor relations. One plant carries out small group activity sessions between the staff of the personnel department or the president and all the production workers.

In this way, we can say that overall the semiconductor industry is at a stage of technology transfer where it is attempting first of all to materialize in America the manufacturing technology proven in Japan. Although the industry is aware of the necessity of the application of the Japanese method to the human management method side, due to its particularity of being a technology and equipment-led industry, it has left this problem for the future.

However, ④ education and training is considered as a supplement to this. The 3.0 industry average is almost identical with the industrywide average (+0.1 point). It is lower than auto assembly (3.4), but higher than the 2.9 of auto parts that equals the industry-wide average. Also, it is sufficiently higher than consumer electronics (2.2). All individual plants, except SB and SE, which are low, are above the industrywide average. In this industry, plants do not necessarily have a system of training skilled workers on the shop floor, centered around OJT combined with job rotation. Rather, they send key personnel to Japan for training. In general, because of dependence on Japan for technology, technicians are sent to Japan for training and from Japan to coach.

Another important point on the personnel management method side is that the labor relationship that comprises the framework for the above method is what is called the nonunion American type. None of the plants have a union, and the industry average for ⑲ Labor Unions is 5.0, top position among the industries. On the other hand, the industry average for ⑱ Job Security is, although slightly higher by 0.1 point than consumer electronics, considerably lower than auto parts (5.0) and the auto assembly (4.2), and very much on the adaptation side. This is a major characteristic of the semiconductor industry. SA, partly due to its length of years of operation, resorted to layoffs five or six times in the past, and SD and SE carried out layoffs in 1985 and 1987, respectively. There have been no layoffs in the other plants, and they appear to want to avoid them as much as possible, although no overt statement has been made that guarantees this. When the cases of actual layoffs are taken into account, it rather closely resembles the American system. This is probably due to the industrial particularity observed in these targeted semiconductor transplants, where on the one hand they have a system of job classifications with comparatively high "barriers" between jobs, and on the other hand they have been under severe pressure from the product-market cycle, called the "silicon cycle." This, too, exemplifies the characteristic of this industry to incline in the direction of adaptation in the area of personnel management.

Summary

The local production of semiconductors by Japanese firms in America is focused mainly on the downstream process, with memory chips as the main product in which Japan holds an edge. In order to allow Japan's strength to truly develop on

American soil, these Japanese firms are bringing-in the manufacturing technology, manufacturing equipment, and related know-how together with components and materials, that has proven itself already in Japan. On the other hand, in spite of such close technological dependence on Japan, the production system on the manufacturing floor itself is not necessarily being advanced through the application of the Japanese method, but shows a strong American character. But, a tendency to push forth the application of Japanese methods on the personnel management side, which is connected with the introduction of Japanese elements, can be observed for the wage system. The specifics of these items give rise to the average picture of the semiconductor industry as belonging to the "result bringing-in and method-adaptation type" when viewed from the perspective of the 4-Perspective Evaluation. Also, in general, the degree of "application" for the semiconductor industry is higher than consumer electronics but lower than automobiles, determine its overall position in the middle.

Finally, let us take a look at the significance that the local production of semiconductors, marked by such characteristics in its development, holds in the American semiconductor market. Japanese semiconductor manufacturers are not only the major suppliers of the world's semiconductor market, but also have appropriated a fair share of the most powerful market, the American market. In 1989, all Japanese manufacturers together held a 25.5 percent share of the American open market, excluding products used within their own companies. We are not able to determine the proportion of local production in that figure. But in the largest case of an individual company for which data are available, local production shared the market fifty-fifty with imports from Japan. At the very least, local production constitutes about 10 percent. We can assume that the others lie somewhere between these two figures. This also means that the relative weight of local production of semiconductors on the American market falls in the middle, between auto assembly and consumer electronics.

In the current semiconductor business slump, there is even some indication of a possible resurgence of U.S.-Japanese friction concerning semiconductors. In some situations, we also see a lower market share for Japanese companies in the American market for DRAM and some other items. In the midst of such a situation, by promoting the transfer of the preprocess, preparing for 4M DRAM production, and finalizing building plans for new full-scale memory plants, we can expect local production to increase in its importance in the American market.

Given this state of affairs, will the application of Japanese methods intensify, with human factors becoming important for the improvement of quality and productivity, and Japanese "superiority" turned into reality in America, thanks to the transfer of Japanese manufacturing technology? Or, will the existing tendencies described above be reinforced, depending on such tendencies as the necessary transfer of new manufacturing technology brought about by the further increase in the integration densities of memory chips, or the changeover of local production to a fully integrated production process as the preprocess is shifted to local facilities, or a shift of focus to higher value-added products like semicustom and custom products? This, and the connections with those differences that stem from the different types of individual companies and plants that have already emerged, will require further examination.[4]

COMPARISON BETWEEN THE FOUR INDUSTRIES

At last, while looking back over the characteristics of auto assembly, auto parts, consumer electronics, and semiconductors, the four industries that we have been analyzing, we would like to briefly compare one industry with another and thus bring this chapter to an end.

The most remarkable characteristic of the auto assembly industry is the high application ratings at each individual plant for each of the groups in the hybrid evaluation, and the high application ratings for method in both human and material aspects. The fundamental factor for this can be found in the Japanese production system itself, for which superiority in competitiveness depends heavily on human-related elements. But for auto assembly, such a tendency is especially strong. In other words, the auto assembly plants cannot really show their strength without active participation in shop-floor operations and the development of broad skills, not only by technicians like maintenance personnel, but also by the production workers themselves, or without the flexible management of a plant that is based on these. And this particularly applies to an industry that embraces such a multitude of various-sized parts, which not only further complicates production control within a plant, but also makes the stable and efficient relations with parts vendors in regard to quality and delivery an indispensable precondition for smooth plant operation. We can say that for these reasons, a strong inclination toward Japanese method application emerges on both the human and material-related sides in the core of the production system inside and outside of the auto assembly plants.

At the same time, when transplanting the Japanese system into the core of plant operations, the question of how to nurture the local soil so that it will best facilitate the transplantation process is of the utmost importance. It is in this light that high application for IV, Group Consciousness, and V, Labor Relations, can be best understood.

Local production by the Japanese parts manufacturers is the way to definitively and efficiently solve the problem of proceeding with the localization of procurement while simultaneously striving for the application of Japanese methods. The local production of auto parts transplants started precisely out of such considerations. Therefore, either in view of the strength of the organized ties between auto assembly manufacturers and parts suppliers in Japan, or the indigenous requests for such local production, it is only to be expected that the application ratings of the auto parts industry would be high, following the example of the auto assembly transplants. Or, if we focus only on the application ratings themselves, the auto parts industry appears to have an inclination toward application that exceeds even that of auto assembly.

However, a closer look at the contents of these application ratings reveals some nonnegligible differences. Simply put, in the case of auto parts, the difference is the high dependence on Japan on the material side centered on production equipment and on the high application rating for the parent-subsidiary relations, which is symbolized by an extremely high ratio of Japanese expatriate employees rather than personnel management methods; in other words, on the strength of authority on the Japanese side. It is a reasonable assumption then, that local production is supported by a very strong tendency to bring-in ready-made material (material-results application) and by dispatching expatriate Japanese employees to lead plant management under the control of the parent company (human-results application).

Contrary to auto assembly and auto parts, the consumer electronics industry, of which the main activity is centered on producing color TVs, is characterized by its remarkably low application ratings. And these low ratings are most obvious in those areas related to personnel management methods, such as work organization and its administration, group consciousness, and labor relations. This may be fundamentally due to the fact that with the exception of picture tube plants, the local production operation is limited to the final assembly process. This limitation obviates the need for highly skilled production workers and maintenance crews because of the simplicity of the process and equipment. Above all, there is also no need for many engineers. In this way it is possible to achieve a level of quality and efficiency that are almost as good as plants in Japan, without sticking too much to Japanese methods in such areas as the development of skills, as long as the equipment is securely in place, the quality control of parts is performed as it should be, and personnel control is carried out properly with clearly defined individual responsibilities. This accounts for the lower application ratings on the side of personnel management in the core.

In the consumer electronics industry also, direct and indirect dependence on Japan is high as far as the production equipment and functionally critical components are concerned, and this constitutes an important pillar in the support of the local production. Also, in the areas of group consciousness and labor relations, that are more directly connected with the sense of values and behavioral patterns of the local society, the inclination toward local adaptation tends to be stronger than is indicated in the low application ratings of the core. It is characteristic of consumer electronics, with its relatively long history in local operations and its localization of management, to be one step ahead of the other industries in its attitude toward local adaptation, as is shown, for example, in its low ratio of Japanese expatriate employees.

The average of application ratings of the semiconductor industry fall in the middle between auto parts, with the highest score, and consumer electronics with the lowest. In addition, its ratings by groups also show a mixture of the characteristics of these two industries. Personnel management methods as, for example, work organization and its organization, have low application ratings similar to consumer electronics. On the other hand, on the side of material-results, including production equipment and parts, its dependence on Japan is high, even higher than in auto parts. The application rating for parent-subsidiary relations is also high, also similar to auto parts.

Finally, it boils down to two fundamental points. One is that in the semiconductor industry, there is a strong tendency to be led by technology. Another is the size of the transplants, which are much smaller than plants in Japan. The production of semiconductors is characterized first of all by the repetition of intricate processes, which make full use of advanced, high-precision machinery. This means that the engineers and the skilled technicians who maintain and adjust the equipment on the shop floor play markedly greater roles than the production workers who perform the simple repetitive tasks. So although the reasons are different than those in consumer electronics, there is very little motive to forcibly introduce Japanese methods in the area of personnel management when the focus is mainly on the production workers. On the one hand, because Japan has an overwhelming edge in the production of memory chips, which is the essential activity of the transplants, and also because the number of technical personnel and their level of expertise are limited due to the scale of the transplants, there is a strong tendency to greatly increase technological dependence on Japan. Furthermore, this is an industry where technical innovation is moving forward at an extremely rapid pace, to the point where even the cause and effect relationship that underlies fluctuations in yield is left totally unclarified, and this spurs on the tendency to want to use parts and equipment that match those of the parent factory in Japan as much as possible. It is also certainly the case that in tandem with the effect of the scale of the transplants, this high degree of dependence on Japan for technology also has something to do with the strong authority wielded by the Japanese parent companies.

7

Types of Japanese Factories Located Overseas

HIROSHI KUMON
KUNIO KAMIYAMA
HIROSHI ITAGAKI
TETSUJI KAWAMURA

In this chapter we attempt to describe the Japanese transplants in terms of a number of patterns in each industrial sector, while focusing on the differences between companies within each of the industrial sectors: auto assembly, auto parts, consumer electronics, and semiconductors. In particular, we shall focus on differences in the application-adaptation balance of the twenty-three items of the hybrid model, as well as on differences and characteristics in the ways human and material elements are transferred in terms of the 4-Perspective Evaluation. By identifying the specific patterns of individual companies, we can better highlight the characteristics of each industrial sector from many angles. This approach will help us simultaneously to identify those patterns that apply to the Japanese corporations that are operating local production facilities in America (the subject of the next chapter) and to study the strong points and problems that each of these patterns implies.

FACTORY TYPES IN THE AUTOMOTIVE ASSEMBLY INDUSTRY

Here we pick six auto assembly plants and present their respective characteristics. In doing so, we will see that the strategies adopted by the parent companies in their advance into North America have shaped the patterns of each of these plants.

Characteristics of the six plants can be stated at the outset. The AA Plant is the Japanese-led high application type. This plant is typical of the auto assembly industry, with its high application/method application approach that has been realized by dispatching massive numbers of Japanese expatriate personnel. By so doing, they have attained the current high level of localization. The AB Plant is the American-led application type. It is 100 percent owned by a Japanese firm, but with Americans given the top plant management positions. The AC Plant, the application-adaptation combined type, is a joint venture with an American company and unionized. It Actively pursues the application of Japanese methods. The AE Plant, the revised method application type, applies Japanese methods after they have been revised in accordance with the experience of others who have made their advance into the United States so as to adjust them to the local business management environment. The AF Plant, the production equipment-led type, is keen to introduce robotics into the assembly line, the most difficult process to automate in an American plant. Finally, the AD Plant is the site adaptation type. On the one hand, it alone is located in Michigan and has accepted labor unions. On the other hand, its number of Japanese expatriates and the amount of Japanese-made equipment installed at its facilities is relatively large.

High Application Type Based on Japanese Personnel: Factory AA

AA is characterized by the fact that it consistently pursues the transfer of manufacturing technology and management control systems by means of a great number of Japanese expatriate. Because this pattern can be relied on for the effective application of Japanese-style management to a transplant and AA has followed it in every way, it can be said to be typical of those types of Japanese corporations that have made inroads overseas. Its success in such a strategy, coupled with the fact that the company's products have gained a high reputation in the American market, enabled the plant to outdistance its contenders in expanding production capacity, as well as in localizing engine production. Also, its degree of recognition in America is high.

As mentioned before, AA Plant is characterized by its high number of Japanese expatriate employees. This no doubt stems from the fact that AA was the first plant to establish itself in America having bet its corporate fortunes on the move. Since then, it has been applying Japanese things to the local site, trying to find its way through practical experience because there was no model to follow. This approach is costly but would surely lead us to expect positive results. Japanese expatriate employees at AA number 350, the highest among Japanese automobile transplants. In addition, there are 200 temporary assignees meant to stabilize operations at its secondary facilities. Contrary to most of the Japanese-owned enterprises that claim they intend to try to turn over the management to the top local executives as soon as possible, this plant asserts that 4 to 5 percent of its total work force will continue to be Japanese expatriates for some time. Japanese involvement is high in the area of management control. That is, there is a higher than average chance that Japanese will be in charge of management-control organizations. Americans and Japanese are paired throughout all departments, except for the public relations section, which is headed by an American. In the other companies in which general manager positions are filled by Americans but where, in many cases, Japanese are assigned as advisors, the practical effect is virtually the same as if these positions were filled by Japanese. However, in AA, the Japanese and American managers are paired; thus the Japanese participation is more thorough. On the shop floors also, there are a number of Japanese coaching jobs, and we especially noticed a predominance of these on the inspection line. From now on, AA will have to address the subject of closer Japanese and American contact in carrying out the transfer of methods. Japanese expatriates will be asked to have contacts with Americans over a broader scope, so that the transfer that has thus far centered around technology will shift to the level of overall management, while American managers will be asked to acquire localized management techniques. They will have to improve the management capability of the American top management through a "tug-a-war" process between Japanese and Americans. This will enable the Americans to advance and will promote the transfer of actual power to them. In addition, it will alleviate the burden of high labor costs due to the expatriate Japanese personnel. In the future their agenda will be the stabilization of business administration through localization of management control.

The selection of the plant site and hiring practices also reflect the philosophy of the plant. In selecting a site, factors such as transportation, parts supply, environmental restrictions, available workforce, and so on were also taken into account. Particularly in regard to the human issue, the emphasis was placed on behavior and work ethics, and so forth. They chose a rural area of Ohio where the workers are from rural communities that put a high value on hard work and have a low population turnover rate. AA utilizes a unique hiring method. Unlike other Japanese transplants, which place an interview at the final stage of a series of tests, in this plant they proceed with interviews repeatedly, through which they judge a candidate's aptitude for the team system and toward company rules like attendance. In regard to hiring, however, the plant has been called to task by government authorities concerning its low hiring rate for minorities; they are correcting this now. Specifically, they modified their hiring policy to expand the area from which people are hired and have begun to hire minorities in proportion to applicants, thereby complying with the actual level of enforcement of the equal opportunity employment law. To better implement the team system, they set aside a total of 15 minutes at the beginning and ending of the shift to conduct a meeting, and clean up and check parts for the following shift. The plant was successful in urging the employees to reject the UAW's effort at unionization by means of such measures as job involvement and creating a sense of unity among the workers. But then AA pays wages comparable to those of the UAW, rather higher than the local standards.

For a while after the start of operation, the main focus at AA had been on technology transfer. But in recent years it has built a training center, and is carrying out a wide range of educational activities. This is a full-scale effort, with special focus on training leaders. Even now, each year team leaders are sent to Japan for training. This would seem to us to agree with their policy to achieve a reliable transfer of technology even if it costs more money.

Next, let us look at the actual performance of the plant operation, at localization and its move toward relative independence of the parent company. Since the start-up of automobile production, AA has proceeded step by step in a very orderly manner, and is not only expanding its production capacity, but also it is on its way to becoming a complete automobile business comprised of research and development, manufacturing, and sales. The motorcycle has bestowed upon its parent company an absolute advantage over other Japanese assembly plants, and indeed it successfully advanced into America on the basis of its motorcycle operation at first. Then, in 1982, it started to produce automobiles. In 1985, it began manufacturing motorcycle engines, and then automobile engines in the following year. As the value of its products rose in the American market, it built a second production line in its auto plant and began production. Nothing could better demonstrate its advanced approach and its relative independence from its parent company, than its "five point plan in North America," made public simultaneously in Japan and America in September, 1987. The plan, targeting 1991, consisted of the expansion of automobile production capacity to 510,000 units through construction of a second plant, the attainment of 75 percent local content in parts through expanded capacity in the engine production facilities in coordination with the former point, beefing up the engineering affiliate as well as product research and development, and expanding exports. This demonstrated that the company was committed, not only to increase its automobile production capacity, but also to the autonomous development of products and sales in the United States. In the middle of the company's vast land holdings equal to that of Setagaya ward of Tokyo, a world-class test course is located. Opposite the first plant, across the test course, a second plant is under construction. We could not help but feel that their plan was proceeding in a successful manner. It is estimated that AA will employ 10,000 people.

Application Type Based on American Personnel: Factory AB

In contrast with AA, AB Plant is characterized by the fact that the management of the plant has been given over to Americans. However, it does not mean that the plant is opting for the traditional methods of American management. Rather, a mixed new management method is beginning to emerge that reflects elements from the history of the American auto industry, and what Americans have been able to understand of Japanese methods. Japanese expatriates normally number fourteen; however, because a second line was under construction within the plant, at the time of our visit the number was twenty. We were told that the number of Japanese would be reduced again at the completion of the plant expansion. This sort of thorough localization of the management class is a particularity of AB. There is no other case that fits this pattern among the Japanese auto transplants. In other words, instead of plant management by Japanese, a surer method of application, this plant has chosen to apply methods by local people, thus placing the priority on human localization. It is blazing a trail, so to speak, that other transplants will adopt in the future. The adaptation aspects of its management were more noticeable than in other transplants.

Since the plant is 100 percent owned by a Japanese corporation, the five board member positions are all securely held by Japanese, with the exception of one, which is held by an American, who is also the president. However, the management class is left in the hands of Americans. The president and five vice-presidents are all Americans. There is only one Japanese vice president, as an advisor. Thus, the roles played by Japanese are limited in comparison with other transplants. Unlike other Japanese transplants, it has Americans placed at the head of all sections. This is due to the strategy of the head office, namely, to localize management from the beginning. They hired a then-vice president of one of the Big Three for the post of the first president. He put into operation management methods he learned from visiting factories in Japan, in addition to his experience in American auto plants. For this reason, now we see his legacy, a mixture of elements from Japan with slight variations and those that have been put into effect after his exit from the post. The current president is a person whom he brought with him when he left the American firm.

There are a number of systems that have been put into operation under the leadership of the former president. Of these, we can cite simplified job classification. We are told that this was carried out under his strong initiative, based on his experience in American auto facilities. Other examples are different uniforms for white collar and for blue collar workers, common cafeterias for all personnel, company meetings, and so forth. Vice-presidents and up have their individual office rooms, although in general, the open-style office arrangement prevails. However, in most cases there is a partition between desks, so unlike other Japanese auto transplants, this is not a fully open style.

The wages are based on the nature of one's duties, but 2.5 years after being hired anyone may become eligible to receive pay for versatility (50 cents/hour). This pay implies that the employee is able to perform five to six different jobs. In fact, however, almost everyone receives it. In that respect at least, its role in promoting the change toward more multiskilled workers can be acknowledged. Moreover, everyone is given a bonus. The combined income of wages (based on one's job classification) and bonuses reaches a level comparable to that of the UAW, we were told.

Promotion from a technician (production worker) to a leader is based on the principle of promotion from within the company, but involves an interesting method. At first, general technicians recommend a fellow worker to be a leader. Then the manager makes a decision. In this regard, other Japanese auto transplants either follow the vacant position method or the immediate superior's recommendation method. Plant AB, on the other hand, opted for its own method that requires the recommendation of fellow technicians. There are six steps in the process of promoting someone to the position of an area manager, who supervises team leaders. These consist of tests, interviews, education, and training. A recommendation from colleagues and the manager is one of the requirements after application for the vacant post, the first step, has been taken.

Next, by examining its production equipment, engine supply, and how it established standards for operations, we can clearly see where it has adapted to local conditions. The stamping equipment and the car body welding processes is Japanese made. The painting line equipment is made in the United States, and the assembly line also is mainly composed of American components. To date the plant has been importing passenger cars engines from its Mexican plant, and engines for trucks from Japan. From now on, truck engines will be imported from both Japan and Mexico, while all passenger car engines will be built in this plant. This signifies a further advance in the local production of engines, including imports from the Mexican facilities. As for the method of establishing operation standards, the work of individual technicians is determined by industrial engineering experts; in short, it follows the American system. In this, then, we felt they had something in common with plants of the Big Three, that is, a relatively long cycle-time, slow speed production lines, and a relatively high number of unattended cars moving on the line. These points made us wonder if the plant has not achieved the Japanese level of productivity, as a result of American management.

The UAW launched a full-scale attempt to unionize the plant in 1989. But the employees turned it down. The main issues were line speed and occupational accidents. Apparently management made counterarguments by presenting certain facts. The plant has an expansion project underway targeted for 1992. Its capacity will increase from 260,000 units to 440,000 units. To accomplish this, the plant will be expanded in all areas. AB will expand and include the stamping, welding, painting, and assembly lines within the same plant facilities.

Application–Adaptation Combination Type: Factory AC

AC Plant, a joint venture with an American company, is of the application-adaptation combined type. It shows the application of Japanese methods in the work organization and in job commitment, while displaying local adaptation in such areas as site selection, the labor union, and the composition of the management class. This type is common to those of companies (AF and AH) transplanted in the form of joint ventures with American partners. It is of particular interest that this is the first Japanese auto assembly transplant that accepted the UAW. Its labor contract and labor-management relationship framework has served thereafter as a model for those plants that did not reject unionization.

AC's pattern was defined by the parent company's strategy for moving into America. Its parent company in Japan was reluctant to accept the idea of local production in a developed country, whereas it regarded the Japanese domestic market as the most important. Nevertheless, after receiving pressure from America to engage in local production, and because its competitors had already proceeded along this line, it belatedly joined the group, typically the latest arrival among the top companies. And typically of its discreet approach, instead of going it alone, AC opted for a joint venture with an American company. The American firm, whose aim was to learn Japanese-style management through the joint venture, decided to leave the management of the plant in the hands of the Japanese partner. It was decided to utilize a plant that had been closed down by the American company. This plant was well known for its rough labor-management relationship and frequent strikes before it was closed down. Therefore, the Japanese took time to negotiate with the UAW beforehand, hiring an ex-Secretary of the Department of Labor as an intermediary and advisor. As a result of such cautious negotiations, they built a friendly relationship with the International UAW as well as with the union region. The parties agreed on a basic philosophy of mutual trust and cooperation between labor and management for the sake of increased productivity. Based on this, they reached an agreement on specific measures, such as hiring ex-union members with priority and job security, simplification of job classification, and adoption of a team system, promoting versatility among workers, and so on. Since in this way the same plant, that had been forced to shut down under American management, was able to succeed by using a combination of Japanese management with the same American workers. In a single bound it raised the opinion of Japanese-style management in the eyes of Americans. The reasons for its success probably cannot be boiled down to one. For the hiring of personnel, it did not automatically hire all the previous employees, but screened them carefully first. Furthermore, the UAW International was gradually coming more and more to see employment as the most important issue. These facts no doubt played an important role in the creation of a cooperative labor-management relationship. Nevertheless, still the single biggest reason may have been the fact that Japanese-style, hands-on, active involvement management approach that places a premium on job security had the advantage over traditional American authoritarian style management with its underlying threat of a layoff. The realization that a relative advantage was to be gained by management, conducted by Japanese executive officers, and combined with high quality and highly efficient automobile manufacturing technology is the real reason for its success.

The Japanese side had the responsibility to manage the plant, although the number of dispatched Japanese personnel is relatively low, numbering thirty-four, or 1.2 percent of the total workforce. This places AC in the middle between AA with many Japanese expatriates and the opposing case, AB with only a few. This is the type most frequently observed among Japanese-owned enterprises and, within this group, AC is among those with fewer Japanese expatriate employees. We were told that in the future a further reduction is in the works through enforcement of the education of the local managerial class.

AC has a labor contract with the union along the lines of generally resolving issues arising in labor relations within the company. New labor agreements have already been concluded, but the basic framework of labor relations has remained unchanged.

Let us take a moment to explain how they handle labor-management consultation and grievances. A labor-management consultation system has been put in place that offers a channel for talks as well as collective bargaining. Through this, a regular two-way discussion of the situation in both the corporation and the union can go forth and function very well as a mechanism for consultation between the two sides. As much as possible grievances are handled in the workplace through a discussion between a team leader or group leader and the workers instead of going through the union. It is therefore rare that a problem is handed over to an external arbitration organization. Also, they have set limitations on which items can be arbitrated, which exclude wages, production standards, the welfare program, health and safety, and other agreed-on items. However, as far as production standards are concerned, which is the issue most likely to be a bone of contention between labor and management in the automobile industry, if labor-management consultation does not yield a satisfactory solution, consultation with the American advisor at AC Plant (ex-Secretary of the Department of Labor) is allowed. And they may invoke the UAW regional representative. In the case of the Big Three, if labor and management cannot find a solution for a grievance concerned with production standards or health and safety through normal channels, the union reserves the right to resort to a strike while their contract is still in effect. However, at AC, the union cannot resort to a strike, and a grievance of this nature is not an item for arbitration, either. This is undoubtedly the reason one route is left open, that is, consultation with the American advisor and the regional representative in regard to production standards. A provision that the union renounces its right to strike regarding changes in production standards is commonly found in the labor contracts of all the Japanese auto transplants who have a union. This could be an indispensable condition for the implantation of a Japanese-style production system, which attaches such great importance to flexibility. However that may be, we found cases where we sensed that the relationship with the union was still at a very delicate stage. In answer to our question of whether it was possible to cut the number of workers once some had become well-versed in their job and had thereby generated spare time, we were told that it would be next to impossible because of the requisite negotiations with the union. Or, we find that because there is antagonism within the UAW regarding its course of actions, especially on the issue of joint participation in labor-management activities, even though a cooperative relationship has been established with the UAW International, a group at the local level may not agree with the position of the UAW International. Even at AC, for example, at the second term election for union officers, a group opposing the executives gained a certain number of committee members from the shop floor.

AC has established Japanese-style plant control methods. When the plant was reopened, a new stamping facility was constructed and robots from Japan were brought into the welding process. As much as possible the other equipment was utilized as it was, including equipment in the paint line. Therefore, AC is not actively bringing-in Japanese material, as plant equipment but plant control methods, on the other hand, such as production control and manufacturing control have become Japanese. For instance, by delegating the authority to stop the line to line workers, the process of problem solving by individual workers or by a team will gain ground. In the case of an American plant, designing of production standards is carried out by the IE section, but in this plant there is no such section. It is said that when it came time to make a full model change, operation standards were brought in from a plant in Japan that was producing the same model. These were given to the team leaders so that they could make their own, and it all went successfully. Another point, to achieve the production system particular to this company, maintenance is critical and therefore the number of maintenance personnel is relatively high. Also, to obtain an additional production of 100,000 pickup trucks annually to replace imports from Japan, in-house welding and assembly lines are under construction, and an additional paint facility will be built. The production is scheduled to start in the fall of 1991.

Modified System Application Type: Factory AE

AE represents the newest type of transplant. Here Japanese management is applied after revising it in accord with the local management environment. AE's Japanese parent company, based on its experiences with the AC Plant, in a joint venture with an American firm, built fully-owned plants in the United States and Canada. One of them, AE Plant, is actively planning and putting into operation measures in the areas of human resources management and production control peculiar to this company, with the aim of actually putting into practice a production system developed in Japan. Moreover, although AE is application intensive, it is characteristic of this plant that the application is not carried out directly, but is somewhat revised and adapted to the American environment. If the plant is opting for such a revised application, it is probably because AE prepared its management-control methods precisely in order to put into practice its own production system, while relying on the experiences of its forerunners and its own experiences in joint operation with an American firm. On the other hand, it did not fail to consider certain areas of the local business environment in its adaptation process. It is making a serious effort to hire minorities and women, taking the equal opportunity employment law into account, and is paying attention to improving cooperation with local communities. The site is located in a rural area not too far from the Kentucky state capital. It has integrated the processes of stamping, welding, painting, and assembly, has a plastic plant, and a test course all situated on its large piece of property. At the time of our survey, a power train plant was under construction for the production of functional parts, such as engines, and so on. Also, a new auto plant targeted for start-up by the end of 1993 of 200,000 units annual capacity will be built on the premises.

Japanese expatriates number seventy-two, representing 2.4 percent of all employees. These figures lie between AA and AB, and are within the range most frequently found among Japanese auto assembly transplants. In the management-control organization in charge of plant management, the president and one vice president are Japanese, and two vice presidents are Americans. Most of the Japanese, except a few general managers, are assigned as advisors to teach American general managers or section chiefs Japanese-style management methods and to serve as a communication channel with Japan. Unlike AC, where unionization was unavoidable because of the joint venture deal, because AE is managed by a single hand, there had been no union at the beginning and, by the time of our visit, there had been no attempt at unionization.

In the area of human resources management, in general, they are introducing Japanese practices that have been revised in the light of traditional American practice and systems. First of all, the company's prudent policy is shown in its management of hiring. Employees, and most of them are from the local state of Kentucky, are hired after going through 9 stages of careful examination. Not experience or skills but comprehension and potential are the most important hiring criteria. As a result, hourly workers with college degrees also increased. The intention of such hiring practices would appear to be the formation of multiskilled workers and the practice of *kaizen*. Moreover, employment of minorities and women has been actively promoted, and hired not only for general production positions, but also for maintenance positions. The company's unique production system requires a fairly high number of maintenance personnel in comparison with other companies. Second, its education and training program is interesting. As for maintenance, they conduct a systematic training program that attaches great importance to the development of multiskilled workers. In consideration of differences with maintenance workers in Japan who acquire intuition and ability through experience, they revised the basic plan that they had brought in from Japan, and drew up a new program jointly with the Americans, consisting of dividing maintenance tasks into 27,000 segments, and systematically arranging them in seven steps, to be acquired one after the other over a period of 3 years at the training center within the plant.

Third, they are pursuing unique experiments in wages. That is, the plant is unusual in that the evaluation of personnel performance is taken into consideration, although to a small degree, in determining wages. Although job rotation is employed with the goal of developing multiskilled workers and an equal distribution of jobs, a difference in degree of skill proficiency, disproportionate workloads, and also differences in working attitude remain. The personnel performance evaluation is used to reflect these in the wages. It does not affect the basic wage, but applies to a portion of the bonus. The basic wage is determined by one's duties, but the personnel performance evaluation plays a role in determining a portion of the biannual bonus. Basically, a bonus the equivalent of 15 percent of 6 months' earnings is paid. Of this, 14 percent is dependent on companywide productivity, quality, safety, and attendance, and 1 percent is determined by the personnel performance evaluation. In the performance evaluation, appraisal by the group leader and that by the worker each receive equal weight. The company intends to maintain its policy whereby the performance evaluation should apply to a portion of the bonus but not to the basic wage. However, it is utilized in one way or another for promotion.

Fourth, let's look at an aspect of the Japanese-style personnel rotation. Job rotation is supposed to be carried out on the authority of a group leader who holds the power to assign jobs. But in practice, it is the team leaders who give the orders. Within a team, jobs are rotated at 2-hour or 1-day intervals. For now the goal is for each worker to master two jobs. The group leader ranks each of the group members in skill proficiency on a scale of one to four. However, because unlike in Japan there exists a difference of wage levels between production and maintenance workers, they cannot create a *kaizen* team by combining these two groups, so they have formed a task force-type improvement team made up of maintenance workers. Unlike in Japan, promotion to team leader or group leader from the rank of production worker is not done on the basis of the recommendation of a direct supervisor. Instead, those who desire the promotion apply for a vacant position, and all applicants undergo training. Those with higher overall scores in training, performance, and in the interview are considered qualified. Management then determines from among these who will receive the promotion. Only in the case of a tie score is seniority taken into account. This could be called a Japanese-American mixed method.

In the United States, where the parts supply environment differs from Japan, AE is assigning more workers to production control than do plants in Japan, by "beefing up the logistics section to serve as a breakwater for the production section, so that production can make better use of Japanese methods." And gradually what is called the just-in-time system (JIT) is being introduced. Japanese-operated parts vendors are used first, and then American vendors. Further expansion of this system is expected. Inside the plant, AE is successfully applying the company's own "soft" production control techniques.

Production Equipment Intensive Type: Factory AF

AF is characterized by the fact that it actively pursued the automation of its assembly line by boldly introducing numbers of robots into the assembly process, the most difficult process to be automated. We prefer to regard it as a pattern wherein the predominance of production equipment in a transplant was given concrete expression. Moreover, this plant far exceeds the facilities of the Japanese parent company in level of automation. AF Plant is a joint venture between one of the Big Three and a Japanese company; therefore, a UAW local was established. The inevitability of unionization might have been one of the reasons a strategy of installing the most up-to-date production equipment at the transplant was adopted. In other words, the existence of a union could become a restricting factor to Japanese-style flexible personnel handling. Annual production capacity is 240,000 units. Total personnel numbers 2,800, which is considerably lower than other Japanese transplants of similar size and facilities. Here the figures show the results of the automation of the assembly line. Although this is a joint venture, the operation of the plant is entrusted to the Japanese side. More executives have been dispatched by the Japanese side, fifty-five, versus eleven from the American partner.

This plant hired maintenance workers before the start-up of operation, immediately sent them to Japan for an 11 month training course and paid special attention to preventative maintenance in instructing them. We can grasp the plant's strategy of the active introduction of robotics from the fact that they sent maintenance workers to Japan at the outset, whereas other Japanese transplants would send people of the leader-class to learn about team systems and operational techniques, or both. However, as automation is promoted in the assembly process, achieving a steady operation became the main concern. In fact, during our visit, the plant was trying to go into full operation with two shifts, and we sensed that they were running into the kind of problems common to all the highly automated factories. Also, we saw a number of cars in the repair area waiting for touch-ups.

After a careful study, the plant was built in a rural area, Bloomington-Normal, Illinois. The plant's facilities are structured around the stamping, welding, painting, and assembly processes. Generally speaking, the automation of three of these, stamping, welding, and painting, is attained almost at the same level by every company, but in the assembly process manual operations predominate. The plant boldly introduced robots into this assembly process, the last to be automated. Specifically, they installed a total of 120 robots throughout the trim, chassis, and final assembly processes, thus automating 22–25 percent of the assembly operations. The line is set up in such a way that manual and robot-run processes alternate. Car bodies are moved along the line by belt conveyors in the manual processes, and by shuttles in the robot processes. The line continuation is ensured by the transfer equipment installed between the conveyors and shuttles. Due to a need to increase the in-process workability for the reason of increased robot-run processes, they adopted a method whereby not only doors but also engine hoods are removed at the beginning of the trim process, and are replaced at the final assembly process by the time mounting operations in the engine room have been mostly completed. The highlight of robotics are the engine and front and rear suspensions mounting robots. That is, an engine and suspension parts come out in their respective positions corresponding to the specified areas at the front and rear of a car body, alongside the body that is laying on a dolly on the shuttle that is halted. They are then mounted to the body automatically. There is a subassembly line adjacent to the shuttle, which transports the parts. There is a group of twelve closely lined up robots having forty-five servo-axes in total, which handle this series of operations.

The labor contract with the union is basically the same as that of AC Plant. They have meetings on a regular basis at a company-wide and at departmental levels. A policy of resolving problems through consultations at the workplace is in effect although the items that may be arbitrated are limited. Production standards, wages, the welfare program, health and safety, and out-sourcing fall outside the range of items that may be arbitrated, and the union is not allowed to strike for these items. Although their labor contract is thus different than those of the Big Three, their labor-management relations are reportedly in good shape. Here are two cases in which we felt the presence of the union. The first one is that, unlike other factories, AF does not have a team leader system but salary-based group leaders who directly control twenty general associates (hourly wage earners) each. This is to avoid a possible situation in which the union could get involved in a matter relating to the promotion of the team leader, because a team leader is an hourly wage worker, and could become a union member. We are told that the direct control by group leaders was working well without problems. Incidentally, the door to promotion from an hourly status to a group leader is not through an application system. Rather a branch manager, an immediate superior, makes the recommendation, and the branch manager's superior, a general manager, approves it. Although this process does not involve Japanese-style workers' performance evaluation, in practice it is the individual's abilities that are evaluated. Second, we were told that job rotation within a group is acceptable, but once it goes beyond the group, the union voices opposition. We are told that it is difficult to carry out a workers' movement beyond the group boundary, even for other plants that do not have a union. AF is currently studying how to deal with this.

Location Adaptation Type: Factory AD

AD Plant is the only Japanese auto assembly facility built in Michigan, and it also accepted the union. It differs from other Japanese companies in that, located near Detroit, it does not employ a rural workforce. Although this is a completely new plant, AD opted for local adaptation in the matter of site location. On the other hand, and perhaps partly because of this, it carried out the human-material application by sending in a massive number of Japanese expatriates, and installing mostly Japanese-made production equipment. This is a unique pattern among Japanese auto manufacturers: Local adaptation in the site location and labor union, and application in human and material matters. AD is among those who joined the race late, starting its transplant operation in the latter half of the 1980s, with production beginning in September, 1987. After start-up, it swiftly revved up the rate of production. In June of the following year, it went to two shifts, and achieved full-time operation as early as September.

Japanese personnel number 219, which is high, superseded only by AA. Of those, 150 are stationed there, and the rest are trainers assigned to the plant on a short-term basis. The top management consists of the president and three vice presidents, all Japanese, and two American vice presidents, in charge of manufacturing and personnel affairs, respectively. In addition, there is a Japanese who has been given the position of representing the advisors.

For the plant site, they chose the previous plant site of an American corporation that has capital invested in their parent company in Japan. This is out of consideration for a condition that requires that "it has to market cars together with" that American firm. The main elements of the production equipment, such as the stamping presses, body construction equipment, welding robots, paint booths and ovens, deodorizing equipment, and paint and assembly robots, were brought from Japan. We noticed an interesting idea employed on its final assembly line. The assembly line is divided up into ten segments, and arranged in such a way that if one line stops it does not affect the other lines. And they have rationalized the parts supply so that it feeds from one side to every line, one after another. They are in the process of adopting methods of removing doors and reinstalling them at the final stage for the sake of workability like AA and AF do.

Next, let us look at particularities in AD's labor management and labor relations. Hiring is carried out by selection through a careful process of tests plus an interview, just as in the other Japanese transplants, with the emphasis placed on team activities. At first they hired experienced maintenance people, all holders of an apprentice card. Because they are located in Michigan, there were plenty of skilled workers, and so they hired them. The labor contract contains a provision for a training program for skilled labor, which will be followed from now on. As the urban workers are likely to take Monday and Friday off, management has ensured a smooth operation by setting up a pool of temporary workers to fill in on these 2 days. Wages started from a level slightly below that of the Big Three, and are supposed to catch up with them by the third and final year of the current labor contract.

As for the relations with the union, they nurtured friendly relations with the UAW International and the region, and built a cooperative relationship with the local as well. However, a changeover of leadership took place among the ranks of the executives of the local in 1989. At first, the management conducted preliminary negotiations with the UAW International, reached an agreement on such matters as the flexibility required for the achievement of the company's production method, *kaizen,* and labor-management cooperation, and in 1985 the two parties exchanged a letter of intent. In 1987, concurrently with the start up of production, the union was formed. The region representative, who had often consulted with the company's management, appointed the chairperson, and the executive body was formed. They made space for the general manager of personnel and the union officials in the same room in the plant, so that labor and management came to work in the same office next to each other. In 1988, a labor contract was sealed. The issues were job classification and seniority, job security, the maintenance training program, overtime, and so forth. Regarding safety, training, small group activities, welfare programs, and so on, they decided to set up a joint labor-management committee to make decisions based on their agreement. Grievances, safety, production standards, and out-sourcing are excluded from those items that can be arbitrated by an outside organization. If these issues cannot be resolved within the company, to reach a final settlement, representative of the UAW region would consult with the vice president in charge of personnel affairs (an American). Also, on these issues the union cannot strike. At start-up, the plant began with such a framework governing labor relations so that the Japanese-style production system could be made to work. But in 1989, at the election of local union executives, the appointed regional chairperson was defeated and replaced by a former maintenance worker, who represented a group critical of the former executives. A situation unpredictable from the very start emerged.[1] The UAW International has chosen to participate in joint labor-management activities, and thus was able to coexist with the Japanese auto manufacturers. Nonetheless, there are a diverse lot of opinions among the members of the local union. It will be interesting to observe how AD will relate to the new union executives. This will have an impact on the methods of technology transfer.

FACTORY TYPES IN THE AUTOMOTIVE PARTS INDUSTRY

The nine autoparts plants that we targeted for our analysis are mostly high application-oriented facilities with an average application rating of 3.6, the highest among the four industrial sectors. Nevertheless, application rating level alone does not necessarily reveal the unique features of the individual plants. Also, the contents of the plants with the same application rating may vary from one plant to another. In this section, therefore, we will try to discover and analyze some characteristic patterns by looking into the composition of the rating for each plant, its relations with its parent company, or its affiliation with an auto manufacturer. Against the background of the framework of our analysis, the first three plants were chosen because their pattern more or less represents typical features of a Japanese auto parts transplant, characterized as it is by high application. The other two plants have been added by way of contrast, since they have unique features in the form of their advance into America, and in that sense may provide an interesting pattern for Japanese transplants in general.

Modified High Application Type: Factory AM

Despite its parent company's long years of experience in doing business in America, AM belongs to the high application group among auto parts transplants. Moreover, its orientation toward application can be found across the board in matters of local business management. Even for those aspects that are difficult to apply in their original form in the local environment, there is a marked intention to carry out application of the Japanese methods, by full use of "revised application" if necessary. This is the most characteristic feature of the plant.

The plant started operations in July, 1986. Its character has been greatly influenced by the fact that its parent company had been operating a local production facility in California since March, 1971, exceptionally early for a Japanese automobile-related firm. Although its operation in California deserves ample credit for pioneering production by Japanese automobile-related manufacturers in America, it was not able to cope with the local production of the sudden influx of auto assembly transplants that occurred in the 1980s. There was the need to expand toward full-scale local production, and AM was built to fill it.

The California plant is located in an industrial zone in a Los Angeles suburb, whereas the new AM plant is located in a small country town in the state of Michigan some distance from the big cities. Beginning with such a plant site policy, AM demonstrated its taste for intensive application of the entire Japanese system. In individual company standard deviation among the 23 items we used for evaluation, its value was 0.72, second place among target companies. Since the top plant (0.69) is on the extreme side of adaptation (the application rating is 2.0), AM's high application rating shows that it, more than the others, has been engaged in a consistent application of all the items. However, any attempt to bring in Japanese methods in their original form naturally runs into constraints imposed by the American environment. AM's attitude in confronting these is to devise new means of application that accommodate the aptitude of the American employees, local systems, and traditional practices. It shares this accommodating attitude toward the use of "revised application" with AE, the auto assembly plant. This may have something to do with the fact that AM is an AE-affiliated parts manufacturer.

Let us take a closer look at this by using the *kanban* as an example. It is not an easy task to implant the Japanese *kanban* system in America. There are two stages in introducing the system. The first one is the physical use of *kanban* cards, but using them alone is nearly devoid of merit. The next stage is aimed at reducing inventory and eliminating waste by utilizing *kanban* cards and to strive to improve quality and efficiency at the same time. At the level of stage one, the system has reportedly achieved 70 percent application between AM and its related parts suppliers, because it is handled by Japanese personnel. Left to Americans, even the bare use of *kanban* cards itself would not be easy. Moreover, for the full *kanban* system to work smoothly, the inventory control system must be changed, even at customer companies, and there must be mutual understanding of matters related to overall production control, including smoothed-out production. Lack of such an understanding, even in dealing with another Japanese-owned firm, is illustrated by the case of an American in charge of ordering who requested "a delivery 2 days ahead of the scheduled date." But AM is making efforts to achieve the system even in America, through an appeal to its customer auto assembly plants.

In this regard, in Japan there exists the so-called "soft system," which operates without manuals to handle the "gray areas" in production control. In other words, this system can easily deal with "abnormal cases" not mentioned in the manuals. In America, however, there is insufficient training to deal with situations that require abnormal situation handling, and manuals would be needed. We heard that there was a decisive difference in this area of production control between Japan and the United States. One rather thought-provoking remark had it that, "It is possible to transplant Japanese methods like the *kanban* system or the piling up of minute improvements, but it requires changes in format and the writing of manuals." In short, although the extent of the practical implementation of the *kanban* system is still far behind Japan at this point, progress is being attempted through revised application that is adjusted to the conditions of the American environment.

Then, let us look at the evaluation of performance. At AM, the performance evaluation is in force for all the employees, and is also utilized for promotions. Specifically, there are eight wage grades from the entry level (i.e., qualified) up to supervisor for each of three job classifications. It takes generally 2 years to be promoted from the first grade to the second grade (proficient) and from the second to the third (advanced) grade. However, depending on the evaluation, one could be promoted in a year. This is having a significant practical effect on the wages as well.

Incidentally, in regard to wages, at the time of our field investigation, AM was working on the idea of switching to a salary system for all, indicating just how strong their orientation toward application was. In America in general there exists clearly marked gaps, between hourly and salary, exempt and nonexempt, and so forth. As an anecdote to these, many of the Japanese companies have been devising ways to promote a Japanese-style egalitarianism, more Japanese than the practices in Japan in a sense. Nevertheless it has proven very difficult to eliminate these gaps themselves. Undaunted, AM tried to introduce a wage system that bears a strong resemblance to those in Japan. In the end, the plan of introducing the all-salary system was dropped (from an interview conducted at the head office in Japan on March 14, 1990). Nonetheless, in the United States where calculating blue-collar workers' pay on an hourly wage basis is an unwritten law, AM should be given high marks for challenging such a traditional practice.

In a case such as this where there is an attempt to implant a full-fledged Japanese system by making full use of revised application, Japanese personnel still play a large and crucial role. Of the approximately 800 employees, there are thirty-four Japanese (4.3 percent). Any reduction in this number would appear to remain rather difficult. Besides, out of eighteen Japanese working in the production-related area, fourteen, including engineers, assume coaching roles and adhere closely to the shop floors. Also, among the ranks of managers, two thirds of those at the level of assistant-manager and above are filled by Japanese. American managers are paired with a Japanese for support. Here we can discern the existence of a tendency for "human-result" application, which is a general characteristic of the Japanese auto parts transplants. It will be interesting to observe their future course and see how far this taste for application will actually penetrate and how well they will be able to transplant the Japanese system.

Application-Adaptation Combination Type: Factory AJ

AJ's application rating is slightly below the average for the auto parts industry, although it exceeds the average of all the studied transplants. Thus, the plant belongs to those on the application side. However, since its establishment, the plant has been actively working for localization, and this has taken root as its external image as well. Therefore, the key point in understanding this plant is to know that despite its adaptation-oriented image, it carries out a number of application-oriented measures. We will attempt to clearly characterize this plant by focusing on how best to understand this combination of an attitude that attaches great importance both to localization and to high application.

First, let us look at its strong attachment to the importance of localization. In response to the advance of AB into Tennessee, AJ started its operation in same area, beginning in February, 1984. Its line of products consists of air conditioners, evaporators, and so on, which are fairly common products at AM. In terms of the affiliation of their respective parent companies, the AE-affiliate AM, is opposed by the AB-affiliate AJ as one competitor to another. AJ's local content was 27 percent when it began operation in 1984, and as a result of its systematic effort to increase this rate it had risen to 81 percent at the time of our investigation. The plant continues to pursue more and more domestic sourcing, for example. At the same time that it is actively following the path to localization in the field of procurement, it has committed itself to a very thorough involvement with the local community. For example, it provided $2 million of the $4 million needed to build an indoor sports stadium in Shelbyville. And regarding friendly relationships with the local communities as important, two local area school teachers are invited to Japan regularly every year. It also offers the public access to its softball and tennis facilities. Furthermore, using the same system as that of AB, it created a committee composed of nineteen local residents so that it would have an opportunity to listen to local advice on a regular basis, once every 2 months. Moreover, AJ is strengthening its cooperation with a research-and-development (R&D) firm its parent company created as a separate company, for the purpose of actively enhancing its R&D capability in America. Also, its parent company has another separate company that owns a test course in Arizona. As a result of such active efforts in research and development, though it still must receive support from Japan, it now has a structure capable of dealing with the joint development of new car models in the United States, even with the Big Three.

In many other ways, too, AJ expresses its all-out attitude toward the importance of localization. However, this attitude of blending into the local environment is not the only trait characterizing AJ. Indeed, where it judges that application should be regarded as the most important, it has the ability to move forward with radically high application. This probably accounts for the fact that it has been able to maintain its competitiveness as a Japanese enterprise. For example, its production equipment, a "material-result" aspect, is exactly the same as that in Japan, and in fact it was installed after having been tried out in Japan. Also, it has been zealously promoting QC-circle and total quality control (TQC) activities, aiming for full participation by everyone and has achieved an 84 percent QC circle participation rate. In the wage systems also, an individual performance evaluation system that affects pay raises is in place. Specifically, there are four job classifications from I to IV, of which III is maintenance and IV is leadman. Of them, the first three classes, including maintenance, are considered to be production workers. Each category has wage grades of one to five, and the raise is supposed to go through these five grades in 3 years. Performance evaluation intervenes, however, to influence the margin of raises. The same thing can be said for AM, but it was difficult to introduce and put into effect such a performance evaluation under the traditional labor-management practices in the American automotive industry. Having dared to carry it out reflects the application-oriented side of AJ.

That such an high application was possible might be due to the fact that the plant was sited in a farming area of Tennessee. Needless to say, the traditional labor-management practices have less influence over the agricultural areas of America. The job turnover rate, for example, is quite low (forty people left the plant over a 6-year period) in an area where the regional annual average is said to be 25 percent. Furthermore, the attendance rate (paid vacations counted as absenteeism) is over 97 percent at worst. These points considered, it would be hard to believe that such high application was possible only because of the site location policy. In order to promote the long-term employment (and many of the other Japanese transplants are devising similar measures), the plant made a commitment, albeit verbal, to a no-layoff policy. Also, the active effort to foster the group consciousness, which is reflected in the above-mentioned introduction of QC circles, may be one of the reasons why the attendance rate is so high.

The point is that some initial application-oriented measures are being gradually modified in the direction of adaptation as greater importance is put on localization. For instance, the plant modified its organizational structure that had had an executive position for a Japanese that fell between the Japanese president and the American senior vice president in such a way that the Japanese would become an advisor. The intention is to give more authority to top American management, with the goal of "putting Americans on the front line, because the customers are Americans, although so far the plant has actually been managed by Japanese." Other measures conducted along the same line to strengthen adaptation were not necessarily this drastic. Nevertheless, they are reflected in the fact that the application rating of the previous survey, although it is not so accurate due to differences in items and in standards of evaluation, has veered toward the adaptation side by two-tenths of a point. To a certain extent this demonstrates a general tendency of Japanese transplants to gradually tone down application, although the taste for it was strong at start-up.

AJ is thus able to keep many application-oriented features by taking advantage of a site location that seemed to be a fertile ground for the application of Japanese methods. At the same time, it avoided as much as possible friction with the local communities by sticking to its attitude of attaching a fundamental importance to localization. These characteristics of AJ, then, constitute one of the typical patterns of the local production facilities of Japanese corporations in America.

Result High Application Type: Factory AO

AO started its operation in May 1988, and we visited there in September of the following year. By then the plant had only a little more than 1 year of experience. Possibly reflecting this, AO's unique characteristics may be seen in its conspicuous attitude of result-application, particularly as it applies to the core of the Japanese-style production system. Its application rating belongs with the highest group among target transplants.

The fact that AO is a joint venture with the largest American car manufacturer may also play a role here. As a general rule, a joint venture with a local American company gives the Japanese side certain advantages, such as lower costs and absolving it from having to pay extreme attention to friction with the local environment. AO's parent company is a nonaffiliated Japanese manufacturer specializing in automotive brake systems. Like AC, although it is a joint venture, the Japanese side has taken all responsibility for manufacturing. Naturally it can be assumed that the American side's main purpose was to acquire AO's high technology in the manufacturing of car brakes. In fact, the investigation team from the American partner company visited the AO plant more than ten times. In addition, like many other

Japanese auto parts transplants, selection of the site, a rural area in Kentucky, may have the use of application-oriented measures more feasible.

Let us attempt to verify our assumption that AO is inclined toward high application in core systems. The job classification is simplified on the shop floor to a mere two categories, production and maintenance. A team leader controls five teams, and each of them is composed of five workers (a group leader leads a team's operation). Under the instructions of the team leader, job rotation is vigorously followed within each team. It takes the form of everybody changing one's post every month. There is a "job training board" on each shop floor, showing how well individual team members have mastered their jobs. There are three distinct colors indicating different levels: Gray, completed; pink, in training; and yellow, novice. This system demonstrates an ongoing effort to develop multiskilled workers in a systematic way. Prior to start-up, the plant had sent team leaders, who play such key roles in on-the-job training, to Japan so they could gain actual experience working on the line. It is said that the management persuaded those who were reluctant to work on the line by telling them, "You will be the ones who are going to teach others". So in the AO plant it happens that a team leader performs some job process by oneself to help out the subordinate team workers, something unthinkable in the usual American system. These team leaders had been recruited from outside during the start-up phase, but thereafter the plant adopted a system of promotion from within the company in which a production worker would become team leader after being a group leader. All workers were made aware of this idea of promotion from within the company through the employee handbook. AO's inclination toward application can also be observed in many other areas. A performance evaluation system is in place "for ensuring good communication" between production workers and their team leaders. In the area of quality control, the quality check by workers themselves is regarded as the most important, and a system where workers themselves can stop the line is being used. However, there still exists some questions as to what extent these applied methods will really take root. Many difficulties can be expected in firmly establishing Japanese methods among American employees. In the case of small group activities, for example, AO is at a stage where it has not reached the point of forming actual groups yet. Therefore, it is probably the expatriate Japanese personnel who are really supporting the critical part of the application of these methods from the side lines. The presence of sixteen dispatched Japanese (including five temporary assistants sent at the expense of the parent company in Japan as the procurement personnel, to be discussed later) versus 138 total employees would seem to suggest this.

At the same time that AO depends on the human-results application from Japan, and has shown an aptitude for very high application, particularly in the core system-related area, it also has quite a strong inclination toward "material-results" application as well. For example, the plant introduced equipment typical of this category that had been developed in Japan specifically for use in America. Although before the start-up the equipment had been tried out in Japan in a fully automated line, because of predicted difficulties in recruiting maintenance workers, eventually its rate of automation dropped below that of Japan. Incidentally, they appear to have difficulty training their maintenance workers. In the first place, due to the location, it is difficult to find maintenance workers locally, which shows up in comments like "They're just a bunch of amateurs. There is no all-arounder." Consequently, direct supervisors and the plant manager must select candidates from among their workers according to their "individual interest and aptitude" who they feel can become capable of handling all the assembly jobs. These candidates are then trained through short-term programs developed in conjunction with a local vocational school. Also, two trainers are sent by the parent company from Japan in rotation as coaches to assist the workers in such areas as maintenance methods, machinery control, and methods of preventive maintenance. They are "not to put their hands on anything themselves," however.

In addition, let us look at the procurement aspect of "material-result." Like other firms, AO attaches great importance to the domestic sourcing of parts, but in doing this, it must confront a number of problems—casting, for example. The company had started its investigation of thirteen local vendors 3 years prior to start-up, and began local sourcing from two of these while providing them with technical assistance. However, the arrangement did not prove to be satisfactory and in the end the plant switched to procurement from Japan. As a consequence AD had to depend on imports from Japan for nearly 100 percent of its procurement for a while after start-up. The plant then organized a local sourcing team composed of five Japanese sent from the parent company to ensure correct technical assistance and to confirm quality, along with two persons recruited locally, and by July, 1989 it was able to set up a system that enabled the local sourcing of 30 percent of all parts.

Thus, AO may be characterized as receiving its support from the results application of human and material. As far as the core system is concerned, it is inclined to the high application of method as well. In this sense, it shows one of the characteristics of the Japanese transplants at the time of start-up. It would be interesting to follow the future course of this plant to see to what extent it can firmly establish the method application in its attempt to fit in with the local environment, given the support of a favorable condition—namely, its joint venture with an American company.

Assembler Support Type: Factory AP

We have chosen the preceding three patterns, as they demonstrate, to our eyes, the typical pattern of Japanese local production facilities in America, using our evaluation framework as the standard. AP is described here not because it is especially remarkable in the application-adaptation relationship, but because its supplementary role to an auto assembly manufacturer provides an interesting case of a Japanese auto parts transplant.

AP started production of stamped parts in August, 1988 in Illinois, and immediately drew public attention because of the manner in which it came into America. It became somewhat famous thanks to the wide media coverage it received. This is because AP's advance into America was directed through its head office in Japan, a company newly created jointly by sixteen medium and small parts vendors, all located in the same industrial park in Okayama prefecture, as a response to the start-up of AF's American operation. At that time, although sixteen vendors strong, they still felt they needed help from AF's head office. For its part, the AF side could easily help them since they presented a single body. This form of overseas advance became a model for medium and small parts manufacturers, who are individually incapable of making advances overseas, but are pressed to do so, in order to deal with the "hollowing out" (vacuum) created in the domestic market when automobile manufacturers themselves move operations abroad.

When one comes to think about the character of AP, it is quite interesting that through the process of determining twenty-three production items at the start-up, AF's parent company had given instructions based on cost calculations. The relationship between AP and AF is probably best expressed by the comment: "We are somewhat like AF's third plant." AP exists by virtue of its incorporation in the local production facilities of an assembly manufacturer, AF. Let us take a close look at this. Among the necessary stamped parts, AF performs in-house production of main-body parts, whereas the various other components are handled by AP. They have a work-sharing relationship. AP exists to function as sort of a handyman for AF. In that sense, AP's presence is indispensable for the assembly manufacturer AF's local production.

Another example concerns a design-change to a component (fuel tank) that AP was purchasing from an American vendor, but this vendor was unable to do the job. It was AP who was able to temporarily deliver replacement fuel tanks. This case is sufficient to point out that a flexibility that allows for quick changes in direction to supplement an automobile assembly plant cannot be expected from American parts vendors at the present time. In addition, AP's role is also important in matters of cost and quality. AP surpasses the auto assembly plant AF in the production technology of small-sized stamped parts. It is said that in general the presence of a parts vendor like AP is necessary if a Japanese automobile manufacturer is going to successfully operate local production facilities in America.

Considering such a relationship, it may be inferred that the AP's production structure is fully unified with AF. Large-sized stamped components that AP handles, other than the main-body, are made locally, from stamping through final assembly. Small-sized components, on the other hand, are made by assembling knock down (KD) parts imported from Japan. Many parts are supplied free of charge from AF, and delivered back to AF after going through the assembly processes at AP. To save freight cost, the KD parts gathered by the head office in Japan from those companies who are participants in the joint operation are also packed together with the KD parts of AF's parent company, and exported to AF. They are then supplied gratis to AP. This has the additional advantage that AP can avoid risks associated with exchange rate fluctuations. Components supplied in this way meet the close tolerance required for robots so they can assemble them without error in the highly automated body assembly line at AF. AP's clientele is limited to AF only at this point, although supplying AD in the future is under consideration. Therefore, under the present circumstances, AP's operation is fully dictated by that of AF.

Various problems are likely to arise after the launch of new models by AF, presumably a few years down the road. However, since start-up, the ever-current primary objective of the plant has been to achieve the same level of quality and productivity as the member companies in Japan. For instance, since the plant uses tools and dies used in Japan, AP places orders from the Japanese head office and the head office ships the tools and dies, along with personnel to assist in doing whatever AP is unable to do locally. Thus, six Japanese engineers are dispatched as the maintenance workers to assist the American maintenance crew of thirteen, six of whom handle die maintenance, and seven, general maintenance. In other areas also, dispatched Japanese personnel are present. Of the 243 total employees, seventeen are Japanese. These include three who have been sent from AF's head office. The plant is characterized by the fact that, in general, the Japanese methods application rating is kept high, in order to attain a unified structure with AF under the leadership of these expatriate Japanese. It ranked second in average application rating among all the transplants.

Promoting the application of Japanese methods requires an appeal to employees' understanding; thus, communication with the employees is regarded the most important. Unlike AF, who has accepted the UAW, AP's position is to avoid unionization if possible. Once before, unionization was attempted by the UAW and the Teamsters, and it was voted down by a large margin. This had made the plant all the more attentive to this area. To give a concrete example, they are conducting talks, called round-tables, of approximately 1 hour duration, twice a month, inviting one person from each section for a total of ten employees. Moreover, except for wages, it appears that various measures are being attempted to eliminate gaps between salary workers and hourly workers in order to promote Japanese-style egalitarianism and to raise their group consciousness and involvement.

Nevertheless, as far as wages are concerned, they are quite cautious in applying the Japanese method. AP has four job classifications for its hourly workers, and its wage system is based on the nature of one's job, with different wages applied to each job classification. The hourly wage corresponding to a given job classification is raised almost every 6 months after the initial trial period has elapsed, and peaks out in each respective job category 2 years after joining the company. (An example of a general production worker's hourly wage would be $8.50). This system deserves credit in that as with the auto assembly plants, the plant has broken down the wall of the American style of strict job classifications, and succeeded in simplifying them. However, it was left with the problem that after 2 years in any given job category, wages would reach the same level. Therefore, they are searching for the ways to generate differences. The performance evaluation system was introduced as one of the means to do this, but at present it is still not reflected in wages or promotions.

AP is a local production facility that made its advance into America at the request of the auto assembly plant AF. It supplements AF, and has established a system for full cooperation with AF. AP exists as a kind of model seen from the perspective of assembly plants in America where, unlike Japan, it is not easy to find this kind of parts vendor.

Advancing in Related Fields Type: Factory AN

AN is a transplant owned by a nonaffiliate manufacturer of stamping dies for automotive applications, which holds the largest market share in Japan among specialty die manufacturers. However, AN, who began its operation in June, 1987, debuted as a panel stamping and subassembly plant. Its intention was to acquire experience in local production in America, by finding its way into a related field at first, not in its own specialty of die making. This plant is added to our list of patterns as such a special case.

Originally AN's parent company had started to study the possibility of an overseas venture prior to the middle of the 1970s. Initially, they were considering an advance into some developing country by means of a joint venture with a local firm. However, since it takes at least 5 years for a die manufacturing operation to start paying off, meaning poor investment efficiency, talks with the prospective partner did not bear fruit. Therefore, in 1978 or so their policy of overseas expansion was redirected to the developed countries, and around 1982 they decided to target America. In the meantime, the company was also being wooed by the biggest American automobile manufacturer to manufacture dies in the United States. Out of deference to their policy to maintain an equidistant diplomacy with all companies, they decided in the end to proceed into "a new business field," with their own specialty, stamping die manufacturing, repositioned as a future goal. Although we have called it a new field of business, considering that the company had recently "extended its business into areas surrounding dies" in Japan, and was operating panel stamping and welding assembly processes, and considering the fact that dies used for its American stamping operation were manufactured by the company headquarters in Japan, it was not actually an advance into a totally new business, but rather an advance into a related field. Incidentally, even while our investigation was underway, they were constructing a die plant to operate their main business, and they were training die workers with the intention of starting the operation as a separate company in 3 years.

AN was "uneasy in the beginning," because it stepped into a related area, but it succeeded in receiving an order for the stamping and subassembly of doors from one of the American Big Three. Although it also supplies AD, by the time of our investigation, deliveries to that American firm had reached upward to 80 percent, which would almost indicate that it was an "affiliate company" of the American company. In any event, its performance has been better than initially anticipated. AN, who has been accumulating operating experience in America in a related business and is conducting the training of the die workers necessary for its main business, is not typical, but it does deserve to be listed as one of the patterns of the American operations of a Japanese auto parts transplant.

However, it is true also that AN has been running into difficulties that reflect the fact that it entered a field where it did not have sufficient technical expertise at home. For instance, they had to ask for coaching by AD's technicians in welding, and appear to be getting AD's advice on many other things as well. The existence of various technical problems is reflected also in the high number of Japanese expatriate personnel, although a fair number of them are needed to train die workers. Seventeen of twenty-seven Japanese expatriates are said to be coaching on the shop floors. In maintenance especially, due to the difficulties of obtaining skilled workers with electrical knowledge, Japanese frequently get directly involved with the job at hand.

In this way, under Japanese leadership, AN shows its strong inclination toward the side of application. On the other side, it is obliged to care about local adaptation under the influence of the site it selected, a suburb not far from Detroit, Michigan. This is reflected in its application rating, which is slightly above the overall average. Let us cite a specific example. In this plant, job classification is simplified to two classes: general (associate) and maintenance (skilled). However, the job rotation, which should be the primary purpose of the simplification of job classification in the first place, was said to not have been implemented yet even within a team composed of five workers. Moreover, although the study to introduce job rotation is ongoing, old workers assert their rights of seniority, we were told. It can be seen from such facts as these that because of the site it selected, in an area within the sphere of influence of traditional American labor-management practices, AN has had no choice but to assume a position, aptly described by comments like, "How to blend in with American culture, that is the key."

AN, with its excellent technology in automotive-application stamping dies, made a temporary inroad into a related field. Its future course will command attention to see how it can utilize its experience in local production, which continues to be a learning process, for the benefit of its future venture within its true specialty.

FACTORY TYPES IN THE CONSUMER ELECTRONICS INDUSTRY

As we saw in Chapter 6, Section C, the consumer electronics industry is characterized by the fact that not only its application rating average is the lowest among the targeted industrial sectors, but the application ratings vary quite widely from one firm to another, both in their average rating for all items and in the ratings of individual items or groups. In this section, we are going to classify the target consumer electronics plants under several patterns, while focusing on the differences and characteristics of individual enterprises, especially in regard to what we called "human" elements and "material" elements, such as production equipment and parts.

Local Adaptation Type

Localization as Part of an Overall Management Strategy: Factory EB
EB is representative of plants with an orientation toward the localization of business administration. Here, "localization" has two meanings. First, it means that the rating for application shown in our hybrid chart is low. And to the contrary, it means there is a very clear inclination toward adaptation to local conditions. As we have said repeatedly, the consumer electronics industry has a low application rating overall. But EB in particular and a few other plants manifest this tendency in the extreme. However, in the case of the EB plant, in addition to this it seems the plant progressed to quite an advanced stage of localization in areas that are not covered by our items of evaluation, such as the localization of the head office function. Therefore, through the combination of these two sides we would like to position EB as a representative plant of the local adaptation type.

First, let us look at the low application side. EB is considerably lower than the home electronics industry's application rating average in each of these groups: I, Work Organization and Administration, II, Production Control, IV, Group Consciousness, and V, Labor Relations. It has much in common with plants that have low application ratings, but EB's extremely low ratings in the items of group I, Work Organization and Administration, particularly stand out.

Before getting into the actual examination of the low application rating, we need to mention the fact that EB is not a newly built establishment, but a color TV plant formerly owned by a major American electric appliance manufacturer that was bought out. This undoubtedly constitutes one of the main factors that dictate how this plant is operated and one of the reasons why its application rating is low.

At first, on-the-floor hourly jobs including maintenance have been differentiated into 100 different job categories, which are ranked across fourteen levels. Wages basically correspond to each respective job rank on a one-to-one basis. For operations, a fixed job-type system was adopted, in which a specific worker repeatedly performs a specific job. For example, in a typical plant in Japan workers are expected to become capable of handling both assembly and adjustment jobs, whereas in this plant, it is a fixed rule that an assembly worker only assembles, and an adjustment worker only adjusts. The promotion from one job rank to another in the production area is done through a system whereby those who have applied for a job posting are selected according to how well qualified they are by virtue of experience and outside professional training or education. For those with similar qualifications, seniority makes the difference. One way or the other, EB is certainly carrying on the typical traditional American style job organization that it received from the former plant.

In production control, group consciousness, and labor relations, the degree to which Japanese methods have been brought in is very low. In a Japanese plant, helping to determine standard times for tasks, and making job assignment based on these, is the job of the supervisor, whereas in this plant these tasks are not assumed by someone in the shop, but by IE. The proper modus operandi here can only be labeled as American in style. Even though small group activities are conducted once a week at lunchtime without pay, there are few participants. The plant has already been forced to lay off workers six or seven times. EB's lack of a union is simply due to the fact that being nonunion was already part of the creed of the American company before the buy-out, and it cannot be attributed to the policy of the Japanese company. Complaints from workers are handled by means of a system of five steps, moving from step one, where the supervisor and worker or workers have a talk, through step five, where they consult with the president, and general manager of personnel. Here, too, they are following in essence a system of the former plant.

On the other hand, although in the initial stage they used the production equipment of the former plant just as it was, by the beginning of the 1980s, 7 years after the buyout, they brought in equipment from Japan, modeling the main line after a plant in Japan over a period of 3 years. Also, it should be noted that just before this, they had transferred the processes of inserting parts into printed board and assembling chassis to their Mexican maquiladora plant, lightening up their own line so that only the final assembly process remained.

EB is one step ahead of the others in the diversification of suppliers for procurement. It started making full use of the maquiladora before the others, as will be mentioned later in this section. Nevertheless, its local content is at almost the same level as other transplants in the industry, and it is not exceptional in the fact that it depends on Japan for the key components.

To sum up, EB is able to stay competitive and to maintain quality by depending basically on Japan or the "Japanized" part in hardware and materials, such as production equipment and critical function components. In the management of personnel, it is stamped strongly with the style of the former plant; in other words, the traditional American style. So it is naturally quite difficult to build a system of meticulous production control peculiar to Japanese firms. For the strength that supports EB's local production, we can probably thank the depth of the business organization that surrounds the plant and the localization of management. The strength of the organization enveloping this transplant, like the worldwide logistic network and the well-equipped American head office, count for a great deal. These are the reasons we can characterize this plant as a case of localization in the context of overall strategic management.

To begin with, it was the first among Japanese electrical appliance firms to establish a maquiladora factory for procurement in Mexico, and is utilizing the maquiladora system to the utmost. Its procurement method network is probably tops in the industry and covers not only Mexico, but also Southeast Asia, Canada, and Europe.

Also, on the side of its local business management in America, including the sales network, we sense the strength and depth of its organizational capability in its linking of American head office functions with plant management. With the creation of the North America TV Division in 1988, a structure was completed for overall control of the EB plant, the maquiladora, the Canadian plant, and also the sales network in all of North America. As a result, EB, which had been seen previously as if it were merely an auxiliary plant for Japan, is gaining relative autonomy, as shown by its ability to join the North America Division in decision making concerning sales prices and planning in the local marketplace.

Maintaining competitiveness through localization of the head office function, based as it is on the "hard" technology of products and production equipment, while control and utilization of the plant's personnel is left to local custom, has perhaps more in common with the image of American-based multinational corporations than it does as a general trait of Japanese manufacturing companies. It fully deserves mention as a possible direction for Japanese firms as their overseas production networks expand further in the future.

Accepting and Modifying Traditional Labor Unions: Factory EC

EC Plant was established upon the buyout of an existing nonprofitable factory. While finding ways to compromise with the union it inherited from the former plant, EC has put the business back on the road to recovery in a short period of time. However, soon thereafter it was confronted with a difficult situation as the relations with the union became aggravated and turned sour. But again it appears to be making progress toward stabilization. It has come through many ups and downs in the process. Experience of this kind contains lessons worthy of contemplation and some interesting suggestions.

Because it started local production by buying out an old nonprofitable factory from an American company, and fully utilizes its maquiladora plant, EC can be classified under the same pattern as EB. Cooperation with a major American distribution corporation plays an important part in its localization of business management. Although their joint venture relationship sustained since the buyout has been recently dissolved, they still maintain an agreement according to which this distribution corporation procures 70 percent of the TV sets it sells from EC.

What most clearly distinguishes EC from EB is that EC has inherited a labor union from the former plant. If we mention EC here, it is primarily because our attention was drawn to the details surrounding its relations with the union. The labor union in question is the IUE, a traditional American-style union, generally regarded as more aggressive than the other labor unions in this field.

As soon as it was bought out, EC began to draw attention nationally and internationally as a success story for Japanese management, because they were able to put a nonprofitable plant into the black very shortly after the buyout, and because it organized a company sports festival involving union members. In spite of this, in the middle of the 1980s and thereafter, it was hit by several serious labor disputes. The situation grew worse until rumor had it that the end of the company was imminent. The root cause may be found in the fact that, although the plant seemed to have captivated its employees by a management style that may even be characterized as warmhearted, its attempt to push through changes in work practices in areas like personnel placement, and so on, ran afoul of the fundamental line of the traditional American type of job control unionism. We still remember clearly the sensational coverage of the story by both the Japanese and American media, turning it all around, so as to make it out as a good example of Japanese-style management, which, groaning in hopeless labor relations, had hit a dead end. In the meantime, mutual distrust deepened and the dispute dragged on endlessly.

Nonetheless, through the interviews and plant tour we conducted in the fall of 1989, we observed some changes in attitude among the union and the employees, that gave us the impression that the intention of the management to strive for a more flexible plant administration, although slowly, had begun to pay off. The underlying reason for this was a strong sense of crisis that had developed among the employees and in the local community due not only to the fact that a considerable reduction in workers had resulted from several layoffs, but to the emerging possibility that even the plant itself would be closed down and the entire manufacturing operation transferred to the maquiladora plant.

As a result, the new labor agreement, revised in 1989, included reduction in a number of job ranks corresponding to wage levels, down from eleven ranks to five. This then created a base that would allow more flexibility in dealing with production adjustment or workload changes. Also, the role of seniority rule in promotions and relocation, although not discarded, seems to have become much more flexible in its application. Until then previously laid-off workers were given the first priority at a time of a production increase, but this was changed so that the plant was allowed to select new employees without the need to distinguish between recalls and new people. Also, from this time onward the labor agreement contained additional phrases that recommend solving grievances basically through consultations between the worker or workers and the supervisor. However, the formal channel via the union continues to exist.

Thus, at EC also, we could probably say that the framework is taking shape for a stable labor-management relation that is at least not hostile, if not positively good. The production that once had plunged to as low as 600,000 units a year had recovered to the level of nearly one million units a year by the time of our survey in September, 1989. A direct result was that the plant proceeded to hire 120 new people, and it is probably correct to assume that operations at EC have restabilized.

These experiences suggest the following:

1. It is not easy to change once-formed job practices. Although a great deal of care and consideration is needed, it is better to bring in totally unfamiliar Japanese systems from the very beginning, thus minimizing friction and discord in the end.
2. The "warmhearted" management posture, issuing from a pet idea of Japanese management, is delicate and easily broken. It would seem that a more stable plant operation is possible under a rather dry, businesslike management style combined with rational measures.
3. If EC has been displaying a degree of high adaptability despite the various problems just described, albeit not so well organized or generally applicable as in the case of EB, it is the experience of EC's parent company, one of the prominent Japanese multinational corporations, in the full use of local management resources that probably should be given much of the credit.

Production Control—Technology-Dependent Type: Factory ED

In short, ED is a plant that is achieving both quality and efficiency at quite a high level for a local production facility through, on the one hand, adopting businesslike American-style methods for personnel management, and on the other hand, building up the total system in an appropriate fashion with the backing of production control technology cultivated in Japan. In other words, this is the plant that embodies in the clearest way the chief characteristics of the consumer electronics industry, that is, a strong inclination to local adaptation in the management of shop-floor personnel combined with a superiority in "hard" technology that includes products, production equipment, and components that provide a critical resource for enhanced competitiveness. Not only can ED boast of top-level production results as an example of a Japanese color TV transplant in America with an annual output of 1.1 million units, but, the range in terms of inches of the line of products it manufactures reflects to some degree its highly efficient operation.

Although ED is not a bought-out factory, but a newly established facility, its application ratings in I, Work Organization and Administration, IV, Group Consciousness, and V, Labor Relations, are either at the same level or lower than EB, while in the area of human-methods it sticks to a generally businesslike local approach. Although the number of job classifications and job ranks are lower than at of EB, on the floor the two systems are basically the same. Wages, for example, correspond completely to respective job ranks. As for matters concerning placement and promotion of workers, and job flexibility, restrictions imposed by seniority and job categories appear to be more strictly applied than at EB. Job rank promotion is done through job-posting, with seniority given first priority in the selection criteria. Maintenance workers positions are filled by hiring experienced people from outside, and production workers must not get involved with maintenance jobs, as this would constitute a violation of job territory.

It is the same thing for the group consciousness and labor relations. Small group activities simply do not exist. The plant has already had to use layoffs. A labor union is present (International Brotherhood of Electric Workers: IBEW), and there was a strike at the time of revision of the labor contract. To handle grievances, a typical American system has been adopted that has a provision for resorting to an outside arbitration organization at the fourth and final step.

The strong point of ED Plant resides in the fact that it is a so-called "green field factory," and it was able to fully utilize the advantage it had due to a lacking of any restrictions that would have come from an existing facility. Thus it has been able to build up a solid system of equipment and production control throughout the period of production increase, beginning in the mid-1980s. A perfect example is its system of operation and quality control by means of computers utilizing bar codes. This was proposed by an American manager in charge of quality control and manufacturing, and both the hardware and software were developed locally. This is a system fitted for mass production by consistent computer control of parts, from input to product output, by means of serial numbers attributed to each one of the sets to be manufactured. When trouble arises, a repair worker inputs data on-site and the problem is then sent out for analysis. Although the computer control scheme itself originates with the local transplant, there is no doubt that the overall system of ED is securely grounded in expertise of production control techniques accumulated by the parent factory in Japan. A result of such a production and quality control system is that the in-line rejection rate is nearly comparable with that of the plant in Japan. Product quality after shipping, too, was given top honors in a *Consumer's Report*.

In short, as stated in the beginning, the characteristic of ED is that while thoroughly introducing a businesslike traditional American approach in the areas of work organization and human control methods, it let production control technology lead the way to a firm consolidation of the production system, thereby achieving the twin goals of high efficiency and high quality.

If one were to presume to fault this approach, it would be in the stiffness of the plant operation. This is not only confined to fixed job categories or the strong influence of seniority. As the plant also lacks the means to foster the group consciousness or motivation among its employees, the problem of how to obtain greater flexibility in the plant operation becomes all the more critical.

Finally, we wonder if there is not a possibility that operating the plant in the pursuit of Japanese-style efficiency within a framework of typical American-style labor relations does not automatically entail dispassionate, business-like American-type disputes.

Twin Factory Core, High Application Type: Factory EA

EA has a high application rating for the consumer electronics industry. Especially in I, Work Organization and Administration and II, Production Control, that is to say, in the core system areas, it exceeds even the average for all industries. However, as we will mention later, it is probably correct to assume that its high application rating in these core areas is made possible through use of its sister maquiladora, located adjacent to the EA Plant—in other words, by selectively limiting the production of the American plant in both volume and models. This is why we called EA a twin-plant core high application type.

Before discussing the core system of EA, let us look at the general characteristics of the plant. First, the plant embarked on local production in America at the beginning of the 1970s, the first in the consumer electronics industry. It was therefore of the earliest period, even ahead of all the companies targeted by our present survey, and it was, moreover, a case of not buying out an existing facility but building a new one. Also, EA is the only Japanese transplant that operates the final assembly of television sets and picture tube production on the same premises.

For a consumer electronics company with a high application rating, EA is the only one that is utilizing a maquiladora plant. A production system is established with the maquiladora and the American facilities functioning as a unified set that allows for the wholesale transfer of small-sized mass production-type products with low added-value to the maquiladora plant, and limits the EA plant to production of picture tubes, a process that is strongly equipment-dependent, and to high value-added products such as multifunction color TV sets and computer displays. It is necessary to remember that its high application rating in the core systems has been realized by being thus selective in both scale and models.

Within the core system, our attention is first drawn to a unique feature of the production equipment. Even in the final assembly line for color televisions, generally not a very automated process, the adjustment process is unmanned and carried out by computers and microprocessors, and a part of the assembly operation is done by robots. Progress in process improvement is engineer-led, so to speak. There are pieces of equipment and expertise that the local plant has developed on its own. This suggests the depth of the accumulation of technical expertise cultivated through long years of experience operating the plant.

Under I, Work Organization and Administration, the job classification and wage systems have certain noteworthy features. Job ranks of supervisor and lower have been greatly simplified to comprise but four ranks, including the leadman who assists the supervisor. As a result, job rotation is of course easy to carry out, and within one supervisor's territory it is actively pursued. This contrasts sharply with the fixed job categories of EB and ED. In the wage systems, pay raises are given according to length of service, with a 7-year cap on service in the same job ranking. The performance evaluation system also counts attendance and the degree to which one has become a multiskilled worker. That differs greatly from the job title-type American system. Its application rating would appear to be fairly high, not only in production technology but also in human management within plant operations. What we have been discussing above is the height of the application ratings of the system, but it is still necessary to question how such aspects as the flexibility of operations management and the long-term formation of a wide range of skills will actually function in practice. Most supervisors in the EA plant have been promoted internally from among production workers. Their role is primarily personnel management. As for the technical side, they are assisted by the so-called leadmen who have been selected from among technicians. As we mentioned in passing in Chapter 6, the more the development of skills is limited in duration and scope, the more difficult it is to obtain human assets good for all actual hands-on tasks, labor management, and control of operations. Even for this plant with its long years of operating experience, it cannot be said that it truly fostered the development of supervisors possessing both technical and management skills. Therefore, as mentioned earlier, improvements in processes are normally limited to those taken under the initiative of engineers. They have yet to reach the stage where improvements are promoted from the bottom up, as can be seen in plants in Japan.

This must have something to bear on its employee turnover rate of near 20 percent annually, which is on the higher side in the industry. The actual impact naturally depends on which group of employees shows a high mobility, but generally speaking it can constitute a restricting factor for a flexible plant operation and the long-term formation of a skilled work force.

In any event, with certain reservations referred to above, EA can be said to have achieved a flexibility in plant operations that is probably quite high for the industry. To do this it has had to limit itself to high value-added products by transferring low value-added products to the maquiladora, and utilize to the full its technology-driven automated equipment, as well as its long operating experience in production and control accumulated by a certain class of highly skilled long-time employees.

Introduction of New American Ideas Type: Factory EI

EI is characterized by two things. One is that, although it is grouped with the consumer electronics industry, the plant is actually dedicated to picture tube production. Second is the fact that it was founded as a joint venture with a major American electric appliance manufacturer. (At present, the joint venture with the American firm has been dissolved and the operation is 100 percent owned by the Japanese firm.)

In the case of this plant also, the application rating is relatively high in the area of its core systems, and it, too, operates a production engineering-led plant. In this sense the pattern is similar to EA above. Also, both of them manufacture picture tubes, and this might be associated with their performance. However, in personnel control methods there is a great deal of difference. EI plant also is striving for flexibility in work organization, and in doing so, it shows its intention to actively introduce systems that are in practice in newly established American nonunion factories.

First, let us look at some features of the personnel control methods at EI. Jobs are ranked by four levels, from production worker to maintenance workers. This figure is relatively low for the industry. Job rotation is carried out within a team of members of the same rank. In view of the nature of the consumer electronics industry, this system is not necessarily aimed at the formation of skills involving employees from a broader base as is the case of the auto assembly industry. Nevertheless, there is no doubt this is a structure capable of flexibly dealing with the adjustment of production volume for various models and changes in the workload that result from technical evolution.

The wages basically correspond to the job ranks, and are raised almost every 6 months with a cap of 3.5 years within each job rank. The rate of pay raise depends on a performance evaluation by one's immediate superior, by a supervisor, for example, in the case of a production worker. In fact, this wage system linked to performance evaluation is a system that had been put into practice by the American electric appliance company, former joint venture partner, at its new nonunion plant, and which was brought in by the American general manager of personnel.

For a plant that operates large-scale machinery such as that used in picture tube production, how to secure a large maintenance crew and how to enhance their abilities is a matter of critical importance. The plant has set up a system enabling it to train its own maintenance workers, while tactfully tying into the skilled worker development program that is a part of the state government's regional education and training program. This skilled worker development program is set up in such a way that EI cooperates by providing engineers as instructors or trainers. Thus it can design the training to fit its production lines, and at the same time, trainees can obtain maintenance qualification for the EI plant at the completion of the program.

In the area of human-methods like job organization and education and training that are directly tied to the core of operations, we can see its predilection for application. Although EI leans toward application, its approach is not to bring in Japanese systems unadulterated. Rather it is attempting to find its way in a very interesting direction by applying the core Japanese methods while utilizing the local environment and resources. Sometimes, it deliberately brings in new American trends to the company (wages and performance evaluation) and, at other times, it takes advantage of systems outside of the company peculiar to the local area (development of maintenance workers).

On the other hand, in IV, Group Consciousness, and V, Labor Relations, its strong inclination toward local adaptation is fairly obvious. Small group activities, although present, is not very active. The company seems to have made no special commitment to a policy of no-layoffs.

The labor union is the IBEW, the same as the former joint venture partner's plant. (The ex-partner's plant is located within the same building). EI says that its management made the first overture. The American general manager of personnel looked favorably on that union as having an understanding of the new trend in America's labor relations. While accepting the labor union, the fact that the plant was able to introduce a system practiced in some nonunion American plants was of course influenced by the basic trends of recent years in labor relations, such as the rise in the importance of the local union and changes in the union's mind-set. However, it also probably owes a great deal to the character of the IBEW, which is regarded as moderate.

The proportion of Japanese expatriates is less than 1 percent. This is extremely low, on a par with AB auto assembly plant. This fact shows that EI can be characterized as having a local adaptation factor on the human side as well.

EI's production equipment is obviously modeled after the Japanese plant. Since the outlook had become favorable for the maintenance capability that had been an initial source of concern, it was possible to install more highly automated machinery at the time EI expanded its production line. Also, at that time, a system to monitor abnormalities in equipment and in the product flow by means of a four-tiered computer system, including mini computers, was introduced. As the data is accessible to everyone, the computer also functions as a means to motivate employees. We are told that the importance of computers is greater than anticipated, in tracking or analyzing trouble spots in a newly-built plant in America that is operated by a group of amateurs, so to speak, with little experience.

In short, EI can be characterized as applying the Japanese system in a more or less straightforward manner on the technical side, in areas such as production equipment, that have a direct impact on production and on quality control. Although also directly connected to production and quality, on the personnel control side, EI accepts the union and at the same time tries to transplant the core spirit of the Japanese method by deliberately utilizing elements and systems observed in the new nonunion American plants. This is a simpler approach than that of AE, an auto assembly plant. Or, the plant could be viewed as representing a kind of revised application approach in the consumer electronics industry.

The biggest problem for EI Plant may boil down to just how to increase security and motivation among its employees who come from a regional labor environment that is characterized by very high job turnover rates. In fact, the job turnover rate at this plant is high indeed, exceeding 30 percent a year, although most of these are nonskilled workers. At EI in particular, besides the dialogue with employees, no special measures are taken to attempt to raise the group consciousness. Therefore, the critical question is how this can avoid affecting flexibility in plant operations, product quality, and job efficiency in the future.

Application-Adaptation Balance Type: Factory EF

EF produces color television sets at the rate of one million units a year, achieving one of the highest output levels among Japanese transplants in America, second only to ED. In addition, its production of microwave ovens reaches as much as 900,000 units, also among the largest production outputs of the Japanese transplants. It assembles laptop personal computers on a small scale as well.

The application rating of EF Plant just equals the industry average. Moreover, we should make special mention of the fact that with the exception of IV, Group Consciousness, that scored a slightly higher rating, all the other ratings of the groups' individual items nearly coincide with the industrial average. In a sense this plant embodies the perfect image of the average Japanese consumer electronics transplant in the United States. However, it is not merely average. Rather, it is an ingenious balance between application and adaptation, bringing-in Japanese methods where appropriate, while taking local conditions into consideration. Its average rating is the result of the convergence of these two tendencies.

The number of job ranks from production worker to maintenance workers is rather higher than ED, for example. Wages correspond one-to-one with these job ranks. However, EF has been gradually cutting down the number of job titles. Furthermore, they are training workers to be able to handle a broader range of jobs. As a result, it enjoys a far greater degree of flexibility with regard to job categories than ED. Job rotations, for example, are carried out among workers of the same job ranking even though their job titles are different.

We can observe an ingenious balance of application and adaptation also in regard to supervisors. To recruit supervisors, the company does not necessarily adhere only to the principle of internal promotion. When a suitable person is not available internally, it hires also from outside through public advertisement. Therefore, unlike factories in Japan, a supervisor is not necessarily a skilled worker who is highly experienced in the shop-floor techniques. The primary roles of supervisors reside in the allocation and management of manpower. Their lack of technical expertise, if any, is compensated for by a group of experienced workers who repair products along with other tasks on the line. By having these workers share the duties of a Japanese-style supervisor, the plant takes the position that this is a case of "two performing as one."

The production equipment also demonstrates a good example of the balance between application and adaptation. Needless to say, the basic concept of the equipment is from Japan. However, for example, on the microwave oven automated line, in recent years there are a certain number of machines that have been locally developed and introduced using local resources. The result has been that the degree of automation of this line would seem to be ahead of the Japanese plants. Moreover, the purpose of pursuing its own development is not merely a response to local limiting factors, such as the quality of the labor force. Its primary object is found rather in making the maintenance jobs at the local facilities easier to perform, and in raising the maintenance capability of the transplant. EF is the most advanced in localization of equipment among all the newly constructed transplants. The fact is that its localization could be said to be one step ahead of the others, thanks to its intention of raising the maintenance capability.

Regarding job security, although the company has not overtly declared any special interest in a no-layoff policy, nevertheless, so far there has been no layoffs. Although the plant is unionized (IBEW), labor relations are in good shape, and no disputes have grown complicated enough to warrant a strike.

We wonder if these smooth plant operations based as they are on such a balanced application-adaptation relationship, may not be largely dependent on a rising group consciousness among workers, initiated by the small group activities. The small group activities of EF Plant could be classified as among the most active of all the target transplants of our current study. Membership of each small group is composed of those working under the same supervisor. Their activities take place twice a month for 2 hours. Although participation of all workers is not mandatory, the participation rate is over 80 percent. The fact that participation rate exceeds 80 percent in spite of a voluntary participation system deserves to be considered as an exception in the American context. But then this may be largely due to the fact that activity is conducted during the normal working hours with the line stopped.

The aim of activity is to instill in the workers an awareness of the importance of quality and productivity and, through this, to promote their interest in participating in the business. In spite of the opinion that productivity is a taboo theme because it is a reminder of cuts in the workforce, EF took the trouble to go ahead with it anyway. Here, we can infer EF's active stance. They did not do this posthaste, without forethought and preparation, however. They carefully and unobtrusively laid the groundwork in advance. An American general manager of personnel affairs repeatedly explained that if a surplus of manpower resulted from the introduction of automated machinery or an increase in productivity, it would be handled not by dismissal, but by natural retirement. Indeed, if the productivity increase also increased sales volume, it would result in an increase in the number of jobs.

Its production scale and its wide range of product models lead us to believe that EF's production control and operations management are quite efficient, and simultaneously very stable and smooth. No doubt EF plant operations gain their support from a combination of an exquisite balance between application and adaptation and meticulous measures to raise the group consciousness and motivation among its employees. The balance is maintained by trying to make use of Japanese methods in a timely manner without forcing them while accommodating different local conditions. The measures to instill a group consciousness and motivation are best seen in its active small group activities.

Nonunion, Labor-Management Cooperation Type: Factory EH

The first feature that strikes us about the EH Plant is that its application rating is the highest among consumer electronics firms. Moreover, like EA, it exceeds the industry average application rating in nearly all of the groups. However, its application rating in the core, in areas such as I, Work Organization and Administration, and II, Production Control, is not especially higher than other companies. Nevertheless, the plant is producing car phones to absorb seasonal fluctuations in demand for its color TV sets and to ensure smooth switchovers between these two lines; it has plans to systematically train about 10 percent of it workers in handling both production lines. This could be regarded as somewhat of a step forward in the development of a multiskilled workforce.

Although the application rating of II, Production Control, is also a little high, the reason can be attributed solely to its high dependency upon Japan for production equipment, and EH has nothing particularly unique to offer here.

This plant's most distinguishing characteristic is found in its efforts, not so much in these core areas, to keep relations with its employees as friendly as possible by striving for good mutual communication. In other words, EH is almost too concerned about how to avoid unionization. They are striving for good communication with their workers by taking advantage of various opportunities, by carrying out, for instance, a personnel meeting once a month for hours with a group of approximately fifteen employees at a time. This is due to a tacit assumption that the nonunion state can be maintained by responding to the employees' expectations and siphoning off their demands.

Rather as an exception in the consumer electronics industry, the plant has explicitly stated its intention to avoid layoffs. The purpose is to attract better talent, but at the same time it could be understood within the context of averting offensives from the union. In an industry that is beginning to accept unionization as more or less inevitable, EH, like EA, is making a strong stand on the side of maintaining its nonunion status, even if it must pay the price for this in various ways, and go to some pains to keep up the cooperative relationship with its employees.

However, there is a little doubt as to the value of this in terms of the collateral security that can be expected or that there is a good deal of significance in avoiding the union by being discreet and spending time and effort to that end. Naturally, if a traditional labor-management confrontation style union were organized, it would be entirely possible that not only the cooperative spirit shared by the workers but also the main point, flexibility in the plant operations, might be blown away. Probably, EH's apprehension about an American-type union stems from such considerations. But, for those plants that have accepted unionization, for example, EF and EI, the cooperative spirit among employees aside, flexibility in organization and worker motivation do not appear to differ markedly from what we find at this plant, even when very conservative estimates are used. This does lead to the interesting question of how different things really are, with and without a union, in American factories that have similar personnel participation levels and flexibility in how they organize their operations. The issue requires further reflection.

FACTORY TYPES IN THE SEMICONDUCTOR INDUSTRY

Materials Application, System Adaptation Type: Factory SB

If we classify the target semiconductor transplants into either "application type" or "adaptation type" according to whether their individual application ratings are above or below the overall average application rating for all the studied transplants, SD, SG, SF, and SC would be of the "application type," and SE and SB of the "adaptation type". These two adaptation type plants were both earlycomers to America, and both had started local production before the emergence of Japan-U.S. friction over semiconductors. Both are large, in employment as well as production. In fact, SB is the largest among semiconductor transplants, and SE ranks third. Both plants have the longest operating experience among their peers.

SB is below the semiconductor industry average in all groups except labor relations, where it matches the industry average. It is definitely a local adaptation type. Especially in the parent-subsidiary company relationship, SB's local autonomy is the highest among the target semiconductor transplants, although its level is slightly lower than that of some of the consumer electronics transplants and one auto assembly transplant, AB. The Japanese expatriate ratio is low. With its low number of expatriates, the authority of the transplant company and the position of top local managers, SB leads the others in localization. SE, on the other hand, is on par with other major companies for these last two items. So localization on the human side is the characteristic of SB. It placed an American in the post of plant manager from the beginning. Also, through our interview, we confirmed that the plant was working vigorously to localize the decision-making process. At SE, the roles held by Japanese are important in the local business management, and its dependence on the Japanese parent company is as high as the other application type transplants. Nevertheless, aside from these differences, SB and SE share many traits in common as adaptation types.

The application rating in procurement is not much different from three of the application type transplants. Its production equipment is basically the same as that of Japan. The "intake" of manufacturing technology from Japan forms the basis for its local production. In fact, at SB it is understood that "production techniques are to be dealt with mainly by Japanese." On the other hand, in regard to the core of the production system, the plant appears to be of the adaptation type, closely resembling the American nonunion high-tech type. In this sense, it may be characterized as a "material-application and method-adaptation type."

SB's work organization and its administration most closely resemble the American type. There are four job ranks for production workers and, separately, three ranks for production technicians who perform maintenance work. This is identical to SE's system. SE's own job classification system was built from a system standardized in America with job titles and wage grades that had been internally adapted. For this reason, the number of job categories is high, and it is very American. However, already at the time of our survey, SE was in the process of revising their system, and we left with the impression that greater simplification was imminent. At SB, we heard nothing of the kind. Job rotation is not carried out on a regular basis at either SB or SE. In the case of SE, as the necessity arises, jobs are rotated within the same production process through reassigning workers to a higher wage job ranking. Coupled with quite detailed job classifications in both plants, the "walls of demarcation" between jobs are high. These fixed job classifications are readily apparent.

Both plants employ the performance evaluation system in the promotion of production workers. At SE the promotion is carried out regularly at the time of yearly review, but sometimes it is also done at the discretion of supervisors. When a vacancy opens up, the job offer is posted. In both plants, in general the basis for promotion is individual ability and talent. The number of years of service is not much taken into account and the traditional seniority rule is not applied.

In such a job classification system, wages basically correspond with job titles. At SE, criteria include, in addition to the average pay raise rate, job categories, years of service (with a 7-year cap), and the results of the annual review. Since the number of job categories is relatively high, and the "walls of demarcation" between job categories are also high, job categories are the basis for determining wages. In fact, we are told that "the degree of difficulty of jobs corresponds to different wage levels." However, the length of service is a part of the criteria, and they also adopt the range rate. Combined then with the results of the annual review, differences between individual workers arise. So, in a sense, it is not a wage system that corresponds directly to job categories. In the process of determining wages, aware of potential union-related problems, the personnel department starts to function as a sort of substitute union. Compared to this, SB appears to be more oriented toward a wage system that corresponds to job categories.

On the side of labor relations also, the two plants are close to American nonunion semiconductor companies. Neither has a union. The personnel department takes an active role in handling grievances on the shop floor, paralleling the job hierarchy with solution channels. Both have methods for listening to the workers in small groups. Both are paying relatively close attention to maintaining good labor relations. This aspect is also shared by SF. SB has had no layoffs throughout its history, but the company has not clearly declared a no-layoff policy, either. SE's position is that resorting to a layoff would have a negative impact on morale. In spite of this, it carried out a small-scale layoff once in the past. Both prefer long-term employment, and have a pension program (401K Plan) linked to long-term employment. However, at SB, we are told that certain problems remain to be solved in regard to incentive measures for long-term employment. SE has certain incentives in place, such as a commendation system and others.

These two adaptation type plants closely resemble American nonunion and high-tech type enterprises in the area of personnel management on the shop floor. We will check on the application type plants, too, but it appears that the difference between application type and adaptation type among the Japanese semiconductor transplants could be in reality a very relative distinction. This is a conspicuous feature of the semiconductor industry, that differs sharply from consumer electronics.

In both plants, in the area of "hard" management, related to production equipment and so on, quality control, maintenance control, and operations management approximates the American method. Both have a rather high number of QC operators, who are different than regular operators, and of specialized inspectors. In this way, they aim to obtain a level of quality on a par with Japan. Equipment maintenance at SE is entrusted to their own engineers, and there is little room left for the participation of production workers. From the beginning, the production equipment and production processes for semiconductors require highly precise adjustment, even in the final process. For this reason, on the quality control side, too, there is a marked dependence on equipment and technology and, in consequence, maintenance becomes critically important. Furthermore, the advanced technical skill required by this maintenance means that a great deal of reliance is placed on specialized technical workers. It would seem from the industrial nature of these characteristics that the application of Japanese methods in the maintenance and quality control of semiconductor production would consist in establishing a feedback system from production to the technical section and to the technical workers and those in Japan as well. However, even from this perspective, the two plants are similar to the American type.

At present, small group activities play only a small part. An attempt has been made at SE, but nothing definite has come of it. We observed such activity only in the inspection arena, although the plant was busily attempting to set up a structure with the intention of turning it into a vital force soon. A suggestion system was introduced for improving operations. At SB, an attempt is underway to correct the American-style vertically segmented relationship and to improve horizontal cooperation in troubleshooting by forming a team when a problem arises. Although the number of teams is small, in addition, zero-defect (ZD) programs are in effect.

Even these two adaptation type plants, which rely on production technology from Japan, are also dependent on bringing-in "results" in the form of production equipment and parts. This is common for the larger semiconductor firms. But beyond this, SB is implanting local American methods for much of the core of the production system, including the management of personnel on the shop floor and management of the "hard" side. Moreover, the control and operation of the transplant is managed with a relatively small number of Japanese expatriates. There is a relatively high degree of autonomy, particularly in the case of SB, from the parent company in Japan. In this sense, while depending on manufacturing technology or its practical application, that is, production equipment and parts from Japan, SB displays its strength. On the human side, localization is highly advanced; thus in the core of the production system, instead of forcing application of Japanese methods, it is basing local production on a rather American-style system. SB has its Singapore plant perform three-fifths of the assembly work, after the preprocess treatment is done at the U.S. plant, and return the product to America. In this, too, it resembles American firms. The significance of the end process, for which the skill factor of production workers counts more than in preprocessing, is diminished here. This fact may be further accentuating SB's adaptation-orientation in the control and operation of work organization.

The two adaptation type plants have been in operation a long time and the production of both is on a large-scale. Therefore, the characteristics of the type we have been examining above can be seen as one typical example of the approach taken by local Japanese semiconductor production facilities in America so far. One interesting point is that SE is going ahead with revision work and a stronger orientation toward the application of Japanese methods can be seen. As a matter of fact, at SG plant, which has the same parent factory as SE and which recently started operations that consists primarily of preprocesses, this orientation is even more obvious. At the time of our visit, preparations were underway at SB, ahead of the other firms, for the local production of 4M DRAM chips, destined to becoming the main force of the next generation. In connection with this move, we suspect that SB's orientation toward the application of Japanese methods to production systems will become even more pronounced from now on and will include the training of production technicians and maintenance workers.

Human Application, Automation Technology Type: Factory SF

When looking at the four application type plants through the 4-Perspective Evaluation, we see their degree of intake from Japan is high on both the human side and the material side, and that they are strongly dependent on Japan. They are seeking to apply Japanese methods to personnel management as well as to material management, that is, to production equipment and operations management. Among these four semiconductor transplants, SF is the second largest in production and number of employees. Moreover, SF is the type led by automation technology as shown by its rather thorough application of automation to production processes in Japan. This greatly effects the company's approach to operating its local production facilities.

The full production of semiconductors at SF started relatively recently in 1985. Its major operations are the integrated production of 256K DRAM chips, the assembly of 1M DRAM chips and production of application specific integrated circuits (ASIC). At the time of our survey, they were in the process of starting up the preprocessing of 256K DRAMs, and just entering into the mass production of ASIC. Preprocessing in semiconductor manufacturing is largely dependent on manufacturing technology that stems from actual operating experience, and the accumulation of detailed know-how is critical. For this reason, it is of the utmost importance to transplant to local facilities manufacturing technology established in Japan, including equipment, parts, and materials. This is particularly true at SF with its technology-led production. The Japanese method application rating is not so high on the human side of management and operations on the shop floors. Given these conditions, SF achieved the largest production output among the four major application type plants. It is engaged in the integrated production of memory chips and is going ahead with the mass production of ASIC. As it makes this transition to a more stabilized operation, we expect to see expanded application of the Japanese method to the human side of management also. In fact, signs of this are already in evidence.

SF's averages in the parent-subsidiary company relationship group and in the production control group are the highest among semiconductor plants. The dependency on Japan for technology and human resources is common among major application type plants, but at SF it is especially pronounced. The proportion of Japanese expatriates is high, and they occupy critical positions in the upper echelons of management. Japanese initiative is the dominant force in decision making on technical matters, production items, investment timing, and so forth.

A clear demonstration of the dependency on Japan for technology is seen in the substantial number of engineers and maintenance personnel sent for training in Japan. Aside from the case of consumer electronics, this is a trait generally observed in the local production operations of Japanese transplants, and it is found in many of the semiconductor plants as well. However, in SF's case, twenty to thirty engineers are dispatched annually on a long-term basis of 1 to 2 years. This is meant to aid in the attempt to transplant indigenous Japanese ways of doing things with the purpose of developing engineers for ASIC design and preprocessing. This can be viewed as a case of an all-out effort to transfer technology. It probably comes from the shift of preprocessing to the transplant that had the effect of deepening dependency on Japan for technology, and strengthened its characteristic orientation toward technology.

The shifting of preprocessing to transplants in America and the subsequent increased dependency on Japan for technology can be observed in other transplants as well. At SC, they were preparing to start the preprocessing by an across-the-board retrofit of their facilities. Part of their effort to transplant the "Japanese system" consists of regularly sending an average of two or three people from among team leaders, managers, and engineers to Japan every month. Specifically for the purpose of the start-up of preprocessing, a training program in Japan has been set up, targeted mainly at the engineer class. Also, production workers, supervisors, and engineering personnel, totaling forty people, are dispatched from Japan to the local facility as coaches. Even for the end processes, where the technology transfer has been completed, Japanese engineers remain for technical coaching and the dependency on Japan for technology continues. Also at SG, a facility newly built mainly for preprocessing and ASIC production, at the stage immediately preceding the mass production of 256K DRAMs, to help initiate 1M DRAM production, thirty or more engineers, supervisors, chiefs, and safety management officers are being sent to Japan annually.

Seventy to eighty percent of SF's production equipment is Japanese. SF belongs to the lower side in the semiconductor industry for procurement of parts and materials from local American vendors, and consequently it is highly dependent on Japan. Although the pieces of production equipment are the same as those used in Japan, for easier maintenance, the extent of the automation that links them is held down, possibly showing the persistent difficulty in instilling full maintenance know-how in the local workers. It is said that equipment maintenance at SF for assembly (the end process) is handled mostly by Americans, but that for the wafer process (preprocessing) Japanese still play an important role. The plant is dependent on Japan as well as expatriate Japanese, for the "hard" side, namely production equipment and its control.

Since the semiconductor manufacturing processes contain a number of black boxes, the accumulation of manufacturing know-how through actual operation experience is essential. Therefore, the basic requirement for the smooth local production of semiconductors is first to apply the manufacturing technology and expertise built up in Japan to production equipment and human resources. However, if we can believe what was pointed out at the interview, "the key to the incorporation of 'Japanese thinking'" in the "techniques for making things" at a local site is "the technicians on the shop floor, and the subsequent strength that these primary players will provide as they grow in expertise 10 to 15 years down the road". A long-term objective is necessary to create a system right on the shop floor, wherein a better understanding of the manufacturing processes by the shop workers enables them to "build quality into processes" and a feeling that they can perform preventative maintenance themselves "deepens skills."

In practice, even at SF we find some inclination to apply Japanese methods to the shop-floor management of workers. The job classification for production workers in the assembly and testing areas is composed of nineteen job categories. This is not a small number. These categories are allocated into three job classes. Overlying these are three distinctions—operator, key-operator, and senior operator—based on the capability of the individual worker. On top of those come the leadmen and the line-technicians, whose role is to respond to major equipment failures. The leadmen ensure that "work management" is carried out effectively, and are divided into two levels, that correspond to pay based on the nature of the duties involved. Among the ranks of production workers, operators are capable of machine operation, key-operators are capable of simple repair jobs, and senior operators are more multiskilled key-operators. It is the system in which the more depth and breadth a worker acquires in one's skills, the higher the rating of one's capability. A higher qualification is dependent on obtaining a certain minimum number of points in the biannual performance evaluation, and then participation in an educational program for the promotion. This is how the process of developing multiskilled workers is evaluated and handled, with great importance attached to it.

The wage system is basically determined by the matrix of job ranks and worker's capability ratings, and differences in wages are generated according to the degree of difficulty of the job. Thus, it corresponds somewhat to job titles. However, as there can be as much as a 10 to 20 percent differential between individual workers due to the performance evaluation, some degree of allegiance to the human factor is taken into account. Actually, this system is a recent introduction. Previous to it, there were eight levels of job grades with their corresponding wages, more of an American-type system. At present, job classifications have been simplified and the progress made by individual workers in their respective skills is evaluated, so the system has been revised toward the side of application.

Another feature of SF is the great degree of importance it attached to labor relations also in connection with its site selection. The site is located in a state that has a low rate of unionization compared with the national average. This indicates that at SF also, the avoidance of unionization has been fairly deliberate. In fact, SF was the object of a union offensive 2 years ago, and countered with careful measures, including wages. It appears that the plant is striving to maintain a nonunion type labor-management relationship. There is no clause-strengthening job security stipulating a no-layoff policy. Instead, a layoff rule that accords with seniority is prescribed. It is American in form. However, so far the plant has never had to lay off anybody, and we heard that they desire to continue avoiding it. Therefore, in practice long-term employment would seem to be viewed by SF as quite important.

SF is attempting to strengthen the overall technical capabilities of its production workers. This is done in view of the fact that, like its parent factory in Japan, the automation of the interface between manufacturing machines has been rather thoroughly implemented, and consequently more importance is given to preventive maintenance. In the quality control area also, the importance of "building quality into processes" by individual workers is being taught. To some extent the plant is seeking to develop Japanese-like shop-floor workers by means of the job classification and wage systems. However, it is said that the quality "depends mostly on the technology" and that, in practice, most areas are under Japanese supervision. The productivity per worker is still behind Japan even in the assembly process (end process), but the difference in yield has disappeared. In preprocessing, however, problems are said to persist. As for job rotation, it is thought that "Carrying it out would be meaningless, unless the workers' skills are at a very high level." Although it is stated that the job assignments can be changed, in actuality jobs appear to be generally fixed. Does this mean that putting into practice a structure to foster multiskilled workers is still premature at this local site? Nothing noteworthy presents itself in the application of the Japanese method in the area of cultivating a group consciousness. Although there is a suggestion system, no small group activities are carried out.

SF then is running a technology-led local production facility, thanks to the thorough automation of production processes pursued by its parent in Japan. This increases its dependence on Japan for equipment and technology. In order to keep a stable operation ongoing in America, the crucial issue will be the development of local engineers, maintenance people, and technicians. To do this, SF has just recently started to promote the development of "deepening one's skills" among shop-floor workers and to nurture technicians to become key workers who are closely involved with the production floor. However, the bulk of this task remains for the future. The transfer of operations including even preprocessing, to the transplant coupled with the sophistication of products manufactured, is expected to increase SF's dependence on Japan in technological and human areas. From the long-term perspective, we feel that the application of Japanese methods will continue to increase because local workers are being trained by means of Japanese methods.

Basic Necessary Personnel, High Application Type: Factory SD

SD provides an interesting contrast with SF. For mass-produced products, it operates only the end process for memory chips. For integrated production including preprocessing it makes only prototypes (samples) of ASIC, based on gate arrays. Production capacity is relatively low, one-fifth that of SB, the largest, and ranks fourth after SE. Its scale in number of employees is the smallest. Its parent company has an advantage over others as the top manufacturer of 1M DRAM chips. But local production figures into this in only a small way with about 10 percent of the corporation's total sales in the American market.

SD started its operation in 1980 by buying out a facility transplanted by another Japanese company that had made inroads into Silicon Valley at quite an early period. In this sense, SD has a long experience operating in America. However, the Silicon Valley has become inappropriate for expansion of mass production facilities, due to the high cost of land and labor and to pollution issues. For this reason, a trend is developing to utilize the valley as a technology center. SD, instead of being a full-scale integrated mass production plant for memory chips, has been established for use as a facility for the fabrication of prototypes by specializing in high value-added ASIC.

In the spring of 1989, an ASIC-dedicated prototype (sample) manufacturing plant was opened. The focus will shift to ASIC, which represents one-fifth of all current production. The company placed five design centers across America, and established the main center within the SD Plant. Along these lines, the plant is operated with a high Japanese method application rating, by a selected and limited number of workers, based on manufacturing technology and its embodiment, the manufacturing equipment developed in Japan.

SD shows the highest application rating among the target semiconductor transplants in job classification, job rotation and promotion, and so on from group I, "Work Organization and Administration." Job classifications for production workers consist of wafer fabrication (preprocessing), assembly (end process), and testing. The job grade starts with "entry" at 6 months after joining the company, then "intermediate," and having become a multiskilled worker, "specialist." One rank higher is "leadman," giving us a total of only four grades. Work on the shop floor is organized around teams that are composed of a supervisor, under whom one to three leadmen are posted at each process, with two to five or six operators under them. Within the assembly (end process), job rotations are frequently carried out for the purpose of transforming production workers into multiskilled workers. In fact, creating the job grade of "specialist," introduced in December, 1988, appears to have been intended as a way to treat workers who reach the status of multiskilled workers. The leadmen are dedicated to their respective processes, while the production workers are dispatched to wherever the operation demands it depending on fluctuations in production, and even the team unit itself is not absolutely fixed. Compared with SF, the normally high "walls of demarcation" of American-type job classifications are not so insurmountable here.

Also, the plant attaches a fair importance to Japanese methods for instilling a group consciousness. Small group activities had been carried out in the past, but did not take root. Instead, 6 months prior to our investigation, the plant had launched a combined group activity and suggestion system and QC circle-style activities, called total preventive maintenance (TPM). Because nearly 10 years of operations in America had "exhausted the introduction of technology from Japan," and because the end process yield had already stabilized at nearly the same level as Japan, to jack up the yield one more notch, it was said to be important to bring out the "will to involve" in the workers.

It seems very difficult to firmly establish the small group activities themselves in the semiconductor transplants in America. Once past the stage where manufacturing technology and physical equipment are brought in from Japan, however, it can be said that more effort is being spent on the creation of the "*genba*ism-oriented methods" themselves. In regard to the wage system, because "there is no relation between job and the wage," the job-correspondence character of wages is weakened. Here, too, a performance evaluation is employed. Moreover, long service is rewarded by incremental annual pay raises so that wages reflect length of service. Also, operators are given an across-the-board bonus twice a year at a fixed rate figured against a half a year's earnings.

It is necessary to discount the supervisor function, as far as the application of the management of the workers on the shop floor is concerned. The first-line supervisor's function is mainly to handle personnel matters, such as interviews for hiring and layoffs, and so on, and to work on production control-related tasks, such as work assignments based on the schedule laid out by a manager in charge of production, and to follow up on the production schedule. It is not part of the first-line supervisor's function to run a job team, or assume responsibility in technical-related matters of production. This is fairly common among all of the target semiconductor transplants. However, promotion to the positions of leadman and supervisor is done primarily from within the company. Although the supervisor function does not include so much application, SD certainly leans most strongly to the application type in comparison with the other semiconductor transplants.

In stark contrast to SF, SD has the lowest application rating in the area of labor relations. Although its position regarding layoffs is "We want to avoid them if at all possible," it carried out a layoff once in the past, and a policy toward job security is not clearly defined. Nevertheless, considering its emphasis on the development of multiskilled workers and on obtaining leadmen and supervisors through promotion from within the company, we cannot simply say it is indifferent to long-term employment. Even that layoff actually occurred as part of a change in direction, whereby the facility was converted to a technology center focused on ASIC. Thus, it would appear that the plant does not necessarily dismiss long-term hiring policies lightly. Its pension system is another factor that encourages long-term employment. Nevertheless, the plant has little inclination to actively apply Japanese methods to their hiring policies and to job security, and in this way it more closely approximates the American type. Perhaps this characteristic is more strongly pronounced here in comparison with the plants of other regions due to SD's location in the Silicon Valley.

As the facility is converted into a technology center, SD seems intent on applying Japanese methods to key local personnel. These form a select group, limited in number, whose purpose is to sustain the production of high value-added products. For manufacturing technology and equipment and parts they are heavily dependent on Japan. And in the operation and administration of the plant, the role of the Japanese expatriates is relatively important. Moreover, it is largely dependent on its Japanese parent company for making decisions critical to the local business operation. Currently, SD's parent company is looking for an American site to build an integrated mass production plant for ASIC. It will be worthwhile to see how much of SD's experience in such an application-oriented shop-floor system will prove useful in the local production of the new facility. Although labeled as an application type, SD may be an exceptional case.

Materials Adaptation, System Application Type: Factory SA

SA provides many contrasts with the transplants of major semiconductor corporations. Particularly in the case of Work Organization and Administration, its application rating is not only the highest in the semiconductor industry but also among the highest for all the target transplants. Whereas in all the other five groups, on the contrary, its rating is below the industry average. So by excluding group I and glancing over the semiconductor industry, SA would appear to be an adaptation type. But it displays application type features in its management and production system. Moreover, SA's most obvious feature is that it is the least dependent on Japan in the material area (production equipment and procurement) in contrast with the transplants of the major firms. Thus, it is classified as a "material-adaptation methods-application type."

Eighty percent of SA's production equipment is made in America. This is probably because originally, SA's Japanese parent company established the plant in the beginning of the 1970s with the aim of mastering American semiconductor manufacturing techniques. The parent company still maintains its fundamental strategy to mainly target the market for relatively low integration products that remain after the major players have shifted their main forces to other areas. Even in the facilities in Japan, half of the equipment (in terms of expenditure) is American-made. Nevertheless, we must not overlook the fact that since at the present time the technological edge belongs to the Japanese side, an effort to bring up the compatibility of equipment with the parent company is being stressed. Currently, the rate of compatibility is 60 percent, and the number of Japanese-made pieces of equipment is increasing.

Localization is progressing rather well also in procurement. Localization here is the most advanced in terms of both local content and sources for parts. Seventy percent of parts and materials is procured from local sources, and of those, 70 percent are American vendors. Thus procurement from local American vendors represents half of the total procurement. However, as far as wafers are concerned, the portion of local Japanese vendors is high at 70 percent. Furthermore, SA provides technical assistance and guidance to these local American vendors. The items of the purchasing contract is typically 1 or 2 to 3 years. Japanese methods are applied on the procurement side and this, too, contrasts sharply with the major corporations.

On the human side also, the ratio of expatriate Japanese is the lowest among the target semiconductor transplants. Thus, the degree to which it "brings-in the results" from Japan is low on both the material and human sides. Nevertheless, the local business operation lacks autonomy in regard to its parent company in Japan, both in terms of the limited delegation of authority and the positions occupied by the top local executives; dependency on the parent company is high. The application ratings of these two items are nearly the same level as all the other transplants of major companies except SB. This probably has something to do with its length of years of operation and the fact that the size of its parent company is small.

On the other hand, contrary to the ongoing progress in localization on the material side, the application rating is high on the method side of personnel management. The job classification has been simplified, and the separation between jobs made less rigid. Job categories for production workers are roughly divided into pre- and end-process. For each job process in these two areas, there is a team organized much like the team in Japan. Each team is composed of a fixed group of eight to fifteen operators. For each process there is a salaried supervisor, assisted by one leadman per shift. The operators are ranked in three job grades, A, B, and C, according to the degree of difficulty of the job. Since about 2 years ago, to develop versatility in its workforce, the plant has been actively conducting job rotation within a team. In each process area, individual job assignments are less fixed. The wages for production workers are determined according to the job grade, years of service, and assessment by means of an annual "performance evaluation." It is said that wages differ from one individual to another, so the system includes some capability to adapt to the human element while based on the job grade. More than half of the supervisors are promoted from within the company, and this figure is expected to increase in the future. As for the function of the supervisor, although we lack sufficient confirmation on this point, we assume that a supervisor oversees a working team together with a leadman. It can be judged that in the areas of the work organization and its administration, Japanese ways of doing things have been introduced to a fair extent.

In the area of instilling a group consciousness, small group activities are the most intense of all the semiconductor transplants. However, the participation rate is still only 30–40 percent, activities are carried out during the normal working hours, and these are said to be strongly imbued with a manufacturing technology-led "top-down" character. However, the small group activities rate here is not so low when compared to the struggling efforts to get it going at the transplants of the major corporations. In the domain of information sharing and a sense of unity, however, Japanese methods are not being actively brought in. In maintenance, quality control, and operations management, all indicators of "hard" management methods, SA shows an application rating almost as high as the "application type" plants of the major corporations.

Thus, the application rate is high for methods of human and material control and operations in those areas pertaining to the core of the Japanese management and production system, and it is characteristic of this plant to actively bring in Japanese methods. From the beginning, SA had strategically positioned itself in Silicon Valley in order to best absorb the local American semiconductor technology. In such a context it has actively applied Japanese methods in the areas of plant control and operations. In this sense, it is unique among the other major semiconductor companies.

8

Overall Evaluation and Prospects

TETSUO ABO

Throughout the preceding chapters we have shown the theory behind our research, its underlying analytical framework, and the various aspects of the analysis and evaluation of our on-the-spot investigation conducted both in Japan and America. The present chapter, then, is not merely a recap of this but an attempt to confront the primary accomplishments of the application-adaptation model analysis carried out up to this point with an evaluation of actual performance in order to arrive at a general assessment of the condition of the transfer of the Japanese system to local Japanese transplants. Due to various difficulties, an evaluation of performance did not appear in our previous preliminary study. The current study also leaves much to be desired in this regard, but without an evaluation of actual performance it could hardly be considered complete. In conclusion, we will attempt to tie together the accomplishments of the present research as a whole and take this occasion to touch upon the areas that impressed us most in the past two investigations and to review within a broader context the significance of the present research in regard to a few issues thus bringing-in future prospects.

APPLICATION-ADAPTATION EVALUATION
OF THE TARGET PLANTS

First, let us present some of the key points of the main characteristics of the application-adaptation evaluation ratings of thirty-four Japanese transplants in four industries that have come to light so far.

1. At a rating of 3.3, the overall average of the hybrid evaluation leans slightly toward the application side, and although Japanese elements predominate somewhat, Japanese and American characteristics are judiciously mixed in nearly equal portions. As far as the evaluation based on our model is concerned, the Japanese transplants as a whole are operating with both Japanese and American elements mixed together. But, of course, when we look at individual industries, at specific items that constitute the model or at individual groups, there are significant variations, and it is necessary to pay full attention to their combinations.

2. Indeed, a fairly large gap can be seen between industries. While auto parts, with a rating of 3.6, and auto assembly at 3.5, noticeably lean toward the application side, consumer electronics at 2.7 has, to the contrary, shifted in the direction of adaptation. With a rating of 3.2, the semiconductor industry, on the other hand, is found in the middle at nearly the overall average.

3. Looking at rating combinations in regard to the six groups, it is interesting to see that items that concern result application of humans or materials in terms used in the 4-Perspective Evaluation, such as Labor-Management Relations (3.6), Parent-Subsidiary Company Relations (3.6), and Production Control (3.3), are aligned on the higher side, whereas Work Organization, the heart of the application of the human method of the Japanese system, at 2.9 is relatively low, and Group Consciousness, which could be considered as a subsystem of the human-method aspect, at 3.2, is high. Superimposing these onto the previous survey, we notice that Labor-Management Relations, Parent-Subsidiary, and Production Control all increased on the application side, even if by a mere 0.1. Work Organization, on the contrary, declined by 0.2. This may suggest that there is a problem here that is greater than the margin of error. Viewed together with the 0.2 rise for Group Consciousness, this could be seen as an attempt to assist the struggling growth of the core part by means of subsystems. On the other hand, the fact that Procurement (3.0) dropped 0.1 compared with the previous study indicates that this material-result application had reached its limit and could advance no farther because of constraints due to localization.

4. The same things can be confirmed through examination of the 23 items. On the side of higher ratings for application, we see Labor Unions (4.4), Production Equipment (4.3), Suppliers (3.9), and Ratio of Japanese Expatriates (3.7). With the exception of Job Classifications (3.7), they all fall under the category of result application of humans and material. We find method application items aligned on the lower side in both the human and material areas, that is, Wage Systems (2.4), Procurement Methods (2.5), Small Group Activities (2.5), Job Rotation (2.6), and Maintenance (2.6). This clearly highlights the strong predilection to directly bring-in the ready-made things of the Japanese system concerning both humans and material, and the relatively weak tendency to bring-in methods. We will discuss the meaning of this in our conclusion, along with the reason for the rise in job classification.

TEN TYPES OF TYPICAL JAPANESE TRANSPLANTS

In the preceding Chapter 7, we brought out in sharp relief the concrete image of transplants in America, through comparative studies of variations in major plants by picking out a few characteristic types from each of the four industrial sectors chosen for this study. In this section, we will select from these types ten plants that bear characteristics that are representative of Japanese transplants but transcendent of individual industrial categories, and compare them.

The point of doing this is as follows.

1. These plants are considered to be those that illustrate the major types of Japanese transplants, have an adequate track record, and are apt to keep their manufacturing operation in America.
2. Therefore, according to their respective experiences, they could also be seen as models presenting a number of choices for Japanese corporations in their drive to locate local production in America.
3. However, these ten plants were not necessarily chosen on the basis of their success in business or the scale of their production. Of course, plants typical of each sector are included, but at the same time, we also picked those that, from the standpoint of our standards for evaluation, include thought-provoking means of transferring Japanese management and production systems.
4. Each of these ten was selected primarily on the basis of the objective analysis of our research but finally with a certain value judgment of our own and represents an aspect characteristic of all the Japanese plants taken up for our study. In other words, to consolidate our present research, we thought it was necessary to not only show the average image common to all the plants, but in the above way, to reveal the overall image of Japanese plants in the United States in a composite, three-dimensional form that would provide some practical benefits for local production.

Now, although in fact these ten plants clearly illustrate the characteristics of their respective industries, they will be presented here from the standpoint of the aspects or characteristics that are generally representative of transplants, over and above the distinction characteristic of a specific industry. The 23-item, 6-group evaluation of the hybrid model is the criteria first used to compare the ten plants and to categorize them into types. However, as we have already stated, the average degree of application is not the only issue here. There is another criterion, the 4-Perspective Evaluation. With this we look at the combinations and balance among elements, or "hybrid", constituting the model, with our focus on the real transplantation of the Japanese system. This is also an important tool.

Japanese-Lead High-Application Type: AA, Auto Assembly

Plant AA, as belonging to the top group of the application-oriented-type, can be called the number one representative of Japanese transplants in America, due to its remarkably high performance as measured by production output. On the other hand, this plant also stands out on the adaptation side in its extension of the meaning of what has been called localization, by the considerable progress it has made in shifting to local production, as typified by its early establishment, high local content, and so forth. Therefore, we cannot simply label it as an across-the-board application type. Certainly, in addition to the usual high-application-orientation particular to automotive plants, AA's overall rating has been pulled sharply toward the application side by the prominence of human-result application, as shown in its conspicuously high ratio of Japanese expatriates and in its site-selection, where the emphasis was on a rural work force. So we could classify it as a human high-application and material adaptation type. But what we have here is a marvelous hybrid pattern of a plant that achieved remarkably high quality and efficiency, and that by producing a great quantity of two major models in many variations, is closing in on the Big Three, and aims to further leap ahead by completing a second plant. But, viewed from a different angle, it cannot be completely denied that the strong orientation toward the human-result application that is at the very core of its strength may, in the end, threaten the stability of long-term operations. The high number of Japanese expatriate employees is a big factor in the inflation of direct and indirect labor management costs, and this may also serve to delay the localization of the trouble management function. Moreover, its apparent partiality toward a certain type of work force and the fact that it is a nonunion plant suggests certain sensitive problems, such as minority issues. Although plant AA's success story is very famous, nonetheless, it is necessary to emphasize at this point that its strong points as well as its problems in, for example, the key role played by Japanese expatriate advisors, can be seen at most of the Japanese transplants in America. (More on this later.)

American-Lead Application Type: AB, Auto Assembly

At any rate, the high-application group is made up of auto assembly and auto parts plants, of which AB stands out in contrast with AA. AB's application rating is quite low in comparison with, needless to say, that of AA, but it is also low compared to the 3.5 average of the auto assembly industry. Among this group it stands out as an example of the adaptation type. This is due to the fact that since the ratio of Japanese expatriates is extremely low, the Americans, who occupy almost all the managerial posts from the president down, understand the parent factory's system, and are trying to apply Japanese methods with the help of this small number of Japanese advisors. Its low score in human-result application is mainly responsible for holding down its overall average. Given this condition, if AB were able to match AA in performance, we could consider it as the most ideal form of a Japanese transplant in America. In reality, however, when judged on production and sales performance, AB's figures are currently not only well below AA's, but below AC and AE as well. The models produced at AB have brought some influence to bear on this problem in connection with changes in marketplace conditions for pickup trucks and with special problems with compact car models, and so forth. But it would still seem to indicate that Japanese-style management of operations, when run by Americans, leaves some considerable gaps in contrast to the case where there is direct control and guidance by the Japanese expatriates. On the other hand, AB has its good points, such as considerable cuts in personnel expenses and its ability to deal effectively at the critical phase of upcoming U.S.-Japan investment friction. Moreover, it is also good at setting up a system of local procurement made up of suppliers based in the United States, like AJ, which will be presented later, and AT, a subsidiary based in Mexico. When both the soon-to-be-launched new models are out, and the construction of its second plant completed, the odds are good that the plant's unique adaptation method will again attract considerable attention.

Adaptation and Application Combined Type: AC, Auto Assembly

In many ways, AC falls in the middle between AA and AB. AC's parent company is typical of Japanese corporations, who belatedly embarked on local production overseas only after being pressed. In fact, its first approach to setting up a plant in America took the form of a joint venture with an American firm. Although the result of careful negotiations and selections, these circumstances lead to the formation of an extremely interesting combination. They accepted the existing plant and the workers of the partner, and the materials and human assets of the UAW-based American corporation facility level as a full set, and managed it jointly with a certain number of expatriate Japanese employees and with about the same number of managers from the U.S. partner. Thus, from the beginning, based on the premise of considerable local adaptation in regard to almost all the elements of the plant management, the Japanese employees, fully entrusted as far as the management of plant-level operations was concerned, have tried to apply the parent factory's methods as much as possible. As a result, it found itself at a midway position in the such major indexes as the overall average of application-adaptation and performance ratings—that is to say, higher than AB but below AA. It was also a valuable experiment to test the degree to which the Japanese-style management could permeate operations and thereby discover how the existing human and material elements and organizations, including the union, have been reworked into the participation-type and flexible steering-type of Japan that leads to the achievement of high quality and efficiency. So it is that there have been major repercussions in the States from this case in particular. Nevertheless, results did not sufficiently satisfy the parent company, a leader in the Japanese production system. Partly because of this, the parent corporation came forward several years later to start operation of its 100 percent-owned "greenfield plant," AE, as described below.

Method Revision and Application Type: AE, Auto Assembly

Thus, ideally, AE aimed at increasing the level of quality in a traditional Japanese transplant in America, while making the most of the valuable experiences gleaned from AC, and also taking into account the broad-ranged studies of the activities at other Japanese plants in the United States, including states such as AA, AB. That is, in terms of our model, a Japanese transplant established up until then was to aim at the application of the Japanese method as is. When this could not be carried out, the transplant was to try adaptation, by introducing American methods (elements). In short, it assumes that the relationship between application and adaptation is basically a relationship of a "choice between two alternatives," whereas the aim of AE was revising the methods of the parent company in advance through positively accepting American methods and conditions, while trying to apply the "logic" of the parent's methods. In other words, the application partly subsumes the adaptation, that is a "revisionist application."

For example, an American method was introduced in the case of the maintenance personnel development at AE. After a thorough analysis, adaptation consisted of converting the Japanese OJT-centered approach into an imposing long-term training program. We could call it pursuit of a more realistic way of applying the parent factory's methods by trying to make the American element compatible with the application. However, as stated above (Chapter 2), our model is primarily constructed as a means of facilitating comparison with parent factories in Japan. It is not easy, however, to bring quality and efficiency (including costs), the fruits of the revised application, up to a level equivalent to that in Japan. But if such an achievement were possible to some extent, we would have here the most ideal form of the international transfer of manufacturing technology. In any event, the fact that the plant is competitive enough within the American market is being borne out by results through the fall of 1990.

Revision High-Application Type: AM, Auto Parts

AM, a typical auto parts plant, has a number of similarities with AE, and ranks highest in application among the ten types. Furthermore, it consistently ranked highly in all categories across the board. Despite its affiliation with AC-AE, as the firm is already a huge corporation in Japan, it was strong enough to start developing local production in America on its own initiative ahead of AC and AE. Therefore, even though it has not been as systematic and logical as AE, the firm has a record of practical experiments in a kind of revisionary application in its use of the *kanban* and wage systems, due in part to its business relationship with auto assembly facilities. AM ranked so highly in application because, first of all, like all other firms in the auto parts industry, it required specialized equipment and many Japanese expatriates in order to carry out the detailed transfer of technology and know-how. In its ability to meticulously promote and control the intake of Japanese methods, including the above-mentioned revisionary application, the plant appears to be able to easily stand comparison with AE, for example.

Application/Adaptation Combined Type: AJ, Auto Parts

Also an auto parts plant, but quite different than AM, AJ is also quite active in localization in conjunction with its high degree of application. But in fact, its overall average rating is slightly below the industry's average. Is this simply because it is an affiliate of AB? But, although it is in the process of transferring more managerial posts to Americans, unlike AB it still appears to be oriented toward application with a high ratio of Japanese expatriate advisors supporting the personnel evaluation system and the QC circle activities. Localization occurs in the intensity of its local content and in the vigorous promotion of exchanges with local communities. Here we can see a facet of the determination of AJ, which is on its way to becoming a world-class parts supplier, in its conscious effort to inhibit the one-sided tendency to lean toward a high degree of application, common in the auto parts industry. On the other hand, in the sense that it offers a particular combination of application and adaptation, there is a similar aspect to previously described AC. But there is an important difference in that for AC, adaptation presupposed a joint venture with an American firm.

Across-the-Board Adaptation/General Strategy Type:
EB, Consumer Electronics and Electric Appliances

In contrast to the high degree of application of the group just described, there is the low-application group—that is, a high-adaptation group that is primarily made up of consumer electronics and electric appliances plants. EB is representative of this aspect of adaptation. EB's overall average is at the lowest level, along with that of ED, among all the target plants. One reason for this is that EB bought a TV plant from an American electric equipment manufacturer and started its operation by taking over the existing equipment and employees, including some of the management personnel. Another was probably that the overseas operations development strategy of its parent company from its early stages had been diversified and general in nature, to a degree not common in Japan. The plant equipment was mostly replaced by equipment from Japan not long after the acquisition. But, aside from this, in those things connected with human resources basically they have organized the plant and its methods of operations along traditional American lines. What enabled the plant to maintain its competitiveness while adapting large American parts of itself to the essence of the human-material-methods of the Japanese system that we constantly emphasize, is EB's diversified strategy. First, on the material side, it was crucial that in addition to replacement with Japanese equipment, it pioneered the usage of foreign factories such as the maquiladora to obtain key components for its supply system. Second, the plant has been supported by the global organization and strategy of a multinational corporation, as shown by the corporation's global logistic network built around the sales network of the U.S. head office. One thing that we should not overlook here is the fact that the production process at this plant is limited to the final assembly in which the equipment and processing operations are relatively simple. If its processing were as complex as is the case in automotive plants, the results might have been quite different.

Production Control Technology Dependency Type:
ED, Consumer Electronics and Electric Appliances

Like the above-described EB, ED also depends on maquiladora for parts supply, and this plant in the same consumer electronics industry possesses the essential conditions to be competitive. Moreover, while adopting a businesslike American approach in the area of personnel management, on the hardware side they carefully brought in production control technology from the parent factory. Characteristically representative of transplants in the consumer electronics industry in recent years, ED has registered top-level results in all areas of production: units, number of models, and quality level. On the shop floors, they are adapting to local methods, such as, for example, in the methods of setting up and operating work organizations, the methods of carrying out quality control and maintenance activities, and in the acceptance of labor unions without forcing too much in the areas associated with human or material methods. On the other hand, they are greatly dependent on material-result application for their strength, by bringing-in products, production equipment, and parts. In this regard, the plant's most striking feature may be its smart way of introducing the operating techniques of its parent factory by adapting them to the prevailing local conditions, as can be seen directly in the use of the bar-code system in operations and quality control. Of course, the success of having such a resolute attitude probably owes itself in good part to the simplicity of the production process. Moreover, further study would be needed to determine to what extent this factory could respond with flexibility, when faced with various fluctuating factors, such as the switchover to different product models, or economic fluctuation, and relations with the labor union in such circumstances.

Application-Adaptation All-Side-Balanced Type: EF, Consumer Electronics and Electric Appliances

Among plants in an industry that is primarily characterized by the adaptation approach, such as the two plants discussed above, there is a group that shows a stronger orientation toward application in certain areas. EF is a plant that commands our attention by virtue of the fact that not only does it find the middle ground between these two groups, but it also displays a remarkable balance in the ratings by group and by item of the hybrid-model. Since there is no big variance between its ratings, a very definitive and tidy graph can be constructed. To sum up, EF is one of a small number of TV plants that consistently delivers high performance. Unlike EB and EC, efficiency and quality are built-in at its own plant, without undue dependence on external conditions (the single exception being the import of chassis from sister plants in ASEAN countries), while a balance is carefully maintained between application and adaptation in all aspects of the management of the transplant. Although it shares in this certain aspects with ED, there are more than a few differences. For instance, although it is a newly built plant, it accepted the union, and thus while avoiding any strikes, it promotes small group activities with zeal, reduces the number of job classifications little by little, and carries out partial modification or development of equipment locally, by itself. It can be labeled as the "local version" of "accumulative-type management", the type particular to companies coming from Western Japan, that accumulates minute techniques and know-how. However, it cannot be said that all this has been necessarily carried out by plan under a well-defined policy. Rather, it is the result of trial and error, experiences piled up one after another empirically by the local staff, under the leadership of Japanese expatriate managers, a few whom have been on assignment there for a long time. Therefore, EF seems well-suited to serve as an honorable example of a transplant in a technical area, namely, consumer electronics and electric appliances. However, its modus operandi is so ingenious that no especially unique feature or particularly decisive factor can be found. So it becomes surprisingly difficult to develop the logic needed to formulate it abstractly as a model.

Human-Adaptation Material-Application: SB, Semiconductors

SB, which, through the scale of its production and its business history, represents the semiconductor industry fell rather short of the 3.2 overall industry average for application. Therefore, since it is of the adaptation-type, it could be said to be rather close to consumer electronics. But, when we look at how it is actually structured, it clearly shows one of the characteristics of a semiconductor plant. That is, on one hand, with almost all the procurement sources for the production equipment and parts being based in Japan, the extent of application in material-result is extremely high for the essential hardware technology. On the other hand, for the application of methods regarding human and material, such as work organization-related items, and items concerned with controlling quality and the maintenance systems, except for the wage system, the degree of application is considerably low. This simply projects an aspect, common to the semiconductor industry, that shows that as long as Japanese technology is securely brought in on the hardware or material side, the organization dealing with human resources and operations can be handled somehow, even in the local way. After all is taken into account, SB's overall average of application is still lower than other semiconductor plants. One can only presume that because SB's parent company is relatively better at product engineering than in production engineering, it places less emphasis than other companies on application on the human-methods side. This type can be seen frequently in the high-tech equipment-dependent industries. In any event, it remains a question whether a little more application of Japanese methods is not needed in the area of training the equipment maintenance crew.

PERFORMANCE AND APPLICATION-ADAPTATION

Through our study so far, it has become clear that most of the target Japanese plants in the United States somehow manage to continue to operate by combining application and adaptation on an individual basis and that a great variety of combinations exist in different industries and from one firm to another. It was our initial objective not only to evaluate the extent of hybridity between application and adaptation, but also to determine the relationship between an actual plant's hybrid combination and business performance. This was also an objective of our previous study, albeit unfulfilled. This time we were determined to achieve our objective, made careful preparations, and pursued it with perseverance. But, we cannot say we necessarily obtained a satisfactory result. In short, while there were not enough consistent data to produce a significant conclusion, we were able to obtain some valuable data that enabled us to further our aims. Here, we will attempt to isolate and describe as many hidden meanings as possible.

Performance Guidelines

First, we will throw some light on exactly what constitutes performance and mention some of the problems in calculating it.

Henceforth, we will take productivity as an index for performance, and compare the performance of transplants with their parent factories. Productivity here means basically the volume produced per worker per hour at a given plant or with a given process, taking into account to some extent a particular cost factor. Many explanations and reservations are required here, but first let us mention some general technical problems in dealing with the material.

1. Although we attempted to ensure that we were comparing identical production processes for each industry, in some cases, like auto parts, it was not possible.
2. Because there were difficulties finding identical product model line-ups (between parent and subsidiary), we later introduced a reduction factor to account for the difference of product mix. For example, we inserted a productivity lowering factor for transplants with fewer models.
3. Since working hours would differ between parent factory and subsidiary (the parent had longer hours), we made adjustments for each firm and industry.
4. We counted the indirect production personnel, including maintenance, quality control people, and expatriate Japanese employees as employees, then later factored this in as a specific cost adjustment factor, that is, a cost increase factor for transplants with a higher ratio of these indirect production costs.

Second, here is a somewhat detailed explanation of major issues in data collection and calculation.

Technically, there are two basic difficulties: Problems endemic to the international comparison of the productivity of an industry, or of companies. In order to accurately compare productivity between two plants, the respective product models and production processes should be the same.

Let us look first at the case of product models. In the Japanese parent factories, there is a rapidly growing trend to manufacture "many-models-in-small-quantity," whereas normally at the transplanted plants, production is restricted to a few models targeted at a specific market. If this is an important difference for us here, and strictly speaking, it is possible that such a comparison would not stand in the first place, it is that the most prominent characteristic of the Japanese-style production system, noticeable since the 1970s, does not only reside in the achievement of a high level of quality and efficiency, but also in the fact that while maintaining these high levels, the system has been able to accommodate minimum lead times while increasing the number of models and options offered in response to the diverse needs of the market. With this in mind we checked for as many product variations as we could in the transplants but, although we could obtain the number of models, it was difficult to learn of detailed differences in options. In the case of automobiles, for example, these would range from items as basic as engine size, number of doors, front wheel or rear wheel drive, and wagon version, to color, type of transmission, seats, and accessories. Then there was the question of how much we should discount the performance of a transplant because of such differences. It is probable that even the firm itself is incapable of accurately calculating this.

Turning to production processes, we find the differences here are chiefly due to the problem of the in-house production ratio. In our study we looked for both those parts of the transplanted process that were most typical for each industry, and at the production process of the plant as a whole. At the local plants, the final assembly process was most typical for automobiles and televisions, and the downstream process for semiconductors, whereas a most typical process could not be determined in the case of auto parts. In any event, it is rare to find a completely identical process in both the parent and the subsidiary plants.

Let us turn now to data collection. As everyone who deals in this knows, most company data is considered secret, and even if the corporations are not named, it is not easy to obtain a sufficient amount of detailed data.

In our study note the following factors:

1. As for the profit figures, since most of the transplants are a 100 percent subsidiary of either a parent company in Japan or of a regional head office in the United States, their financial management is handled by means of consolidated accounting systems, and therefore figures cannot be extracted for an individual plant or business unit. Consequently, as mentioned below, we were forced to rely solely on the macro-data available from the U.S. Department of Commerce or JETRO publications.

2. Because of this, the study had to be based primarily upon comparisons of productivity but, because the objects of study in this area are exceedingly numerous, and also because it was extremely difficult to prepare comparable data from both parent and subsidiaries, we were not able to persevere long enough to obtain sufficient data from all the plants. Nevertheless, we were able to get the minimum amount of data needed to conduct a parent-subsidiary comparison for key plants in each industry with the exception of the auto parts industry.

3. Looking at each industry, we have gathered sets of data for 70 percent of the plants in the consumer electronics industry, but not quite 40 percent in auto assembly. In the semiconductor industry, although we obtained data on more than half of the plants, truly comparable data was obtained on approximately 40 percent. The auto assembly and semiconductor industries stood out for their strict attitude toward keeping secrets. For auto parts we collected data for 80 percent. This may have been due in part to the fact that, because products and processes differ so much from one plant to another, we were content to ask them to quantify the gap in productivity between parent and subsidiary in rough figures only.

In contrast to quantitative indexes that present bare figures, the various cost factors required to generate results are often ignored in comparisons of productivity. But their inclusion implies several problems, as described below.

As opposed to these indexes, there are those that commonly indicate the performance of a transplant but do not lend themselves well to a direct comparison with the parent in terms of good or bad results. These are easy-to-understand indexes such as production volume (or dollar amount), market share, the layoff rate, or rates of absenteeism, and they can be effectively used as occasion demands. These figures are especially useful when contrasting the performance of transplants, apart from a comparison with their Japanese parent, with similar plants of competing American firms since, in the end, this is a matter of survival for the transplants.

Productivity Comparison for Japanese Transplants

In this section we will deal with the evaluation of actual performance.

Consumer Electronics

Let us begin with the consumer electronics industry, for which the data is the most complete. By determining the ratio of television sets assembled per worker per hour on the final assembly line of the six color television plants for which we obtained data, and comparing it with their respective parent factories, we can point out the following:

1. The nominal average rate of productivity of the six transplants relative to their respective parent factory is slightly more than 80 percent.
2. Not only could we see no clear correlation between the application rating, based on the average of the 23 items for each plant, and the above-mentioned rate of productivity, but there is even a tendency for a transplant with a lower degree of application to show a higher productivity rate.
3. In the number of production models (different sizes), transplants have five to six models, whereas parent factory could have seven to twelve sizes. On an average, the transplant's figure is 60 percent of that of the parent.

Thus, regrettably, we did not observe differences in the rate of productivity that might correspond precisely to the degree of application of each plant. Also, due to the limited amount of data available, we cannot draw a definite conclusion on this point. At any rate, for the productivity of these processes, the parent-subsidiary nominal difference is about 20 percent. But, if we take into account not only the number of models, but also the differences in systems and functions, the actual difference could probably reach 30 percent, or about 70 percent of the parent factory. Moreover, when comparing television plants, it is necessary to bear in mind that only the final assembly line exists to be sampled, an area where it is hard to show differences in productivity. Furthermore, some of the Japanese parent factories that supposedly provide the basis for comparison are in the process of shedding the title of mass production factories as their main production shifts to developing countries, primarily in Asia. In short, these facts suggest that the United States is no longer a country suited to television assembly as illustrated by the fact that only a fraction of the manufacturing process remains there by way of a sort of compensation for securing a market for sales. It is quite understandable that there is barely one company surviving among competing American manufacturers.

Auto Assembly

We have data for a practical comparison for only three factories, partly because some of the other transplants were not yet in full operation at the time of our study. Here, also, we can point out the following in regard to the final assembly process (data applicable to the whole plant was also taken into account):

1. The nominal average rate of productivity for the three transplants compared to their respective parents is slightly under 70 percent.
2. There is no clear correlation here either between the application rating based on the average of the 23 items for each plant and the rate of the number of assembled vehicles per worker compared to the parent plant. However, the number of plants with data available were probably insufficient to address this question.
3. Only one of the three transplants has two production models; the other two had only one. (Overall, three out of nine transplants make two mod-

els and the others one.) The parent factories, on the other hand, have three or more basic models, and four to five models if we include variations. Moreover, the parent factories had double or triple the number of major options as the transplants, five to seven as compared to barely three.

4. Transplants have two to four times as many quality control and maintenance workers taken together per vehicle as do their respective parent factories. Such a gap is particularly pronounced for quality control personnel. The ratio of quality control personnel to overall personnel is also about double, with 5 to 6 percent for parent factories and 10 to 12 percent for the transplants.

Thus, also in the automobile industry, the simplest comparison of productivity shows the transplants to be approximately 30 percent lower than their parent factories. However, here, the following cost factors should be brought in.

1. Because the processes are all technically complex, differences in the degree of model mixes that combine models and types is of much greater significance than in other, less complex, production and it is necessary to give full weight to the impact of this on productivity.

2. Costs are incurred by automobile factories through their common practice of assigning Japanese employees to work in the United States and Americans to Japan. Assigning Japanese overseas, the majority of whom are managers and section chiefs, is said to cost (salaries, taxes, allowances, travel expenses, etc.) about twice what would be paid to them in Japan. So the nearly four hundred Japanese middle management employees of a certain US transplant, just counting full-timers, is costing about twice as much as it would in Japan. In addition, there are about half this number of temporarily assigned trainers and others. These Japanese employees are not only indispensable for assuming the responsibility of general management, but also in performing the important role of training, especially of quality control and maintenance workers. But in Japan, for the most part, this is handled by on-the-job training, and does not require special expenditures.

Naturally, every company has a policy to gradually reduce the number of these Japanese employees. The actual pace of reduction, however, is slow. Some even assert that it will be impossible to realize such a reduction in the near future when the time comes for a model-change, or if there is a certain amount of localization of R&D or procurement. Moreover, every firm, in the early stages at least, sends to Japan over 100 U.S. team leaders, and quality control and maintenance workers. Such special expenditures, even if they are covered in part by a state government subsidy, must add up to a considerable amount.

3. Besides the above-mentioned expenses incurred for training quality control and maintenance workers in Japan and America, there are additional cost factors due to the fact that more such people are employed, at higher wages, with a separate wage system that differs from that in Japan. (Even the auto industry, which reduced job classification dramatically, could not remove this classification.) This can be restated as a question of how much extra expenditure is necessary for a transplant to maintain the same level of product quality as its parent factory in Japan.

4. For increases in expenses incurred by local sourcing of parts and resources, it goes without saying that the level of cost, quality, and just-in-time delivery found in Japan cannot be expected. Furthermore, there is a question of "local content". Because of this, transplants must, with considerable effort, call in Japanese manufacturers to assist the local manufacturers and to conduct the receiving inspection, all of which add to the expense. A senior coordinator in charge of production control at one new plant emphasized that such additional expenses were unavoidable as a first line of defense in bringing the shop-floor environment as close as possible to that of the parent factory. These three major cost increase factors are indeed characteristic of the overseas production by Japanese firms. But, in the case of auto assembly, they are strikingly apparent. Incidentally, other than these, problems of a high termination and absenteeism rate, frequently observed in other Japanese factories located overseas, are virtually nonexistent in auto assembly, running 1 to 8 percent and 2 to 5 percent, respectively. This is probably because these employees are people who have joined their companies only after severe competition, in the two or three digits ratio range, who have a strong desire to enter a local Japanese auto plant, with a view toward receiving a high wage, far above the regional average and comparable to the UAW's.

Considering this, it would not be incorrect to state that the real efficiency of auto assembly transplants, with supposedly the same quality level and with cost factors taken into account, does not exceed 60 percent of that of the parents. Therefore, in strictly economic terms, it is still more advantageous for Japanese manufacturers to export from Japan, even paying all the export costs (freight, insurance, packing, and custom duties), that are commonly estimated at being in the range of 15 percent of the shipping price. Nevertheless, cars manufactured by the Japanese transplanted factories, almost without exception, continue to expand their share of the U.S. market at the expense of the Big Three, proving their edge in performance over U.S. companies, as will be described below. We probably should say that they are achieving their expected goals to some extent, while paying the cost of localization.

Semiconductors

Here, we were able to gather sufficient data on four factories. One was dropped, however, because it cannot be necessarily considered a mass production plant. Besides these factories, there were those that could provide data on only production volume or number of employees. When the above-mentioned factories happened to lack data on production models, quality control, or maintenance workers, and so on, this data was used as a supplement, albeit with certain conditions attached.

Here we can point out the following facts.

1. The nominal productivity rate of transplant to parent is a little under 80 percent.
2. When productivity, converted to 256KDRAMs, based on the number of units produced per worker in the downstream process of semiconductors, is compared with the degree of application in individual factories, again, nothing significant emerges.
3. With regard to the difference in product mix, as far as the mass produc-

tion factories are concerned, transplants had two product types, and the parents four. But some transplants with small-scale production were making three types.

4. In the comparison of the number of quality control and maintenance workers per unit of production volume, transplants have a rate slightly more than double that of their parent factories. This is about the same as the rate for most of the consumer electronics factories (including picture tube plants), although we did not mention it earlier, as well as about equal to that of the auto assembly factories already mentioned. One interesting aspect here is that while the number of maintenance workers in semiconductors and consumer electronics tends to exceed significantly that of quality control, with automobiles it is just the opposite, as mentioned before.

Thus, it would appear that according to the simple productivity comparison, the level of productivity among the semiconductor transplants is not so low, with the exception of the one that is not a mass production plant. The difference in product mix also seems to be not as big as the case of consumer electronics and automobiles, due in part to the fact that these are semifinished products. However, this applies only to the downstream process, where it is generally accepted that a difference of productivity is relatively hard to see. Differences will probably become greater as these factories get into full operation. (There was only one plant in which the upstream process was fully operational at the time of our study, and two other plants had just started.)

By looking at the cost aspect, corresponding to the indications gleaned from analyses conducted so far, the ratio of maintenance workers stands out, showing that this industry is the equipment-led type, highly dependent on the direct acquisition of materials, including parts. We notice here two of the three major cost factors mentioned earlier. And the percentage of Japanese employees, being the third cost factor, also is found to be a little higher than in auto assembly, following behind auto parts. In short, local production for semiconductors is more expensive than for automobiles.

In the final analysis, in a comparison of the productivity itself, the difference between parent and subsidiary in semiconductors appears not to be considerable but, their method of bringing-in a Japanese plant virtually "as is," would seem to entail a significant cost burden. With this in mind, then, the real productivity rate is probably slightly under 70 percent. But in the mass production of memory chips, the transplants are steadily replacing U.S. manufacturers in the U.S. market, a market protected by the Japanese-U.S. Semiconductor Agreement since 1986.

Auto Parts

As mentioned earlier, it was difficult to obtain data for auto parts that could be compared in concrete terms. We have no recourse but to base our evaluations on the approximate productivity differences given to us by the companies concerned. In general, we asked them to indicate in approximate numbers the degree of productivity achieved by the transplant as compared with the parent factory. However, one of the major parts manufacturers who responded made an extra effort to determine comparative figures of piecework time (total process time per completed product) after it was adjusted by differences in processes. This provided us with a standard for a fairly close comparison of physical productivity.

The following points emerged from the six factories that responded with figures among the eight factories asked, with the exclusion of one that is producing different items than its parent.

1. The productivity rate of transplants vis-a-vis their respective parent factories ranged from 70 to 95 percent. Not every case fit the picture, but here at least we did see a general tendency toward a correlation between the extent of application and productivity.
2. The average productivity rate was just under 85 percent.
3. For this industry more than others, we may need to discount a substantial portion of the productivity of the transplants by factoring in differences in product mix. Although we are unable to show this with figures, we see in the transplants a mere fraction of the diverse lineup of products produced in their parent factories.
4. From the perspective of the three main cost increase factors, just as with auto assembly, we may say that local production for this industry is rather expensive. Partly because of the generally small size of their facilities, the fact stands out that the ratio of Japanese expatriates is extraordinarily high. (See Table 3-3).

We have said that a certain correlation can be seen between the degree of application and productivity only in the case of auto parts; this can be tentatively explained as follows. Most of the auto parts manufacturers that we have studied, despite their late arrival, and in response to a call primarily from Japanese auto assembly manufacturers, are showing the strongest orientation toward application. This takes the form of the direct import of equipment and human assets from Japan, which provides them with a corresponding increase in productivity. Since under these conditions, the above-mentioned figures concerning productivity are susceptible to reflecting to some extent the subjective standpoint of the Japanese employees who are actually working on the application, this could have the effect of inflating both figures. In any event, in the case of auto parts, the relationship between the specific application points and productivity appears to be rather straightforward. This may reveal the quickest way to tie these two, the application points and productivity, together. Needless to say, in these cases, the question of applying the methods of the Japanese system or of using a revised application adapted to local conditions, and so forth, are issue for the future, except in certain plants.

Moreover, even this productivity, which is considered high, is not necessarily profitable once some discount factors and cost questions are considered. The actual number may indeed be around 70 percent. For those parts manufacturers who initiated transplant operations in the America within the last 2 or 3 years, in particular, the question for the time being is not profit, but rather first how to supply their affiliated assembly manufacturers with parts of satisfactory quality and under acceptable delivery terms. Their move toward a strong result application-orientation could be in part a manifestation of this. There is no doubt that in this way the auto parts transplants are also beginning to pressure the American parts companies, first with higher rates of local production going to Japanese assemblers, and second with an increase in the rate of supply to the American assemblers.

So far we have been studying the relationship between application and adaptation, as well as the competitive relations with U.S. companies in four industries, by comparing the performance of the transplant, primarily in terms of productivity, with that of their respective parent factories.

Let us summarize the results.

1. In a comparison of simple productivity, the rate of the transplant to its parent factory is the highest in the auto parts industry (a little under 85%) then, in decreasing order: Consumer electronics (a little above 80%), semiconductors (a little under 80%), and auto assembly (a little under 70%). The plain nominal average is slightly less than 80%. However, the real productivity rate of transplants must reflect cost factors such as product-mix, the Japanese expatriate employees ratio, difference in number of quality control and maintenance workers, and so forth. When these are taken into account, the order from high to low (70% to 60% of the parent factory) is: Consumer electronics, auto parts, semiconductors, and auto assembly.

2. As long as we tried to see the relationship of performance to application-adaptation through an average of the degree of application, no correlation could be found, not only for individual factories, but also for each industry. By industry, only in auto parts did the data show the highest value for both the physical productivity rate and the degree of application. However, since a different method of calculation was employed in this case, the real values, after correcting the calculation and adding certain cost factors, showed on the contrary that consumer electronics, with the lowest degree of application, demonstrated the highest rate of productivity.

The auto parts industry seems to be aiming at immediate results by directly importing materials and workers, whereas the consumer electronics industry seems to be operating in a smarter way by making the most of their longer experience in the market. But in fact they are only operating only the relatively easy parts of the production process. So both leave something to be desired as a model of full-fledged local production. Therefore, to really proceed with our investigation of this correlation between application and performance, we would need to consider the relationship between performance and the groups and individual items that make up our model. Unfortunately, however, the performance data provided by the present study is insufficient for such an analysis to be of genuine significance.

3. Nevertheless, the correspondence of the average degree of application of 3.2 for the transplants that provided full data (3.3 for the targeted factories overall) with productivity rates slightly less than 80% as the nominal average and 60% to 70% in reality, may be of some significance. This means that when a transplant shows that it has applied more than half of the parent factory's Japanese-style production system as shown on our model, its productivity rate vis-à-vis the parent factory is from 60% to 70%. Of course, this does not immediately indicate that there is a simple

positive correlation between the degree of application and the productivity rate. This was made clear by the fact that individual correlation was virtually nonexistent. At any rate, such a relation probably indicates that the transplants are achieving an efficiency of far more than half that of the Japanese parent factory, through an almost fifty-fifty hybrid that has emerged from the struggle between application that brings in Japanese strong points and adaptation that accommodates itself to the American environment.

4. What Japanese transplants in these four industries mean to the American market will depend on how well they are able to compete, given the level of quality and production discussed above. Let us examine this point in the next section.

IMPACT ON THE AMERICAN ECONOMY
AND INVESTMENT FRICTION

Now let us turn our attention to the impact of Japanese transplants on the American economy with a particular focus on their competitiveness in the American market. Let us present our conclusion first by saying that in general the transplants, given the level of productivity described above, are quite capable of eroding the market share of American factories, in a market protected by a voluntary restriction on exports, various trade agreements, and customs duties. As a result, American factories are now being replaced by Japanese transplants. On one hand, this contributes to shoring up declining American industries and to increased employment. But at the same time, it is also a condition contributing to intensification of investment friction.

Impact on the American Economy

At first, let us look at the market share situation for each industry in America. (Refer to the relevant sections in Chapter 5 for more details.)

1. For the auto assembly industry, in an American automotive market that appeared to be further weakened in 1990, 1 year after our survey, Japanese cars including exports held a 29.9% share. (By American brand cars, but including those supplied on an OEM basis from Japanese plants based either in Japan or America, another calculation is possible in which the number would be around 33%.) Of this 29.9%, 11.4% were made in America. Likewise, this would be 15% if we included those supplied to the Big Three by the Japanese transplants, including joint ventures. In 1987 the figure for local production was 4.7% (23.7% together with imports), so the recent rapid growth of local production is quite obvious.

2. At this point we are not yet at the stage where we can calculate the market share for each of the individual parts in the auto parts industry. Over the 3-year period following our previous survey, all the major parts manufacturers have set up their production facilities in America in a rapid response to the lineup of the auto assembly plants. While a number of difficulties persist, they are increasing their deliveries to the American assemblers as well.

3. For consumer electronics and electric appliances, let us consider the case of color televisions. At the time of the survey, TV sets made by the Japanese transplants accounted for around 50% of total American domestic production. The rest was shared among the French Thomson, the Dutch Philips, and the only American firm, Zenith, about which we often hear of selling-out deals, and Korean companies. Adding in an estimated amount of OEM-based supply to American firms, to Thomson and the others, plus imports made by Japanese companies including those from Japanese-controlled factories in Taiwan, Singapore, or other countries, the share of the Japanese corporations in the overall American market can be estimated at over 40%. Although as described earlier, right after our previous survey the structure of the local production of TV sets underwent a violent transformation in order to cope with the appreciation of the yen, resulting in a gradual diminishing of the importance of the U.S. facilities; behind it all the overwhelming predominance of the Japanese companies still persisted.

In the past, the Japanese share was 90% of the American market for microwave ovens, of which production lines are often seen attached to those of TVs in television plants; but in recent years, tight competition with products from newly industrializing economies, like Korea, has put more pressure on these transplants than was the case with TV sets, to the point where we have begun to see some of them forced to consider stopping production.

4. In semiconductors also, Japanese products are rapidly expanding their share of the U.S. market, primarily with mass-produced memory chips, up to 25.5% in 1989 from 13% in 1986, based on of the total amount of money for all items included.[1] The retreat of American corporations became more and more apparent as one after the other of the major manufacturers such as Motorola and National Semiconductor, were forced to stop producing memory chips (SRAM) in the sluggish semiconductor market of 1990.[2] However, a semiconductor transplant's dependency on Japan is quite direct in many respects, such as production engineering, material and procurement, and so on. Indeed, it is virtually impossible to run a large-scale transplant that is comprised of upstream processes. Therefore (varying over a range from 10% through 50%), the proportion of local production has traditionally never been very high in what the Japanese companies sell on the American market. However, due to a general exacerbation of trade friction and to the long-term view of the American market, the major Japanese manufacturers, in contrast with the American firms, are more active in the construction of new facilities, including upstream process lines.

In addition to these four industrial sectors, local production is also on its way to becoming firmly established among the general machinery and steel industries, which we dealt with through questionnaires (Chapter 4). In short, the assembly and processing type of local American production of the major Japanese industries has reached the point where it is ready to substantially influence the level of performance, such as in the area of competitiveness, of the entirety of their respective industries in the United States. That is, Japanese transplants, which are replacing American company plants in each of these industries, are preventing the retrogression of the industry and contributing to the revitalization and development of it.

As stated earlier, it is not possible to obtain data concerning the profitability of the factories studied. But, by looking at the total profits earned by American subsidiaries of Japanese corporations, according to sources like the U.S. Department of Commerce, while commerce and others (finance, etc.) are making a fair profit, the manufacturing sector has been consistently registering losses. For example, losses for 1988 and 1989 were $87 million and $452 million, respectively.[3] For the time being, we can assume the following reasons were behind this:

1. Most transplants have been in operation only for a short time.
2. The head offices of Japanese companies do not necessarily think their transplants must pay their own way alone, but think of them in combination with the export of finished products or related parts from Japan.
3. As usual, emphasis is placed on securing long-term market share. Although these considerations include those that are open to criticism from America, such as items that are involved with local content, or the issues of transfer pricing as a means of circumventing local taxes, we will not address such topics here. The important point in relation to the present study is the fact that these Japanese transplants content themselves with such a low level of profitability and are destined to become an ever-growing presence in the American market for some time.

However, when statistically calculating the degree of direct contribution local activities of Japanese companies make to the American economy, we find that it is still not very substantial. For instance, in the case of employment, which is the easiest to see, in 1988 the American subsidiaries of Japanese companies, excluding banking firms, employed 401,000 people, representing 11% of all the American subsidiaries of foreign companies. (Britain 20%, Canada 19.4%). This comprised a mere 0.5% in the total employment of the United States. (Likewise, the manufacturing industry provides a bit less than 1%, the electric and electronic equipment industry 1.5%, and the automobile sector 2.7%.) Naturally, this is not limited to the factories alone, but includes all employment associated with each of these industrial sectors. Also, in general, the employment figures of Japanese transplants tend to appear quite low relative to the results of production and actual sales (about 3% of sales in the manufacturing industry, including imports), because they have a far slimmer workforce than their American counterparts. It would also be necessary to take into consideration the fact that the employment growth rate of the Japanese-owned companies registered 37% and 32% in 1987 and 1988, respectively, far exceeding the overall average of 10.14% for the U.S. subsidiaries of foreign companies.[4]

In this perspective, although the scale of the American production of the Japanese manufacturing firms cannot be thought of as very large yet, we would like to focus our attention on the force with which they have come to threaten a critical portion of the domestic production base of the American corporations in the little more than 10 years since their "reluctant" beginning in the second half of the 1970s. Because at this point most of the Japanese transplants, except those of consumer electronics and electric appliances, are yet at the stage of barely completing the transition to across-the-board full-scale production, such a force can be expected to come into its own as a mighty economic power in the years ahead. It should be sufficient for concerned parties in both Japan and America to consider that in the near future, products made by the Japanese transplants will take 30–50% of the U.S. market share.

The remarkable and widely known progress of the Japanese products and plants in America is having a profound impact on corporate America's management attitude itself. Some firms are even trying to introduce Japanese methods. There is no space here to pursue this topic, but note that at present, those that have been successful are corporations, like Motorola, that were different from the start than those on which we based our American traditional model. Therefore, the extent of their influence cannot be considered to be very great.

U.S.-Japan Investment Friction

At this point, everybody is wondering about such questions as how the replacement of the plants of American companies by Japanese transplants will affect American industry, and the future course of U.S.-Japan investment friction that can be expected to occur along with it. We cannot afford to get deeply involved with either of these issues in the present study, but at least we can say the following based on what we have examined so far. First of all, in purely economic terms, the Japanese manufacturing firms' direct penetration into American industry should be welcomed. In transplanting into American industry the production technology for which Japan has an edge, they function as a check to its retrogression in international competitiveness. By doing so, they play an important role in maintaining employment, just as does the direct investment in developed countries by a number of multinational corporations. At present, then, the nature of the ownership of the Japanese transplants offers no obstacle to the incorporation of Japanese technology into the production base of American industry and to it becoming a part of American economic power.

Moreover, the Japanese transplants make an important contribution to the improvement of America's external trade balance by first, reducing the volume of imports, mainly from Japan (accompanied, however, by a transition period of decreasing imports of finished products and an increase in imports of parts), and by somewhat increasing exports through reverse exports to Japan, Europe, and so forth, both of which are obviously beneficial in respect to the balance of trade; and second, by an improvement in the balance of capital, although the outflow of investment profits will become a problem in the future. At the present time, however, the profit for Japan's direct investment in America's manufacturing sector is negative; consequently, it poses no immediate problem. Moreover, generally speaking, when profits are made, particularly in the case of a manufacturing business, it is natural that a fair amount of them will be reinvested locally. The balance, of course, will return to the investor country.

Friction arising in spite of these facts cannot but be attributed to nationalistic feelings in regard to the nationality of ownership. But, as we mentioned in Chapter 1, historically it has been Japan that has clung to these feelings most tenaciously among developed nations, and Japan could hardly be the one to throw the first stone here. Also, in the case of Japanese corporations, it could be pointed out that there is a tendency to deliberately incite this issue directly and indirectly in conjunction with characteristics of Japanese-style management and production itself. Generally speaking, it could be called a frictional heat generated because of differences in national character, when a system conceived to function at its best in an inwardly-oriented homogeneous society is enticed into being used in a mobile and diverse society.

First of all, it is difficult to make progress in the localization of materials and human resources. As we have seen thus far, the domestic sourcing rate for parts of around 60% is a level probably still not satisfactory to local parties. However, from the viewpoint of the Japanese companies, this is not simply due to the desire to import parts from Japan. There exists in Japan many long-term reciprocal relationships, such as *genba* (work-site)-style arrangements, governing exchanges between an assembly manufacturer and its parts suppliers.[56] Not only are cost, quality, and delivery matters reviewed on a daily basis, but even cooperation on technical development is carried on through such exchanges. Consequently, it is not an easy task to switch this relationship over to local parts suppliers. So it is that even the local sourcing rate mentioned above was partly comprised of procurement from the Japanese parts transplants. This leaves open the possibility that the question of applying the country origin rule comparable to that of Europe will emerge. Another thing concerning materials that also stands out is the fact that the most equipment is brought in from Japan.

In the case of human resources, the biggest problem is the high ratio of Japanese expatriates. As stated earlier, this not only deprives local white-collar workers of opportunities for promotion, but also serves to limit their practical action and authority.

Second, there is the situation in which the very act of applying the Japanese method clashes with the American's way of working, their sense of values, or both. Not only the activity style of *kaisha*ism,[7] through which the job in the company ends up absorbing almost the entire life of each employee, is bound to impose a sort of strain on the American worker's own perception of everyday life, but also, when seen from outside of the local communities, the restricted way of behavior of such a company seems peculiar. Inside the plant, the slow-going promotion and the work assignments based on multiskilled or generalist workers that blurs responsibilities and spheres of authority may raise resistance, especially among the white-collar and skilled workers. The simplification of job classification may be welcomed by production workers as egalitarianism. On the other hand, it may create a conflict with the American unions that strive for job security by preserving many corporate job classifications. Another tough issue is that in the zealous effort to create a homogeneous environment within the company there is, in the end, a tendency to exclude minorities in various ways.

Third, for a Japanese transplant to be accepted as a "good corporate citizen" is not as easy as it sounds. Yet, at this time, compared with 3 years ago, great progress has been made, and a rating of 2.3 shows that it is approaching a level comparable with that of corporate America (1.0 is the same level as American companies). But the nature of the difficulty here is totally different than that of the other 23 items. In the first place, the parent companies in Japan have acquired relatively little know-how. So all they can do is adapt themselves by learning from the American corporations. This is surely at odds with the fact that the Japanese system has been formed by absorbing the abilities and energies of its workers into the corporate organization. This system itself not only markedly lacks just those elements that would enable a corporation to become a citizen open to the outside, but actually promotes the opposite. This is why we have treated this item separately in our model.

The Japanese corporations are unable to handle this problem without a totally new way of thinking. It will never become a reality before ways of doing things are changed at the head offices, as well as within Japanese society. It is an issue directly connected with the essential part of the Japanese corporations' "internal internationalization". Therefore, we assume this matter will require much more time and effort. Adding to that, we could hope that such trial and error, coupled with the experience of the Japanese corporate expatriates and their families[8] and the resulting effect of this feedback on Japan, will lead to a review of the dark side of the corporate society, Japan. In fact, we are already seeing some possible signs of this. Nevertheless, in view of the fact that this movement is accompanied by the difficult question of how far Japanese-style management will be able to maintain its original efficiency while undergoing such changes, our understanding of the model just does not allow us to feel as optimistic as some observers would appear to be.

In this way, both Japanese corporations and their transplants in the United States will continue to face the challenge of how to combine the local application and adaptation of Japanese methods in their effort to further internationalize. When all is said and done, Japanese hybrid-type transplants will firmly establish themselves in American industry, albeit with a level of efficiency inferior to their parent factories. And American economic society will be able to do nothing but accept them. Certain elements of the revisionist format may be expected to feed back to the parent factories in Japan as well. Thus we come at last to consider the question of how to assess the results of the current study from the standpoint of our fundamental question, which is: How possible is the international transplantation of Japanese-style management and systems of production?

SUMMARY

Overall Assessment

Finally, a summation is in order. Regarding the transfer status of the Japanese management and production system at the target Japanese transplants in America, our overall assessment is as follows:

The overall hybrid degree rating of 3.3 for the Japanese transplants, evaluated by means of our application-adaptation international transfer model, remains, numerically at least, slightly in favor of application from Japan. However, by taking into consideration the difficulty repeatedly emphasized throughout this study of transplanting the Japanese system in America, frankly, it should be regarded as a level of application far greater than expected. The corresponding performance compared to the parent factories in terms of real productivity after adjustment by cost factors, was found to be within a range of 60–70 percent. Although only a few transplants have become profitable on their own, in general they are superior to the facilities of American corporations in competing within the American market and are in the process of replacing them. In this sense, we can conclude that the transfer of the parent factory's system to the local transplants has been successfully achieved, at least for now.

But then we have to look at the substance behind the numbers. A degree of application just past the midpoint should not necessarily lead us to think that the level itself is low. Rather, it might be better to assume that this is the most relevant level for the transfer of a management system to a country of far different environmental conditions. However, the next real question is how the various elements within the system combine with one another to make up a rating of 3.3, because it is quite possible that differences in the stability and potentialities of a transferred system will depend on the contents themselves. The most important characteristic of the current application-adaptation hybrid situation can best be seen in terms of the 4-Perspective Evaluation. On one hand, we have the strong dependence on the direct intake of ready-made Japanese elements for production control (especially equipment) and procurement (including those supplied by Japanese-owned vendors) on the material side and typically a mass expatriation of Japanese on the human resources side. On the other hand, there is a weak intake of methods both as applied to materials and human resources, such as work organization, quality control, and maintenance.

These provide a combination of contrasts. Their multifaceted aspects have been seen through a correlation analysis of their elements (Chapter 5), and these have been given credence through the results of the questionnaires that were based on different data sources (Chapter 4). As long as this situation prevails, the efficiency and quality level can be maintained. But it hardly need be repeated that any advancement in the real transfer of the Japanese system will be difficult.

Though we stated above that the intake of methods is weak, the 2.9 average among four industries concerning Work Organization can be regarded as the minimum level for the system to function. Some of them ranked highly, like the auto assembly industry, with its 3.3. However, we need to pay careful attention to this point. Further familiarity often reveals that although a given Japanese system or way of doing business has been introduced in form, it functions in quite a different way in practice. (Here, an alternate and contrary approach deserves our attention—that is, the revisionary application that consists rather of taking on the American form of something and then attempting to transplant within it the logic of the Japanese system. Please refer to the "Impressions" below.)

For instance (all this has been introduced in Chapters 1 through 5), the number of job classifications were radically reduced to from one to three, and this in turn opened the way to the adoption of a flexible work organization and training methods. Nevertheless, due to difficulties in changing over from the American-style wage and salary systems, which depend strictly on job descriptions, it still was not possible to evaluate the skills that are formed over a long period of time within a company and to have them reflected in wage and salary levels. Or, although having somehow managed to introduce a personnel assessment system based on individuals and have it also apply to production workers, in many cases this turned out to be simply another application of a performance evaluation system that already exists in America, one that not only has its own format and requires the signature of the person evaluated, but which is limited in its use to that of a very small point of reference for part of a bonus or promotion. Also, we see job rotation being utilized mainly to distribute workloads more equitably, and small group activities being carried out in normal working hours under orders.

If we take into consideration the way these functions are actually applied, the differences with Japan loom larger. However, given the current level of application we cannot continue without mentioning the extremely critical role of Japanese employees as, so to speak, the ultimate factor in enabling day-to-day routine operations to run. And when it comes to more major changes that affect all processes, such as the introduction of new models, model changes, or adding a new production line, then the role of Japanese employees becomes decisive. We could say that the complexity of the problem can be well seen through the fact that frequently it is in those very factories that are positively pursuing local production, including some capability for development work, where the number of Japanese is noticeably high. As will be described below, they keep an eye on all areas, perform the function of go-betweens at various levels, and their overall expertise and know-how fill up any cracks or gaps between the parent and child. They are certainly the living embodiment of Japanese management. We may go so far as to say that the greatest strength and uniqueness of the Japanese system can be seen in the fact that such a system is able to develop such human assets.

From the opposite perspective, the question is how many Japanese transplants currently are capable of standing on their own feet without any Japanese expatriates employees or with their numbers drastically reduced. (There is an extremely exceptional case among the Japanese transplants in the UK. See Chapter 1, note 2.)

It is a question of the long-term stability of these plants. As mentioned earlier, this is also probably the reason why we have found virtually no American company that has succeeded in adopting the Japanese methods. (This is a different issue than the fact that the management methods of what has been called an excellent company in America have some similarities with those of Japan.) What is the combination and level of application-adaptation proper for the items and groups of the international transfer model, in order for transplants to become independent of the direct import of Japanese elements? Naturally, it is possible to draw up a recommended hybrid factory model on paper, one that emphasizes the side of methods. However, given the present situation, where we are not able to satisfactorily collect reliable data on productivity and profitability about factories that have at most only about 10 years experience, it would be irresponsible to produce a too-facile answer to this question.

Impressions of the Field Study in the United States and Future Prospects

In the previous section we summarized the essential parts of the results of our present research. In this section, then, we will refer to a few points that particularly impressed us in our field research in the United States during the summer and autumn of 1989, and we will reflect upon the implications of our evaluation, and look at future prospects.

Although it flowed naturally from our theoretical hypothesis, we were impressed first of all by the keen realization that the "movement of people" is one of the key issues for the U.S. transplants of Japanese firms. To organize and utilize people in the Japanese way of *genba*ism, the first step is to keep people in the organization. [*Genba*ism ("work-site-orientation") means, approximately, that it is most important to be on the spot, involved, and all members' taking part in what is actually going on.] Without this we are unable to do anything. Within Japan, of course, the mention of lifetime employment evokes no special response, since it is simply taken for granted. But during our visits to American factories, we were made keenly aware of the seriousness of the problem at every level.

For openers, a 10% annual termination rate for blue-collar workers is not rare in corporate America. Even those Japanese transplants that have been making a concerted effort to lower this have had a hard time breaking the 10% mark. Add to this a layoff and the problem of worker changeover further intensifies. Faced with workers of whom more than a third are renewed every year, there is here a fundamental limitation to any effort to develop multitalented workers through repeated on-the-job training and to the training of team leaders as key personnel who have a comprehensive understanding of the complexities of the workplace. Furthermore, the rate of supervisors and white-collar managers who quit their jobs is often higher than that of the blue-collar workers, and these are the very people who are leading workers and controlling shop floors and plants. In fact, since the 3-year period of the previous survey, we encountered a number of cases where many of the American managers whom we had met before had left for other jobs. Therefore, the number of Japanese executives, who assume responsibility in a consistent way, cannot be reduced. But here, too, there is changeover, since they normally return to Japan after at most 5 years.

Thus, there is a continuous turnover of workers at these transplants at any given level, with the rare exception of a few Japanese 10-year veterans. For the Japanese-style system to actually take root, then, entails the serious problem of how it is able to compromise with this situation. Of course, those Japanese transplants, such as the auto assembly manufacturers, that operate on a large scale and that are relatively stable are attempting to come up with as many countermeasures as they can to hold the movement of people to a minimum level. Then, too, the settling rate of the American managers looks to be high. (One meets the same people years later.) But, in any case, we would like to reemphasize the fact that it is this great difference in premise between the United States and Japan that is most fundamental to all of the application-adaptation issues.

Second, and this relates to what has just been said and the point has been repeated in the earlier study, the role of Japanese expatriate employees is definitely critical in the transfer process of the Japanese system. But what caught our attention this time was the presence of a number of people holding a position that does not conform to anything in the usual organizational structure, who are called "coordinators" or "advisors." This may be partly due to a shortage of open managerial and leadership positions because of the high number of Japanese employees but, this possibility aside, it would seem more likely to mean that while U.S. personnel are officially placed in as many managerial positions as possible in an attempt to further "localize" personnel, Japanese employees are given the task of assisting them as a kind of *kuroko,* an assistant hidden in background in traditional Japanese Noh and Kabuki, as a shadow cabinet, if you will. This could be said to be a clever Japanese way of handling the problem, but it involves not only very delicate problems in the relationship with the American managers, but may adversely affect the morale of the Japanese employees as well. In such a relationship, we cannot help but wonder how long their tolerance of each other can go on.

Although it is a simple matter to point out such problems in applying the "human-result" approach, many of these problems are intimately connected with the strength of the Japanese methods themselves, and the proposal to just mechanically isolate them as "illogical Japanese peculiarities" is not easy to apply in actual situations. Rather, Japanese companies should seek to find out what possible hybrid combinations will be acceptable in the environments of various foreign countries, even if these are rather less efficient, and at the same time continue to preserve their basis of competitive strength.

Third, and this is related to what has just been said, it is noteworthy that those most zealous in attempting to implement the "revised application" approach that we have discussed previously are, for the most part, the "coordinators." This brings in the question of how, given a full appreciation of the difference in environmental conditions between the United States and Japan, to reshape the essence or logic of a system constructed in Japan, or in the parent factory, in such a way that allows it to become acclimatized to the American soil. This is neither a simple application nor a simple adaptation, but an extremely interesting and challenging experiment, and it is probably the only way that the Japanese method will ever be able to really take root in a country outside Japan. But the chances of this actually happening, especially with cost concerns taken into account, is still unknown.

Fourth, one thing we began to notice this time, was the attempt, after simplifying the job classifications, to evaluate certain individual workers who had been grouped under the same job category, and to utilize this for raises and promotions. This is a noteworthy step beyond the first stage where the wall of the American job classifications was broken down. If this were done carelessly within the American environment, there would be the risk of creating confusion in the relationship between wage differences and job divisions. In other words, some of the doubt we felt last time remains as to how far they can go in maintaining such an extreme simplification of job classifications. Moreover, it should be remembered that it is not so easy to avoid the problem of "favoritism" when faced with the task of carrying out individual personnel evaluations of a large number of team members in a society that is made up of such a diversity of people. (In the first place, this very problem is one the historical factors behind job-control unionism that attempts to eliminate ambiguity from the allotted share of work for each individual and the basis of its assessment, by defining the scope of job responsibility (see Chapter 2).

Fifth, what new light, then, does our fact-finding surveys and analyses of the transfer across national borders of the above-described Japanese-style management and production system throw on the theory of Japanese management?

It was not the aim of the present study to treat this in an exhaustive way. Nevertheless, by observing conditions surrounding the places where this system has collided with an alien system, certain things have been clarified. Certainly, it has become clear that the import of Japanese-style "methods" is no easy task, and that even if the methods associated with a particular Japanese system or structure do manage to get transferred, there is no guarantee that they will function as they did in Japan. This would further support the view that it is not possible to fully understand the Japanese system apart from the social and cultural environmental conditions that lay behind it.

The point that characterizes the Japanese management system that has been made clear through these international comparisons, seems to boil down in the end to a question of demarcation—that is, how a member of an organization defines the area of one's job responsibility and the state of consciousness that accompanies work activities. Our investigation and analyses also supports the common assertion that it is *genba*ism that gives rise to the various facets of the methods of the Japanese system, and it is this same *genba*ism that is at the very root of their practical functionality. In short, we have observed a strong tendency for members of Japanese organizations and workplaces to feel over a long period of time a sense of oneness with their organization and its relations—relations that include not only other firms within the corporate group, but also even suppliers. In working and competing together, these members transcend their job description or their allotted role in business relations and thereby reenergize their respective organizations, and this is an important source for a wide variety of innovations and improvements. Each member, thus committed, is predisposed to expand one's area of responsibility indefinitely, limited only by individual capability, always in the end supported by the sense of unity, of belonging to the same group, of "us" or "our company."

Also, regarding the formation of multiskilled work training, commonly formulated as the core of the Japanese system, there is plenty of room to question how long it can be advanced efficiently without *genba*ism as a precondition with its broad interest toward the workplace and where the work tends to involve everybody. Needless to say, Japanese corporations have various devices that foster such an atmosphere in the workplace, such as long-term employment, the combination of a highly seniority- and individual-oriented wage system together with performance ratings, and so forth. But our study has made it clear that there is also a certain limit to the transplantation of such devices into a society that places a high value on the precise demarcation of job descriptions to correspond with the diverse abilities of the people, that are objectified as "qualifications," and where the activities of the entire organization are organized through a structure of differentiated work.

Thus, one of the important roles of those expatriate Japanese, who have became a well-nigh indispensable element in the transplants, may very well be able to go around forming the ties of *genba*ism between American workers who tend to retreat into specialization or an inflexible differentiation of work. Naturally, the knowledge and know-how of these Japanese employees is essential but, if that were all, it could be transferred sooner or later. However, if their real role is to deal with people's consciousness or behavioral orientation, not easy things to shape in American society, then Japanese employees such as these will have to remain a long time to continue to provide a "cover" for these differences.

As the sixth and final point, let us give one noteworthy case of the feedback effect that the experience of local production in the United States brought to Japanese-style management. One of the major automobile manufacturers in Japan decided in 1990 to make a great change in its policy of locating domestic factories, and made public, one after the other, its plans to build new factories across the Japanese archipelago in places such as Kyushu, Tohoku and Hokkaido. Because the company had traditionally centered its growth in an enormous corporate town with a number of its own plants and most of the related parts vendors arranged in nearby proximity in a specific area of the Chubu region, creating an extremely efficient microcosm, with such things as the "just-in-time" linkage of goods with manufacturing processes, the announcements caught the public by surprise.

However, to anyone who knew what was really going on at the company's U.S. transplant operations, such a move was not totally unexpected. Of course, the direct cause of this policy shift was to deal with the labor shortage of recent years. But, even so, for this typical Japanese corporation with its strong tendency to turn inward, traditionally attached to the geographical efficiency of its particular area, to be able to make such a rapid change in its way of thinking, could only be due to the experience and confidence it had accumulated through somehow having managed to put a local operation on track in such a diametrically opposite environment as that of the site in the United States. In that sense, this could be called one case of "internalized internationalization."

Epilogue

More than One Hundred Years: A Historical Overview of Japanese Direct Investment in the United States

MIRA WILKINS

For over 100 years Japanese businessmen and bankers have made direct investments in the United States. The principal sectors for their investments have been finance, trade, shipping, and insurance. Until the last 2 decades, the share of manufacturing and real estate investments has been small. The new stakes in manufacturing have occurred along with the growing sales of innovative Japanese products in the American market, actual or threatened restraints on Japanese exports to the United States, and the currency realignments that strengthened the yen vis-à-vis the dollar (and were tantamount to raising the price of Japanese exports to America). The yen-dollar ratios and the lowering of Japanese capital export restrictions in recent years have opened the way for the Japanese—with their new capital surpluses—to make large U.S. real estate investments. Likewise, Japanese banks, insurance companies, and trading companies have expanded in this country— assuming new functions as their U.S. assets increase. Japan's domestic economic growth has brought to it great wealth, and the limited, undramatic early direct investments have now been supplemented by an acceleration of giant new activities, along with well-publicized billion-dollar acquisitions. At the start of the 1990s, Japanese direct investments in the United States are sizable and conspicuous.

In 1989, Americans purchased more Honda Accords than any other car. About 60 percent of the Honda Accords had been built at a Japanese-owned plant in Marysville, Ohio. The remainder were made in Japan by the same multinational enterprise.[1] For many years before World War II, Ford cars, assembled in Japan, had held the largest share of that market.[2] It had taken roughly 50 years for the

This chapter first appeared as an article entitled "Japanese Multinationals in the United States: Continuity and Change, 1879–1990," in *Business History Review* 64 (Winter 1990): 858–929. Reprinted by permission of the publisher.

reverse to occur. The strangeness to Americans of a Japanese multinational offering the best selling automobile in the United States tends to cloak the long history of Japanese direct investment in this country. What is new today is not the existence of Japanese multinationals nor their presence in this country, but some of the specific U.S. sectors that are attracting the Japanese, the size of Japanese direct investments, and their significance in the American economy.

This epilogue is designed to provide a context for the study of Japanese direct investments in U.S. manufacturing facilities presented earlier in this volume. It is included in order to show where these specific involvements in manufacturing fit into the overall, long history of Japanese direct investments in this country. The present book has studied Japanese automotive and electronics plants and production systems in the United States with an application-adaptation model. This epilogue offers a narrative on the rise of and characteristics of all Japanese direct investments in America—in services and real estate as well as in manufacturing. It positions within the broad historical sequence the particular Japanese activities in consumer electronics, semiconductor, and automotive manufacturing.

THE EARLIEST JAPANESE DIRECT INVESTMENTS IN THE UNITED STATES

Japanese direct investments in the United States have long been important for the Japanese economy. They provided the means by which Japanese foreign trade connections were pursued. In the years 1880–1914, the Japanese increasingly took over from foreigners the organization of their own international trade and made direct investments abroad to do so.

The earliest Japanese direct investments in the United States appear to have occurred in the late 1870s. Mitsui & Co. opened an office in New York City in 1879. By 1881, fourteen Japanese trading companies with a total of thirty-one employees had branches in that city. These firms needed men resident in the United States to process transactions. Meanwhile, in 1880, the Yokohama Specie Bank, the predecessor of the Bank of Tokyo, had set up an agency in New York City, principally to arrange the financing of Japanese trade. New York was by the 1880s the financial and commercial capital of the United States.

Subsequently, Yokohama Specie Bank established itself on the West Coast (San Francisco and later Los Angeles) and in Hawaii. Japanese shipping companies installed personnel at offices in West Coast port cities; men were required there to handle the needs of the shippers. The third major locale of Japanese firms in pre-World War I America was in Texas, where between 1910 and 1913 the three major Japanese trading companies that dealt in raw cotton exports *from* the United States initiated purchasing outlets; the Japanese wanted to inspect what they were buying.[3]

With the exception of a Kikkoman factory to make soy sauce, which a Japanese scholar has identified as built in Denver, Colorado, in 1892, all the Japanese direct investments in the United States before 1914 were in service sector endeavors—that is, in trade, finance, shipping, and insurance. Japan's "Big Three Service Enterprises," Mitsui & Co., Yokohama Specie Bank, and Nippon Yusen Kaisha

(N.Y.K.)—the shipping company—were active in the United States. A fourth key service enterprise, Tokio Marine Insurance Company, likewise, did business in this country. These four specialized firms often cooperated with one another.[4]

The size of the overall Japanese investment in the United States was small (by 1914 about $25 million). The level of employment was tiny (Mitsui, among the largest Japanese firms in America, had only twenty-eight employees in its New York City office in 1910).[5] Compared with the huge European portfolio and direct investment in the United States in the late nineteenth and early twentieth century, the Japanese presence was slim. Total foreign investment in the United States in 1914 was about $7.1 billion.[6]

Nonetheless, from the standpoint of the *Japanese* economy, the stakes of the Japanese multinationals in the United States in the years before World War I were of profound consequence. Japanese silk exports to the United States were vital to Japanese economic development, generating foreign exchange for imports.[7] Japanese trading companies, the Yokohama Specie Bank, the shipping companies, and the insurance enterprise—that is, Japanese multinationals in the service sector—assisted this commerce in a material manner. Increasingly, the Japanese organized and directed their own export expansion. The same was true of imports. The Japanese were buyers of American railroad equipment, machinery, and, most crucial, raw cotton for their innovative cotton textile industry. The Japanese companies' outlets in the United States contributed the service infrastructure for a substantial portion of such imports from America; in 1914, one Japanese trading company, Mitsui & Co., by itself was handling more than 30 percent of U.S. raw cotton exports to Japan.[8]

1914–1941

During World War I and in the interwar years, the fundamental characteristics of Japanese direct investments in the United States did not alter substantially. Japan emerged from the war a stronger nation, a creditor in international accounts. The Panama Canal opened in 1914, which led to greater Japanese-U.S. commerce. Table E–1 provides the only available figures on Japanese direct investment in the United States before World War II. The figures given in this and subsequent tables are stock figures, representing the level of Japanese direct investment in the United States. As noted (in the source portion of Table E–1), the Japanese percentages of total *direct* investments in the United States indicated on that table are probably an overestimate. Table E–2 gives, for the single year when such information is available before World War II, the composition of the investments; it shows that roughly 98 percent of the investment was in service sector activities. All evidence indicates that this make-up of investments was typical of the entire interwar period.

After World War I, U.S. companies made major investments worldwide, dwarfing foreign direct investments in the United States; the latter, nonetheless, continued. Since Japan was an ally of America in World War I, the war created no major discontinuity (such as was the case with German direct investment in the United States). Until the late 1930s, as one would expect, U.S. business investments in

Table E–1. Japanese Direct Investment in the United States, 1914–1941 (Book Value in Million U.S. Dollars and Percentages)

Year	Total	As Percent of Total Direct Investment in the United States
1914, June 30	25	1.4
1929, Dec. 31	45	3.2
1937, Dec. 31	41	2.1
1941, Dec. 8	35	1.5

Source: 1914 total: Mira Wilkins, "Japanese Multinational Enterprise Before 1914," *Business History Review* LX (Summer 1986), 209; 1929 total is based on the U.S. Department of Commerce figure on all Japanese investment in the United States of $50 million; from my own research, I estimated that about $5 million was portfolio investment; 1937 and 1941 totals: Mira Wilkins, "American-Japanese Direct Foreign Investment Relationships, 1930–1952," *Business History Review* LVI (Winter 1982), 507. Between June and December 1941, the Japanese government withdrew $27 million, held for it by the Yokohama Specie Bank, equivalent to nearly half the assets of the bank in New York (Alien Property Custodian, *Annual Report, 1944*, 58). I have no idea how this affected the *book value* (as given above) of Japanese direct investment in the United States. I calculated the percentages based on total direct investment figures for 1914 and 1929 from Cleona Lewis, *America's Stake in International Investment* (Washington, D.C.: Brookings Institution, 1938) and for 1937 and 1941 from the U.S. Departments of Commerce and Treasury. I believe that the denominator in each case is too low and thus the Japanese percentage of the total is exaggerated.

Japan were larger than Japanese direct investments in the United States (there had been a sizable expansion of U.S. business in Japan in the 1920s). By 1940–1941, Japanese restrictions on U.S. enterprise in Japan caused such a decline in U.S. direct investments there that Japanese direct investments in the United States actually exceeded U.S. direct investments in Japan.[9] Yet, whereas well over half of the U.S. direct investments in Japan was in manufacturing, all through the interwar period Japanese direct investments in manufacturing in the United States remained minimal (see, for 1937, Table E–2).[10] The composition of Japanese direct investments in the United States also departed sharply from that of overall foreign direct investments in this country. In 1937, of the total foreign direct investments in the

Table E–2. Japanese Direct Investment in the United States, By Sector, 1937 (Book Value in Million Dollars and Percentages)

	Million $	%
Finance	21.8	53
Distribution	16.5	40
Transport	1.8	4
Manufacturing	.9	2
Total	41.0	100

Source: Mira Wilkins, "American-Japanese Direct Foreign Investment Relationships, 1930–1952," *Business History Review* LVI (Winter 1982), 507. These are year-end figures. "Finance" appears to include banking. Percentage total is off because of rounding.

United States, 39 percent was in manufacturing, 22 percent in finance, 15 percent in petroleum, and 14 percent in transportation; the remaining 10 percent was divided among distribution, mining, public utilities, and other sectors.[11]

As Table E-1 shows, the size of Japanese direct investments in the United States in the interwar period was larger in total than before World War I. Specifically, in finance, there were more Japanese banks with outlets in America. These banks were engaged in international transactions, mainly related to Japanese trade. In 1914, the Yokohama Specie Bank had been the only Japanese bank in the United States; it was joined in New York City by the Bank of Taiwan (which entered in 1917), the Sumitomo Bank (1918), the Bank of Chosen (1919), the Mitsubishi Bank (1920), and the Mitsui Bank (1921). All remained active in that city until Pearl Harbor. These six Japanese banks in New York City had agencies, licensed under New York State law, under which law they were not allowed to take deposits.[12] The Bank of Japan also had a New York outlet that "did not engage in banking activities for which a license . . . [was] required by the state of New York."[13] Yokohama Specie Bank in New York, in addition to its trade related activities, aided the Japanese government in handling negotiations on government bond issues and obtained foreign exchange for the payment of interest on Japanese government borrowings.

On the West Coast—operating under state laws—in Washington and California, new subsidiary banks and branches of Japanese banks began operations. Some took deposits; those that did not handled foreign exchange, trade finance, and remittances to Japan. Newcomers after 1914 in the state of Washington included the Yokohama Specie Bank's Seattle branch, established in September 1917, and designed for foreign trade financing (it did not take deposits),[14] and the Sumitomo Bank of Seattle, incorporated in 1919.[15] In March, 1925, the Sumitomo Bank of California, Sacramento, was organized; it was a deposit-taking institution.[16]

The Yokohama Specie Bank did by far the largest business of all the Japanese banks, and its U.S. assets were the greatest.[17] In the 1930s, its branches and agencies financed over half of Japan's imports from the United States.[18] It also participated in a major fashion in financing Japan's exports to America, probably financing an even larger percentage of the total.[19] That bank became a training school for Japanese bankers. The bank recruited graduates from Japanese universities, such as University of Tokyo and Tokyo Commercial College (the predecessor of Hitotsubashi University). The education process (which involved a move every 2 or 3 years) would begin at the bank's headquarters in Yokohama; then the man would be dispatched to Shanghai and/or Bombay to learn about the silver exchange business; only later would he be assigned to New York and/or London. Thus, a Yokohama Specie Bank employee in New York would have had international experience elsewhere and would have been already qualified in foreign exchange transactions; he obtained a further education in New York. The bank, in short, gave on-the-job training in the interwar years to a new generation of Japanese men, who became highly knowledgeable in the complexities of international banking.[20]

In addition to the above-mentioned Japanese banks' activities in America, the Fujimoto Bill Broker Bank, Osaka (the predecessor to Daiwa Securities) set up the Fujimoto Securities Company in 1923 that started offices in San Francisco and in New York.[21] A few years later, in 1927, Nomura Securities, also headquartered in Osaka, joined its rival in New York.[22] These securities companies apparently aimed to encourage Americans to buy Japanese government bonds and also sought to give Japanese investors access to American-issued securities. Each of the securities companies seems to have assumed that Japan would return to the gold standard earlier than it actually did and wanted to be poised to take advantage of the opportunities when that occurred. (Japan returned to the gold standard for a short period—January, 1930 to December, 1931).

By the 1930s, when Japan began to have major deficits in its trade accounts, accompanied by serious foreign exchange difficulties, and as the depression in America curtailed all securities dealings, there was no future for these securities firms. Japanese aggression in Manchuria made Japanese government bonds even less attractive to Americans. After the Japanese Capital Outflow Prevention Act of 1932 and the strict foreign exchange laws that became effective in May, 1933, these firms' business declined further; Fujimoto appears to have closed its American offices in about 1933, while Nomura shut its New York office on December 31, 1936.[23]

Before World War I, only one Japanese marine insurer did business in the United States; by the time of World War II, three Japanese insurance companies had a U.S. presence.[24] The year-end 1937 figures on Table E–2 covering "finance" seem to include the banks and insurance companies.

While in the interwar years the dollar value of Japanese direct investments in finance was larger than that in distribution, the number of Japanese firms with U.S. offices that participated in trade was far greater than the number taking part in finance. All the major Japanese general trading companies had branches in the United States; these were engaged in exporting, importing, and third-country trade in a variety of different products. The preeminent trading company continued to be the earlier leader, Mitsui & Co., which by 1941 had offices in New York, San Francisco, and Seattle.[25] Mitsubishi Shoji Kaisha (Mitsubishi Trading Company), founded in Japan in 1918, started American branches in Seattle (1921–taking over the existing office of Mitsubishi Goshi that was established in 1918), New York (1921), and San Francisco (1926). Added Japanese general trading companies with New York offices included Suzuki Shoten (until it went bankrupt in Japan in 1927), Iwai Shoten, Okura Shoji, Takashimaya Iida, Gosho, Nihon Kiito, Asano Bussan, and Ataka Shokai. Suzuki, before 1927, had branches in Seattle, Portland, Houston, and Fort Worth, as well as New York. So, too, Asano Bussan and Okura had branches in Seattle, San Francisco, Los Angeles, and New York.[26] Other specialized trading companies that only handled the major Japanese export—raw silk—had offices in New York. Likewise, specialized trading companies in raw cotton exported from the United States to Japan and maintained their offices in Texas.[27]

The Wall Street Crash (1929) and the subsequent depression in America reduced the market in the United States for luxury goods; Japanese silk exports to the country fell off dramatically. Already in the late 1920s, silk prices had begun the decline. At their peak in 1925, Japanese raw silk exports, principally to the United States, had equaled 37 percent of the value of Japanese exports to all foreign countries.[28] Despite the Wall Street Crash, as noted earlier, Japan in January, 1930 went back on the gold standard (it had gone off the gold standard in 1917). The return was brief, and in December, 1931 Japan had to devalue the yen.

During the 1930s, the yen continued to depreciate; Japan's losses in silk exports were more than offset by that nation's overseas sales of cotton and rayon goods, as well as a wide range of low-priced manufactured items; some of these products went to America, but most were sold in Asia. Nonetheless, Mitsui and Mitsubishi began exporting to the United States canned crabmeat and canned tuna, pottery, cheap glass, cotton textiles, toys, and novelty items; yet 1937 aside, all during the 1930s raw silk (at the greatly reduced volume) still represented over 50 percent of Japanese exports to the United States.[29]

Despite Japan's desire to diversify exports to the United States, as the country industrialized in the 1930s and supplied its military needs, Japan had become an even larger *importer* of materials and equipment from the United States. While Japan remained America's largest customer for raw cotton, the new exports to Japan aided that rapidly industrializing country. Japan's trade balance with the United States, which had been positive in the 1920s, became negative.[30]

In arranging the newer Japanese exports to the United States and the newer U.S. exports to Japan, the Japanese trading companies increased their importance. While most of the Japanese trading companies in the United States had established themselves before the 1930s, there were some fresh entries. Kanematsu opened offices in New York and Seattle as late as 1936.[31] Despite the many Japanese trading firms, there was substantial concentration in their activities. In 1939, the four leading Japanese general trading companies (Mitsui & Co., Mitsubishi Shoji, Okura Shoji, and Asano Bussan) handled more than 44 percent of Japanese exports to the United States and fully 57 percent of U.S. exports to Japan.[32] The existence of zaibatsu interconnections undoubtedly was associated with this concentration, albeit all the Japanese trading companies appear to have handled business for firms outside as well as inside its group.

By 1940–1941, Mitsubishi Shoji—with its branches at Seattle, New York, and San Francisco—had as its principal activity the export of steel, steel scrap, machinery, petroleum, fats, and fertilizers from the United States to Japan and the import of silk from Japan to the United States. When, after Pearl Harbor, the Alien Property Custodian seized the U.S. properties of Mitsubishi, one asset was a continuous steel billet mill that was being built on order for Japanese use in Manchuria. The mill, which was 90 percent completed, had a book value of $725,000.[33]

The significance of these trading companies in Japanese-American commerce and Japanese economic development is hard to exaggerate. The trading companies through their U.S. offices served the changing requirements of numerous Japanese firms that wished to sell in and buy from America, firms that had neither the size nor skilled manpower to undertake such foreign trade on their own.[34] As in the case of the Yokohama Specie Bank, the trading companies created through the hiring and further training of university graduates a cadre of professionals knowledgeable in the complexities of international trade.[35] These men understood how to handle foreign exchange transactions, were familiar with customs regulations, and knew shipping routes and schedules. They were experts.

In addition, the trading companies' American offices became conduits by which technology spread from the United States to Japan. The methods ranged from (1) the negotiations for the export of full plants (as in the case of the steel billet mill referred to above), (2) the transfer of technological knowhow and plans (and arrangements on licensing), and (3) the intermediation in discussions between Japanese business and U.S. multinationals that had investments and that wished to invest in Japan. Any Japanese businessman visiting the United States would typically have appointments and schedules set up for him by a trading company office.[36]

An added important Japanese investment in distribution was that of Yamanaka and Company, Ltd., of Osaka, which had three American subsidiaries—in Boston, Chicago, and New York City—where it had stores to sell Chinese antiques. The New York store was inaugurated around 1900 and the others thereafter. In season, the regular stores opened branches at U.S. resorts, Bar Harbor, Newport, and Palm Beach.[37]

Typically, the imports and exports handled by Japanese trading firms or the imports sold by Yamanaka in the United States were carried on Japanese ships. Japan had become a major shipbuilder and maritime nation. Indeed, during World War I, the Seattle branch of Mitsubishi Goshi (opened in 1918) had as its first purpose the export of iron and steel to Japanese shipbuilders that had orders from the U.S. Shipping Board.[38]

Usually, Japanese shipping companies had branch offices on the West Coast and in New York. Included were Kawasaki Kisen Kaisha, with branches in New York, San Francisco, and Seattle; Nippon Yusen Kaisha, which had seven American branches; and Osaka Shoshen Kaisha (controlled by Sumitomo), which had a New York branch, as did the Yamashita Line and Kokusai Kisen Kaisha Ltd. The Mitsui Line was a department of the trading company. In the period 1927–1936, on average, Japan's merchant fleet carried roughly 73 percent of Japanese exports and about 63 percent of its imports.[39]

What all this meant was that—even more than in the period before 1914—the Japanese banks in the United States financed Japanese trade; Japanese insurance companies insured the cargoes; the Japanese trading companies with offices in this country handled the bulk of Japanese commerce (including the movement of intangibles, technology transfer, and assisting the arrangements for American companies' joint ventures in Japan),[40] and last but not least, Japanese ships transported the goods in both directions. On an ever larger scale, Japanese direct investments in the United States offered the business infrastructure for Japanese commerce. Briefly put, Japanese trade was more important to Japan than to any of that country's trading partners. If the Japanese did not undertake to pursue this trade to their own advantage, they would lose out. So the Japanese developed specialists in all facets of international commerce, who cooperated with one another. Thus, even though the dollar amount that the Japanese had invested in business in the United States in the interwar years was relatively minor compared with the total foreign direct investment in the United States, the value of this stake for the Japanese economy was nonetheless substantial.

Moreover, and interestingly, "Japan-bashing" (it was not called that) based on U.S.-Japanese economic relations mounted in America in the 1930s, and, as in more recent times, it was more associated with concerns over trade than over investment, yet the two were closely linked. In the 1930s, while most Americans knew nothing of the Japanese direct investment patterns, they did read in their newspapers that American steel scrap was contributing to the build up of Japan's military might (and they did know that Japan had been the aggressor in Manchuria, and in China, and then farther afield). Likewise, although in the 1930s Japan was America's largest single customer for raw cotton, the growing Japanese cotton textile industry meant that the Japanese trading companies were seeking to export finished cotton goods to the United States. During the 1930s this provoked intense hostility, government hearings, and formidable discussion. Were Americans being put out of work because of Japanese textile imports, goods made with "coolie wages"? American immigration walls had excluded cheap labor from the Orient, while—as the complainers maintained—U.S. law permitted "the products of his work to flood our markets at prices with which the most efficient domestic producer cannot compete." And, it was not only the domestic market that seemed in jeopardy. Low-priced Japanese goods were selling well in third countries, with the perceived consequences that American exports were lower and American jobs lost. The response in America was anything but friendly.[41]

WORLD WAR II AND ITS IMMEDIATE AFTERMATH

On July 26 (but effective June 14), 1941, as Japanese troops spread into Indo-China, President Franklin Roosevelt froze Japanese assets in the United States; all financial and export-import transactions came under U.S. control.[42] As indicated in Table E-1, the freeze does not seem to have been fully enforced, since between June and December of 1941 the Japanese government was able to withdraw $27 million that was held for it by the Yokohama Specie Bank's New York agency.[43]

After Pearl Harbor, the U.S. Treasury Department began to take over Japanese assets in the United States. President Roosevelt on March 11, 1942, authorized the formation of the Office of the Alien Property Custodian, which would seize the properties of all enemy (including Japanese) firms in the United States. Subsequently, nineteen Japanese banks and insurance companies were liquidated; by far the largest was the Yokohama Specie Bank (assets about $55.6 million). Likewise, the offices of the Japanese trading companies and of the shipping companies were closed down and their U.S. properties sold. The Alien Property Custodian alerted museums to the splendid Chinese antiques in the stores of the Yamanaka subsidiaries and tried to make it easy for the museums to buy these magnificent art works. By June, 1945 the Alien Property Custodian had vested 169 Japanese firms with assets of almost $104 million; it continued to liquidate these assets. If the reader compares this dollar sum with the Yokohama Specie Bank's assets given above, the preeminence of that one bank is evident.[44]

Once the war was over, Japan as the defeated nation was subject to the occupation by allied forces. The Occupation set out to assist Japan on the route to recovery on a democratic basis. This meant many economic reforms that had impact on the future of Japanese investments in the United States. First, the holding companies at the pinnacle of the zaibatsu were dissolved. A directive from the Supreme Commander of the Allied Forces, dated July 3, 1947, eliminated the old holding company, Mitsui & Co.[45] Trading companies that had been part of a formal group, connected by family ownership, now became independent. Yet, in the case of Mitsui, a new Mitsui & Co. emerged eventually out of the dissolution; other trading companies persisted; and as the postwar years passed, the prewar enterprise groups, although they were never formally reunited, consulted and often acted in concert. In the prewar period there had never been a one-to-one synchronization of the international business of zaibatsu firms. What in time reemerged after the war was not unlike the prewar interfirm cooperation.[46] Second, Toyota, which had started vehicle production during the 1930s, was in April, 1945, designated a Mitsui-affiliated restricted company (Mitsui affiliated companies had owned 13.7 percent of Toyota shares). This had important consequences on the business structure of Toyota's postwar international investments.[47] Third, the Japanese banking system was reformed. The Yokohama Specie Bank disappeared to be replaced in 1946 by the Bank of Tokyo, which inherited the Yokohama Specie Bank's business and personnel, along with their know-how and international expertise.[48] Fourth, the Occupation imposed a network of regulations, including those governing international transactions. Until August, 1947, it conducted all Japanese international trade; then it allowed Japanese trading firms to resume exports and imports.

By 1949, the General Headquarters for the Supreme Commander for the Allied Forces (as the Occupation was called) began to turn more economic policy decisions over to the reconstituted Japanese government; under the Foreign Exchange and Foreign Trade Control Law of 1949, every Japanese investment abroad had to be approved by the Japanese Ministry of Finance. The Japanese intended to use scarce capital resources at home.[49]

About this time, the first postwar Japanese investments in the United States started; Japanese trading companies were formally permitted to establish overseas offices, beginning in August, 1950.[50] A survey by the Ministry of International Trade and Industry in September, 1950 revealed 131 Japanese trading companies with foreign offices; while I have not seen the survey, possibly some of these outposts were in the United States.[51] By 1952, Japanese trading companies had offices in New York. In that year, when the Occupation ended and Japan once more became politically independent, there already existed a small amount of Japanese direct investment in the United States. On the basis of this interest, no one could have predicted the future.

FROM 1952 TO THE START OF THE 1970S

When in the 1950s, Japanese direct investment in the United States started to resume, the United States was the undisputed world leader. The United States came out of the war with formidable economic strength. American business abroad became ever more in evidence. Yet, at the same time, there continued to be foreign direct investments in the United States with Japanese businessmen and bankers among the investors. The first Japanese direct investments in the United States in the postwar period were for the most part of exactly the same sort as in the prewar years, that is, those of Japanese trading companies and financial institutions. Fuji Shoji Kaisha America, Inc., Tokyo Boeki Kaisha, Inc., and Tozai Koeki Kaisha, Inc. were among the pioneer U.S. subsidiaries of Japanese trading companies to set up business in America after the war. These three firms merged on July 11, 1954, into Mitsubishi International Corporation, incorporated in New York.[52] Daiichi Bussan (the immediate successor to the Mitsui Trading Company) had opened its first branch in the United States in 1951.[53] By the end of the decade it would have twelve offices in the United States and Canada.[54] Sumitomo Corporation of America was established in New York City in March, 1952.[55]

The Japanese Ministry of Finance maintained strict controls on banking abroad,[56] yet it approved certain U.S. endeavors. The Bank of Tokyo, with the old staff of the Yokohama Specie Bank, had vast international experience. Soon, it was in New York, with an agency. On October 28, 1952, it incorporated the Bank of Tokyo of California.[57] The *form* its banking operations took in the United States was—as had been the case in times past—determined by state government regulations. The next month the Sumitomo Bank reestablished itself in California with the Sumitomo Bank of California, San Francisco, with a branch in Los Angeles.[58] Ironically, as these new activities were undertaken, the *Annual Report* of the Superintendent of Banking (California) was reporting on the liquidation of the banks' prewar facilities in California.[59] A newcomer to California banking was the Sanwa Bank, which by June, 1953 had organized its first base in California.[60] Nomura Securities reestablished its prewar New York office in 1953.[61] In 1955 the Bank of Tokyo formed in New York City the Bank of Tokyo Trust Company, to engage in general banking as well as international activities; because New York law at that time still forbade branches, foreign banks created trust companies that could conduct domestic banking activities.[62] In 1961, the New York Banking Law would be changed: foreign banks were allowed to have branches in that City (but they could not have both agencies and branches; the Bank of Tokyo kept its status as an agency, using the Bank of Tokyo Trust Company for its general banking business).[63] By 1959, the Bank of Tokyo of California had its head office in San Francisco, with branches in Gardena and Los Angeles and assets of $37.6 million; the Sumitomo Bank (California) had its head office in San Francisco, with branches in Los Angeles and Sacramento and assets of $34.8 million; while the Sanwa Bank in San Francisco had assets of $33.1 million.[64] Thus, despite Japanese government restrictions on its banks' activities abroad and on capital exports, the Japanese perceived it to be in their interest to allow the banks (as they had allowed trading companies) to enter the United States—aiding commerce as well as restoring and enhancing Japan's standing in the world economy.

The Japanese made manufacturing investments in resource-procurement in the United States, in 1953–1954, in Alaska Lumber & Pulp Company and Alaska Pulp, Inc., for example. Alaska Lumber & Pulp Company was owned by 140 Japanese wood-using firms and trading companies, along with some Japanese government agencies.[65]

In addition, a very few innovative Japanese manufacturers began to bypass the trading companies and to start their own sales organizations in the United States. Their behavior was not unlike that of American companies in the late nineteenth century, which bypassed independent wholesalers and export companies and integrated forward into handling their own sales. While in the post-World War II era the characteristics of Japanese industry changed dramatically, within Japan there remained the realization that because the country had no basic raw materials, it had to export to get foreign exchange for the required imports. Yet, it was less clear that the Japanese trading companies—that specialized in primary products and small volume diversified exports—could handle the volume foreign sales of the new industrial goods that were being produced and whose producers hoped to sell them abroad; thus, some Japanese companies in the newer industries that required specialized sales promotion (including advertising and brand name recognition) considered forward vertical integration into foreign distribution to encourage exports. It is also important that nylon first appeared in 1939 and after the war a host of new synthetic fabrics substituted for natural fibers. This not only meant that silk stockings were no longer worn, but cotton textile exports would no longer have their prewar significance. The Japanese did become involved in synthetic fabrics, and for a while this sector seemed important. Yet the fantastic Japanese domestic economic growth of the postwar era was not based on textiles, but on other new, modern industries.

Of the mid-1950s, Akio Morita of the SONY Corporation writes, "I was not the only Japanese doing business in New York. . . . Many, if not most of them, relied on the giant Japanese trading companies that understood foreign markets and had established offices overseas."[66] Morita's company was one of those that had the kind of innovative products that the trading companies did not understand. So, too, first in radios and then in television sets and other goods, Matsushita Electrical Industrial Company had exported to the United States; in 1959 it organized its own sales subsidiary.[67]

Likewise, in the automobile industry, as early as October, 1957 Toyota had formed Toyota Motor Sales, U.S.A.[68] Toyota managers in Japan were aware that European models, especially Volkswagens, were selling in the United States. The new subsidiary appointed distributors and dealers. Yet, the first Toyotas introduced into the U.S. market attracted few American buyers and the Japanese company in December, 1960 decided to cease passenger car exports to the United States. Toyota Motor Sales, U.S.A. shut down most of its U.S. activities—retaining only a skeleton staff.[69]

Nineteen fifty-nine is the first postwar year for which the U.S. Department of Commerce published statistics on the book value of Japanese direct investment in the United States. Before that the amounts were considered too small to segregate. The Department of Commerce figures, as presented on Table E–3, suggest that in the period 1959–1973, Japanese direct investments (these are stock figures) never exceeded 1.7 percent of total foreign direct investment in the United States. The percentages are less than in 1929 and 1937 (see Table E–1 above).[70]

The Department of Commerce figures in Table E–3 are in many ways unsatisfactory. First, direct investments in banking may be in the "other" category in 1959–1960, but do not seem to be included subsequently (even so, compare the asset figures of Japanese banks in California, given above, with the direct investment figures provided on Table E–3 and one can see serious problems). Second, the investments in trade were not separated from other investments (except in 1959, see note d). Third, some of the investments indicated as in manufacturing (1959–1971) may be more properly classified under trade, thus exaggerating the manufacturing percentage of the total investment. Fourth, the negative Japanese direct

Table E–3. Japanese Direct Investment in the United States—Position at Year-End,
1959–1973 (Book Value in Millions of U.S. Dollars and Percentages)

Year	Total	Percent of FDI in U.S.	Distribution of Japanese DI by Sector			
			Manufacturing	Petroleum	Finance & Insurance[a]	Other
1959	80	1.2	*b*	*c*	16	64[d]
1960	88	1.3	NA	NA	NA	NA
1961	92	1.2	NA	NA	NA	NA
1962	112	1.5	51	−2[e]	19	44
1963	104	1.3	55	*c*	19	33
1964	72	.9	54	*c*	20	−1[e]
1965	118	1.3	56	*c*	22	40
1966	103	1.1	60	*c*	22	21
1967	108	1.1	64	*c*	25	19
1968	181	1.7	65	*c*	33	83
1969	176	1.5	67	*c*	39	70
1970	229	1.7	70	−3[e]	43	120
1971	−227[e]	*f*	76	*c*	50	−353[e]
1972	−154[e]	*f*	72	*c*	57	−283[e]
1973	259	1.4	129	*c*	81	48

Source: 1959–1960: U.S. Department of Commerce, *Foreign Business Investment in the United States* (Washington, 1962), 34–35; 1961–1970: Robert B. Leftwich, "Foreign Direct Investments in the United States, 1962–71," *Survey of Current Business,* February 1973, 36; 1971–1973: *Survey of Current Business,* October 1975, 41.

Key: NA: Not available. (*a*) Excludes banking. (*b*) Included in other. (*c*) No investment. (*d*) This "other" figure included $12 million in trade. (*e*) A "minus" figure means that the capital flow that year (or in a prior year) to Japan exceeded the recorded book value of the foreign direct investment. (*f*) Not meaningful.

Note: This table suggests (inappropriately) that in 1973, 50 percent of Japanese direct investment in the United States was in manufacturing. Likewise, in other years the percentage of the total investment in manufacturing seems not to reflect reality. The principal reason that the table misrepresents the ratios was that the investments in trade were often not meaningfully rendered. In 1973, specifically, the trade investment was reduced owing to parent-affiliate intercompany loans, creating obvious distortions in the data.

investment figures require explanation: the large negative total in 1971 was the result of an anticipation by Japanese businessmen that the yen would appreciate against the dollar. Accordingly, U.S. affiliates of Japanese trading firms prepaid their parents for imports (thus, lending to their parents); this is reflected in the negative $353 million in the 1971 "other" column. The 1972–1973 figures are, likewise, distorted by the responses to the changes in foreign exchange relationships.[71]

Yet in 1962 the U.S. Department of Commerce noted that "Japanese direct investments in the United States now are considerably larger than ever before; manufacturing investments of some size have been established, while old trading and financial firms have returned and new ones are being initiated."[72] The reference to manufacturing investments "of some size" was probably to the resource-oriented plants in Alaska (see above).

During the 1960s, Japanese activities in the United States continued to be closely linked with Japanese trade with this country. U.S. affiliates of Japanese companies dominated American commerce with Japan. For 1974, U.S. affiliates of Japanese firms handled 94.4 percent of U.S. exports to Japan and 85.8 percent of U.S. imports from Japan![73] The reason for this was (1) the experience of Japanese firms in handling this trade and (2) the continuing importance of this trade to Japan. Most in evidence in conducting this trade were the Japanese trading firms, but some of the Japanese exports to the United States were now being handled by the distributing companies set up by Japanese manufacturers who were paying more attention to American sales—and U.S. sales networks. SONY, for example, established in 1960, SONY Corporation of America, which during the 1960s created its own sales organization in the United States, marketing first imported transistor radios and then television sets.[74] Matsushita Electrical Industrial Company acted in a parallel manner. So, too, Oki Electric Industry Co. Ltd., in Japan, began to sell equipment for telephone exchanges. It formed an American marketing subsidiary, which in 1968 acquired one-third of the shares of one of its important distributors.[75] In 1964, Toyota Motor Sales, U.S.A. resumed passenger car imports into the United States and appointed new independent distributors; its dealer organization expanded from 200 in 1964 to 719 in 1967. Nissan Motor Corporation similarly established a sales network in the United States in the 1960s, as did Honda Motors. By contrast, Mazda, the latecomer in the U.S. market, used the distribution system of C. Itoh & Co., a Japanese trading company.[76] Americans' image of Japanese manufactured goods, based on the 1930s imports, had been that of cheap products. And, at first, the Japanese did seek to compete on the basis of price; at the same time, they sold high quality products.

By the 1960s, some Japanese firms began to invest in manufacturing in the United States, for sales in the United States. Yoshi Tsurumi identified one such investment in 1958; none between 1958 and 1965, and then another eight companies that started plants in America between 1965 and 1969.[77] The firms that invested in making goods in this country in the 1960s to serve the U.S. market were not numerous. Some, such as the chemical company Sekisui, were unsuccessful; Sekisui soon withdrew, unable to compete.[78] Some came in almost by accident: Mitsubishi Heavy Industry had exported its light aircraft to the United States for private planes; its Texas importer desired to build the fuselages in the United States and the Japanese company, to spur sales of the rest of the plane, agreed; 2 years later (in 1969), the Texan went bankrupt and Mitsubishi Heavy Industry acquired his American firm.[79] There were Japanese manufacturing investments in textiles and zippers.[80] One expert on Japanese multinational enterprise, Michael Yoshino, would write that the few Japanese manufacturing investments in the United States of this time were "idiosyncratic in character."[81] In most cases, the manufacturing facilities designed to reach the U.S. market were small (one firm had thirteen employees; on average they employed about forty to fifty people).[82] Yoshino attributed the absence of important Japanese direct investments in manufacturing in the United States to serve the U.S. market to the fact that most Japanese companies had acquired their technology and marketing skill from American enterprises— and thus had, or so it seemed, no advantage in the American market.[83] Wages in the United States were far higher than in Japan; language was a difficulty. Moreover, why manufacture in the United States if the market could be reached by exports? The 1962 U.S. Trade Expansion Act had lowered duties, and the American market became the most open in the world. Thus, the typical Japanese direct investments in the United States before the early 1970s were those of trading companies, those for procurement of raw materials, sales networks for Japanese manufacturers, and banking investments (designed to facilitate trade). These latter were, however, becoming impressive.

During the 1960s, Japanese banking investments in the United States grew, so that by 1972 Japanese bank agencies in New York held over half of the resources of all the foreign bank agencies in that city. The agencies were heavily committed to servicing the major Japanese trading companies and aiding Japanese trade. As of early 1974, the Bank of Tokyo Trust Company was the largest foreign-owned bank in New York. By then, the Bank of Tokyo was operating on an interstate basis in the United States. Aside from its interest (shared with the Industrial Bank of Japan) in the Bank of Tokyo Trust Company, it owned the Bank of Tokyo of California, had joint ownership of a Chicago affiliate, had a Chicago branch, and the New York agency. The Bank of Tokyo made available its services in aiding U.S. businesses investing in Japan, and Japanese businesses investing in the United States.[84]

Using data from Japanese sources (as distinct from the information on Table E–3), Terutomo Ozawa concluded that in 1973 about 77 percent of Japanese foreign direct investment in the United States was in commerce, banking, insurance, and other services.[85]

1971–1990

If the numbers given by the U.S. Department of Commerce on the level (stock) of Japanese direct investment in the United States, given on Table E–4 are accepted, in 1989 (the latest figures) only 25 percent of the total Japanese foreign direct investment in the United States was in manufacturing, with the bulk of the other 75 percent in commerce, banking, finance, insurance, and real estate. This suggests that despite the sizable rise in investment over the years (as shown on Table E–4), the basic composition had not changed. Once again, the reader must be wary; the appearances may be deceptive. There were in the 1970s and 1980s real changes that go far beyond the obvious size and relative importance of the Japanese stakes. Nonetheless, the Japanese figures do remain in contrast with the general profile of foreign direct investors in the United States: In 1989, 40 percent of the total foreign direct investment in the United States was in manufacturing (compared with 25 percent in the Japanese case).[86]

In the early 1970s, Japanese businessmen adopted new strategies. During the late 1960s, concerns had arisen in America over recurring deficits in the U.S. balance of payments. The United States had been financing the economic growth of the rest of the world. Yet with imports rising, some of the U.S. commitments to free trade seemed to be dissipating. In the context of U.S. worries over imports, Japanese manufacturers were accused of "dumping."[87] In 1970, Japanese television makers, including SONY, were named as defendants in an antitrust suit.[88] In 1971, for the first time in the twentieth century, it appeared that the United States would have a deficit in its trade balance. The response was the "Nixon shock" and the devaluation of the dollar. The effect of the currency realignment was that Japanese exports

Table E–4. Japanese Direct Investment in the United States—Position at Year-End, 1974–1989 (Book Value in Millions of U.S. Dollars and Percentages)

| Year | Total | Percent of FDI in U.S. | Distribution of Japanese DI by Sector | | |
			Manufacturing	Trade[a]	Other[b]
1974	345	1.3	330	−442c	457
1975	591	2.1	325	−221[c]	477
1976	1,178	3.8	304	329	545
1977	1,741	5.1	325	824	592
1978	2,749	6.5	474	1,522	753
1979	3,493	6.4	696	1,767	1,030
1980	4,225	6.2	837	2,307	1,081
1981	6,993	7.7	1,158	4,197	1,638
1982	8,742	8.6	1,485	5,317	1,940
1983	11,336	8.3	1,605	8,057	1,674
1984	16,044	9.7	2,460	9,689	3,895
1985	19,313	10.5	2,738	11,796	4,779
1986	26,824	12.2	3,578	13,687	9,559
1987	35,151	12.9	5,345	15,352	14,454
1988	53,354	16.2	12,222	18,390	22,742
1989	69,699	17.4	17,255	21,005	31,439

Source: 1974–1977: *Survey of Current Business,* Aug. 1978; 1978–1982: ibid., Aug. 1983; 1983: ibid., June 1985; 1984–1985: ibid., Aug. 1987; 1986–1988: ibid., Aug. 1989; ibid., June 1990.

Key: (a) This is given as "trade" in the *Survey of Current Business* through 1984; from 1985, it is given as "wholesale trade." (b) "Other" is the total of Japanese direct investment in the United States minus the Japanese direct investments in "trade" and "manufacturing." The principal categories of Japanese investments included under the rubric "other" are those in "finance," "insurance," and "real estate"—and "banking," when after 1983 direct investments in banking are segregated by the U.S. Department of Commerce. (c) A "minus" figure means that the capital flow to Japan in that year or prior ones reduced the book value by an amount that was greater than the recorded book value of the foreign direct investment.

Note: This table starts with 1974, using figures based on the major benchmark survey made for that year, which resulted in sizable revisions in the earlier published 1974 figures (the revisions reduced the earlier provided Japanese direct investment figure for 1974; compare the figures for 1974 not given in any table herein but in *The Survey of Current Business,* October 1975, 41, with the revised ones given above). Thus, Tables E–3 and E–4 represent different series.

to the United States became more expensive. (The exchange rate went from 357 yen to the dollar before the "shock" to 301 yen to the dollar at the start of 1973.)[89] The currency adjustments—and others that followed with floating rates—altered the cost structure for Japanese enterprise in the United States. The stronger Japanese currency made properties in America cheaper. For the Japanese, costs of U.S. production (translated into yen) did not seem so prohibitive. Figure E–1 shows the decline in U.S. prices vis-à-vis Japanese ones and the fluctuations in the exchange rate, 1973–1988.

Yet, even before the Nixon shock and the devaluation of the dollar, SONY Corporation had concluded that it would be prudent to manufacture in the United States; the threats of protectionism, the antidumping suit, and the antitrust action were considerations. Also, and as important, SONY by 1970 had created a national

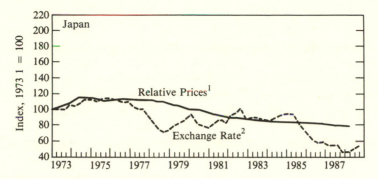

Figure E–1 Japanese-U.S. Exchange Rates and Relative Prices, 1973–1988

1. Ratio of Japanese GNP implicit price deflator to U.S. GNP implicit price deflator.
2. Foreign exchange value of the dollar.

Source: Economic Report of the President, 1989, 111, relying on data from the U.S. Department of Commerce, International Monetary Fund, and Council of Economic Advisors.

marketing organization in this country; it was aware that there was a large demand for its products. And, as Morita later explained, why pay the costs of shipping from Japan; an added advantage of producing "onshore" was that the company could more easily "fine-tune production depending on market trends."[90] The Nixon shock made SONY's plans even more viable. In 1972, SONY opened a color television factory in San Diego, California, its first U.S. manufacturing facility. The plant had 250 employees.[91]

Meanwhile, in the mid-1960s, protectionist sentiment in the United States had begun to arise in relation to the sizable Japanese exports of ball bearings to this country. The U.S. Defense Department placed restrictions on the procurement of foreign manufactured ball bearings for military use, insisting that the critical nature of this product required U.S. production for security of supply. Like SONY, the ball bearing companies had developed large U.S. sales. In 1971, Toyo Bearing established its first manufacturing facility in the United States, and in the next 2 years the three other principal bearings makers in Japan started U.S. plants.[92]

During the 1970s, the key Japanese consumer electronics firms (concerned over future U.S.-imposed obstacles to Japanese exports) resolved to produce in the United States to meet U.S. market demands. SONY (see above) was followed by Matsushita Electric Industrial Corporation (1974-Illinois); Sanyo Electric Co. (1977-Arkansas); Toshiba (1978-Tennessee); Sharp Corporation (1979-Tennessee); and Hitachi (1979-California). At all these Japanese plants color television sets were made.[93] Some manufacturers built new factories and others acquired U.S. companies (or divisions of American companies) and their facilities.

The next wave of entries into manufacturing was in semiconductors (sometimes involving the same firms as in consumer electronics). Just as the Japanese makers of color television sets had been stimulated to start producing in America by rising U.S. worries over imports, so, too, after an antitrust suit was brought against NEC and other Japanese producers (in 1975), semiconductor firms began to consider production in Americans' home territory. The antitrust charges were dismissed, but the U.S. industry's antagonism to imports did not abate and protectionist measures seemed imminent. In 1978, NEC acquired its first American company; Hitachi and Fujitsu followed with investments in 1979; Toshiba in 1980; Hitachi again in 1981; NEC built its own new American plant in 1982; Mitsubishi entered in 1983.[94] As noted, some of these companies were in both consumer electronics and producer goods. The influx continued in the mid-1980s.[95] In 1987 Fujitsu announced that it would purchase an 80 percent stake in Fairchild Semiconductor Corporation, which along with its existing holdings would have made Fujitsu the leading semiconductor firm in the world. Fairchild Semiconductor was a major defense supplier. American manufacturers (and the U.S. Defense Department), already disturbed by the growing Japanese presence, were now outraged; Fujitsu decided not to make the acquisition.[96] The fury was specifically aimed at the Japanese firm, for Fairchild was already controlled by a French multinational enterprise.[97] Instead, Fujitsu built a new plant in Oregon.[98] In 1989, Kyocera Corporation, Kyoto-based maker of ceramic semiconductor parts, took over AVX Corporation, an American electronics firm (price: $561 million).[99] This was an expansion of Kyocera's U.S. business; it already had other American plants.[100]

In the late 1980s, attracted by low cost land and the availability of skilled labor, more than fifty Japanese companies invested in Oregon, including NEC, Fujitsu, Kyocera, Epson, and Sharp (in the "Silicon Forest," as a contrast to California's "Silicon Valley," where the Japanese were encountering substantial hostility). What was becoming evident by the late 1980s was that the Japanese electronics companies were developing multiplant, multiproduct operations in the United States and that their enterprises were at the cutting edge of technology. Some of the entries had been in new activities; others, acquisitions. The latter were often the most visible—and thus more likely to receive (at least at origin) a negative public response.

The invasion had started with SONY's opening of its San Diego plant in 1972. Its initial investment there was very small. In 1988 SONY paid $2 billion for the record business of CBS, Inc., and if that were not spectacular enough, in 1989, SONY made the $4.8 billion purchase of Columbia Pictures and of Gruber Peters Entertainment Corporation. That takeover ranked in the top ten acquisitions in America in 1989. Its rival, Matsushita, followed in 1990 with a $6.6 billion takeover of MCA/Universal, which was the largest Japanese acquisition in American history. Both purchases represented the extension of "hardware" firms into important entertainment software developments.[101]

The size of the new activities was impressive. Less than 2 decades before, investments by Japanese manufacturers in the United States were in the thousands of dollars; while many in the 1980s and at the start of the 1990s were in the millions, some were in the billions. The strengthening of the yen vis-à-vis the dollar (see Figure E–1) encouraged these moves.[102] Twenty years earlier, employment at Japanese manufacturing subsidiaries was judged large if it numbered in the hundreds; by the 1990s certain individual Japanese electronics companies employed thousands of Americans at their multiplant, multiregional, multiproduct, multifunctional operations.[103] There continued to be concerns about the national security consequences of some of the investments in electronics.[104]

If the Japanese electronics companies have achieved an important position in America, this is also true of Japanese firms in the automobile industry. The pattern of penetration was similar. There were exports first; marketing organizations set up in the 1960s and 1970s; and then in the 1980s, manufacturing in the United States. U.S. protectionist measures and the potential for more protectionism, "voluntary export restraints" (on the part of Japan; first introduced for automobiles in 1981), the currency realignments that changed the costs, plus, and probably most influential, high U.S. demand for Japanese products, served to encourage these new investments.

The first of the Japanese vehicle producers to manufacture in the United States were not the car but the motorcycle companies. They already had a large share of the U.S. market.[105] In the mid-1970s Kawasaki Heavy Industries constructed a plant in Nebraska to manufacture motorcycles.[106] Honda came next, announcing in October 1977 that it would build motorcycles in Ohio.[107] This Honda plant would become the locale where Honda automobiles were subsequently made.

Then, one after another, in almost a staccato sequence, Japanese car companies began to enter the United States with new facilities and new processes of manufacturing (including plant management systems). All came after the introduction of voluntary export restraints. Honda produced its first car at Marysville, Ohio, in 1982 (the pioneering Japanese car maker in this country); Nissan went to Smyrna, Tennessee, and its first Tennessee vehicle was made in 1983; Toyota, in a joint venture with General Motors, had its first car, a Chevrolet Nova, move off the assembly line at Fremont, California, in 1984; Mazda followed in Flat Rock, Michigan, in 1987; Mitsubishi began producing at Normal, Illinois, in 1988; Toyota, now on its own, made its first Kentucky-built Camry at its modern plant in Georgetown in 1988; and Isuzu/Fuji's first output in Lafayette, Indiana, was in 1989. These were giant projects with employment in the thousands. By the end of the 1980s, Toyota's investment in Kentucky was $1.1 billion.[108] In each case, the Japanese multinationals had to learn how to combine the operations of their existing U.S. distribution organizations—established to sell imports—with their new U.S. manufacturing facilities.[109]

At the same time, and closely linked, parts and equipment suppliers from Japan invested in the United States to meet the needs of the car and truck manufacturers. New Japanese investments in steel were made in the 1980s, said to be associated with the Japanese car makers' requirements. In 1983, the Japanese tire company Bridgestone bought an unprofitable radial truck tire plant in Tennessee from Firestone Tire & Rubber Company; in 1988, it acquired all Firestone's tire factories; the price was $2.6 billion. Overnight, Bridgestone moved into the top rank of world tire makers. The acquisition was the largest single investment to that date by a Japanese investor. It was surpassed in 1989 and 1990 by the earlier mentioned investments by SONY and Matsushita.[110]

Japanese investments in real estate were also sizable. In the 1960s the Japanese had been buying hotels in Hawaii, to serve the affluent Japanese tourist.[111] At the start of the 1970s, with the appreciation of the yen and relaxation by the Japanese of restrictions on capital exports, Japanese investments in real estate accelerated rapidly.[112] Japan in December, 1980 passed a Foreign Exchange Control Law that more sharply reduced the restraints on capital outflows. As one author has put it, before December, 1980, capital outflows from Japan were prohibited unless specifically permitted (but in the case of the United States, they were often specifically permitted); after that date, capital outflows were permitted unless specifically prohibited.[113] Increasingly, Japanese liberalization of capital exports opened the way for the large investments in manufacturing that we discussed earlier—and also those in real estate—which might not have been authorized otherwise.[114]

During the 1970s, and especially in the 1980s, Japanese investors' stakes in real estate moved from Hawaii to the U.S. mainland, and by the late 1980s, the Japanese were prominent as buyers of urban properties, particularly on the west coast and in New York City, but also in Atlanta. The main attention was to office buildings and hotels. By the late 1980s, the Japanese investments in real estate became dramatic. A 1989 book reported that 70 percent of downtown Los Angeles was Japanese-owned.[115] In New York City, there were spectacular purchases, including Rockefeller Center (in which the Mitsubishi Estate Company acquired a sizable equity interest), the Exxon building (purchased in 1986 by Mitsui Fudosan), and two-thirds of Citicorp Center (1987, Dai-Ichi Real Estate Company).[116] These direct investments reflected the new capital surpluses in Japan.

Meanwhile, what was occurring with the past patterns of investments by Japanese trading companies and financial institutions? Regrettably, the figures on Table E–4 that show the sizable Japanese direct investments in trade do not divide these investments between Japanese manufacturers and Japanese trading companies. Japanese manufacturing companies with branded products have usually developed their own U.S. distribution organizations, as we have noted; Japanese trading companies, while still of major importance in Japan's global position, seemed perhaps of less significant vis-à-vis Japanese businesses' direct investment in the United States, at least those *to meet American demand.*

Nonetheless, the principal Japanese trading companies have continued to invest in trade and manufacturing in the United States. Mitsui & Co. had in 1983 sixteen offices in U.S. cities around the country.[117] According to Robert Lawrence of the Brookings Institution (as quoted in the *Wall Street Journal,* February 26, 1990), affiliates of Japan's six key trading companies accounted for about 60 percent of all U.S. exports to Japan.[118] These experienced firms knew *Japanese* requirements and had advantages in conducting such trade. Moreover, their largest investments in manufacturing seem to have been in resource-providing entities that both serve the U.S. market *and* export from the United States (the trading companies could handle their exports). Thus, major investments of Mitsui & Co. have included those in Alumax, Inc. (an integrated manufacturer of aluminum products); Gulf Coast Grain, Inc. and United Grain Corp. (in the grain business); and Neptune Packing Corp. (a canner of tuna fish).[119] Leading trading companies—Mitsui & Co., Mitsubishi International Corporation, C. Itoh & Co., and Nissho-Iwai Corporation—were also taking minority positions in small and not so small U.S. companies, frequently in high technology fields.[120] Many of such "venture" capital projects provided information to the Japanese investors; presumably, these were projects that would develop profitably, at which time the trading companies would bring in more specialized Japanese enterprises. By the end of 1989, Mitsui & Co. had seventy-five U.S. affiliates, in which it held an interest of more than 35 percent; the president of Mitsui, U.S.A. announced that by the end of 1990, he hoped to have double that many affiliates.[121] Clearly, the trading companies—not only the largest one, Mitsui & Co.—maintain a significant presence in the United States, have important investments, and continue as in the past to provide trade and information conduits, and the basis for strategic alliances. Their activities, although far more extensive than in earlier times, in broad terms resemble those of the past.

By contrast, Japanese financial institutions have taken on a new and extraordinary role within the American economy. In the early 1970s, the Japanese Ministry of Finance relaxed its restrictions on Japanese banks developing overseas operations. The Foreign Exchange Control Law of 1980, as noted, sharply reduced capital outflow restraints. As a consequence of these measures, Japanese banks have greatly enlarged their U.S. business.

Every Japanese bank that entered the United States wanted to be in New York City (the nation's financial center), and every major Japanese bank had an agency or branch there. Yet, the biggest developments, principally acquisitions, were in California. Sanwa Bank (which had been present in that state since 1953) organized in 1971 the Sanwa Bank of California (a state-chartered banking subsidiary), and in the 1970s Sanwa purchased several local California banks—Hacienda Bank, Golden Gate Bank, and First City Bank—and created the Golden Gate Sanwa Bank; in 1986, Sanwa nearly quadrupled its network of branches when it bought Lloyds Bank's $3 billion asset California subsidiary (Lloyds Bank of California). The next year (1987), the already huge Bank of Tokyo of California acquired California First Bank, with its network of over 100 branches, and in 1988, the latter bought Union Bank, San Francisco, from the British, Standard Chartered PLC. Meanwhile, Mitsubishi Bank (which had set up the Mitsubishi Bank of California in 1971 and had expanded in a modest manner) in August 1983 had bought BanCal Tri-State Corp., the owners of the Bank of California; this gave Mitsubishi Bank operations in California, Washington, and Oregon.[122] By the end of 1986, in addition, in California, Mitsui Bank, Tokai Bank, Dai-Ichi Kangyo Bank, and the Sumitomo Bank all owned banks and took part in full-service domestic banking. By 1989, Japanese-owned banks controlled about 25 percent of the state's banking market, up from 13 percent in 1986.[123] By that year, ten Japanese banks had 424 branches in California.[124] American bankers attributed the Japanese expansion in this state to "razor-thin" pricing.[125]

It was not only in California (and on the West Coast) that Japanese banks made significant inroads. They were by the 1980s on a national scale providing letters of credit for municipal bond offerings, offering commercial credit across the country, and helping with real estate financing for American as well as Japanese customers.[126] In the 1950s, 1960s, and 1970s, Japanese banks had aided and assisted Japanese trading companies, industrial enterprises, and investors in real estate. By the 1980s, Japanese banks were providing services for U.S. and European corporations on a major scale. In September, 1989, Dai-Ichi Kangyo Bank agreed to purchase

60 percent of Manufacturers Hanover Corporation's CIT Group for $1.28 billion; the CIT Group was a leading finance company with fifty offices throughout the country.[127] When that acquisition agreement was made, aside from its business in California, the Dai-Ichi Bank had a New York branch and offices in Chicago and Atlanta; it had over $30 billion in assets in the United States.[128]

At the end of 1988, the leading Japanese banks in America (measured by assets) were the Bank of Tokyo ($44.2 billion), Mitsubishi Bank ($32.7 billion), Fuji Bank, Ltd. ($31.1 billion), Dai-Ichi Kangyo ($30.6 billion), Sanwa Bank ($28.8 billion); Industrial Bank of Japan ($28.7 billion); and Sumitomo Bank ($22.2 billion).[129] In 1989, the Bank of Tokyo employed 9,000 people in the United States (and only 5,000 in Japan).[130] Four Japanese-owned firms—Nomura Securities Company, Daiwa Securities Company, Nikko Securities Company, and Yamaichi Securities Company—were not only important in the New York money market, but by the end of the 1980s the "Big Four," as they were called, served as primary dealers in buying and selling U.S. Treasury bonds. These firms had become significant participants in mergers and acquisitions, particularly in assisting Japanese acquisitions of American companies and also serving other nonJapanese enterprises. While not giants in their own right, they could draw on the vast resources of their parent firms.[131] They had extensive international experience and knew the Eurobond and Euroyen markets.

Japanese insurance companies became major investors in America, using their surplus funds. Once Japanese insurance companies had insured cargoes. Now their business was entirely different. They were now financial intermediaries. They were doing what the Japanese banks (and securities companies) were doing—introducing Japanese monies into the American economy. Indeed, Nippon Life Insurance Company acquired a stake in Shearson Lehman Bros. (the "securities arm" of American Express), while Yasuda Mutual Life Insurance obtained a minority holding in Paine Webber. Along the same lines, Sumitomo Bank had bought an interest in Goldman, Sachs, while the Industrial Bank of Japan had acquired Aubrey G. Lanston (a primary dealer in U.S. government securities); Nomura Securities obtained an interest in Nomura Wasserstein Perella Company.[132]

In short, if the role of Japanese manufacturing companies and Japanese investors in real estate in the United States in the late 1980s had become impressive, that of Japanese financial institutions had become equally, and perhaps even more, striking. Foreign investors in the United States in times long past had had leadership in particular high technology industries—from radio communication to rayon (the first synthetic fabric)—so that was not new.[133] The rapidly expanding Japanese manufacturing activities in America in the 1980s was in that tradition. Although it is novel to have the Japanese in the lead, it is not unique to have a foreign direct investor taking the initiative. Similarly, the British and the Dutch at various times in American history have had major U.S. real estate holdings.[134] Yet, not since the British had had investments in the Bank of the United States (before the War of 1812) and in the Second Bank of the United States and its successor (before its bankruptcy in 1841) were foreign investors in a prominent role in domestic banking on a national scale.[135] The entry of foreign banks, and in the lead Japanese banks, on an interstate basis, gave American banks leverage to press for interstate banking. Foreign banks before 1978 had the possibilities of operating on a national scale in a way forbidden to American owned banks. Likewise, Japanese banks were getting around the U.S. prohibitions against securities affiliates. The activities of Japanese financial institutions in the United States were awesome. By the end of the 1980s, Japanese banks were foremost among foreign banks in the United States.[136]

THE RECENT INVESTMENTS

As Japanese direct investment has soared (and Japanese direct investments moved to over 10 percent of the total direct investments in the United States—see Table E–4), the investors were obtaining remarkably low returns on their U.S. holdings. Table E–5 gives the rates of return on Japanese direct investments in the United States for 1985–1989. As the sums invested became larger, the rates of return came to seem even more dismal. Why were the 1987–1989 recorded level of return so low? Some have suggested that Japanese companies look to the long term and do not care about immediate returns, their shareholders being less demanding than American ones. Other possible explanations include: (1) Because of the strength of the yen (see Figure E–1), many Japanese investors were tempted into takeovers at what seemed—in terms of yen—to be "bargain" prices; yet, in terms of dollars the Japanese may have overpaid, and the low stream of earnings expressed in dollars could reflect the overpayment.[137] (2) For new investments, high start-up costs could explain low returns (this is the long-term argument in another guise). (3) Costs of doing business in America may have been higher and revenues lower than anticipated (the U.S. market is difficult to penetrate). And (4) possibly the figures are deceptive and the actual returns are higher.[138]

In the manufacturing sector during the late 1980s, every year losses were recorded; this seems to be particularly related to the newness of the investments. While the profits performance of the Japanese automobile manufacturers in the United States are not available, scattered evidence indicates losses. The returns in the real estate sector have been poor—and in 1987 were negative.[139] Recently, the president of Mitsui U.S.A. was quoted as saying that when Japanese trading companies invested in U.S. manufacturing enterprises, they were not so much interested in a high return on these investments as in increasing the trade flows that the trading companies would handle.[140] Ultimately, however, the high returns should

Table E–5. Rates of Return on Japanese Direct Investment in the United States, 1985–1989 (Percentages)

	1985	1986	1987	1988	1989
All Japanese direct investment in U.S.	8.8	5.2	2.7	3.3	2.1
Manufacturing	−7.5	−7.0	−0.6	−0.5	−2.4
Trade	11.9	5.7	4.4	5.7	1.9

Source: Survey of Current Business, August 1987, August 1989, and August 1990. A negative percentage indicates losses.

be reflected in the trading companies' business. And, in fact, the only respectable returns shown in Table E–5 are those of the trading companies in 1985. In California, where the Japanese banks are so outstanding, they have not been as profitable as their U.S. counterparts.[141] The *Wall Street Journal* reported in October, 1989 that the Big Four Japanese securities firms—Nomura, Daiwa, Yamaichi, and Nikko—had been "only marginally profitable, if at all in the U.S."[142] Indeed, quite a large number of Japanese investments in the United States have been over the decades (and not just in the years indicated on Table E–5) unsuccessful—if success is defined by profitability—and there have been retreats (based on failures) as well as the more publicized rash of new entries.

The low recorded U.S. returns in the late 1980s notwithstanding, measured by book value, Japanese direct investment in the United States passed 15 percent of the total foreign direct investment in the United States in 1988 (see Table E–4). That year, the Japanese became second only to the British in their foreign direct investment in the United States (using the same criteria, the British were, however, still far ahead, with over 30 percent of the foreign direct investment total).[143]

In the late 1980s, there remained only one U.S.-based color television producer, Zenith. Japanese firms dominated this market, selling output principally from their U.S. plants.[144] The new Japanese stakes in automobile manufacturing are substantial, even though the market share in this industry is not as high as in color television sets. Japanese car sales in 1989 (both made-in-America cars and imports) equaled 30 percent of the market, up from 25 percent in 1987.[145] The Japanese in the late 1980s ranked first—by far—compared with other foreign nationalities in their holdings of U.S. banking assets; Japanese banks' share of U.S. banking assets (10.1 percent as of June 30, 1988) was large,[146] but not as great as the *market* share in key manufacturing industries—from color television to automobiles. Perhaps, however, it is inappropriate to compare market shares in consumer durables with asset shares in the banking sector.[147] But, banking is not just any industry; the 10 percent asset share might be perceived as creating more public policy concerns than the far larger market share in color television sets, or even for that matter in automobiles.

Table E–6 contains a profile comparing Japanese and British *nonbanking* direct investments in the United States in 1988, the latest year for which such information is available. These figures (unlike the book value of direct investment ones) place Japanese firms in first place among foreign companies in the United States in terms of assets and sales. The relatively small number of employees and the very high average compensation relates to the different industry composition of Japanese and British investments (the large Japanese stakes in real estate ventures and in trading companies mean fewer employees relative to assets and sales than those in other sectors).

By the end of the 1980s and the start of the 1990s, Japanese direct investments in America struck symbolic chords. All at once, America was not America any more. Honda had a place in the Detroit Hall of Fame. Automobile shows featured Japanese products (some but not all made in America). Americans felt uneasy when they read that from 1987 to the start of 1990, General Motors and Chrysler had shut seven U.S. automobile plants, employing about 20,000 persons, while in the

Table E–6. A Comparison Between Japanese and British Nonbank U.S. Affiliates, 1988

Basis for Comparison	Japanese	British	All Foreign
Total assets (in million dollars)	275,038	194,064	1,147,237
(as percentage of all foreign)	(24.0)	(16.9)	(100.0)
Total sales (in million dollars)	225,319	142,336	853,349
(as percentage of all foreign)	(26.4)	(16.7)	(100.0)
Net income (in million dollars)	615	3,645	11,561
(as percentage of all foreign)	(5.3)	(31.5)	(100.0)
Employee compensation (in million dollars)	15,117	22,009	112,370
(as percentage of all foreign)	(13.4)	(19.6)	(100.0)
Number of employees	401,000	734,800	3,682,200
(as percentage of all foreign)	(10.0)	(20.0)	(100.0)
Average compensation per employee			
(in dollars per annum)	37,698	29,952	30,517
(as percentage of all foreign)	(123.5)	(98.1)	(100.0)

Source: Survey of Current Business, July 1989, 129; these figures are based on ultimate beneficial owners; the average compensation is the employee compensation divided by the number of employees.

same time span five new Japanese automobile plants had opened, employing just over 11,000.[148]

Headlines screamed, "America turns into a big garage sale."[149] The imagery was not a happy one. The 1989 Mitsubishi Real Estate Company's purchase of 51 percent of Rockefeller Center and the Sony Corporation's acquisition of Columbia Pictures triggered deeply hostile feelings. These were further accentuated when in 1990 Matsushita bought MCA/Universal. "Would American movies take on a Japanese cast?" the *Wall Street Journal* asked.[150] From coast to coast, around the nation, the very core of America's heritage seemed in jeopardy. A 1989 *Newsweek* poll found that 43 percent of Americans considered Japan a greater threat than the Soviet Union and this was before there was a general acceptance of the end to the Cold War.[151] New words and phrases entered Americans' vocabulary, "Japan-bashing," "Japanphobia," and "sake-sippers beholden to Japan" (the last a reference to individuals who thought the Japanese were not all that terrible). Negative emotional reactions rise and fall. In the late 1980s and at the dawn of the 1990s they had reached a new peak.

By 1990, the Japanese direct investment in the United States was conspicuous and substantial (even though measured by book value, British direct investment in the United States was larger than that of the Japanese). In overall terms, it could be argued that Japanese direct investments in the United States were not that impressive, considering the general resources of the nation. There seems no question, however, that in a number of important sectors, Japanese business investment had become pivotal.

Japanese businessmen marveled at the paradox of U.S. consumers' desire to purchase Japanese goods from cars to desktop computers and of American state governors' begging for more Japanese investment, while numerous Americans *at the very same time* resented the Japanese "invasion" of U.S. markets. Yet this paradox of ambivalence is historically an inherent part of the experience of all multinational enterprise. The visceral responses in America are in keeping with past reactions when once before the United States was—as it is today—a large recipient of foreign investment[152], and also with European responses when in the 1960s there were worries over the American "invasion."[153] Until the 1980s, Japanese investments in the United States were not large enough to sustain long periods of antagonism. This is no longer the case. If the experience of the history of British investors in the United States and American business abroad is any guide, Japanese investment in America will continue to be welcomed and despised—at the same time. Practically every country, the United States included, wants foreign direct investments, but *only on its own terms,* terms that shift in different times and circumstances.

CONCLUSIONS

For more than 100 years, Japanese foreign direct investment has existed in the United States. Over most of that long period, interrupted by World War II, the size of the investment expanded on a modest basis. Not until 1977 did Japanese foreign direct investment in the United States exceed 5 percent of the total, and not until the 1980s did it become of consequence in the U.S. economy.

By contrast, before World War I, the Japanese direct investments in America were of significance for the *Japanese* economy. There was throughout a substantial role of service sector direct investments, linked at origin with Japanese needs and requirements. The Japanese to encourage trade made direct investments. They were not unique in doing so; foreign direct investments of other nationalities had also been made to spur commerce. The British, as an island nation, dependent on trade often combined in clusters trading company, banking, insurance, and shipping direct investments.[154] What seems unique about the Japanese is how long the service sector involvements vis-à-vis those in manufacturing have persisted as characteristics of Japanese investment in the United States. Thus, in 1937, when Japanese service sector direct investments in America represented 98 percent of the total, the British had 55 percent of their U.S. direct investments in manufacturing and petroleum.[155] Similarly, whereas 75 percent of Japanese direct investment in the United States in 1989 was in the service sector and real estate, the British have 57 percent in manufacturing and petroleum.[156]

Yet, much of the evolution of Japanese multinational enterprise as seen in its stakes in America is far from distinctive to the Japanese. Like direct investors from other countries, the Japanese have used their special advantages and experience in their international and, specifically, their U.S. expansion. The service sector activities in the United States once linked with international trade have in recent years served the Japanese and others in *U.S.* transactions: U.S. distribution organizations set up to sell Japanese exports now sell Japanese and others' products made in America; trading companies make sizable investments in raw material processing and in venture capital projects (and the markets served are both domestic and international); banks that financed Japanese trade, now also finance U.S. mergers and acquisitions; insurance companies that once were confined to insuring cargoes, have invested their capital surpluses in a range of American endeavors. The service activities have, in short, taken on new functions. The Japanese have built on their earlier advantages.

Years ago, I found a pattern in the growth of American multinational enterprise, one evolving from a single center to a polycentric structure, where within individual host countries, the U.S. multinational developed over time significant multiplant, multifunctional organizations.[157] The same pattern is evident in the evolution of Japanese multinationals, as seen in their U.S. investments. Today's stakes of the Japanese in the United States combine the continuity of past experience with the novelty for the Japanese multinational of greater size and diversity, innovative processes and product offerings, and for the first time, important impacts on the *American* economy.

Notes

Chapter 1

1. See Ozawa, 1979, Kojima, 1978, and the Institute of Social Science, 1990, ch. I.

2. For product and process technology, see Abernathy (1978); for labor-saving and material-saving innovation, see Vernon (1966), for accumulation-oriented technology, see Yoshihara (1983) and Imai (1988). Mechanics- and electronics-oriented technology were mentioned by Professor J. Zysman in answers to Abo's questions at the American Center in Tokyo on January 23, 1991. Of course it is also possible that certain countries may excel at technology that serves both types of models. In fact this pattern has recently been observed in Japan.

3. Dunning, 1981, Part 1.

4. Abo, 1981.

5. Buckley, 1987.

6. Yoshino, 1977.

7. Trevor, 1983.

8. Agreement with the union at a Nissan plant in Britain has resulted in a combination of simplification of the job classification system and personnel evaluation that effects wages and promotion, thus coming quite close to the Japanese model (formally similar to the evolution form seen among certain plants in the United States). The above is from Wickens (1987, Chapter 8) and an interview at the plant with Abo (December 10, 1990). Surprisingly, at Calsonic plant, which supplies parts to the same British Nissan plant, there are no Japanese expatriates, all of the work being carried out by British personnel (same plant interview). At any rate, it appears that British plants are recently more flexible than their U.S. counterparts when it comes to adopting Japanese methods.

9. The earliest representative study is by Abegglen (1958). Studies by Japanese researchers have focused on distinctive features of the Japanese system, such as "enterprise unions" or the "seniority system," for example, the Institute of Social Science, ed. (1950) and Okochi, Ujihara, and Fujita, eds. (1959).

10. For example, since before the war, typical Japanese family-owned businesses have been able to guarantee neither efficiency nor quality. It is common knowledge that Japanese products before and until shortly after the Pacific War were known as "cheap and inferior". On the other hand, there is some very interesting research revealing the implementation of rationalization through the enterprise-specific labor relations among certain small and medium businesses as early as the interwar period. (Banno, 1991). It is also well known that there is a rather considerable difference in the performance of Japanese public and private enterprises, although their management systems are similar in respect of a number of practices, such as lifetime employment, seniority system, and frequent job rotation.

11. Hall, 1979.

12. Yasumuro, 1982.

13. See Koike (1977) and Koike and Inoki, eds. (1987). Moreover, even strong supporters of the view that elements of the Japanese system are universal and compatible with other systems have recently become more flexible. Koike (1990) admits that there are limits to compatibility when he

says that ". . . concerning compatibility of the Japanese system, because of a long and persistent industrial tradition in Western Europe and the United States, changes may provoke exorbitant costs". On the other hand, he stresses the compatibility of this system to Southeast Asian countries, which lack a similar industrial tradition.

14. Shimada, 1988.

15. Baba, 1991, Matsumoto, 1991.

16. Kumazawa, 1989.

17. Totsuka, 1990.

18. See the following books: Cohen and Zysman (1987), Dertouzos et al. (1989), Womack et al. (1990), Porter (1990), Clark and Fujimoto (1991), and Kenney and Florida (1991, 1992).

These books all focus on the importance of the competitive advantage that Japanese industry gained from the production system or manufacturing technology. However, with some exceptions of Poter, to a certain extent, and Kenney and Florida, they do not recognize the importance of the Japanese culture as an environmental precondition for such a system. Instead, most of them emphasize the role of the Japanese government's industrial policy.

For example, Womack et al. provide an excellent description of the efficient and superior performance of the "lean production system," but they stress that "lean system" does not necessarily equate with "Japanese system". They emphasize the "universal" nature of "lean system" unrelated to Japanese culture (pp. 8–10). However, it would be difficult for them to offer a persuasive explanation of the sufficient conditions of "dynamic work team," which they identified as "the heart of the lean factory" (p. 99), without taking the Japanese sociocultural background into account. How easy is it for all the employees who live in a society where the "demarcation" principle active in work rule has been firmly established from top to bottom, to have overall understanding of the environmental context of their plant, and to be able to promptly cope with the problems that arise? It has been our observation that Japanese society is among the very few wherein there is a distinct "all member-involvement consciousness" or group orientation as opposed to "demarcation."

Womack et al. also mention the important role of teamwork in the product development organization by referring to Clark and Fujimoto's research result (Ch. 5). But here again we should point out the difference between the "top-down" leadership of product managers in a western company and the Japanese-style leadership provided by "heavyweight" product managers who achieve cross-functional coordination in product development activities ranging from concept creation, designing, and process engineering to marketing [see Clark and Fujimoto, Ch. 9]. However powerful the authority of "heavyweight" product managers may appear, it does not derive simply from a higher managerial position within the company. Their power stems from practices that are less "demarcation"-style or worksite-oriented, and that are supported by a companywide sense of teamwork that bridges authority of the various sections from sales, through production and research and development, as well as by a sense of intercompany involvement that is felt by assemblers and parts suppliers.

Chapter 2

1. Shimada, 1988.

2. This research maintains essentially the same theoretical and analytical frameworks adopted in our previous book (Institute of Social Science [Abo. T. ed.], 1990). However, developments in subsequent research and surveys led to some important changes and improvements.

First, in addition to the "application" focus of the hybrid analysis, the previous research introduced a different analytical viewpoint. It divided items and groups into two major categories: groups I, Work Organization and Administration, II, Production Control, and III, Procurement, were classified as "application" groups, and groups IV, Group Consciousness, V, Labor Relations, and VI, Parent-Subsidiary Relations, were classified as groups to be evaluated primarily with respect to their "adaptation" to the local environment. It was considered valid to focus on local "adaptation" because the items classified accordingly offered a high degree of resistance to the "application" of the Japanese management and production system. In the present research, that approach was not employed. Instead, there is a consistent focus on "application" in the form of the "international transfer model." Reasons for this change in approach are given in Chapter 1.

Second, those elements for which data showed clear evidence of reflecting local conditions or a particular managerial environment were treated separately as "environmental conditions." Examples include local labor or transportation conditions determined by plant location, as well as different plant management strategies determined by the parent company, or by different forms of ownership, such as a joint venture. The "pattern analysis" is an attempt to correlate and discover meaningful relationships between these "environmental conditions" and the various patterns of local production and management exhibited by the local plants.

Third, the following changes and additions were made to the groups and items comprising the "hybrid model":

1) "Operations management" became a fourth item added to group II, Production Control, in order to allow a more comprehensive evaluation of the Japanese-style production operations at local plants.

2) Procurement, which was group V in the previous study, was promoted to group III, because it is directly related to the production system and could therefore be best regarded as a "secondary core" group following core groups I, Work Organization and Administration, and II, Production Control. This also served to emphasize the significance of Group Consciousness, which changed from group III to group IV, as a part of the subsystem that supports the "application" intensive core groups. Also, item 13, Procurement Method, was added to group III, Procurement, in order to better evaluate local application of the Japanese-style procurement system.

3) The items in group IV, Group Consciousness, were extensively rearranged. Job Security was removed and placed in group V, Labor Relations. Of course job security does have the effect of increasing employees' group consciousness, but it was also considered to be part of an general managerial framework that is a precondition for other policies, such as worker training or education. Finally, certain items which were dealt with individually in the previous study (Open-style Office, Uniform, Socializing, and Company Meetings) were combined with other measures that promoted the characteristic sense of group consciousness, to become two items, namely, Information Sharing and Group Identity.

4) What was group IV, Employment Situations, in the earlier study became group V, Labor Relations. By separating those elements that are general, fixed, preconditions for local management as "environmental conditions," this group is reorganized into four items. This emphasizes their significance as a framework for the local application of the Japanese-style production system. Also, the names of the items in group VI, Parent-Subsidiary Relations, were changed and the focus of the evaluation was slightly shifted.

3. Some additional comments regarding our methods in creating this model are in order. Our primary focus is measuring the degree of local application of the Japanese-style management and production system by Japanese companies in order to have a solid grasp of the situation regarding local production. The most fundamental objective in building a model for the Japanese and American systems consisted of establishing its evaluation criteria. This required construction of a theoretical image of the Japanese management and production system in accordance with its underlying logic that Japanese companies actually pursue and then abstract its essential elements. In accordance with that theoretical image, the Japanese way of approaching each element became one set of references, and the completely opposite American approach to the identical aspects of the system became a counterpoising set of references. This set of references constituted a coordinate axis with which to evaluate the conditions of each local plant. Of course, this ideal "model" does not actually exist at any plant, American or Japanese, in the United States or in Japan.

The American "model" presented in this book is based on one of postwar, dominant trends. For this reason, the model may be too close to a traditional plant pattern and may thus fail to adequately reflect more recent changes. In recent years there have been various changes in the traditional pattern of management and production systems and in postwar labor relations. Moreover, the existence of companies whose approach to management has always differed from the traditional pattern has also come to light. These matters deserve careful attention because they alter the conditions of the managerial environment and affect the conditions that restrict application of the Japanese system at the local plants, as well as give rise to differences between industries. However, the extent to which these changes to or deviations from the traditional pattern have taken root, or whether they actually constitute a dominant trend, are subjects that now require careful study. In fact it should be possible to gain a clear understanding of those changes and deviations by establishing the traditional pattern as a set of comparative standards.

4. An influential view expressed by Kazuo Koike is that the principal characteristic of the Japanese production system can be found in the "skill" formation that takes place at the shop-floor level. He stresses the significance of the "practical methods of OJT," interpreting "the nucleus of modern technical skills" as "the ability to perform the multiple duties belonging to various workstations" as well as "the mental dexterity (that consists of) the ability to deal with . . . unusual situations . . . and change" (Koike, 1987, pp. 7–17). We have learned much from Koike's interpretation of "modern technical skills" and the significance that he attaches to OJT. We believe that training in multiple skills, which enables workers to perform numerous job tasks, and the Japanese principle of workplace organization that is rather free of the sense of fixed job assignments, have a systematic and mutually supportive relationship. The Japanese-style management and production system is built out of the close relationship and intricate interplay between these factors and other elements, such as the function of supervisors, small group activities, seniority wages, and long-term employment. The "mental dexterity" and the accumulation of "multiple technical skills" by workers whose high productivity and high quality production characterize the Japanese workplace are also the product of this "system." We therefore approached this research from these aspects of the "system." Our method involved resolving the "system" into its constituent elements, exposing the "application-adaptation" relationship of the different aspects of these elements, and thus investigate the international transferability of the Japanese-style management and production system.

5. Hirohide Tanaka states that Japanese labor management is chiefly characterized by the fact that "there are generally few elements to a *job*" (Tanaka, 1988, pp. 97–99). He states that "Fundamentally, (Japanese labor management) is the same as that in the United States. They were both formed and have developed under mass production technology systems" (p. 44) and "they are both job-based systems, that can be easily compared in on the basis of a single dimension, namely how they insert the "human" element". In this respect we basically agree with Tanaka.

6. In regard to "corporate-specific skills" of the internal labor market theory, Koike tries to offer an explanation in terms that emphasize the variations of "career path" settings and the internal promotion system that provides corporate specificity. However, since "corporate specificity" of skills in Japan is considered more closely related to job improvements and know-how accumulated on the shop floor, we have sought to distinguish this notion through our use of the term "internal plant skills." Although from this perspective it is difficult to quantify the degree of corporate specificity related to particular "skills," it does seem that examples abound where this is much greater than Koike allows. Although Koike's explanation may be suitable for describing "corporate specificity" in the American system, it is probably less suitable for describing a Japanese enterprise. See Koike and Inoki, eds. (1987, p. 15). For the significance of job improvement activities, see Imai (1988).

7. Important research has been published on the characteristics of the Japanese production system since the main parts of the present publication were first completed. Concerning the auto industry, Womack et al. (1990) characterized the Japanese system as the "lean production" method meticulously contrasting it with the mass production systems in Europe and the United States. This research supplements our own studies on the auto industry in that it takes performance evaluations into account, and it addresses areas that we did not cover, such as the Japanese product development system and customer relations. See also Chapter 5, note 1.

Suzuki Ryoji (1990) also shares our focus on the Japanese system when he says "the Japanese system is a combination of JIT production and Japanese work organization" (p. 92). He emphasizes the idea that the Japanese production system is the source of the international competitiveness of Japanese processing and assembly industries. He also explicitly asserts that Japanese work organization is a necessary condition for the existence of JIT.

However, since he concentrates on the production system, he fails to completely clarify the relationship between the production system and other aspects of the management system, or its socioeconomic basis. He points to three characteristics in his comparison between Japanese and American systems, (1) finely demarcated job classifications and the accompanying rigid job assignment, (2) specialization (inflexibility), and (3) individual responsibility (absence of the group) (ibid., pp. 46–49). Although these characteristics might be considered to fundamentally correspond to the mass production system, in addition to such "technical" arguments, they can also be considered to correspond to the "job control unionism" type of labor relations. Another important and related point concerns the historical-social conditions pertaining to external social customs and systems.

The characteristic of the workplace described as "individual responsibility (absence of the group)" must also be thought of as a synthesis of the social system and the managerial environment. Research in this area has been published by Gordon, et al. (1982). Suzuki also points towards the "counter regulations" (ibid. p. 48) in reference to mass production based upon large lots and continuous production.

The same problems turn up in regard to the Japanese "production system." We consider all systems, customs, and types of behavior, inside and outside the company, to be very important for supporting the Japanese production system. This raises important issues such as the cultural environment as well as historical and social contexts. In that sense it is quite likely that the production system in concrete terms is not a mere consequence of a purely technical logic of production. For this reason, the "system's" international compatibility is likely to become an important issue, particularly in relation to conditions that are fundamental to its existence.

Chapter 5

1. Correlation coefficients were also calculated for all items by industry. However, due to the small sample for each industry it was necessary to combine the auto assembly and parts, and the consumer electronics and semiconductor industries into "auto industry" and "electronics industry," respectively.

2. Correlation with size and character of the parent companies are also intriguing; however, because of the difficulty in knowing how to treat joint ventures, particularly between Japanese enterprises, it was decided not to include these elements. Whether the investment was a joint venture or not is also an important consideration, but since joint ventures were restricted to the auto industries, and did not appear among either the consumer electronics or semiconductor industries, it was decided not to include this element, either.

Chapter 6

1. Womack and his associates (Womack et al., 1990) called the Japanese production system a "lean production system", and considered it to be a new production system that is changing the automobile industry by replacing the old mass production system. Upon studying automobile factories throughout the world, they point out that the efficiency and quality of the "lean production system" are superior to the mass production system. This is a valuable study, for it assesses the worldwide significance of the Japanese method with the focus on production control. (For some criticism regarding Womack's book, see Note 18 in ch. 1.)

2. This according to the yearly editions of *Ward's Automotive Yearbook* and to *Ward's Automotive Reports,* Vol. 66, No. 1, January 7, 1991. The above-mentioned market share require the following qualifications: First, some station wagons, minivans and multipurpose models are not included in the passenger car category. Second, only those cars that display the original brand are counted, both locally manufactured cars and imports, and those supplied to the Big Three, either from Japan or from U.S. transplants, are not counted as Japanese cars. If, for example, we add Japanese imports to the Big Three to the 1990 numbers, the total market share for Japanese cars would be 29.9 percent.

Chapter 7

1. AD Plant has recently concluded its second term labor contract with the UAW local. Those basic provisions regarding the team system that would enable the Japanese-style job organization, and forfeiture by the union of the right to strike for matters of safety and production standard remain unchanged. This is according to a telephone interview carried out from the company's head office in Japan, and the *Nihon Keizai Shinbun* (newspaper) March 16, 1991.

2. However, this only refers to individual plants. When the focus includes activities carried out by the American head offices of these transplants, that oversee both sales and production, the con-

sumer electronics industry has more companies that are active in these areas than the other industries have. Henceforth, persistent programs that closely adhere to individual communities will probably increase in importance.

3. Besides information obtained from the transplants at the time of our survey, calculations are based on the following sources: Electronic Industry Association; *Electronic Market Data Book* 1989; *Television Digest,* Aug. 6, 1990; US Dept. of Commerce; Bureau of the Census; *US Imports for Consumption and General Imports,* 1989.

4. The figures concerning semiconductor market share in America are based on data we received through our survey of the different companies, as well as from *Data Quest.*

Chapter 8

1. *Data Quest,* January 1987, January 1990.
2. *Nihon Keizai Shinbun* (newspaper), August 25, 1990.
3. USDC, *Survey of Current Business,* August, 1990, p. 43.
4. *Survey of Current Business,* July and August, 1990.
5. Hashimoto, 1991.
6. Asanuma, 1984a.
7. Baba, 1991.
8. Kumagai, 1994.

Epilogue

The first rendition of this paper was stimulated by Professor Tetsuo Abo's Toyota Foundation Research Project; he wanted data to put today's Japanese investment in the United States in a historical context. I have learned my Japanese business history from Professors Keiichiro Nakagawa, Tsunehiko Yui, Tetsuo Abo, Hiroaki Yamazaki, and Nobuo Kawabe, and am in their debt. My special thanks go to Steven Tolliday and the two anonymous reviewers for their valuable suggestions.

1. *Miami Herald,* Jan. 6, 1990.
2. Wilkins, 1990, pp. 43–44.
3. On the pre-1914 history, I have relied on data developed for Wilkins, 1986, pp. 199–231. See especially, pp. 218–21. Mitsui's first New York office was a short-lived venture, closed at the start of the 1880s, and reopened in the mid-1890s.
4. On Kikkoman, Kinugasa, 1984, p. 57; on the "big three," Wray, 1989. On the insurance company, see Wilkins, 1986, p. 221.
5. Wilkins, 1986, pp. 209, 222.
6. Wilkins, 1989.
7. Sugiyama, 1988, p. 80; on the growing U.S. importance to Japanese silk exports; by 1896/1900, 57.8 percent of Japan's raw silk exports went to the United States.
8. Wilkins, 1986, p. 200.
9. This was the surprising finding of Wilkins, 1982, pp. 504–507.
10. Ibid., p. 506.
11. Percentages based on U.S. Department of Commerce, Bureau of Foreign and Domestic Commerce, *Foreign Long-term Investments in the United States 1937–39* (Washington, 1940), 34.
12. Based on the Annual Reports of the Superintendent of Banks, New York. U.S. law made no provision for foreign bank branches or agencies; thus state law prevailed. New York State law did not allow foreign bank "branches," only "agencies" that could make loans but could not by law take deposits.
13. Alien Property Custodian, *Annual Report for Year Ending June 30, 1944,* 58n.
14. As noted in the text above, before World War I the Yokohama Specie Bank had branches in San Francisco, Los Angeles, and Honolulu. The date of establishment of the Seattle branch comes from the records of Yokohama Specie Bank, RG 131, National Archives, Suitland, Md, I am indebted to Professor Y. Homma for this information. See *Polk's Bankers Encyclopedia 1926.*

15. The Sumitomo Bank of Seattle had three Americans among its five directors, but was in the eyes of one Japanese observer "more correctly called a branch of the Sumitomo Bank of Osaka than a joint enterprise." Odate, 1922, pp. 81, 84.

16. In 1924 the Sumitomo Bank, headquartered in Osaka, acquired the assets of the insolvent Nippon Savings Bank, Sacramento, and in 1925 established the Sumitomo Bank of California, Sacramento. Earlier (August 1916), the Sumitomo Bank had opened a branch bank in San Francisco; in 1924 it opened in Los Angeles. Cross, 1927, IV, pp. 274–75, 696, 699, and II, pp. 764, 787–88. As noted in the text above, it started in Seattle in 1919. Curiously, Odate (whose book was published in 1922) did not seem to be aware of Sumitomo's branch bank in San Francisco (as reported by Cross). Data in the Superintendent of Banks, California, *Annual Reports,* confirm the accuracy of the information furnished by Cross.

17. An example of the type of business it did was its role in the $25 million Japanese Currency Stabilization credit of November 21, 1929. On November 19, 1929, J.P. Morgan & Co., Kuhn, Loeb & Co., the National City Bank, and the First National Bank, New York, at the request of the Japanese government and the Bank of Japan, agreed to grant the Yokohama Specie Bank Ltd. a revolving credit for $25 million; the negotiations were through Yokohama Specie Bank in New York; the collateral delivered by the Yokohama Specie Bank to J.P. Morgan & Co. consisted of Japanese government bonds equal in value to at least 120 percent of the advance. See U.S. Senate, Committee on Banking and Currency, *Stock Exchange Practices, Hearings,* 73rd Cong., 1st sess. (1933), pt. 1, 251–52.

18. Wilkins, 1982, p. 508.

19. For suggestions along this line, see Yamazaki, 1992. This paper has material on the accounts of the New York agency of the Yokohama Specie Bank in the 1920s and 1929–1931.

20. Ibid.

21. Cross, 1927, III, p. 266, says 1923; Paul J. Hauser, Daiwa Securities America Inc., to Mira Wilkins, Feb. 22, 1989, gives a 1924 date. In 1927, Kuhn, Loeb & Co. made a $1 million broker's loan to Fujimoto Securities Corporation (which was repaid in three months); the collateral consisted mainly of Japanese imperial government bonds, City of Tokyo bonds, and also a diversified set of bonds, including Buenos Aires, Brazilian, and Italian bonds. *Stock Exchange Practices, Hearings,* pt. 3, 1404–5.

22. Nomura Securities Company in New York furnished me (June 29, 1988) with data on the company's history, indicating that in March, 1927, Nomura Securities opened an office in New York City. (The material claims that Nomura was the first Japanese securities company in the United States; it was not; Fujimoto Securities was the first).

23. Data from Nomura Securities Company, June 29, 1988, and from Daiwa Securities, Feb. 22, 1989.

24. The largest was the Tokyo Marine and Fire Insurance Co. (the successor to Tokio Marine Insurance Co.); the two others were the Sumitomo Marine and Fire Insurance Co. (licensed in New York State in 1921) and the Meiji Fire Insurance Co. (licensed to do business in New York and Illinois in 1931). *New York Times,* December 11, 1941.

25. Wilkins, 1982, p. 508.

26. Ibid., p. 509; Yamazaki, 1987, pp. 34, 56; Kawabe, 1987, p. 81; Kawabe, 1980, p. 17. Kawabe is excellent on the activities of the Mitsubishi Shoji in the United States before World War II. On the Seattle branch, see ibid., pp. 34, 36, 49. The reader is also directed to Kawabe, 1989, pp. 177–189.

27. Yamazaki, 1987, pp. 24, 28, 34, and Kawabe, 1987, p. 81.

28. Lockwood, 1954, pp. 398 (1925 peak). Kawabe, 1980, p. 20, has figures that indicate that the dollar value of Japanese silk exports *to the United States* peaked in 1929 and then fell off sharply. In the years 1924–1929, Japanese silk exports to the United States represented between 82 and 84 percent of all Japanese exports to this country. Between 1930 and 1932, they hovered around 79 percent of exports, although the dollar amounts had gone down dramatically.

29. Lockwood, 1954, p. 398, 401; Kawabe, 1987, p. 87; and Kawabe, 1980, p. 20.

30. Lockwood, 1954, p. 401.

31. Kawabe, 1987, p. 88.

32. Kawabe, 1980, p. 26.

33. Alien Property Custodian, *Annual Report for . . . 1944,* 81–82.

34. For details on the role of Japanese trading firms in Japanese imports and exports in the period 1921–1925, see Yamazaki, 1987, pp. 24–31.

35. Yoshihara, 1987, pp. 340–341.

36. On technology transfer, see Wilkins, 1982, p. 509; Kawabe, 1987, pp. 80, 82; and Kawabe, 1980, pp. 18, 35, and passim. Major joint ventures *in Japan* between American and Japanese companies took place in the interwar years. No one has done research on the extent to which preliminary negotiations for such joint ventures were undertaken through American offices of the *Japanese* trading companies and where exactly the Japanese direct investments *in the United States* fit into these Japanese-American relationships in Japan. Mason, 1992, is suggestive in this regard, but the subject requires more systematic study. There is no question, however, that the trading companies' presence in the United States served as an information channel and a communicator of technologies from the United States to Japan; more research is necessary on the specific details of the technological transfer and the relative importance in this regard in different industries of the Japanese trading company versus the American direct investor in Japan. The use of service companies to ferret out information and to transmit technology was not distinctive to Japanese business. My current research indicates that Chemnyco, Inc., in New York, in the interwar period served that function—for I.G. Farben.

37. Alien Property Custodian, *Annual Report for . . . 1944,* 83–84.

38. Kawabe, 1987, p. 82.

39. Wilkins, 1982, p. 509; Lockwood, 1954, p. 349.

40. See note 36 above. That note notwithstanding, this generalization is based principally on my rethinking about my own earlier research on American business abroad.

41. See Herzberg, 1988, pp. 70–81, on cotton textile imports; the quotation is on p. 79. This book is very good on U.S.-Japanese economic relations in the 1930s.

42. Wilkins, 1982, p. 510. The freezing of Japanese assets in the United States was one of a number of steps that the United States took in view of the worsening economic and political relations in the late 1930s. For a sequence of U.S. economic actions affecting Japan, 1938–1941, see Wilkins, 1973, p. 373.

43. Alien Property Custodian, *Annual Report for . . . 1944,* 58.

44. Wilkins, 1982, pp. 512–14. Note that the figures given on Tables E–1 and E–2 above are book value ones; measures of foreign companies' "assets" in the United States cannot be reconciled with these numbers.

45. Mitsui & Co., 1977, pp. 139, and 146–52 (for the process of dissolution).

46. For a number of years, foreigners were told that the relationships between Japanese companies were "very different" from those before the war; by the 1980s there was no disguising the cooperation between group members. The Mitsui & Co. *Annual Report 1983,* 75, published in English, listed the "Major Group Companies, Getsuyo-Kai (Monday Conference) Members." See also Wassmann and Yamamura, 1989.

47. Toyota Motor Corporation, 1988, p. 97. Under the dissolution rules, Toyota, as a "restricted concern," could not open a new branch or new division; Toyota Motor Company was, moreover, by 1949–1950 at the brink of bankruptcy. Toyota sources suggest that the separation of Toyota Motor Sales from Toyota Motor Company was at the insistence of the banks. Toyoda, 1987, pp. 99–101, 158–59. In any case, the sales company for Toyota, Toyota Motor Sales Company (established in 1950) was separately incorporated, separately financed, and separately managed. It was run by the legendary sales manager, Shotaro Kamiya. In 1982, only after Kamiya's death in 1980, were the manufacturing and sales companies merged. Ibid., pp. 157–61.

48. Wilkins, 1982, p. 516.

49. Ibid.

50. Mitsui & Co, 1977, p. 144. Even earlier, some had sent representatives abroad to make "market surveys." Sen Yurugi went to the United States in July, 1949 on behalf of Daiichi Bussan (one of the companies to emerge out of the dissolved Mitsui & Co.); ibid., p. 166–67.

51. On the survey, see Mitsui & Co., 1977, p. 144. A tabulation of foreign direct investment in the United States by the U.S. Department of Commerce found Japanese interests in this country in 1950 to be negligible. Wilkins, 1982, p. 516.

52. Wilkins, 1982, p. 516.

53. Mitsui & Co., 1977, p. 168.

54. Ibid., p. 199.

55. Yamamura, 1989, p. 141.

56. Channon, 1988, p. 30.

57. Superintendent of Banks, California, *Annual Report for 1953,* 130, and Lees, 1976, p. 31.

58. Superintendent of Banks, California, *Annual Report for 1953,* 139, and Lees, 1976, p. 31.

59. Superintendent of Banks, California, *Annual Report for 1953,* 8.

60. Ibid., 138.

61. *Euromoney,* April 1988, 16, and booklet, Nomura, "The Evolution of the Tokyo Capital Market and Nomura Securities," n.d. (1988).

62. Lees, 1976, p. 26. According to Lees, by 1974 and possibly at origin, the Bank of Tokyo Trust Company was owned by the Bank of Tokyo and the Industrial Bank of Japan. The background material is based on data I have collected from the Superintendent of Banking, Albany, New York.

63. Lees, 1976, pp. 12–13.

64. Superintendent of Banks, California, *Annual Report for 1959,* 115, 127, 126. The assets are as of June 30, 1959.

65. Ozawa, 1979, p. 12, and Crowc, 1978, pp. 242–243.

66. Morita, 1986, p. 86; see also, Ozawa, 1979, p. 12.

67. Kinugasa, 1984, pp. 30–32.

68. It had a capital of $1 million and was half-owned by Toyota Motor Company and half by the Japanese sales company, Toyota Motor Sales Company (see note 47, above).

69. The early story of Toyota in America is told in Kamiya, 1976, pp. 74–83; Toyoda, 1987, pp. 120–121; and Toyota Motor Corporation, 1988, pp. 165–168.

70. Table E–3 stops in 1973. There was a major benchmark survey made for the year 1974, with the result of sizable reduction in U.S. Department of Commerce Japanese direct investment figures for 1974. Table E–4 starts with the revised figures for 1974.

71. The explanation is given in the *Survey of Current Business,* February 1973, 31. Note that the "minus" numbers are lower in 1972 than 1971 as the loans from affiliates to parents were reduced.

72. U.S. Department of Commerce, *Foreign Business Investments in the United States* [Washington (1962)], 7. Reprinted in Mira Wilkins, ed., *Foreign Investments in the United States* (New York: Arno Press, 1977).

73. U.S. Department of Commerce, *Foreign Direct Investment in the United States,* 9 vols. (Washington, 1976), I, 35–37 (henceforth cited as *Benchmark Survey, 1974*).

74. Morita, 1986, pp. 93–96, on the financing of the new American sales subsidiary. Nomura Securities served as comanager with Smith Barney when, in 1961, SONY issued Japan's first ADRs (American Depository Receipts) on the New York market. See Nomura, "The Evolution of the Tokyo Capital Market," booklet, n.d.

75. Abo, 1984, p. 26, and Wilkins, 1979, p. 16.

76. Toyota Motor Corporation, 1988, pp. 167, 209–213; Wilkins, 1979, p. 113.

77. Tsurumi, 1976, p. 104.

78. Morita, 1986, pp. 128–29.

79. Tsurumi, 1976, p. 108.

80. Ibid., p. 106 (Yoshida K.K. in zippers), p. 120 (the Tsuzuki Cotton Spinning Company in 1965 with a spinning mill).

81. Yoshino, 1976, p. 80.

82. Tsurumi, 1976, p. 108.

83. Yoshino, 1976, p. 80.

84. Lees, 1976, pp. 27, 26, 49–50, 30.

85. Ozawa, 1979, p. 112. These figures make much more sense than the ones on Table E–3 (see text above for the problems with the numbers on Table E–3).

86. *Survey of Current Business,* August 1990.

87. Morita, 1986, pp. 175–76, for a 1968 antidumping case against SONY.

88. Ibid., p. 176.

89. International Monetary Fund, *International Financial Statistics, Supplement on Exchange Rates* (Washington, 1985), 67.

90. Morita, 1986, p. 129.

91. Ibid., and Morita and Ishihara, 1989, p. 46.

92. Yoshino, 1976, p. 81; see Tsurumi, 1976, pp. 108–111, on NMB, another of the early ball bearing companies in the United States. Concerns over the Japanese role in the U.S. ball bearings industry continued in the 1980s. See Gordon and Lees, 1986, pp. 211–212; U.S. Senate, Committee on Armed Services, Subcommittee on Preparedness, *Sale of New Hampshire Ball Bearings, Inc. to the Japan-based Minebea Company, Hearings,* 98th Cong., 2d sess. (1984); and Glickman and Woodward, 1989, p. 267.

93. Abo, 1984, p. 9.

94. Encarnation, 1986, pp. 129–130.

95. *Wall Street Journal,* Nov. 14, 1988, ran a long list of "selected Japanese direct investments in the U.S. electronics industry," 1985–1987. The investments were typically under $50 million and often minority interests in existing companies. Many were under $10 million.

96. Tolchin, 1988, p. 12.

97. Ibid., pp. 12, 269. The French firm was Schlumberger, Ltd.

98. Glickman and Woodward, 1989, p. 268.

99. *Wall Street Journal,* Nov. 10, 1989. A half-billion dollar investment in 1989 was not "large," but what is important here is that in ceramic semiconductor parts the Japanese were making vital innovations and had real advantages.

100. Tolchin, 1988, pp. 9, 109.

101. *Wall Street Journal,* Jan. 21, 1988, and Jan. 2, 1990. The CBS Records Group that SONY acquired had plants in fourteen countries, and subsidiaries, joint ventures, and licensees in more than fifty nations. Ibid., Dec. 24, 1987. The acquisition of CBS Records was arranged in 1987 and finalized very early in 1988. Ibid., Nov. 27, 1990, on the Matsushita acquisition.

102. The investments were in keeping with those of investors from other foreign countries whose currency was strong in relation to the dollar. Before 1984, there had been no foreign take overs of over $1 billion. In 1985 there were two; in 1986, five; in 1987, six; and in 1988, twelve. *Survey of Current Business,* May 1989, 23.

103. SONY, of course, did, but so did others. For example, Mitsubishi Electric ran a full-page advertisement in the *Wall Street Journal,* April 19, 1988, explaining that it assembled televisions in Santa Ana, Calif.; had a semiconductor assembly and testing plant in Durham, N.C.; a television and cellular mobile phone assembly plant in Braselton, Ga.; as well as an automobile parts plant in Cincinnati, Ohio. It employed almost 3,000 Americans.

104. In 1988, a U.S. affiliate of a Japanese metal, petroleum refining, and petrochemical company acquired an Illinois-based manufacturer of computers and electrical products, which had large defense contracts. The acquisition was "to obtain access to the U.S. company's research and development expertise in electronic parts manufacturing—particularly in the manufacture of copper foil, a material used in printed circuit boards." The U.S. federal government was concerned and only approved the acquisition when the Japanese agreed to put the U.S. company's defense operations into a trust that would be run by the existing U.S. management. *Survey of Current Business,* May 1989, 23–25.

105. I do not have the 1970s figures, but in 1985, four Japanese motor cycle makers—Honda, Kawasaki, Yamaha, and Suzuki—accounted for approximately 94 percent of the American market. *Wall Street Journal,* Sept. 16, 1986.

106. Yoshino, 1976, p. 82.

107. Wilkins, 1979, p. 114.

108. Based on data collected by a group headed by Professor Tetsuo Abo of the University of Tokyo, plus U.S. press reports.

109. The learning process differed by company. Initially, the managements of U.S. manufacturing and of U.S. marketing were separate, with each reporting back to decision-makers in Japan. In the case of Toyota, it was not until 1982 that its manufacturing and sales companies were merged *in Japan* (see note 47, above). At the start of the 1990s, Toyota in the United States still had separate

companies to handle manufacturing and sales, albeit by the end of the 1980s there was increasing communication *in the United States* between the managements of the manufacturing and sales companies.

110. Tolchin, 1988, pp. 81–83; *Wall Street Journal,* Feb. 18, 1988, and March 21, 1988. On its relative size, see *Survey of Current Business,* May 1989, 23.

111. See Crowe, 1978, p. 204 and Heller, 1973 and 1974.

112. *Benchmark Survey, 1974,* I, 186.

113. Makin, 1989, p. 81.

114. I believe that even with strict capital export restraints, the investments in U.S. manufacturing would have been authorized (since they were a response to potential protectionism); without capital liberalization, the real estate investments probably would not have been allowed.

115. Franz and Collins, 1989, p. 21.

116. *New York Times,* Nov. 12, 1989.

117. Mitsui & Co., Ltd., *Annual Report 1983.*

118. *Wall Street Journal,* Feb. 26, 1990.

119. Mitsui & Co., Ltd., *Annual Report 1983.*

120. *Wall Street Journal,* Nov. 2, 1989.

121. Ibid. And, in how many more companies did Mitsui & Co. have less than a 35 percent interest?

122. The Bank of California in 1905 had purchased the London and San Francisco Bank, Ltd., one of the early British banks in California. See Wilkins, 1989, pp. 459–61.

123. Lees, 1976, p. 31; Channon, 1988, pp. 30–32; 1989 figures in *Wall Street Journal,* Oct. 12, 1989; *New York Times,* Oct. 1, 1989; *Wall Street Journal,* Feb. 17, 1989 (on Bank of Tokyo's California acquisitions).

124. *New York Times,* Oct. 1, 1989.

125. *Wall Street Journal,* Oct. 12, 1989.

126. Ibid.

127. Ibid.; the *New York Times,* Oct. 1, 1989, gave the price as $1.4 billion.

128. *New York Times,* Oct. 1, 1989.

129. Ibid. This includes all branches, agencies, and subsidiary banks. It does not include the Dai-Ichi Kangyo 1989 acquisition of the CIT Group.

130. Ibid.

131. For an interesting article on Nomura, see *Wall Street Journal,* April 1, 1987. See also *Euromoney,* April, 1988, 16. Nomura and Daiwa became primary dealers in December, 1986, Nikko in 1987, and Yamaichi in 1988. Their status was reconfirmed by the Federal Reserve in August, 1989. See *Wall Street Journal,* Aug. 22, 1989.

132. See *Wall Street Journal,* April 1, 1987, and Nov. 10, 1989; and Glickman and Woodward, 1989, p. 60. Along the same lines, Yamaichi Securities acquired an interest in the Lodestar Group and Nikko one in the Blackstone Group. Lodestar and Blackstone were described as take over and merger "boutiques." *New York Times,* June 11, 1989.

133. See Wilkins, 1989.

134. Ibid.

135. See ibid. on the early dominant role of the British. In the 1860s and 1870s, British-owned banks were major participants in California banking, so there is precedent there. Ibid., pp. 135, 459–63.

136. Channon, 1988, p. 33.

137. This may have been particularly true in 1988 and 1989 in real estate. I calculated the rate of return for Japanese investment in that sector for 1988 at 1.7 percent, and for 1989 at 2.3 percent. Based on data in *Survey of Current Business,* August, 1989, 52, 57, and ibid., August, 1990, 46, 51. In 1987, Japanese companies had losses on their real estate investments. Ibid., August, 1989, 57.

138. All multinational enterprises have a certain amount of flexibility as to where they take profits; if U.S. operations have low profits or losses, it is possible that the profits may be recorded elsewhere, in complementary activities. The U.S. Internal Revenue Service has become suspicious. A U.S. law passed on December 19, 1989, gave U.S. tax authorities a broad mandate to assess taxes on foreign-owned companies that do not comply promptly with all the I.R.S.'s requests for records.

Japanese companies seemed especially vulnerable. See *New York Times,* Feb. 18, 1990. In 1990 there were Congressional hearings, looking into alleged Japanese tax evasion. One possible reason for the low profits that is *not* tax-related might be that the Japanese have fears of being targets in U.S. anti-dumping litigation. Pricing inputs from Japan at a high level would reduce the profits of the U.S. affiliate. High profits *in Japan* of some companies suffering losses in the United States added to suspicions that their U.S. accounts did not reflect realities.

139. For the losses of *all* foreign investors in the United States involved in manufacturing "motor vehicles and equipment," 1985–1989, see *Survey of Current Business,* August 1990, 55. On real estate, see note 137, above.

140. *Wall Street Journal,* Nov. 2, 1989.

141. *New York Times,* Oct. 1, 1989.

142. *Wall Street Journal,* Oct. 24, 1989; *Euromoney,* April, 1988, 16, reported that during Nomura Securities' first 27 postwar years in America, it made little or no money; it nonetheless persisted. The *Wall Street Journal,* June 5, 1989, obtained before-tax results for the Japanese "Big Four" securities firms in the United States for year-end 1988; all experienced large losses (that greatly offset the prior year's modest profits); in the 6 months ending March 31, 1989, Nomura and Yamaichi posted losses once more, while Daiwa and Nikko had minimal profits. The *New York Times,* June 11, 1989, ran an article entitled "Japan's Washout on Wall Street," calling the efforts of these Japanese securities firms "the biggest flop by a major Japanese industry trying to crack the American market."

143. *Survey of Current Business,* August, 1989.

144. Graham and Krugman, 1989, pp. 40–41.

145. *Wall Street Journal,* Aug. 29, 1990.

146. Graham and Krugman, 1989, p. 22.

147. I am sure that it would be inappropriate to compare banking asset shares with asset shares of companies devoted to automobile production (these are entirely different measures).

148. *Wall Street Journal,* Feb. 2, 1990.

149. *Miami Herald,* Nov. 3, 1989.

150. *Wall Street Journal,* Nov. 27, 1990.

151. See report on it, in *Miami Herald,* Nov. 3, 1989.

152. See Wilkins, 1989, especially Chapter 16. Some of the rhetoric and emotional responses are similar: In times past Americans criticized British investment, claiming that we were losing to British investors what we had won in 1776; now the phrase is that we are losing to Japanese business what the victory brought in 1945.

153. See Wilkins, 1974, pp. 345–46. In the 1960s American business was welcomed in Europe for the technology and management methods it brought, but resented for its very presence.

154. For some of the "clusters" of British foreign direct investment worldwide, see Wilkins, 1988, pp. 265–70.

155. U.S. Department of Commerce, *Foreign Long-Term Investments in the United States 1937–39,* (Washington, D.C., 1940), 34.

156. *Survey of Current Business,* August, 1990, 46.

157. Wilkins, 1974, pp. 414–22.

Bibliography

Abegglen, James C. *The Japanese Factory.* Cambridge, Mass.: MIT Press, 1957.

Abegglen, James C., and George Stalk, Jr. *Kaisha: The Japanese Corporation.* New York: Basic Books, 1985.

Abernathy, William J. *The Productivity Dilemma: Road to Innovation in the Automobile Industry.* Baltimore: Johns Hopkins University Press, 1978.

Abernathy, William J., Kim B. Clark, and Alan M. Kantrow. *Industrial Renaissance: Producing a Competitive Future for America.* New York: Basic Books, 1983.

Abo, Tetsuo. "American Automobile Enterprises Abroad during the Interwar Period: Case Studies on Ford and General Motors with Emphasis on the Process of their Multinational Adaptation to Local Climates". *Annals of Institute of Social Science* (Tokyo: University of Tokyo, 1981), 22:183–224.

———. "U.S. Subsidiaries of Japanese Electronics Companies Enter a New Phase of Activities". *Annals.* op. cit., 1984. 26:1–32. and Occasional Papers. 1985, 47. *Social and Economic Research on Modern Japan.* Berlin:Verlag Ute Schiller.

———. "The International Business Activities of General Electric Company, 1920–1940". *Annals.* op. cit., 1986, 27:54–79.

———. "A Report of On-the-Spot Observation of Sony's Four Major Color TV Plants in the US, UK, West Germany and Japan". *Annals.* op. cit., 1987, 29:1–39. And *Industrial Cooperation Between Europe and Japan,* ed. Joop A. Stam. Dept. of Modern Japanese Studies. Rotterdam: Erasmus University, 1989.

———. "The Application of Japanese-Style Management Concepts in Japanese Automobile Plants in the United States". in *Die Zukunft der Arbeit in der Automobilindustrie,* ed. Ben Dankbaar, Ulrich Jürgens, and Thomas Malsch. Berlin: Wissenshaftzentrum, Ed. Sigma, 1988.

———. "The Emergence of Japanese Multinational Enterprise and the Theory of Foreign Direct Investment". In *Japanese and European Management,* ed. Shibagaki, Kazuo, Malcolm Trevor, and Tetsuo Abo. Tokyo: University of Tokyo Press, 1989.

———. "ITT's International Business Activities, 1920–1940". In *The Growth of Multinationals, The International Library of Critical Writing in Business History I,* ed. Wilkins, Mira. Aldershot: Edward Elgar, 1991. And *Annals* op. cit., 1983, 24:104–123.

———. "Japanese Motor Vehicle Technologies Abroad in the 1980s". In *The Transfer of International Technology,* ed. Jeremy, David J. Aldershot: Edward Elgar, 1992.

———. "Overseas Production Activities of Nissan Motor Co,: The Five Large Plants Abroad". In *Managerial Efficiency in Competition and Cooperation: Japanese, West- and East-European Strategies and Perspectives,* ed. Sung-Jo Park. Frankfurt and New York: Campus Verlag and West View, 1992.

Altscheler, Alan, et al. *The Future of the Automobile.* Cambridge, MIT Press, 1984.

Aoki, Masahiko. *Information, Incentives, and Bargaining in the Japanese Economy.* Cambridge: Cambridge University Press, 1988.

———. *Nihon-kigyo no Soshiki to Jyoho* (Organization and Information of the Japanese Enterprise). Tokyo: Toyo keizai Shimposha, 1989.

Asanuma, Banri. "Nihon ni okeru Shohin Torihiki no Kozo" (Contractual Framework for Parts Supply in the Japanese Automotive Industry). *Keizai-Ronso.* Kyoto University Economic Society, 1984a, Vol. 133, 3:137–58.

———. "Jidosha Sangyo ni okeru Buhin Torihiki no Kozo: Cyosei to Kakushinteki Tekio no Mekanizumu" ("The Organization of Parts Purchases in the Japanese Automotive Industry"). *Kikan Gendai Keizai,* 1984b, 58:38–48.

———. "Nihon ni okeru Meka to Sapuraiya no Kankei" ("Manufacturer-Supplier Relationships in Japan and the Concept of Relation-Specific Skill"). *Keizai-Ronso.* Kyoto University Economic Society, 1990, Vol. 145, 1♦2:1–45.

Baba, Hiroji. "Gendai Sekai to Nihon Kaisha-shugi" ("Modern World and Japanese KAISHA-ISM"). in *Gendai Nihon shakai I* (Contemporary Japanese Society I), ed. Institute of Social Science. Tokyo: University of Tokyo Press, 1991.

Banno, Junji. "Sen Zen Nihon ni okeru Shakai Minshu-shugi,' 'Minshu Shakai-shugi,' 'Kigyo Minshu-shugi'." (" 'Social Democracy', Democratic Socialism', and 'Corporate Democracy' in prewar Japan") in *Gendai Nihon Shakai.* (Contemporary Japanese Society) Vol. 4, Institute of Social Science, University of Tokyo, University of Tokyo Press: Tokyo, 1991.

Brown, Clair, and Michael Reich. "When does Union-Management Cooperation Work?; A Look at NUMMI and GM-Van Nuys". Prepared for the Conference, "Can California Be Competitive and Caring?" UCLA. May 6, 1988.

Buckley, Peter J. *The Theory of the Multinational Enterprise.* Uppsala: ACTA Universitatis Upsaiesis, Studia Oeconomiae Negotiorum 26, 1987.

Buckley, Peter J., and Mark Casson. *The Economic Theory of the Multinational Enterprise.* New York: Macmillan, 1985.

Chang, C.S. *The Japanese Auto Industry and the U.S. Market.* New York: Praeger, 1981.

Channon, Derek F. *Global Banking Strategy.* New York: Wiley, 1988.

Cohen, Stephen S., and John Zysman. *Manufacturing Matters.* New York: Basic Books, 1987.

Clark, Kim B., and Takahiro Fujimoto. *Product Development Performance.* Boston: Harvard Business School Press, 1991.

Cole, Robert E., ed. *The Japanese Automobile Industry.* Michigan Papers in Japanese Studies, 1981, 3.

Cole, Robert, and D. R. Deskins, Jr. "Racial Factors in Site Location and Employment Patterns of Japanese Auto Firms in America". *California Management Review,* 1988, Fall:9–22.

Cross, Ira B. *Financing an Empire: History of Banking in California,* 4 vols. Chicago: S.J. Clarke, 1927.

Crowe, Kenneth C. *America for Sale.* Garden City, N.Y.: Doubleday 1978.

Cusumano, Michael A. *The Japanese Automobile Industry.* Cambridge: Harvard University Press, 1985.

Dassbach, Carl H.A. *Global Enterprise and the World Economy: Ford, General Motors, and IBM, The Emergence of the Transnational Enterprise.* New York: Garland Publishing, Inc., 1989.

Dertouzos, Michael L., Richard K. Lester, and Robert M. Solow. *Made in America: Regaining the Productive Edge.* Cambridge, Mass.: MIT Press, 1989.

Doeringer, Peter B., and Michael J. Piore. *Internal Labor Markets and Manpower Analysis.* Lexington, Mass: Heath Lexington Books, 1971.

Dore, Donald P. *British Factory—Japanese Factory.* Berkeley, California: University of California Press, 1973.

Dohse, Knuth, Ulrich Jürgens, and Thomas Malsch. "From 'Fordism' to 'Toyotism'?: The Social Organization of the Labor Process in the Japanese Automobile Industry". *Politics & Society,* 1985, Vol. 14, 2:115–46.

Dunning, John. *International Production and the Multinational Enterprise.* London: George Allen and Unwin, 1981.

Dyer, Davis, Malcom S. Salter, and Alan M. Webber. *Changing Alliance.* Boston: Harvard Business School Press, 1987.

Edwards, Richard C. *Contested Terrain: The Transformation of the Workplace in the Twentieth Century.* New York: Basic Books, 1979.

Encarnation, Dennis J. "Cross Investment: A Second Front of Economic Rivalry," in *America versus Japan,* ed. McCraw, Thomas K. Boston: Harvard Business School Press, 1986.

Feldman, Richard, and Michael Betzold. *End of the Line*. New York: Weidenfeld and Nicholson, 1988.

Florida, Richard, and Martin Kenney. "Transplant Organizations: The Transfer of Japanese Industrial Organization to the U.S". *American Sociological Review*, 1991, Vol. 56, June:381–98.

Franz, Douglas, and Catherine Collins. *Selling Out*. Chicago: Contemporary Books, 1989.

Fucini, Joseph J., and Suzy Fucini. *Working for the Japanese: Inside Mazda's American Auto Plant*. New York: The Free Press, 1990.

Fuss, Melvyn A., and Leonard Waverman. *Costs and Productivity in Automobile Production: The Challenge of Japanese Efficiency*. New York: Cambridge University Press, 1992.

Garrahan, Philip, and Paul Stewart. *The Nissan Enigma: Flexibility at Work in a Local Economy*. London: Mansell, 1992.

Gelsanliter, David. *Jump Start—Japan Comes to the Heartland*. New York: Farrar, Straus, and Giroux, 1990.

Glickman, Norman J., and Douglas P. Woodward. *The New Competitors: How Foreign Investors are Changing the U.S. Economy*. New York: Basic Books, 1989.

Gordon, David M., Richard Edwards, and Michael Reich. *Segmented Work, Divided Workers: The Historical Transformation of Labor in the United States*. New York: Cambridge University Press, 1982.

Gordon, Donald D. *Japanese Management in America and Britain*. Aldershot: Avebury, 1988.

Gordon, Sara L., and Francis A. Lees. *Foreign Multinational Investment in the United States*. New York: Quorum Books, 1986.

Graham, Edward M. and Paul R. Krugman, *Foreign Direct Investment in the United States*. Washington, D.C.: Institute for International Economics, 1989.

Gronning, Terie. "Japanese-related Plants in North America: The Case of Mazda". *Ritsumeikan Sangyo Shakai Ronshu*. Ritsumeikan University, 1990, Vol. 25, No. 4:155–88; Vol. 26, 2:207–248.

Halberstam, David. *The Reckoning*. New York: William Morrow and Co., Inc., 1986.

Hall, Edward Twitchell. *Beyond Culture*. Garden City, N.Y.: Anchor Books, 1976.

Hanawa, Gi' ichi. "Nissan, Hatsu no Amerika kojyo Seiko-ki" ("Nissan: A Case of the First Successful Transplant in the U.S."). In *Ibunka no naka no Kigyo Shinshutsu* (Overseas Production Operations in the Different Culture). Tokyo: NHK Hoso Kenshu Center, 1989.

Harvard Business School. *Sanyo Manufacturing Corporation—Forest City, Arkansas*, 1982, 9–682–045, Rev. 11/82. Boston.

Hashimoto, Juro. *Nihon Keizai Ron: 20 shisutemu to Nihon Keizai* [Japanese Economy: 20 Century System and Japanese Economy]. Kyoto: Minerva Shobo, 1991.

Hazama, Hiroshi. *Nihonteki Keiei: Shudan-shugi no Kozai*. (Japanese-style Management: Dark Sides and Bright Sides of Groupism). Tokyo: Nihon Keizai Shimbunsha, 1971.

Heller, H. Robert, and Emily E. *The Economic and Social Impact of Foreign Investment in Hawaii*. Honolulu: Economic Research Center, University of Hawaii, 1973.

———. *Japanese Investment in the United States: With a Case Study of the Hawaiian Experience*. New York: Praeger, 1974.

Herzberg, James. *A Broken Bond: American Economic Policy Toward Japan, 1931–1941*. New York: Garland Publishing, 1988.

Hymer, Stephen Herbert. *The International Operations of National Firms: A Study of Direct Foreign Investment*. Cambridge, Mass.: MIT Press, 1976.

Hofstede, Geert. *Culture's Consequences: International Differences in Work-Related Value*. Beverly Hills, California: Sage Publications, 1980.

Holusha, John. "No, Utopia, But to Workers It's a Job". *The New York Times*. Sunday, 29 January, 1989.

Hood, Neil, and Stephen Young. *The Economics of Multinational Enterprise*. London: Longman, 1979.

Iacocca, Lee. *Iacocca: An Autobiography*. New York: Bantam Books, Inc., 1984.

Ikemoto, Kiyoshi, Ueno Akira, and Ken'ichi Yasumuro. *Nihon Kigyo no Takokusekiteki Tenkai* (Multinationalization of Japanese Enterprises). Tokyo: Yuhikaku, 1981.

Imai, Ken' ichi, and Ryutaro Komiya, ed. *Nihon no Kigyo* (Japanese Enterprises). Tokyo: University of Tokyo Press, 1989.

Imai, Masaaki. *Kaizen (Ky'zen), the key to Japan's competitive success.* New York: Random House Business Division, 1988.

The Institute of Economic Study, Chuo University. *Jidosha Sangyo no Kokusaika to Seisan System* (Internationalization of the Japanese Auto Industry and Its Production System). Tokyo: Chuo University Press, 1990.

Institute of Social Science, University of Tokyo (Abo, T. ed.). *Local Production of Japanese Automobile and Electronics Firms in the United States.* Research Reports No.23. Tokyo: Institute of Social Science, 1990.

Institute of Social Science, University of Tokyo, ed. *Sengo Rodokumiai no Jittai* (Labor Unions in the Postwar Japan). Tokyo: Nihon Hyoronsha, 1950.

Ishii, Shoji. "Hokubei ni okeru Nikkei Jidosha Sangyo no Genchika Senryaku" ("Localization Strategy of Japanese-Affiliated Auto Companies in North America"). *Kaigai Toshi Kenkyushoho.* Nihon Yushutunyu Ginko. Kaigai Toshi Kenkyusho, 1990, 2:1–38.

Ishikawa, Kaoru. *Nihonteki Hinshitu Kanri* (Japanese-Style Quality Control). Tokyo: Nikka Giren, 1981.

Ishizaki, Teruhiko. *Nichibei Keizai no Gyakuten* (Reversed Economic Status of the U.S. and Japan). Tokyo: University of Tokyo Press, 1990.

Itagaki, Hiroshi. "Nihonteki Seisan Shisutemu no Tokucho to Kaigai heno Iten Kanosei" ("Characteristics and Transferability of Japanese Production System"). *Journal of Saitama University, Social Science,* 1989, 37:57–79.

———. "A Comparative Study on the Japanese Production System in the U.S.A. and Taiwan". Euro-Asia Management Studies Association Conference. Fontainebleau. October 17–19, 1991.

Iwauchi, Ryoichi, et al. *Kaigai Nikkei Kigyo to Jinteki Shigen: Genchi Keiei to Chuzai'in no Seikatsu* (Japanese-Related Plants Overseas and Human Resources). Tokyo: Dobunkan, 1992.

James, Barrie G. *Trojan Horse: The Ultimate Japanese Challenge to Western Industry.* London: W.H. Allen and Company Ltd., 1989.

Jürgens, Ulrich. "Internationalization Strategies of Japanese and German Automobile Companies". Paper Presented at the Symposium on "Production Strategies and Industrial Relations in the Process of Internationalization". Tohoku University and the German Institute of Japanese Study. Sendai. October 14–16, 1991.

Kamiya, Shotaro. *My Life with Toyota.* Toyota City: Toyota Motor Sales Company, 1976.

Kamiyama, Kunio. "Nihon Kigyo no Zaibei Genchi Seisan no Jittai ni tsuite" ("On the Local Production of Japanese Companies in the United States"). *Annals of the Society for Industrial Studies, Japan,* 1987, 3 (March):55–71.

———. "Nihon Kigyo no Amerika ni okeru Genchi Seisan no Jokyo: 1988 Nen 8 Gatsu Genchi Chosa" ("On the Local Production of Japanese Companies in the United States: Based on Field Research in August 1988"). *Josai University Bulletin,* Josai University, The Department of Economics, 1989, Vol. 9, 1 (January):45–62.

———. "Nihonteki Chingin Shisutemu ni tsuite" ("On the Japanese Wage System"). *Oita University Economic Review,* 1990, Vol. 41, 5 (January):39–62.

———. "Makiradora ni okeru Nikkei Denki Kojo" ("Japanese Electronics Plants under the Maquiladora System"). *Annual Reports of Josai Graduate School of Economics,* 1992, 8 (March):57–79.

Katz, Harry C. *Shifting Gears—Changing Labor Relations in the U.S. Automobile Industry.* Cambridge, Mass.: MIT Press, 1987.

Katz, Harry C., and Charles F. Sabel. "Industrial Relations and Industrial Adjustment in the Car Industry". *Industrial Relations,* 1985, Vol. 24, 3 (Fall):295–315.

Kawabe, Nobuo. "Development of Overseas Operations by General Trading Companies, 1868–1945," in *Business History of Trading Companies.* eds. Yonekawa, Shin'idri and Hideki Yoshihara. Tokyo: University of Tokyo Press, 1987.

———. "Japanese Business in the United States Before World War II: The Case of Mitsubishi Shoji Kaisha, the San Francisco and Seattle Branches." Ph.D. diss., Ohio State University, 1980.

————. "Japanese Business in the United States before the Second World War: the Case of Mitsui and Mitsubishi," in *Historical Studies in International Corporate Business,* eds. Teichova, Alice., Maurice Lévy-Leboyer, and Helga Nussbaum. Cambridge, Cambridge University Press, 1989.

Kawamura, Tetsuji. "Dainiji Taisen Shoki Amerika Kokubo Seisan Taisei no Tenkai" ("Development of the U.S. Defense Production System during the Early Stage of the World War II Period"). *The Teikyo Keizaigaku Kenkyu* (The Teikyo University Economic Review), 1986–1991, Vol. 20, 1:419–86; Vol. 21, 1♦2:380–430; Vol. 22, 1♦2:427–96; Vol. 24, 1:385–465; Vol. 24, 2:328–426.

————. "Dainiji Taisen Amerika Senji Keizai to Sengo Keikijunkan no Henyou" ("The U.S. War Economy in World War II and Its Effects on the Postwar Business Cycles"). *The Teikyo Keizaigaku Kenkyu.* The Teikyo University Economic Review, 1991, Vol. 25, 1:267–478.

Keefe, Jeffrey H., and Harry C. Katz. "Job Classifications and Plant Performance in the Auto Industry", *Industrial Relations,* 1990, Vol. 29, (Winter): 111–18.

Keller, Maryann. *Rude Awakening.* New York: William Morrow and Company, Inc., 1989.

Kenney, Martin, and Richard Florida. *Beyond Mass Production: The Japanese System and Its Transfer to the U.S.* New York: Oxford University Press, 1992.

Kinugasa, Yosuke. "Japanese Firms' Foreign Direct Investment in the United States—the Case of Matsushita and Others," in *Overseas Business Activities,* eds. Okochi, Akio. and Tadakatsu Inoue. Tokyo: University of Tokyo Press, 1984.

Kochan, A. Thomas, Harry C. Katz, and Robert B. Mackersie. *The Transformation of American Industrial Relations.* New York: Basic Books, 1986.

Koike, Kazuo. *Shokuba no Rodokumiai to Sanka: Roshikankei no Nichibei Hikaku* (A Comparative Study of Industrial Relations on the Shop Floor between the U.S. and Japan). Tokyo: Toyo Keizai Shimposha, 1977.

————. *Understanding Industrial Relations in Modern Japan.* London: Macmillan, 1988.

————. "Nihongata Seisan Hoshiki no "Tsuyosa" wo Saguru" ("Searching the Competitive Advantage of Japanese-Style Production System). *Ekonomisuto.* Tokyo. August 20, 1990.

Koike, Kazuo, and Inoki Takenori, eds. *Jinzai Keisei no Kokusai Hikaku.* [International Comparison of Human Resource Training]. Tokyo: Toyo Keisai Shimposha, 1987.

Kojima, Kiyoshi. *Japanese Direct Foreign Investment.* Tokyo: Charles E. Tuttle Co., 1978.

Kujawa, Duane. *Japanese Multinationals in the United States.* New York: Praeger, 1986.

————. "Flexible Production Systems and Japanese Multinationals' Experiences in the U.S. Automobile Industry: Strategic Imperatives and Strategic Dividends". The 20th Anniversary World Conference (of AIB Japan). Tokyo. July 4–6, 1990.

Kujawa, Duane, and Mamoru Yoshida. "Cross-Cultural Transfers of Management Practices: Japanese Manufacturing Plants in the United States". Annual Meeting of the Academy of International Business. Chicago, 1987.

Kujawa, Duane, and Daniel Bob. *American Public Opinion on Japanese Direct Investment.* New York: Japan Society, 1988.

Kumagai, Fumie. "Amerika Genchi Seisan no Hikaku Bunkaronteki Kousatsu". ("A Comparative Cultural Study on the Local Productions of Japanese Firms in the US"), in *Seisan Sisutemu no Nichi-bei Hikaku* (Comparative Studies on Japanese and US Production Systems), ed. Abo. Tetsuo: Kyoto, Minerva Shobo, 1994 (forthcoming).

Kumon, Hiroshi. "Zaibei Nikkei Jidosha Kigyo no Sagyo Soshiki" ("Work Organization of Japanese-Affiliated Automobile Plants in the U.S.A."). *Society and Labor,* 1990, Vol. 1, 37:49–94.

————. "Beikoku Jidosha Sangyo no QWL". ("QWL in the American Auto Industry") *O'hara Institute for Social Research Journal.* 1990, 381:1–12.

————. "Japanese-Affiliated Automobile Plants in the U.S. and Taiwan". Euro-Asia Management Association Conference. Fontainebleau. October 17–19, 1991.

————. "Multinationalization of Toyota Motor Corporation". *Journal of International Economic Studies.* Hosei University, 1992, 6:80–99.

Kumazawa, Makoto. *Nihonteki Keiei no Meian* (Bright Sides and Dark Sides of Japanese-style Management). Tokyo: Chikuma Shobo, 1989.

Law, Christopher M. *Restructuring the Automobile Industry: National and Regional Impacts*. London: Routledge, 1991.

Lee, Albert. *Call me Roger*. New York: Contemporary Books, Inc., 1988.

Lees, Francis A. *Foreign Banking and Investment in the United States*. New York: Wiley, 1976.

Levin, Doron. *Irreconcilable Differences—Ross Perot versus General Motors*. Boston: Little Brown and Company, 1989.

Lichetenstein, Nelson, and Stephen Meyer. *On the Line: Essays in the History of Auto Work*. Urbana and Chicago: University of Illinois Press, 1989.

Lockwood, William W. *The Economic Development of Japan*. Princeton: Princeton University Press, 1954.

Makin, John H. "The Effects of Japanese Investment in the United States," in *Japanese Investment in the United States,* ed. Yamanura, Kozo. Seattle: Society for Japanese Studies, 1989.

Mann, Eric. *Taking on General Motors*. California: UCLA, 1987.

Mason, Mark. *American Multinationals and Japan: The Political Economy of Japanese Capital Controls, 1899–1980*. Cambridge, Mass.: Council on East Asian Studies, Harvard University, 1992.

Matsumoto, Koji. *The Rise of the Japanese Corporation System: The Inside View of a MITI Official*. London: Kegan Paul International, 1991.

Milkman, Ruth. *Japan's California Factories: Labor Relations and Economic Globalization*. California: Institute of Industrial Relations, UCLA, 1991.

Millstein, James E. "Decline in an Expanding Industry: Japanese Competition in Color Television". In *American Industry in International Competition: Government Politics and Corporate Strategies,* ed. John Zysman and L. Tyson. Ithaca: Cornell University Press, 1983.

The MIT Commission on Industrial Productivity. The Working Papers of the MIT Commission on Industrial Productivity. Vol. 1. Cambridge, Mass.: MIT Press, 1989.

———. *The US Semiconductor, Computer, and Copier Industries*. The Working Papers of the MIT Commission on Industrial Productivity. Vol. 2. Cambridge, Mass.: MIT Press, 1989.

Mitsui & Co., *The 100 Year History of Mitsui & Co., Ltd., 1876–1976,* Tokyo: Mitsui & Co., 1977.

Miwa, Yoshiro. 1989. "Shitauke kankei: Jidosa Sangyo no Kesu". ("Sub-contracting Relations: Cases for Auto Industry"), *Keizaigaku Ronshu,* University of Tokyo, 1989, Vol. 55, 3:2–30.

———. *Nihon no Kigyo to Sangyo Soshiki* (Japanese Firms and Industrial Organization). Tokyo: University of Tokyo Press, 1990.

Monden, Yasuhiro. *Toyota Production System*. Atlanta: Industrial Engineering and Management Press, 1983.

Morales, Rebecca. "Work Organization, Technology, and Labor Relations in the U.S. Automobile Industry". In *Technology and Labor in the Automobile Industry,* ed., Sung-Jo Park, 105–138. Frankfurt: Campus, 1991.

Morita, Akio. *Made in Japan*. New York: Dutton, 1986.

Morita, Akio, and Shintaro Ishihara. "The Japan that can say 'No'," typescript (1989).

Morris, Jonathan, and Rob Imrie. *Transforming Buyer-Supplier Relations: Japanese-Style Industrial Practices in a Western Context*. London: Macmillan, 1992.

Moritz, Michael, and Barett Seaman. 1981. *Going for Broke: The Chrysler Story*. Garden City, N.Y.: Doubleday, 1981.

Nakane, Chie. *Japanese Society*. California: University of California Press, 1973.

National Academy of Engineering. The Competitive Status of the U.S. Electronics Industry. Washington, DC: National Academy Press, 1984.

Nitta, Michio. *Nihon no Rodosha Sanka* (Worker's Participation in Japan). Tokyo: University of Tokyo Press, 1988.

———. "Nihon Kigyo no Taibei Chokusetsu Toshi to Roshikankei Senryaku Shiron" ("An Essay on Industrial Relations Strategy of the Japanese Firms in the U.S."). *Annual Report of the Academy of Social Policy.* No. 34. Tokyo: Ochanomizu Shobo, 1990.

Northwestern University, Center for the Interdisciplinary Study of Science and Technology. *The U.S. Consumer Electronics Industry and Foreign Competition, 1980*.

Odate, Gyoju. *Japan's Financial Relations with the United States.* New York: Columbia University Press, 1922.

Ono, Taiichi. *Toyota Production System: Beyond Large-Scale Production.* Cambridge, Mass.: Productivity Press, 1988.

Okamoto, Yasuo. "Takokuseki Kigyo to Nihon Kigyo no Takokusekika" ("Multinational Enterprise and the Multinationalization of Japanese Business Enterprise"), *Keizaigaku Ronshu,* University of Tokyo, 1987, Vol. 53, 1:2–37; Vol. 54, 3:67–92; Vol. 55, 2:43–76; Vol. 56, 1:52–100.

Oshima, Taku, ed. *Gendai Nihon no Jidosha Buhinkogyo* (Automobile Parts Industry in Modern Japan). Tokyo: Nihon Keizai Hyoronsha, 1987.

Okochi, Kazuo, Shojiro Ujihara, and Wakao Fujita. *Rodokumiai no Kozo to Kino* (Structure and Functions of Labor Union). Tokyo: University of Tokyo Press, 1959.

Ozawa, Terutomo. *Multinationalism, Japanese Style.* Princeton: Princeton University Press, 1979.

Parker, Mike. *Inside the Circle.* Boston: South End Press, 1985.

Parker, Mike, and Jane Slaughter. *Choosing Sides.* Boston: South End Press, 1988.

———. "Management by Stress: Behind the Scenes at Nummi Motors". *The New York Times.* December 4, 1988.

Piore, Michael J., and Charles Sabel. *The Second Industrial Divide: Possibilities for Prosperity.* New York: Basic Books, 1984.

Porter, Michael E. *Competitive Strategy.* New York: The Free Press, 1980.

———. *Competitive Advantage.* New York: The Free Press, 1985.

———. ed. *Competition in Global Industries.* Boston: Harvard Business School Press, 1986.

———. *The Competitive Advantage of Nations.* New York: The Free Press, 1990.

Rubenstein, James M. *The Changing U.S. Auto Industry: A Geographical Analysis.* London: Routledge, 1992.

Sakuma, Ken. *Kokusai Keiei to Nihongata Roshikankei* (International Business and Japanese-Style Labor Relations). Tokyo: Yuhikaku, 1987.

Sasaki, Takao, and Hideki Esho, ed. *Nihon Denshi Sangyo no Kaigai Shinshutsu* (The Advance of Japanese Electronics Industry into Foreign Countries). Tokyo: The Hosei University Press, 1987.

Shibagaki, Kazuo, Malcolm Trevor, and Tetsuo Abo, ed. *Japanese and European Management.* Tokyo: University of Tokyo Press, 1989.

Shimada, Haruo. *Hyumanuea no Keizaigaku* (Economics of Humanware). Tokyo: Iwanami Shoten, 1988.

Shimokawa, Koichi. *Jidosha Sangyo Datsu Seijyuku Jidai* (Beyond the Maturity: The Auto Industry). Tokyo: Yuhikaku, 1985.

Shishido, Zen'ichi, and Atsushi Kusano. *Kokusai Goben: Toyota-GM Joint Venture No Kiseki* (International Joint Venture: Toyota and GM). Tokyo: Yuhikaku, 1988.

Shook, Robert L. *Honda: An American Success Story.* New York: Prentice-Hall Press, 1988.

———. *Turnaround: The New Ford Motor Company.* New York: Prentice-Hall Press, 1990.

Smitka, Michael J. *Competitive Ties: Subcontracting in the Japanese Automobile Industry.* New York: Columbia University Press, 1991.

Sugiyama, Shinya. *Japan's Industrialization in the World Economy, 1859–99: Export Trade and Overseas Competition.* London: Athlone Press, 1988.

Suzuki, Naotsugu. *Amerika Shakai no Naka no Nikkei Kigyo: Jidosha Sangyo no Genchi Keiei* (Japanese-Affiliated Firms in the U.S.: Local Plants Management of Automobile Industry). Tokyo: Tokyo Keizai Shimposha, 1991.

Suzuki, Ryoji. "Nihonteki Kigyo Shisutemu to Kokusai Kyoso Ryoku." ("Japanese Firm System and International Competitive Advantage"), *Economy and Management* (Sapporo University), No. 2, Vol. 21, 1990.

Tanaka, Hirohide. *Nihonteki Keiei no Romukanri* (Human Resources Management of Japanese-Style Management). Tokyo: Dobunkan, 1988.

Tolchin, Martin and Susan. *Buying into America,* New York: Times Books, 1988.

Tolliday, Steven, and Jonathan Zeitlin, ed. *The Automobile Industry and Its Workers.* New York: St. Martin's Press, 1987.

Totsuka, Hideo, and Tsutomu Hyodo, ed. *Roshikankei no Tenki to Sentaku: Nihon no Jidosha Sangyo* (Transformation and Alternatives of the Industrial Relations: A Case of the Japanese Automobile Industry). Tokyo: Nihon Hyoronsha, 1991.

Toyoda, Eiji. *Toyota: Fifty Years in Motion.* Tokyo: Kodansha, 1987.

Toyota Motor Corporation. *Toyota: A History of the First 50 Years.* Toyota: Toyota Motor Corporation, 1988.

Trevor, Malcolm. *Japan's Reluctant Multinationals.* New York: St. Martin's Press, 1983.

Tsurumi, Yoshi. *The Japanese Are Coming,* Cambridge, Mass.: Ballinger, 1976.

United States Department of Labor. *Production Practice and Strategies of Foreign Multinationals in the United States: Case Studies with a Special Focus on the Japanese.* Vol. 2. Washington, D.C.: USGPO, 1985.

United States General Accounting Office. *Foreign Investment: Growing Japanese Presence in the U.S. Auto Industry.* Washington, D.C.: USGPO, 1988.

United States International Trade Commission. *Color Television Receivers and Subassemblies Thereof.* Washington, D.C.: USGPO, 1980.

———. *Television Receivers from Japan.* Washington, D.C.: USGPO, 1981.

———. *Color Television Receivers from Republic of Korea and Taiwan.* Washington, D.C.: USGPO, 1984.

Vernon, Raymond. "International Investment and International Trade in the Product Cycle". *Quarterly Journal of Economics,* 80, 1966, 2: 190–207.

Warshofsky, Fred. *The Chip War: The Battle for the World of Tomorrow.* London: Macmillan, 1989.

Wassmann, Ulrike, and Kozo Yamamura. "Do Japanese Firms Behave Differently? The Effects of *Keiretsu* in the United States," in *Japanese Investment in the United States,* ed. Yamamura, Kozo. Seattle: Society for Japanese Studies, 1989.

Wickens, Peter. *The Road to Nissan: Flexibility, Quality, Teamwork.* London: Macmillan, 1987.

Wilkins, Mira, and F.E. Hill. *American Business Abroad: Ford on Six Continents.* Detroit: Wayne State University Press, 1964.

Wilkins, Mira. *The Emergence of Multinational Enterprise: American Business Abroad from the Colonial Era to 1914.* Cambridge, Mass.: Harvard University Press, 1970.

———. "The Role of U.S. Business," in *Pearl Harbor as History. Japanese-American Relations 1931–1941,* eds. Borg, Dorothy. and Shumpei Okamoto. New York: Columbia University Press, 1973.

———. *The Maturing of Multinational Enterprise: American Business Abroad from 1914 to 1970.* Cambridge, Mass.: Harvard University Press, 1974.

———. *Foreign Enterprise in Florida.* Gainesville, Fla.: University Presses of Florida, 1979.

———. "American-Japanese Direct Foreign Investment Relationships, 1930–1952". *Business History Review* , LVI, Winter 1982.

———. "Japanese Multinational Enterprise before 1914," *Business History Review,* LX, Summer 1986.

———. "The Free-Standing Company, 1870–1914: An Important Type of British Foreign Direct Investment," *Economic History Review,* 2nd Ser., XLI May 1988.

———. *The History of Foreign Investment in the United States to 1914.* Cambridge, Mass.: Harvard University Press, 1989.

———. "The Contributions of Foreign Enterprises to Japanese Economic Development," in *Foreign Business in Japan before World War II,* eds. Udagawa, Masaru. and Takeshi Yuzawa. Tokyo: University of Tokyo Press, 1990.

Wilkinson, Barry, Jonathan Morris, and Nick Oliver. 1989. "Japanizing The World: The Case of Toyota". Paper Presented to the APROS Conference on Organizations, Technologies, and Cultures in Comparative Perspective. Australian National University. Canberra. December 13–15, 1989.

Womack, James P., Daniel T. Jones, and Daniel Roos. *The Machine that Changed the World.* New York: Rowson Associates, Macmillan Publishing Co., 1990.

Wood, Stephen, ed. *The Transformation of Work?.* London: Unwin Hyman, 1989.

Wray, William D. *Mitsubishi and the N.Y.K. 1870–1914: Business Strategy in the Japanese Shipping Industry.* Cambridge, Mass: Harvard University Press, 1984.

———. "Japan's Big Three Service Enterprises in China, 1896–1936," in *Japan's Informal Empire in China, 1895–1937*. eds. Duus, Peter, Ramon H. Myers, and Mark Peattie. Princeton: Princeton University Press, 1989.

Yabe, Takeshi. *Nihon Kigyo wa Sabetsu-suru* (Discriminations in Japanese Firms). Tokyo: Diamondsha, 1991.

Yamamura, Kozo, ed. *Japanese Investment in the United States*. Seattle: Society for Japanese Studies, 1989.

Yamashita, Shoichi, ed. *Transfer of Japanese Technology and Management to the ASEAN Countries*. Tokyo: University of Tokyo Press, 1991.

Yamazaki, Hiroaki. "The Logic of General Trading Companies in Japan," in *Business History of Trading Companies*. eds. Yonekawa, Shin'ichi and Hideki Yoshihara, Tokyo: University of Tokyo Press, 1987.

———. "The Yokohama Specie Bank during the Period of the Restored Gold Standard in Japan [January 1930–December 1931]," in *Finance and Financiers in European History*, ed. Cassis, Youssef. Cambridge: Cambridge University Press, 1992.

Yanarella, Ernest J., and William C. Green. *The Politics of Industrial Recruitment: Japanese Automobile Investment and Economic Development in the American States*. New York: Greenwood Press, 1990.

Yates, Brock. *The Decline and Fall of the American Automobile Industry*. New York: Empire Books, 1983.

Yoshida, Mamoru. *Japanese Direct Manufacturing Investment in the United States*. New York: Praeger, 1987.

Yoshihara, Hideki. "Nihon Kigyo no Seisan Gijutsuno Kokusai Iten" ("International Transfer of Japanese Firms' Production Technology"), *Bijinesu Rebyu*, No. 3, 4, Vol. 30, 1983.

———. "The Business History of Sogo Shosha in International Perspective." in *Business History of Trading Companies*. eds. Yonekawa, Shin'ichi, and Hideki Yoshihara, Tokyo: University of Tokyo Press, 1987.

Yoshino, Michael Y. *Japan's Multinational Enterprises*. Cambridge, Mass.: Harvard University Press, 1976.

Index